The Bluegrass Hall of Fame

Inductee Biographies 1991-2014

By Fred Bartenstein, Gary Reid & Others

ISBN 978-0-9897544-1-5

LOC/PCN: 2014947814

© 2014 International Bluegrass Music Museum

All rights reserved. No part of this book may be used or reproduced in any manner whatsoever without written permission except in the case of brief quotations embodied in critical articles and reviews.

Direct all inquiries to: Holland Brown Books, 2509 Portland Avenue, Louisville, KY 40212.

Printed in China

Cover Photos: all credited inside except for Bill Monroe and the Blue Grass Boys (Philip Melnick, 1963); Doug Dillard, Rodney Dillard, Dean Webb, and Mitch Jayne (Nobuharu Komoriya, 1989); Peter Kuykendall (courtesy of *Bluegrass Unlimited* magazine, 1996); Janis, Little Roy, Miggie, Polly, Pop, and Wallace Lewis (Ronald Stuckey, 2001); and Everett and Bea Lilly (Richard D. Smith, courtesy of County/Rebel Records, 1972).

Contents

Foreword, by Joe Wilson vi
Introduction, by Gabrielle Gray xi

1991
Bill Monroe 2
Earl Scruggs 6
Lester Flatt 10

1992
The Stanley Brothers
    Carter Stanley 14
    Ralph Stanley 18
Reno and Smiley
    Don Reno 22
    Red Smiley 27

1993
Mac Wiseman 30
Jim and Jesse
    Jesse McReynolds 34
    Jim McReynolds 39

1994
The Osborne Brothers
    Bobby Osborne 42
    Sonny Osborne 46

1995
Jimmy Martin 50

1996
Peter Kuykendall 54
The Classic Country Gentlemen
    Eddie Adcock 58
    John Duffey 62
    Tom Gray 66
    Charlie Waller 70

1997
Josh Graves 74

1998
Chubby Wise 78
Carlton Haney 82

1999
Kenny Baker 86

2000
Lance LeRoy 90
Doc Watson 94

2001
The Carter Family
    A.P. Carter 98
    Sara Carter 103
    Maybelle Carter 106

2002
The Lilly Brothers and Don Stover
    The Lilly Brothers 109
    Don Stover 116
David Freeman 120

2003
J. D. Crowe 124

2004
Curly Seckler 128
Bill Vernon 132

2005
Red Allen 136
Benny Martin 140

2006
The Lewis Family 144
Syd Nathan 150

2007
Howard Watts ("Cedric Rainwater") . 154
Carl Story 158

2008
Bill Clifton 162
Charles Wolfe 166

2009
The Lonesome Pine Fiddlers 170
The Dillards 176

2010
John Hartford 182
Louise Scruggs 186

2011
Del McCoury 190
George Shuffler 194

2012
Doyle Lawson 198
Ralph Rinzler 202

2013
Tony Rice 206
Paul Warren 210

2014
The Original Seldom Scene
    Mike Audridge 214
    John Duffey 62
    Ben Eldridge 218
    Tom Gray 66
    John Starling 222
Neil Rosenberg 226

The International Bluegrass
    Music Museum 230

Contributors 233

Index 234

...it sparkles still,
and speaks to the soul.

Foreword: They changed the world...

I wish you could have been with me, dear reader, in the mid-forties when it began. The weekly bath for little boys came in a Number 3 washing tub in water heated by a wood stove. Feeling very clean and smelling of the flower scent mom had put into the large white cake of home-made soap, I sat in a circle before the Crosley radio with batteries bulging from its back to listen to the *Grand Ole Opry*.

The crowds lifted the rafters of the Ryman Auditorium with their roaring approval of a young banjoist named Scruggs who never said a word. His sparkling sound went into thousands of hollows like ours, and it sparkles still, and speaks to the soul.

Nothing created on our shores is more instantly recognized as "American" than this music called bluegrass.

This is a collection of biographical material about musicians who changed the world they inherited. They changed it suddenly and dramatically, and their creations are still evolving and reaching into the future.

Many of them are from a time, a time after a great war had ended, when their nation felt free to create a new and better world. They are from the ascending side of progress, and felt free to adjust and improve, to reach for greater quality, to assert their sound.

They were all born in the United States, and the art form they made reflects American history and values, yet their creations have been adopted and adapted by people in scores of distant places. Millions turn to that sparkling stream of sound, knowing instantly that it speaks to their souls. Nothing created on our shores is more instantly recognized as "American" than this music called bluegrass.

Working people invented this music, using concepts, songs, and instruments borrowed from earlier styles of music. Many had walked behind horses and mules on upland farms. They had mined coal and tended cotton-weaving machines. They had moved to Detroit to build cars, and to Maryland and Pennsylvania to pick mushrooms, build dams, and fix anything that needed fixing. Most are from the Southern mountains, a place that has long produced more sons and daughters than it had places at the table. After the war they left in a steady stream, a greater outpouring than that of the Dust Bowl. Their sparkling new music became a favorite sound in the honkytonks, bars, and construction-worker dives in Dayton, Cincinnati, Baltimore, and Washington, D.C.

It was a commercial music from its outset. One paid an admission fee, and sat down to hear a concert. The instruments had been used for many generations for dance forms of folk music where the musicians sat down to perform, and the audience stood up and danced. But this new music was for listening. It involved the lost loves of ancient balladry, dead mother stories from Victorian parlors, hot "breaks" from several instruments, and vocal harmonies that could wring the heart.

It also involved the microphone, an innovation of the early twentieth century that enabled the amplification necessary for bluegrass: the subtle mix of solo voice, harmonies, the lead "breaks" and "turnarounds" by fiddle, banjo, mandolin, and guitar. It enabled the rhythmic "chop" and other backup timekeeping.

This is a collection of biographical material about musicians who changed the world they inherited.

Radio was by far the most important medium in the spread of this music. The larger 50,000-watt stations, such as Nashville's WSM, let millions hear bluegrass on its *Grand Ole Opry*: the pivotal first band (Monroe, Scruggs, Flatt, Wise, Watts) debuted on this station. But local radio was even more important: local daily "live" shows by scores of bands became part of daily life. Few of these artists were paid by their stations, but they could promote paying gigs at an endless series of schoolhouses and small halls: the aptly named "kerosene circuit."

Bluegrass often benefited from accidental juxtapositions. Ola Belle Reed built her New River Ranch performance park in Maryland, 400 miles north of her birthplace on Grassy Creek, a stream that tumbles into the New River on the Virginia-North Carolina Blue Ridge. Her little park, and Sunset Park at Oxford, Pennsylvania, put mountain-born bluegrass and old-time music performers within easy driving distance of New York and Washington's folk music circles. They yearned for roots, these urban seekers who had sat at the feet of Richard Dyer-Bennett, Alan Lomax, and Pete Seeger. Ola Belle welcomed them with open arms.

Poverty is the father of bluegrass. Even in its halcyon early years, the founders barely made ends meet. The foot soldiers of bluegrass, these men and women who attempted to make a living performing it, often starved out. The "day jobs" they accepted to save body and soul ranged across the employment landscape. Carl Sauceman told of a fiddler who sidelined as a safecracker. It fed on passion, on love, on roots that run deep, and a yearning to improve the musical future.

Throughout his long career, Bill Monroe carried on a killing pace of touring, an endless series of one-nighters. Time away from loved ones and very poor pay led to major turnover in his band. But in time this turnover was understood as a blessing. Monroe chose fine artists, schooled them in his reach for perfection at a furious pace, and many of them soon had fine bands of their own, adding to the reach of the music.

Even Monroe had to be told that bluegrass had been invented. Among those who informed him was Don Reno. When Earl Scruggs left the Blue Grass Boys, Monroe brought in Jackie Phelps to play electric steel guitar. Nothing was said about the absence of the banjo at the next *Grand Ole Opry* broadcast. Listening in North Carolina, Reno realized what had happened and immediately left for Nashville. Arriving there, Reno was told that Monroe and his band had left for a performance in North Carolina. So the intrepid Reno reversed his direction on US Highway 70, returned to North Carolina, and there he found Monroe. The band was already on stage, so Reno uncased his banjo, tuned for seconds, and walked unannounced onto the stage. Monroe strode over to the bold young veteran of war on the Burma Road. "You're Don Reno, aren't you?" Monroe inquired. "I've been thinking about calling you."

Journalists, folklorists, and musicologists still struggle to explain bluegrass.

Ozark musicians such as Vern Williams and Ray Park and a talented band called the Dillards drifted westward and took the sparkling new sound to California, Oregon, and Washington State. The Lilly Brothers and Don Stover left the coal-mining region of the Cumberland Mountains in West Virginia and carried their exciting brand of bluegrass to a dive in a low-rent part of Boston that police dubbed "the Combat Zone." They remained for eighteen years, performing seven nights a week for sailors, Harvard and MIT students, and an incredibly diverse gaggle of New Englanders who were soon making brilliant contributions to the music. Among these acolytes were Bill Keith, who popularized a melodic banjo style, and Joe Val, an Italian typewriter repairman with a soaring tenor voice that could shatter crystal, who later founded his own New England Blue Grass Boys.

The industrial heartland of Ohio, Indiana, Illinois, and Michigan made rich contributions to bluegrass. Many of the great performers who worked there are in the Hall of Fame, but please do not assume that all who made bluegrass are listed here. Nothing could be farther from the truth. Many thousands from across the nation have been steeped in this burst of creativity, including brilliant artists who did not care for the poor pay, living in motels, and riding every day. Moreover, it is still being made and, though I obviously care for the early inventors, who am I to doubt that some of the best contributions are still to be made?

When I hear a Japanese, Czech, or Russian bluegrass band, I know a very kind compliment is being paid to the working people of our nation, and it makes me smile.

The converts made by the missionaries that went north, west, and overseas were initially attracted to the instrumental sounds rather than to the lyrics of bluegrass songs. Most had not left a home in a hollow or ever owned even one good coon dog. So the finest of the new urban bluegrass bands sang compositions reflecting the pain and angst their stuck-on-the-beltway urbane fans would better understand.

Journalists, folklorists, and musicologists still struggle to explain bluegrass. They often compare it to jazz, pointing to the virtuosity inherent in both forms, and say bluegrass borrowed its soloing of instruments from jazz. This is dubious, as some of the earliest country groups to go on radio – such as the immensely popular Hill Billies in 1925 – featured solos on guitar, banjo, fiddle, and uke on many of their songs. Some assume the knife-edged coal-mining ridges and hellfire religion of southwestern Virginia inspired the brooding homeplace-obsessed music of the Stanley Brothers. Yet Jim and Jesse McReynolds, another set of bluegrass brothers from another mountain farm just over a few ridges and miles to the south from the Stanleys, gave sad songs a happy turn and helped inspire the musical generosity of the Grateful Dead. So we should ask those who write about bluegrass to assume very little, and to be careful. The creativity of the masters listed here is as complicated as that of other great masters.

As bluegrass music was still getting started, a half dozen bands called "The Country Cousins" arose across the nation. One of them, performing in 1955 on WATA in Boone, North Carolina, had a theme song with a wry twist that echoes the humble beginnings and the out-beyond-the-stars cosmic reach of this music from the people:

> Where did he come from?
> Where did he go?
> Where did he come from?
>   Cotton-eyed Joe?
> From over the Blue Mountains,
> Near the land of Nod,
> Digging taters, seeking God.

— JOE WILSON, FRIES, VA AND TRADE, TN, 2014

Introduction

The International Bluegrass Music Museum is located along the banks of the beautiful Ohio River in downtown Owensboro, Kentucky, the closest city to Bill Monroe's birthplace in nearby Rosine. Among the Museum's most popular attractions are the bronze plaques and displays of artifacts connected with members of the Bluegrass Hall of Fame. Visitors from all over the world come to learn about the men and women who created and developed this distinctive form of music that is enjoyed by tens of millions.

Since 1991 the Museum's sister organization, the International Bluegrass Music Association, has overseen elections to the Hall of Fame (formerly known as the Hall of Honor). Each year a nominating committee creates a slate of 10 to 15 candidates. From these names, electors cast ballots to narrow the nominees to 5 finalists. There are more than 200 electors who themselves have participated actively in bluegrass for at least 10 years, and who merit respect and recognition for their accomplishments and/or knowledge in one or more aspects of the field. After the five finalists have been selected, the electors again vote to select the inductees for that year. In some years there are additional slates, restricted to early contributions or non-performing candidates. The names of the newest Hall of Fame inductees are made public immediately following the final stage of balloting and the formal induction takes place during the annual International Bluegrass Music Awards Show. Later in the year a separate celebration takes place at the Museum, as the plaques of new inductees are unveiled in the Hall of Fame gallery.

...the Museum identified the need to make available to the public more extensive biographical information on the Hall of Fame members,...

In 2009 the Museum identified the need to make available to the public more extensive biographical information on the Hall of Fame members, who now number more than fifty and many of whom are retired or deceased. We wanted carefully researched and engagingly written profiles, which would capture not only the essential facts and career accomplishments of these iconic musicians but also a sense of their personalities and their impact upon fellow musicians and fans. We engaged knowledgeable authors – people who knew most of the inductees on a first-name basis – to write the biographical sketches. The texts were reviewed by other experts in bluegrass music history for accuracy of fact and interpretation. The biographies were displayed on the Museum's website and by 2014 all of the inductees had been profiled.

Fred Bartenstein, one of the principal authors, suggested that we gather the material into a book with photographic portraits, many never-before published. *The Bluegrass Hall of Fame: Inductee Biographies 1991-2014* is a handsome addition to the libraries of music lovers everywhere, and a standard reference work for those seeking to learn about the lives of the earliest and most influential practitioners of bluegrass music. Bartenstein, whose bluegrass involvements date back a half century, has written and researched extensively on bluegrass topics. He generously volunteered to re-edit the profiles and coordinate the publishing project. The International Bluegrass Music Museum is deeply grateful for his timeless gift.

A brilliant and multi-colored mosaic emerges in this historical work, a portrait of life in the early to mid-20th Century...

There were other important collaborators to this volume. It represents the largely uncompensated work of many, a labor of love for bluegrass music, its musicians, and its history. Joe Wilson, a former Museum Trustee and Founder/Chairman Emeritus of the National Council for The Traditional Arts, generously contributed a heartfelt and beautifully written foreword. Gary Reid, another principal author, proprietor of Copper Creek Records and an extensively published author on the Stanley Brothers and other pioneering bluegrass artists and record labels, fact-checked the entire manuscript and helped to locate photographs. Other authors of the profiles included Neil Rosenberg, the dean of bluegrass historians, and Steve Spence, a bluegrass musician and former magazine editor. Dan Loftin, Alan Whitman, Doc Hamilton, *Bluegrass Unlimited* magazine, Museum staffer Lauren RaShae Jennings, Tim Davis from the Country Music Hall of Fame, Carl Fleischhauer, and Frank Godbey provided immeasurable assistance in searching out and selecting the perfect photograph for each inductee. Charley Pennell contributed the Index. Another Museum Trustee, Gill Holland and his associate Stephanie Kertis of Louisville, Kentucky, lent their extensive publishing and business expertise to the shaping of key production decisions. Bob Bingenheimer of Bridge Communications, Yellow Springs, Ohio, designed the book. Four Colour Print Group produced the handsome volume now before you. Photographers and owners of the portraits either donated or accepted token payment for their beautiful work; we are especially grateful that they had the foresight to make and preserve these historic photographs through many decades.

A brilliant and multi-colored mosaic emerges in this historical work, a portrait of life in the early to mid-20th Century, fitted piece by piece into the archives of cultural history by more than four dozen iconic, pioneering artists and their sidemen and women. Their remarkable collective story is, for the very first time, being told and shown on the pages of this book.

In some cases, profiles are provided for individual members of a collective inductee – such as The Stanley Brothers or The Country Gentlemen – in order to highlight their particular contributions and later, separate careers. Where the collective is more easily understood as a unit – such as The Lewis Family, The Dillards, or The Lonesome Pine Fiddlers – a single profile is provided.

Their remarkable collective story is, for the very first time, being told and shown on the pages of this book.

Additional Hall of Fame inductions are made every year, and we envision revised and expanded editions in the future. Factual corrections and additional information for this purpose can be directed to the International Bluegrass Music Museum. We are always happy to welcome your visits and contributions – financial or material – toward our vision to be the world center for the presentation and preservation of the history, culture, and future of bluegrass music.

— GABRIELLE GRAY, EXECUTIVE DIRECTOR,
INTERNATIONAL BLUEGRASS MUSIC MUSEUM,
OWENSBORO, KY, 2014

The Inductees of the International Bluegrass Music Hall of Fame

William Smith "Bill" Monroe ❙ 1991

Remembered as the "Father of Bluegrass Music," Bill Monroe is better understood as a master chef or chemist, blending earlier musical elements into an exciting new form. Bill often spoke of wanting to bring "ancient tones" into his sparklingly innovative music. These included fiddle and bagpipe sounds imported from the British Isles, African-American blues and holiness gospel, American Great Awakening hymnody, as well as hill country dance music and the thrilling new rhythms of hot jazz. His distinctive contribution was blending these influences with an equal measure of his own passionate soul and artistic inspiration to create and evolve what would become a genre of its own, named in honor of Monroe's band, the Blue Grass Boys. It can fairly be said that every bluegrass band on earth draws inspiration from the musical contributions of Bill Monroe.

"You know, I never wrote a tune in my life. All that music's in the air around you all the time. I was just the first one to reach up and pull it out."
- "Bill Monroe Has Lots to Sing but Little to Say" by Jason DeParle, in Ewing, Tom, *The Bill Monroe Reader*, 2000.

Bill Monroe was the youngest of eight children born to a western Kentucky farm family in Rosine, Ohio County, not far from Owensboro. Suffering from crossed eyes that weren't corrected until his teens, the young man endured teasing and visual difficulties that haunted him for life. The family loved music, and Bill proved an apt performer on mandolin, guitar, and vocals. He left school in the fifth grade, began work as a laborer at eleven, and was orphaned at seventeen. Soon after, he joined older siblings in the Chicago area, where he found work in the oil

Born: September 13, 1911, Rosine, KY

Died: September 9, 1996, Springfield, TN

Primary instrument: Mandolin

"There was three of us brothers to start with, that tried to play music and, of course, they was older than I was, and one of 'em – Birch – wanted to play the fiddle. Charlie loved the guitar... So I got the mandolin, I wound up with that."
- "Bill Monroe: King of Blue Grass Music," interview with Doug Benson in Ewing, Tom, *The Bill Monroe Reader*, 2000.

Composed:

BMI's database credits Bill Monroe with 267 published compositions, co-compositions, and arrangements. A few of his original songs and collaborations are:

"Kentucky Waltz" (*Billboard* peak at #3, 1946)

"Wicked Path of Sin" (*Billboard* peak at #13, 1948)

Bluegrass Hall of Fame Inductee Biographies \ 3

"Little Community Church" (*Billboard* peak at #11, 1948)

"Toy Heart" (*Billboard* peak at #12, 1949)

"Scotland" (*Billboard* peak at #27, 1958)

"Uncle Pen" (*Billboard* peak at #1, 1984 for Ricky Skaggs)

"Walk Softly On This Heart of Mine" (*Billboard* peak at #25, 1989 for The Kentucky Headhunters)

"*Blue Moon of Kentucky*"

"*Blue Grass Breakdown*"

"*Raw Hide*"

Early influences:

Pendleton "Uncle Pen" Vandiver, fiddler, Ohio County, KY

Arnold Shultz, guitarist and fiddler, Ohio County, KY

Jimmie Rodgers

Prairie Ramblers

"I wanted a style of my own and that's what I finally came up with."

- "Bluegrass Touches - An Interview with Bill Monroe" by Charles Wolfe, in Ewing, Tom, *The Bill Monroe Reader*, 2000.

Came to fame with:

The Monroe Brothers, 1934-1938

Performed with:

The Monroe Brothers, 1934-1938

Bill Monroe and the Blue Grass Boys, 1939-1996

Led the way:

- Pioneered bluegrass music and set its standard for more than half a century.
- *Grand Ole Opry* member, 1939-1996.

industry. A few years later, he and brothers Charlie and Birch became exhibition square dancers for the *WLS Barn Dance*. Charlie and Bill left their day jobs in 1934 to form the Monroe Brothers, the hottest of the mandolin-guitar duets popular in that decade.

Radio, concerts, and recordings, mostly in the Carolinas, launched the duo to prominence with songs such as "What Would You Give in Exchange for Your Soul," "Drifting Too Far From the Shore," and "New River Train." The brothers quarreled and split in 1938. Bill decided to modernize and enlarge his musical vision with a larger string ensemble, which he eventually named the Blue Grass Boys in honor of his home state. In 1939, on the strength of his adaptation of Jimmie Rodgers's "Mule Skinner Blues," he was inducted to the *Grand Ole Opry* on WSM, Nashville, as a life member.

Over the next five decades, Bill Monroe led a band through

"There are a lot of young bluegrass groups coming along now that are out of this world, boy. They can really sing the harmony and play the music… They're all over the country, and I like to hear them play."

- "Bill Monroe" (interview) by George Gruhn, in Ewing, Tom, *The Bill Monroe Reader*, 2000.

which scores of talented musicians served their apprenticeship. Among Blue Grass Boys alumni who made their later mark in bluegrass, country, folk, and other genres were Clyde Moody, Howdy Forrester, Stringbean (David Akeman), Carl Story, Chubby Wise, Lester Flatt, Earl Scruggs, Benny Martin, Jim Eanes, Don Reno, Vassar Clements, Mac Wiseman, Jimmy Martin, Gordon Terry, Carter Stanley, Sonny Osborne, Bobby Hicks, Kenny Baker, Don Stover, Eddie Adcock, Dale Potter, Buddy Spicher, Del McCoury, Bill Keith, James Monroe (Bill's son), Peter Rowan, Richard Greene, Byron Berline, Doug Green, and Roland White.

The sound that came to be known as bluegrass wasn't born fully formed. It constantly evolved as Bill Monroe merged his creative inspirations with the talents that passed through his band. In the late 1930s and early 40s, the Blue Grass Boys played in a raggy, syncopated, and improvisatory style that evoked both the black string bands of an earlier era and the simultaneously emerging form of western swing. During this phase, the fiddle became the central voice of the instrumental ensemble, and high-pitched solos, duets, trios, and quartets provided a rich variety of vocal material.

With Earl Scruggs's entry into the Blue Grass Boys in 1945, bluegrass music first employed the five-piece ensemble for which it has ever since been recognized: plucked string bass, steel-string guitar, mandolin, fiddle, and banjo played in the three-finger style that Scruggs made wildly popular. During the three years that Bill Monroe, Lester Flatt, Earl Scruggs, Chubby Wise, and Howard Watts were together, their performances and Columbia recordings set a standard that have ever since been recognized as a high water mark for the form.

After Flatt and Scruggs split off to form their own group, Bill Monroe took his sound in new directions. Autobiographical songs, faster tempos, a more dynamic instrumental attack, and eventually double and triple-fiddle arrangements characterized the great music the band made for Decca in the 1950s. In his fifties and a veteran performer, Bill Monroe wasn't content to rest on his laurels. As the folk music craze swept North America, the traditional roots embedded in his music brought it to the attention of new audiences in the colleges and urban centers outside the heartland of the Appalachian region and mid-south where bluegrass had flourished.

The 1970s and 1980s saw a proliferation of bluegrass festivals, labels, radio programs, and media coverage. Bill Monroe was the recognized patriarch of an entire genre of music, which was by then spreading worldwide. In the final quarter century of his life, Bill Monroe received the recognition and approval of peers for which he had hungered as a child. The broader world of the arts and culture recognized Bill Monroe as one of the leading innovators and musical figures of the twentieth century. The "Father of Bluegrass Music" died a few days short of his eighty-fifth birthday after a series of health challenges, through which he continued to perform for appreciative audiences, almost to the end.

— FRED BARTENSTEIN

- Country Music Hall of Fame, 1970.
- First Bluegrass Grammy Award, 1989.
- Bluegrass Hall of Fame, 1991.
- Grammy Lifetime Achievement Award, 1993.
- National Medal of Honor, 1995.
- Rock and Roll Hall of Fame, 1997.

By the way:
- Sang bass in the Rosine Methodist youth choir at age 12 or 13.
- Purchased Brown County Jamboree Park in Bean Blossom, IN in 1951 and produced one of the earliest and longest-running bluegrass festivals there, starting in 1967.
- Toured with a tent and a semiprofessional baseball team in the 1940s (Bill played shortstop).
- Many of his songs were autobiographical (e.g., "Letter from My Darling," "Little Georgia Rose," "Uncle Pen").
- In June, 1985, at Shoney's Restaurant in Nashville, paid the tab for lunch at the meeting that led to formation of the International Bluegrass Music Association.

Earl Eugene Scruggs | 1991

A mild-mannered North Carolinian from a mill town would strike few as a world-renowned, influential musician and composer. Earl Scruggs, once compared to violinist Niccolo Paganini, not only pioneered the three-finger banjo but played it to standards of taste and technique unmatched by thousands of disciples over seven decades. He was an important figure in the birth of the bluegrass genre, and also brought his artistry to the fields of country, folk, and rock, to college campuses, and to television and the movies.

Earl Scruggs's father was an old-time banjo player, but died when Earl was four. Older brother Junie, who also played banjo, had moved out on his own before Earl developed his early musical interests into a style around 1934. Brother Horace, a guitarist, and neighbor Dennis Butler, a fiddler, were the young man's earliest jamming partners. By the age of thirteen, he had purchased his own banjo and by fifteen he was performing professionally on the radio. Music and textile mill work alternated until Scruggs decided to become a professional performing artist at the end of World War II.

After a brief stint with "Lost" John Miller and the Allied Kentuckians, which brought him to Nashville, Earl Scruggs successfully auditioned for Bill Monroe and the Blue Grass Boys. Lester Flatt, Chubby Wise,

> *"Everybody's all worried about who invented the style and it's obvious that three-finger banjo pickers have been around a long time – maybe since 1840. But my feeling about it is that if it wasn't for Earl Scruggs, you wouldn't be worried about who invented it."*
> - John Hartford, quoted in Barry Willis, *America's Music: Bluegrass*, 1989.

Born: January 6, 1924, Flint Hill Community, Shelby, NC

Died: March 28, 2012, Nashville, TN

Primary instrument: Banjo

Composed:
BMI's database credits Earl Scruggs with 156 published compositions, co-compositions (many with Lester Flatt), and arrangements. A few of his original songs and collaborations are:

"Cabin on the Hill" (*Billboard* peak at #9, 1959)

"The Legend of the Johnson Boys" (*Billboard* peak at #27, 1962)

"My Saro Jane" (*Billboard* peak at #40, 1964)

"Foggy Mountain Breakdown" (*Billboard* peak at #58, 1968)

"Don't Get Above Your Raising" (*Billboard* peak at #16, 1981 for Ricky Skaggs)

"Earl's Breakdown"
"Flint Hill Special"
"Randy Lynn Rag"
"Shuckin' the Corn"

Early influences:
Rex Brooks
Dennis Butler
Maybelle Carter
Smith Hammett
Fisher Hendley
Snuffy Jenkins
Mack Woolbright

Came to fame with:
Bill Monroe and the Blue Grass Boys, 1945-1948

Performed with
Carolina Wildcats, Gastonia, NC, 1939

Morris Brothers, Spartanburg, SC, 1939

Carl Story and the Rambling Mountaineers, Asheville, NC, 1942

"Lost" John Miller, Knoxville/Nashville, TN, 1945

Bill Monroe and the Blue Grass Boys, 1945-1948

Lester Flatt, Earl Scruggs and the Foggy Mountain Boys, 1948-1969

Earl Scruggs Revue, 1969-1980

Solo act with various collaborators, 1980 - 2012

Led the way
- Introduced "Scruggs-style," the model for virtually every subsequent banjo player in bluegrass music.
- Co-led the first nationally and internationally prominent bluegrass act.
- *Grand Ole Opry* member, 1955-1969.
- Country Music Hall of Fame, 1985.
- Bluegrass Hall of Fame, 1991.
- National Medal of Artistic Achievement, 1992.
- Million-Air Award from BMI celebrating one million broadcasts of "Foggy Mountain Breakdown," 1994.

Howard Watts, Earl and Bill made up the classic edition of that band between summer, 1945, and spring, 1948. Surviving airchecks from *Grand Ole Opry* performances document the electrifying effect the act had upon audiences. The warmest ovations greeted Earl's radically new banjo solos – the loudest, fastest, and smoothest anyone had ever heard. Announcer George D. Hay gave "Earl Scruggs and his fancy banjo" equal billing with bandleader Bill Monroe.

Tired of the constant touring, Flatt and Scruggs resigned from the Blue Grass Boys and decided to seek local radio work together in a succession of southern markets. They built a band called the Foggy Mountain Boys (named after a Carter Family song, "Foggy Mountain Top"), and populated it mostly with fellow alumni of Bill Monroe's band. Mercury and Columbia recording contracts were negotiated, and the banjo was prominently featured on 78 and 45 rpm singles released just as DJ radio and jukeboxes came into popularity. The band worked territories around Danville, Virginia; Hickory, North Carolina; Bristol, Virginia/Tennessee; Lexington, Kentucky; Tampa, Florida; Roanoke, Virginia; Raleigh, North Carolina; Knoxville, Tennessee; and Richmond/Crewe, Virginia – spawning banjo enthusiasts and future banjo stars at every stop.

> *"I never felt that I should quit what I had done all my life after I left Monroe, and let him go ahead and do it, and me try to learn a new style."*
>
> - Quoted in Barry Willis, *America's Music: Bluegrass*, 1989.

In 1955, at radio sponsor Martha White Mills' insistence, the Foggy Mountain Boys were added to the *Grand Ole Opry* roster and were henceforth based in Nashville. Prominent members of the band included guitarists Jim Eanes and Mac Wiseman; mandolinists Curly Seckler and Everett Lilly; fiddlers Benny Sims, Benny Martin, and Paul Warren; bassists Jody Rainwater and Jake Tullock; and Dobro player Josh Graves. Ironically, given their earlier desire to reduce touring, Flatt and Scruggs did the most traveling of any *Opry* act in the 1950s, covering both live performances and a circuit of radio and television stations in the days before technology supported syndication. Widely popular for an energetic and thoroughly rural style centered on Earl's riveting banjo, they thrived during the early rock 'n' roll era when many of their bluegrass and country contemporaries struggled.

Astute business manager Louise Scruggs helped Flatt and Scruggs to capitalize upon a string of important opportunities. These included the soundtrack and appearances in television's *Beverly Hillbillies*, concerts at colleges and other venues associated with the folk music boom, capitalization on the movie *Bonnie and Clyde*'s use of "Foggy Mountain

Breakdown," and, on the band's Columbia LPs, material from new songwriters such as Bob Dylan, Johnny Cash, Tom T. Hall, and Utah Phillips. Earl's growing interest in new musical genres and performing with sons Gary, Randy, and Steve led to a parting of the ways with Lester Flatt in 1969.

"You just can't make a living on the road unless you've got a record on the charts or some tie-in with a TV show or something. We were forced to do something that was of commercial benefit to us, regardless of the flack."
- Quoted by Lawrence Talbot in Bear Family box set *Flatt & Scruggs 1964-1969, plus*

For a decade, the Earl Scruggs Revue was a popular act, mostly in youth markets, including scores of college appearances. Musicians such as Charlie Daniels, Jody Maphis, Josh Graves, Vassar Clements, Lea Jane Berinati, and a procession of musical celebrities enhanced the long-haired sons' country rock. Banjo icon Earl Scruggs remained the center of audience and media attention, changing his style very little. Health challenges led to Earl's retirement from the road in the late 1970s.

The public never lost its fascination with Earl Scruggs. Jam sessions at Earl and Louise's house in Madison, Tennessee, continued to attract the A-list of performers from bluegrass and related genres throughout the eighties and nineties. Occasional guest appearances with artists like Ricky Skaggs and Tom T. Hall kept him in the recording game. In 1997, bolstered by recent advances in pharmaceuticals and medical care and a huge market demand, Earl decided to accept a limited number of personal appearance dates, media appearances, and recording invitations. All were hugely successful. Widowed at the age of eighty-two, Earl Scruggs continued to receive accolades from new generations as well as surviving contemporaries from the dawn of the bluegrass era. In March of 2012, he died of natural causes at a Nashville hospital at the age of eighty-eight.

"We did a live TV show in 1960 for NBC... where I met this sax man named King Curtis... King turned me on to the new sound, and that stuck in my mind... I guess I'd just gone my limit with bluegrass."
- Quoted by Lawrence Talbot in Bear Family box set *Flatt & Scruggs 1964-1969, plus*

— FRED BARTENSTEIN

- Grammy Award for Best Country Instrumental, 2002.
- Star on Hollywood Walk of Fame, 2003.

By the way:
- Finger-picked guitar on gospel and Carter Family songs, to differentiate the Foggy Mountain Boys' sound from Bill Monroe's.
- J.D. Crowe, a pre-teen in 1949 and 1950, sat on the front row as often as he could to study Earl Scruggs's banjo playing at WVLK in Versailles, near Lexington, Kentucky.
- Wrote the banjo instrumental "Randy Lynn Rag" in honor of Randy Lynn Scruggs's birth in 1953.
- Wife Louise Scruggs (1929-2006) was the first prominent female business figure in country music.
- Piloted his own plane to distant concert appearances, beginning in 1957.
- Wrote an instruction manual: *Earl Scruggs and the Five-String Banjo* and invented Scruggs tuners, used to accurately and quickly change a string's pitch during performance.
- Spoke publicly against the war at the 1969 US Vietnam Moratorium in Washington, D.C.
- A catalyst in organizing appearances by country music legends on the Nitty Gritty Dirt Band's historic *Will the Circle Be Unbroken* album, 1971.

For more information on the history of Flatt and Scruggs, see profiles of Lester Flatt, Josh Graves, Louise Scruggs, Curly Seckler, and Paul Warren.

Lester Raymond Flatt \ 1991

Lester Flatt's grandfatherly emceeing style, relaxed southern singing voice, solid rhythm guitar playing, and songwriting endeared him to generations of bluegrass and country music fans. A member of the classic edition of Bill Monroe and the Blue Grass Boys, Lester's star burned even brighter when he and Earl Scruggs formed a partnership in 1948, heading the Foggy Mountain Boys. Mercury and Columbia records, WSM radio, the *Grand Ole Opry*, constant touring, a Martha White Mills-sponsored television show, themes to *The Beverly Hillbillies* and *Bonnie and Clyde*, and full participation in the folk revival ever widened Lester Flatt's visibility and influence. After splitting with Earl Scruggs in 1969, Lester headed a crack bluegrass ensemble, the Nashville Grass, on Nugget, RCA, and CMH records right up to the year of his death at the age of sixty-four in 1979.

Lester Flatt was born to a musical farming family in central Tennessee, near Sparta. He started on banjo, but switched to guitar at the age of seven. Lester played with a thumb and finger pick, as did most country guitarists in the 1930s and 1940s. He left school at twelve, married singer Gladys Stacey at seventeen, and alternated between textile millwork and music for a decade before committing to a professional music career after a bout with rheumatoid arthritis. Lester sang tenor, first with Clyde Moody and then with Charlie Monroe, before permanently switching to lead upon joining the band

"In their twenty-one years together, Flatt and Scruggs had more impact on the music, in my opinion, than anything that's gone on before or since."

- Lance LeRoy, quoted in Barry R. Willis, *America's Music: Bluegrass*, 1989.

Born: June 19, 1914, Duncan's Chapel, Overton County, TN

Died: May 11, 1979, Nashville, TN

Primary instrument: Guitar

"That little run you hear on the guitar, and hear so many people doing today – I used that for a time setter; we were playing so fast we had to have something to come back in on, and it fit perfectly."

- Quoted by Bill Vernon in "A Conversation with Lester Flatt," *Muleskinner News*, August, 1972.

Composed:

BMI's database credits Lester Flatt with 168 published compositions, co-compositions (many with Bill Monroe or Earl Scruggs), and arrangements. A few of his original songs and collaborations are:

"Sweetheart You Done Me Wrong" (*Billboard* peak at #11, 1948 for Bill Monroe)

Photo: Alan Whitman

"When You Are Lonely" (*Billboard* peak at #12, 1949 for Bill Monroe)

"Cabin on the Hill" (*Billboard* peak at #9, 1959)

"The Legend of the Johnson Boys" (*Billboard* peak at #27, 1962)

"My Saro Jane" (*Billboard* peak at #40, 1964)

"Don't Get Above Your Raising" (*Billboard* peak at #16, 1981 for Ricky Skaggs)

"Backin' To Birmingham"

"Crying My Heart Out Over You"

"Get in Line Brother"

"I'm Going To Sleep With One Eye Open"

"I used to write practically everything we did. Maybe they weren't good, but they were original, and they were selling."
- Quoted by Bill Vernon in "A Conversation with Lester Flatt," *Muleskinner News*, August, 1972.

Early influences:
Monroe Brothers

Came to fame with:
Bill Monroe and the Blue Grass Boys, 1945-1948

Performed with:
Charlie Scott's Harmonizers, Roanoke, VA, 1935

Clyde Moody and the Happy-Go-Lucky Boys, Burlington, NC, 1940

Jim Hall and the Crazy Mountaineers, Burlington, NC, early 1940s

Charlie Monroe and the Kentucky Pardners, Winston-Salem, NC, 1943-1945

Bill Monroe and the Blue Grass Boys, 1945-1948

of Charlie's younger brother Bill in 1945.

It must have been a heady experience to appear on the *Grand Ole Opry* and record for Columbia records in Chicago with the Blue Grass Boys. But by this time Lester Flatt was a seasoned professional, and emceed stage shows for the more reticent Monroe. Like contemporaries Frank Sinatra with the Harry James and Tommy Dorsey bands, and Tommy Duncan with Bob Wills and the Texas Playboys, Flatt was prominently featured as a crooning vocalist. Lester's wife missed him during the long road tours, and soon was also employed by the Monroe organization, selling concessions. When banjo player David "Stringbean" Akeman left the group, Flatt didn't share Monroe's enthusiasm for finding a replacement – until he heard young Earl Scruggs play the instrument in an exciting new style at an impromptu backstage audition. In a 1979 interview with Don Rhodes for *Pickin'*, Lester recalled telling Bill, "Hire him no matter what it costs."

After three years of stardom as sidemen, Flatt and Scruggs decided that they were ready to co-lead their own organization. In 1948, they founded the Foggy Mountain Boys. Relations with their former employer were cordial until Flatt and Scruggs made a guest appearance on the *Grand Ole Opry*. This was a few years before they became permanent members in 1955, at the insistence of Martha White Mills. Bill Monroe considered this direct competition for his artistic and economic niche and tried to block the decision, but was unsuccessful. He and Flatt didn't speak until a 1971 reconciliation at Bean Blossom, Indiana.

The Foggy Mountain Boys worked hard at a series of small radio stations before landing a fifteen-minute, 5:45 am slot in 1953 on WSM: *Martha White Biscuit Time*. This, and a television show which followed two years later, were syndicated to other southern markets. Before videotape came into use, the group was forced to travel to these locations for the broadcasts. A bus was fitted out for the band and they traveled more extensively than any other *Grand Ole Opry* act.

"I remember the first time I heard [the Monroe Brothers] – I really liked them from the start, because it was singing like we used to do at home. When I went to work with Bill, I didn't have any problem, because it fit right in there."
- Quoted by Bill Vernon in "A Conversation with Lester Flatt," *Muleskinner News*, August, 1972.

"People will say to me, 'I see you on television, and you're the most relaxed guy I ever saw.' I just can't do it any other way. I have to be like I am at home – if I can't… I might as well forget it."
- Quoted in Bill Vernon, "A Conversation with Lester Flatt," *Muleskinner News*, August, 1972.

Hugely successful for two decades on the air, on records, and on stage, Flatt and Scruggs finally split in 1969 after differences about musical direction. Earl wanted to play more modern music with his sons. Uncomfortable singing Bob Dylan and other folk material demanded by a Columbia record contract, Flatt headed out on his own to play a much more traditional brand of bluegrass. Martha White sponsored a "name the band" contest. The winning entry, "Nashville Grass," was a pun on the currently popular act Danny Davis and the Nashville Brass.

Lester Flatt made some strong recordings as a solo act, including three albums of duets with former associate Mac Wiseman. His appearances, with a crack ensemble of side musicians, were enthusiastically received on the burgeoning bluegrass festival scene. But health problems arising from a 1967 heart attack led to an open-heart operation, lowered stamina, reduced touring, and eventual retirement early in 1979. Flatt persuaded Curly Seckler to continue the Nashville Grass, and died a few months later. In her song, "The Day That Lester Died," Claire Lynch spoke for the entire bluegrass community, "The songs will live on, we'll sing them again, but somehow it will never be the same."

> *"[Earl Scruggs and I] thought when we first started, they wanted something a little more modern, but they wanted 'Salty Dog Blues,' 'Roll in My Sweet Baby's Arms,' and numbers like that, so we wound up doing them."*
>
> – Quoted in Bill Vernon, "A Conversation with Lester Flatt," *Muleskinner News*, August, 1972.

— FRED BARTENSTEIN

Lester Flatt, Earl Scruggs and the Foggy Mountain Boys, 1948-1969

Lester Flatt and the Nashville Grass, 1969-1979

Led the way:

- Lead singer and guitarist for the classic edition of the Blue Grass Boys.
- Co-led the first nationally and internationally prominent bluegrass act.
- Popularized the famous "Lester Flatt G-run" among rhythm guitarists.
- Hosted the first widely syndicated bluegrass television show.
- *Grand Ole Opry* member, 1955-1979.
- Country Music Hall of Fame, 1985.
- Bluegrass Hall of Fame, 1991.

By the way

- Lived on Old Hickory Lake, just north of Nashville, where he enjoyed fishing with his wife Gladys.
- Mentored Marty Stuart, who joined the Nashville Grass and moved in with the Flatts at the age of 12.
- Bluegrass and country star Keith Whitley could do a close imitation of Lester Flatt's distinctive speaking voice. Lester enjoyed hearing it, and holding conversations "with himself."

For more information on the history of Flatt and Scruggs, see profiles of Earl Scruggs, Josh Graves, Louise Scruggs, Curly Seckler, and Paul Warren.

THE STANLEY BROTHERS

Carter Glen Stanley | 1992

Born: August 27, 1925, Big Spraddle Creek, Dickenson County, VA

Died: December 1, 1966, Bristol, TN

Primary instrument:- Guitar

"Pee Wee [Lambert] played the mandolin and Ralph he played the banjo, just forefinger and thumb, and Carter he was learning Lester Flatt strokes. They was getting pretty good at it 'cause they practiced; they didn't fool around."

- Fiddler Leslie Keith, describing the Stanley Brothers' band as he joined it in 1947, in Bob Sayers, "Leslie Keith: Black Mountain Odyssey," *Bluegrass Unlimited*, December 1976.

Composed:
BMI's database credits Carter Stanley with 127 published compositions (20 in the name of his half-sister, Ruby Rakes), co-compositions (many with Ralph Stanley), and arrangements. A few of his original songs and

Carter Stanley and his younger brother Ralph grew up in the remote coal and timber fields of southwestern Virginia where they spent most of their lives. Father Lee Stanley was a powerful singer in the Appalachian tradition, which his boys also experienced at the McClure Primitive Baptist Church. Mother Lucy Smith Stanley was accomplished at the clawhammer-style banjo. Both widowed in previous marriages, Lee and Lucy separated when Carter was thirteen or fourteen and Ralph was twelve. The boys were close companions and shared a strong interest in the mountain music that surrounded them. They played widely at family and community gatherings, graduating from imagined instruments of kindling wood to the guitar (Carter) and banjo (Ralph) as young teenagers.

After graduating in 1943 from Ervinton High School in Nora, Virginia, where he was class president, Carter served two years in the Army Air Corps. Committed to a professional music career, Carter joined Roy Sykes and the Blue Ridge Mountain Boys in 1946, playing daily on WNVA in nearby Norton, Virginia. When Ralph was discharged later that year, Carter and bandmate Pee Wee Lambert left their group to form the Stanley Brothers and the

"Carter Stanley had an unusual voice, a rare, rich, mellow and pure sound that seemed to flow effortlessly from him. His voice could be so tender at times yet so powerful as well. His voice seemed to pull on emotions he held deep inside. He had the unique ability to paint a picture with words when he sang."

- Daughter Jeanie Stanley in liner note to *Baby Girl: A Tribute To My Father Carter Stanley*, CMH Records, 2005.

Photo: © John Byrne Cooke, 1964

Clinch Mountain Boys. Winning an audition on Bristol's brand-new station WCYB, the group performed daily on the noontime *Farm and Fun Time* for most of the next twelve years. Recordings with Johnson City, Tennessee's Rich-R-Tone label began in 1947.

At first, the Clinch Mountain Boys played in an old-time style reminiscent of Mainer's Mountaineers. Carter's songwriting was a distinctive feature of the band's appeal. "Mother No Longer Awaits Me at Home" and "The Girl Behind the Bar" were followed by "Little Glass of Wine," which became a regional hit. The influence of Bill Monroe and the Blue Grass Boys and Bill's alumni Lester Flatt and Earl Scruggs soon had the Clinch Mountain Boys playing a unique fusion of mountain music and the emerging bluegrass style.

collaborations are:
"I'll Take the Blame" (*Billboard* peak at #86, 1980 for Ricky Skaggs)
"Could You Love Me One More Time"
"The Fields Have Turned Brown"
"Going To the Races"
"Harbor of Love"
"I'll Just Go Away"
"Lonesome Night"
"The Lonesome River"
"Nobody's Love Like Mine"

"Think Of What You've Done"

"The White Dove"

"[M]ost songs I have written at night… I remember very well when I wrote 'The White Dove.' We was coming home from Asheville, North Carolina, to Bristol, Tennessee, and I had the light on because I wanted to write it down and Ralph was fussing at me for having the light on. He was driving and he said the light bothered him, but he hasn't fussed anymore about that."

– Interview with Mike Seeger in March of 1966, quoted by Gary Reid in liner notes to *The Early Starday/King Years, 1958-1961*, Starday/King Records, 2003.

Early influences:

Lee and Lucy Stanley (parents)

Carter Family

Grayson and Whitter

J.E. and Wade Mainer

Monroe Brothers

Bill Monroe and the Blue Grass Boys

Came to fame with:

The Stanley Brothers, 1946-1966

"The Stanley Brothers had a song called 'Little Glass of Wine' and they impressed me with the fact that they actually got a big U.S. Mail sack of letters every day requesting them to sing it, and so naturally we hopped into a session on that."

– Rich-R-Tone Records owner James Stanton, quoted in Rounder Collective, brochure notes to *The Rich-R-Tone Story*, 1974.

In 1948, the popular act's signing to Columbia prompted Bill Monroe to leave that label. During the next several years, the Stanley Brothers developed an innovative style of trio singing. Carter sang the verses solo; on choruses Ralph harmonized on a higher tenor line while Pee Wee Lambert sang an even higher baritone part on songs like "The Angels Are Singing," "The Lonesome River," and "The White Dove."

A slow period in the winter of 1950-1951 led to a brief hiatus in the Stanley Brothers' performances and Columbia recordings. Bill Monroe called upon Carter as a replacement for Jimmy Martin as lead singer with the Blue Grass Boys. Bill's anger toward the Stanleys, whom he felt were copying his music, soon dissipated and the three remained friends for the rest of their lives. In July of 1951, Carter recorded six numbers with Bill Monroe, including the notable duet "Sugar Coated Love" and quartets "You're Drifting Away" and "Get Down on Your Knees and Pray." By October, the Clinch Mountain Boys were back together and hotter than ever.

In 1953, the band moved from Columbia to the Mercury label. This proved a lucky move, as Mercury producer Dee Kilpatrick loved the hard-edged Appalachian sound and stuck with the Stanley Brothers as rock 'n' roll's emergence altered or destroyed the careers of many of their peers. Carter felt the Mercury recordings of the next five years were the brothers' best. In 1958, the band relocated to Live Oak, Florida, to help relaunch the *Suwanee River Jamboree* on radio station WNER. That year, they joined King Records of Cincinnati, where they remained until Carter's death.

King's Syd Nathan encouraged the band to de-emphasize the fiddle,

"Once I saw the Stanleys fill an auditorium that would seat 450 people to capacity twice on a single Saturday night… in a town of 1,200 and a county of 10,000. Forced to leave after the first show so that people outside could get in for the second show, I examined the shiny new Cadillac they had parked near a rear door. Then I joined others who had gathered at the open windows to hear more good bluegrass until the second show ended; they emerged, still dripping sweat, and signing the song and picture books they sold. From the beginning they combined the graceful vocal harmonies of a 'brother' act with hard-driving instrumentation to produce a music with power and depth. I thought then that it was the best music I'd heard, and time has had very little effect on that opinion."

– Joe Wilson, "Bristol's WCYB: Early Bluegrass Turf" in *Muleskinner News*, October 1972.

banjo, and mandolin in favor of a two-guitar sound. Nathan also pitched honky-tonk flavored material he felt would more likely appeal to a country music audience. The Stanley Brothers' only charting single, "How Far To Little Rock," peaked at number seventeen in *Billboard* in 1960. Ironically, it was the folk music audience that carried the Stanley Brothers to global prominence and appearances in the 1960s.

A brooding personality, a decade of road travel away from home and the mountains he loved, and meager financial rewards for his strenuous musical labors perhaps contributed to Carter's deepening alcoholism. His health suffered, and bandmates Ralph Stanley and George Shuffler increasingly filled Carter's roles as emcee and lead singer. Carter appeared at the first multi-day bluegrass festival in Fincastle, Virginia, Labor Day Weekend of 1965, where he triumphantly reprised his recordings with Bill Monroe in the Sunday afternoon "Story of Bluegrass." December 1, 1966, two months after his last concert at Monroe's Brown County Jamboree in Bean Blossom, Indiana, Carter Stanley died of liver failure. He was forty-one.

— FRED BARTENSTEIN

> *"Music was his first love – his life – and he gave it the best he had to give at all times. Sick or well, sad or happy, for Carter Stanley the show went on… [H]is music, his dreams, the things he stood for, live on."*

- Daughter Doris Stanley Avery, letter to the editor, *Bluegrass Unlimited*, July 1976.

Performed with:

Roy Sykes and the Blue Ridge Mountain Boys, Norton, VA, 1946

The Stanley Brothers and the Clinch Mountain Boys, 1946-1951

Bill Monroe and the Blue Grass Boys, 1951

The Stanley Brothers and the Clinch Mountain Boys, 1951-1966

Led the way:

- Co-led the second band to achieve commercial success playing the new (and as yet unnamed) style of bluegrass.
- A major contributor to the "mountain" and "lonesome" sounds of bluegrass.
- Writer of much of the core song repertoire and some of the most affecting lyrics in bluegrass history.
- Instrumental Group of the Year, Country and Western Jamboree readers' poll, 1955.
- Played the prestigious Newport Folk Festival in 1959, the first year bluegrass was included.
- Bluegrass Hall of Fame, 1992.

By the way:

- An informed student of early country music, imparting that knowledge to new audiences during the 1960s folk music era.
- Reportedly turned down Bill Monroe's 1951 offer to retitle his act "Bill Monroe and the Stanley Brothers."
- In his early twenties on a radio broadcast, unthinkingly dedicated the song "Lonely Tombs" to "all you folks that's not feeling well."

THE STANLEY BROTHERS

Ralph Edmond Stanley | 1992

After graduating from high school in May of 1945 at the age of eighteen, Ralph Stanley was inducted into the army. He served a year with the occupation forces in Germany. His administrative talents were recognized there and he was urged to reenlist but decided instead to study veterinary medicine. Arriving home, Ralph was taken by his father directly from the railroad station to a radio broadcast in Norton, Virginia, where he performed with his brother and Roy Sykes and the Blue Ridge Mountain Boys. Carter Stanley and Pee Wee Lambert soon left that band to form the Stanley Brothers and the Clinch Mountain Boys.

Ralph began playing banjo in a two-finger style reminiscent of Wade Mainer. He heard the emerging three-finger style from Snuffy and Hoke Jenkins, and adapted a distinctive variant in 1948, while both the Stanley Brothers and Flatt and Scruggs were appearing on WCYB, Bristol.

Ten years of regional stardom followed, centered on WCYB radio's daily *Farm and Fun Time* radio program. The Stanley Brothers were picked up by national labels Columbia, and Mercury, but found themselves unable to break out of performance circuits where bluegrass was most accepted: North and South Carolina, Tennessee, Kentucky, Virginia, and West Virginia; and areas where Appalachians migrated for employment in Ohio, Michigan, Maryland, and Pennsylvania.

> *"My mother used to pick the banjo… I call it the clawhammer. Actually drop thumb is what she did…. She told me she played all night a many of a night for square dances…. I was about twelve when I first picked up the banjo."*
>
> - Quoted in Fred Bartenstein, "The Ralph Stanley Story: An Interview" *Muleskinner News*, March, 1972.

Born: February 25, 1927, Big Spraddle Creek, Dickenson County, VA

Primary instrument: Banjo

Composed:
BMI's database credits Ralph Stanley with 227 published compositions, co-compositions (many with Carter Stanley), and arrangements. A few of his original songs and collaborations are:

"Big Tilda"

"The Darkest Hour is Just Before Dawn"

"A Few More Seasons"

"Hard Times" (instrumental)

"I'm Lonesome Without You"

"I'm Lost, I'll Never Find the Way"

"Let Me Love You One More Time"

"Wonderful World Outside"

Early influences:
Lucy Smith Stanley (mother)

Primitive Baptist Universalist Church

Photo: Alan Whitman

"Fiddling" Arthur Smith
J.E. and Wade Mainer
Snuffy and Hoke Jenkins
Bill Monroe and the Blue Grass Boys
Earl Scruggs

Came to fame with:
The Stanley Brothers, 1946-1966

Performed with:
The Stanley Brothers and the Clinch Mountain Boys, 1946-1966

Ralph Stanley and the Clinch Mountain Boys, 1967-present

Led the way:
- Co-led the second band to achieve commercial success playing the new (and as yet unnamed) style of bluegrass.

- A major contributor to the "mountain" and "lonesome" sounds of bluegrass.

- Instrumental Group of the Year, *Country and Western Jamboree* readers' poll, 1955.

- First bluegrass band to play the prestigious Newport Folk Festival, in 1959.

- First bluegrass act to record a cappella gospel hymns, 1971.

- Honorary doctorate in Music, Lincoln Memorial University, Harrogate, TN, 1976.

- Bluegrass Hall of Fame, 1992.

- *Grand Ole Opry* member, 2000-present.

- National Heritage Fellowship, National Endowment for the Arts, 1984.

- Living Legend award, Library of Congress, 2000.

1958 brought major changes in the Stanleys' career. They moved to Live Oak, Florida to help relaunch the *Suwanee River Jamboree*, and soon picked up a television and radio circuit for the Jim Walter Homes Corporation. That year they began recording for Starday and King, labels focused on ethnic niches overlooked by mass media. Ralph managed the band's business affairs and, as Carter's health began to fail, found himself increasingly fronting the band as lead singer and master of ceremonies.

"When I got out of the army I was a'gonna train for a veterinary — what I had in mind to. Decided different. Carter mostly decided for me."

– Quoted in Fred Bartenstein, "The Ralph Stanley Story: An Interview," *Muleskinner News*, March, 1972.

The Stanley Brothers were discovered by new audiences, not only in the Deep South, but in cities, at colleges, and in Europe, as the folk music boom of the early 1960s spread. In 1965, they drove from Florida to the first multi-day bluegrass festival in Fincastle, Virginia. Carter's death in December of 1966 came before the festivals grew into a viable performance circuit.

Ralph faced a true dilemma as he entered his forties. Should he change careers in order to better provide for his growing family? Or should he revamp the Clinch Mountain Boys? King Records' Syd Nathan and the fans urged the latter course, and soon Ralph was running the roads again, in a station wagon with Curly Ray Cline, Melvin Goins, and a nineteen-year-old Larry Sparks. In April of 1968, Ralph moved from Florida back to his childhood home in Dickenson County, Virginia, where he began a Memorial Day bluegrass festival in 1971.

"[When I decided to reform the Clinch Mountain Boys after Carter's death] there wasn't too much else I was qualified to do… I got letters by the hundreds from fans asking me to, and that encouraged me. I didn't know much else to do, except going down to labor and hard work, and I never did like that… I wanted to keep as near as I could the same sound, but I guess maybe it didn't. Sort of… I don't know what you would call it: a lonesomer sound… a mountain sound, or something."

– Quoted in Fred Bartenstein, "The Ralph Stanley Story: An Interview," *Muleskinner News*, March, 1972.

In 1970, Ralph and the band (Roy Lee Centers, Curly Ray Cline, and Jack Cooke) were late to a show in West Virginia. As he arrived, he heard fifteen-year-olds Ricky Skaggs and Keith Whitley filling in with songs of the early Stanley Brothers. Recognizing both their love for his music and amazing talent, Ralph Stanley added the duo to the group for two summers and whenever else they could get away from school.

Ralph Stanley mentored many other fine musicians over the years, including guitarists Ricky Lee, Junior Blankenship, Charlie Sizemore, Sammy Adkins, Tony "Renfro" Profitt, James Alan Shelton, and (son) Ralph Stanley II; mandolinists Ron Thomasson, John Rigsby, and (grandson) Nathan Stanley; fiddlers James Price, Todd Meade, and Dewey Brown; and banjo picker Steve Sparkman.

An endless string of recordings emerged on King, Rebel, Columbia (again) and numerous smaller labels. The Clinch Mountain Boys have headlined for the entire four decades of bluegrass festivals. The movie *O Brother Where Art Thou* (2000) brought Ralph Stanley's music to the largest audiences of his career, and led to a Grammy award for "O Death."

"[I'd like to be remembered] as a fella that give the best of my life to bluegrass music; done my best to do it the right way [and] never lower the name down… [of] a music that I respect and love."

- Quoted by Barry Willis in *America's Music: Bluegrass*, 1989.

After performing professionally in seven decades, the octogenarian began to slow down a bit. Son Ralph Stanley II heads the Clinch Mountain Boys on a number of their dates. But Ralph, Sr. can still be heard occasionally on the *Grand Ole Opry* and major concert events. His career is well-documented in the Ralph Stanley Museum on Virginia's Crooked Road at Clintwood and in a 2009 autobiography coauthored with Eddie Dean.

— FRED BARTENSTEIN

By the way:

- As a child, was too bashful to sing and play in front of others. Performed in the kitchen for neighbors sitting in the living room.
- Dry sense of humor and a practical joker. Once sent a novice sideman to fire his brother Carter from the Stanley Brothers.
- Filled in with Bill Monroe and the Blue Grass Boys briefly after banjoist Rudy Lyle was drafted. A bad auto wreck in 1951 sidelined his career until the Stanley Brothers reunited.
- Active in regional Democratic politics. Ran unsuccessfully for Clerk of Courts and Commissioner of Revenue in Dickenson County, Virginia, 1970. Served on the Dickenson County School Board. Recorded a radio spot for the Obama campaign, 2008.
- Honorary chairman of the International Bluegrass Music Museum's initial campaign, "Building on a Legacy," 1994
- Nationally lionized in the wake of the movie *O Brother Where Art Thou* (2000) and the *Down From the Mountain* Tour (2001-2002), but continued to live and drive a Jaguar on mountain roads near his remote childhood home.

For additional early history, from childhood through the Stanley Brothers and 1966, see Carter Stanley's profile.

Donald Wesley "Don" Reno | 1992

Don Reno burned with creative intensity. From his youngest years through a distinguished career in music, he was always "on" as a showman, vocalist, multi-instrumentalist of prodigious talent, songwriter and composer. He generously devoted time and attention to fans and fellow artists. Never content with the status quo, he pushed edges, cross-fertilized musical genres, and invented styles to fit the times – picture a bluegrass Chuck Berry.

What stands out in remembering Don Reno was his energy. He was capable of writing ten or fifteen songs at a stretch. He could hold an audience's attention for every moment of his live performances. He worked marathon recording sessions and traveled hundreds of miles between shows. Coming of age in the Depression and World War II, Don never achieved great economic success. Rock 'n' roll arose just as his career began to blossom. Although he earned fame, the attention he received from the recording and broadcast industries and the size of his audiences suffered accordingly.

Don Reno's legacy in bluegrass was under-appreciated in earlier days. His approach to music was more innovative than traditional, so he received less attention from folk scholars than some of his peers. He wasn't based in Nashville, and recorded for labels that had regional or limited distribution. But new generations continue to discover and treasure Don Reno's huge recording catalog and a few surviving live show tapes and videos.

"Anything that I ever had in my head, it seemed like I could put on the neck of an instrument."

– Quoted in Bill Vernon, "The Don Reno Story, Part 1: The Early Years," *Muleskinner News*, June 1973.

Born: February 21, 1926, Spartanburg, SC

Died: October 16, 1984, Charlottesville, VA

Primary instruments (he played and recorded on all bluegrass instruments):
Banjo, Guitar

Composed:

BMI's database credits Don Reno with 229 published compositions, co-compositions (some with Red Smiley), and arrangements. A few of his original songs and collaborations are:

"Jimmy Caught the Dickens (Pushing Ernest in the Tub" (*Billboard* peak at #27, 1961)

"Soldier's Prayer in Viet Nam" (*Billboard* peak at #46, 1966)

"Banjo Riff"
"Charlotte Breakdown"
"Country Boy Rock 'n' Roll"
"Drifting With the Tide"
"Get Behind Me Satan"
"I Know You're Married"
"I'm Using My Bible for a Roadmap"

Don Reno was born in Spartanburg, South Carolina, and reared in nearby Clyde, North Carolina. His immediate family wasn't musical, but much-older brother Harley married a girl whose brothers had a band. From that source, Don was exposed to fiddlers Art Wooten and Tommy Magness. The first time he picked up a banjo, at the age of five, he found that he could play "Brown's Ferry Blues." He and a friend improvised a banjo, and Reno owned a guitar by the time he was eight. Snuffy Jenkins was his direct influence for a three-finger banjo style. With eclectic musical tastes, Reno injected blues and jazz into his playing. He wavered between guitar and banjo, and was a star on both.

Before his teens, the young man was performing on the radio, first as a solo act on guitar and harmonica, then as a banjoist for the Morris Brothers. Earl Scruggs visited the radio station where they played, and replaced Reno with the Morris Brothers in early 1942. Don went on to Arthur Smith and his Crackerjacks, where he played a variety of instruments and performed comedy. In 1943, Bill Monroe came through town and offered Don Reno a job as his first banjo player.

> *"[Bluegrass is] the music that gives you a feel. It'll make you laugh, it'll make you cry, it'll make you want to dance. There's about seven moods in bluegrass music and when you get your mood changed about seven times in thirty minutes, you've got a tiger by the tail, I'll tell you."*
>
> – Quoted in Peter Wernick, "Interview with Don Reno," *Bluegrass Unlimited*, February 1967.

Reno, however – determined to join the Army – passed his physical, and was inducted in March of 1944. He turned down a musician posting (terming it "a chicken job") and served as company barber in Burma and China. After the war, he operated a South Carolina grocery store and played jazz and country music at night.

In 1948, hearing on the *Grand Ole Opry* that Earl Scruggs had left Bill Monroe, Reno drove to Nashville and, finding the band on tour, followed them to Taylorsville, North Carolina. Without invitation, he uncased his banjo and joined the group onstage in the middle of their performance. Reno stayed with them until July of 1949, sharing the stage at various times with Lester Flatt, Chubby Wise, Joel Price, Jackie Phelps, Benny Martin, and Mac Wiseman, and doubling as left fielder and third baseman with Monroe's baseball club.

Weak from a recurrence of malaria contracted in the service, Reno left the Blue Grass Boys and formed the first edition of the Tennessee Cut-Ups in South Carolina with nephew Verlon Reno. Later in 1949, he was called to Roanoke, Virginia, to work with Tommy Magness and the Tennessee Buddies. North Carolinian Red Smiley was already in

"Let's Live for Tonight"
"Maybe You Will Change Your Mind"
"No Longer a Sweetheart of Mine"
"Talk of the Town"

Early influences:
Delmore Brothers
Tommy Magness
Blue Sky Boys
Shelton Brothers
J.E. Mainer's Mountaineers
Snuffy Jenkins

Came to fame with:
Don Reno, Red Smiley and the Tennessee Cut-Ups, 1951-1964

Performed with:
The Morris Brothers, Spartanburg, SC, 1940
Arthur Smith and the Crackerjacks, 1940-1943, 1952-1955
Carolina Hillbillies, Spartanburg, SC, 1943-1944, 1948
Bill Monroe and the Blue Grass Boys, 1948-1949
Don Reno and the Tennessee Cut-ups, 1949, 1965, 1966, 1977-1984
Tommy Magness and the Tennessee Buddies, Roanoke, VA, 1949-1951
Toby Stroud and the Blue Ridge Mountain Boys, Wheeling, WV, 1951
Don Reno, Red Smiley and the Tennessee Cut-Ups, 1951-1964
Don Reno, Benny Martin and the Tennessee Cut-ups, 1965-1966
Don Reno, Bill Harrell and the Tennessee Cut-Ups, 1966-1977

Bluegrass Hall of Fame Inductee Biographies | 23

RENO AND SMILEY

Left to right: Ronnie Reno, Steve Chapman, Don Reno, Red Smiley at Mocking Bird Hill, Anderson, IN, 1962.

Photo: Ann Milovsoroff

Led the way:

- Pre-empted by Earl Scruggs as the first prominent three-finger banjo player during Reno's World War II service, went on to create a distinctively different banjo style, featuring single-string and jazzy chordal phrases adapted from the guitar.
- First prominent flat-picking lead guitarist in bluegrass.
- With Arthur Smith, recorded top-ten hit "Guitar Boogie" on the guitar in the mid 1940s and the original release of "Feuding Banjos" in 1955.
- Reno and Harrell were the first country act to perform at the United Nations in New York City.
- Bluegrass Hall of Fame, 1992.

By the Way

- Could play banjo or guitar in any key without a capo.
- Mentored fourteen-year-old Hank "Sugarfoot" Garland in a twin electric guitar combo, 1948.
- None of the members of the classic Tennessee Cut-Ups were from Tennessee.
- Released the single "Jimmy Caught the Dickens" as "Chick and his Hot Rods," out of concern that Reno and Smiley fans wouldn't appreciate the rockabilly arrangement.
- Sons Ronnie, Dale, and Don Wayne all went on to prominence in bluegrass and country music after performing with the Tennessee Cut-Ups.

the group. Reno and Smiley found that their talents meshed well and decided to team up in South Carolina and re-form the Tennessee Cut-Ups. Their first sixteen recordings for King, made in January, 1952, included their first release, "I'm Using My Bible for a Road Map." By the time that enduring hit was released, the Cut-Ups had disbanded and Don Reno had rejoined Arthur "Guitar Boogie" Smith on radio and television in Charlotte.

Reno and Smiley continued to record before reforming as a touring act in 1955 with their classic band: Mack Magaha on fiddle, John Palmer on bass, and country music impresario Carlton Haney as manager. Their first session together, in August, 1956, produced "Country Boy Rock 'n' Roll," "No Longer a Sweetheart of Mine," and their most popular composition, "I Know You're Married (But I Love You Still)."

During the next decade, the Tennessee Cut-Ups were red hot in the southeast and mid-Atlantic, appearing on television in Richmond, Petersburg, Roanoke, and Harrisonburg, Virginia, and Washington, D.C. The band's alter egos – Chicken Hotrod (Don), Pansy Hotrod (Red in a dress) and the Banty Roosters – were particular audience favorites. Don's son Ronnie joined the band on mandolin in 1956 at the age of eight. In late November, 1964, Don Reno and Red Smiley dissolved their partnership so Don and Ronnie could move back to South Carolina and work more road dates than their local live television schedule permitted. In February, 1965, Reno and Smiley reunited briefly to play their first and only college concert, at Temple University.

In September, 1965, Don Reno and his reformed Tennessee Cut-Ups appeared at the first multi-day bluegrass festival, at Fincastle, Virginia. There he announced a short-lived partnership with fiddler Benny Martin. From late 1966 to early 1977, Don Reno teamed with Bill Harrell. Red Smiley came back from semi-retirement and toured with them from 1969 until his death in early 1972. A variety of other musicians in this era included fiddler Buck Ryan and bassist Ed Ferris. Younger sons Dale and Don Wayne joined in the late 1970s on mandolin and banjo, respectively. The end of a legendary career came in October, 1984, when Don Reno succumbed to a staph infection after an operation for clogged arteries.

— FRED BARTENSTEIN

> *"Most of the time we'd leave here and we didn't even know what songs we was gonna [record]. Don would write most of 'em on the way to Cincinnati."*
>
> – John Palmer, quoted by Gary Reid in liner notes to *Don Reno and Red Smiley and the Tennessee Cut-Ups, 1951-1959*, King Records, 1993.

RENO AND SMILEY

Arthur Lee "Red" Smiley ∫ 1992

Red Smiley came to prominence during an era when bluegrass music was a subset of country music. His records played on country jukeboxes and country radio. He appeared on bills with major country stars and hosted them as guests on his television show. His performing years stretched from the brother duets and string bands of the thirties to the honky tonk shuffles of the fifties, sixties, and early seventies. He and his fans both enjoyed mainstream country music, and it was a staple of his repertoire. Although Red was one of the few early bluegrass stars who didn't apprentice with Bill Monroe, he performed almost entirely with acoustic instruments and within the bluegrass idiom. A mild-mannered gentleman, Red Smiley was beloved by audiences and fellow artists alike throughout his all-too-short career.

Born Arthur Lee Smiley in mountainous western North Carolina, his red hair suggested the nickname "Red." Little is known about Smiley's childhood and early life, although his family was said to be educated and his father was a friend of mountain

Born: May 17, 1924, Marshall, NC

Died: January 2, 1972, Richmond, VA

Primary instrument:- Guitar

"[Red Smiley] played quintessentially tasteful rhythm guitar. His signature runs and fills were not particularly complex, but they stood out from those of other bluegrass guitarists. This was, in part, because many of Red's vocals were played out of a D position on the guitar – in a lower range than the keys in which many of his contemporaries sang. Red's songs thus lent themselves to backup guitar phrases noticeably different from the Lester Flatt G-run family of licks... "

- Jack Tottle, in liner notes to *Don Reno and Red Smiley on Stage*, Copper Creek Records, 1996.

"Not content to limit themselves to replays of their recorded hits, Don Reno, Red Smiley and their band would launch into a high-energy showcase of original bluegrass, adaptations of old-time tunes, popular country songs from the top 40 charts, and lovely gospel harmony numbers. At times they would even change into outlandish costumes backstage to do silly but endearing skits as Chicken and Pansy Hot Rod, Jeff Doolytater and Mutt Highpockets."

- Jack Tottle in liner notes to *Don Reno and Red Smiley on Stage*, Copper Creek Records, 1996.

Bluegrass Hall of Fame Inductee Biographies ∫ 27

Composed:

BMI's database credits Red Smiley with 77 published compositions, co-compositions (many with Don Reno) and arrangements. A few of his original songs and collaborations are:

"Brighter Mansion Over There"

"Cruel Love"

"Drifting With the Tide"

"If It Takes Me a Lifetime"

"I'm Gone, Long Gone"

"Maybe You Will Change Your Mind"

"Tally Ho"

"There's Another Baby Waiting For Me Down the Line"

Early influences:

Blue Sky Boys

Delmore Brothers

Wiley Morris

Ernest Tubb

Came to fame with:

Don Reno, Red Smiley and the Tennessee Cut-Ups, 1951-1964

Performed with:

Zeke Morris, Johnson City, TN, 1944

Sauceman Brothers (Blue Ridge Hillbillies), Asheville, NC, 1944

J.P. Sauceman and the Carolina Ramblers, Knoxville, TN, 1945

Tommy Magness and the Tennessee Buddies, Roanoke, VA, 1949-1951

Toby Stroud and the Blue Mountain Boys, Wheeling, WV, 1951

Don Reno, Red Smiley and the Tennessee Cut-Ups, 1951-1964

Red Smiley and the Bluegrass Cut-Ups, 1965-1968

---

music scholar and performer Bascom Lamar Lunsford. According to Barry Willis in *America's Music: Bluegrass*, Red was inspired by two hobos playing in Bushnell, North Carolina, when he was about seven. By the late 1930s, he was playing on WROL in Knoxville.

Smiley joined the Army in 1942 and was seriously wounded in Sicily, when a bomb exploded and ripped through his chest. He lost a lung and was hospitalized for almost two years, singing for fellow patients at Walter Reed Army Medical Center in Washington, D.C. After discharge, he attended diesel mechanic school in Nashville, Tennessee, where he first saw Don Reno on stage at the *Grand Ole Opry* with Bill Monroe, but didn't meet him. He also performed in East Tennessee and western North Carolina with well-known musicians Zeke Morris, Red Rector, Fred Smith, and the Sauceman Brothers.

In 1949, Red joined fiddler Tommy Magness's band at WDBJ radio in Roanoke, Virginia. Hearing that Don Reno had left the Blue Grass Boys, he convinced Magness to call and offer him a job. Don accepted and came to Roanoke, where he and Red first met. Soon after, they recorded four Reno-penned sacred songs for Federal, a subsidiary of the Cincinnati-based King label. Although their personalities and styles were very different, Red and Don

> *"Reno and Smiley's ability to entertain was noted on one occasion while appearing at the Terrace Ballroom… in Newark, New Jersey. Don and Red were the opening act for Ray Price…. Following their show Reno and Smiley were showered with an amazing five encores…. Subsequently, both Ray Price and Jim Reeves included in their performance contracts a clause stating that they would not follow Reno and Smiley on stage."*
>
> – Eddie Stubbs in liner notes to *Don Reno and Red Smiley on the Air*, Copper Creek Records, 1996.

realized that the combination was magical. After Tommy Magness retired, both joined Toby Stroud's Blue Mountain Boys in Wheeling, West Virginia, for a short stint.

King Records' Syd Nathan called, offering to record Reno and Smiley alone. In 1952 the pair went to Cincinnati and recorded a session, which included "I'm Using My Bible for a Roadmap." Red subsequently went back to Asheville and worked as a mechanic with the North Carolina State Roads Commission, playing some with Bill Monroe alumnus Wilbur Wesbrooks. Don went back with Arthur "Guitar Boogie" Smith and the Crackerjacks in Charlotte, North Carolina.

The King records began to sell and more sessions were held, in 1953 and 1954. A man in Richmond badly wanted to produce a live show with Red and Don, so during the Easter weekend of 1955 they got the bass player and fiddler from the last session out of their South Carolina cotton mills and went to Richmond. It was at this time that Red Smiley, Don Reno, John Palmer, and Mack Magaha first played together on a stage. The Saturday night before their stage show the group played the *Old Dominion Barn Dance*, a radio show held in Richmond.

After that appearance, the *Barn Dance* offered them a regular job at eighty dollars a show. They accepted and Don Reno, Red Smiley and the Tennessee Cut-Ups were born. In December they took on Carlton Haney as manager and went on to break box office records wherever they appeared – releasing a single record every six weeks. They started the first early morning country music TV show in Roanoke, Virginia, on December 31, 1956. *Top o' the Morning* appeared every weekday until 1968, and was soon followed by a Saturday night radio barn dance in Danville and a weekly TV show in Harrisonburg.

Touring was restricted by the heavy TV schedule and by Red Smiley's health. The war injuries and diabetes sapped Red's strength, and he lost almost 100 pounds in the decade following 1955. An amicable parting of the ways occurred in late November of 1964, shortly after fiddler Mack Magaha left to join Porter Wagoner in Nashville. Don took the band name and his mandolin-playing son Ronnie. Red kept bass man John Palmer, the bus, and the Roanoke and Harrisonburg TV shows.

Smiley recruited fine musicians for his Bluegrass Cut-Ups. They worked on the WWVA Jamboree in Wheeling, West Virginia, and recorded five albums for Rimrock and Rural Rhythm, most since reissued on CD. When *Top O' the Morning* was cancelled in 1968, Red retired and the band continued as the Shenandoah Cut-Ups. That year, Smiley recorded ten sides for Major with electric country backing. Although they sounded good, and "Best Female Actress of the Year" got some airplay, a country career was not in the cards for Red.

Bored at home, Smiley joined up with Don Reno and his current partner Bill Harrell and toured with them for several years. In 1971, he began to suffer mild heart attacks and took seriously ill during a flu epidemic late in that year. He died on January 2, 1972, at the age of forty-seven. He was buried at the Dehart Cemetery in the Jackson Line Community of Bryson City, NC.

— FRED BARTENSTEIN

Don Reno, Red Smiley, Bill Harrell and the Tennessee Cut-Ups, 1969-1971

Led the way:

- Introduced to bluegrass a smooth, lower-pitched vocal style, influenced by mainstream country music of the time.
- Co-led one of the earliest and most entertaining bluegrass acts in history.
- A pioneer in bringing bluegrass to television, performing more than 3,000 weekday broadcasts over the years 1956-1968.
- Bluegrass Hall of Fame, 1992.

By the way:

- Aspired to a solo country music career, which he pursued briefly in Ohio before teaming with Don Reno in Tommy Magness's band, and again in 1968 after retiring from a daily television program in Roanoke, Virginia.
- Played guitar on the first major-label bluegrass album by a female, *Rose Maddox Sings Bluegrass*, 1962.
- Wore a dress made by Mack Magaha's mother and a wig bought in New York City as "Pansy Hot Rod" in the Tennessee Cut-Ups' comedy routine.
- Owned a restored Model A Ford, with which he was pictured on an album cover and in the opening sequence to Reno and Smiley's earliest television shows in Roanoke.

Malcolm B. "Mac" Wiseman \ 1993

Mac Wiseman had a successful career in country music, as a sideman with major artists, and as a soloist before the term "bluegrass" came into common use. But his first and only top-ten records built on other phenomena – the popularity of a Disney television series ("The Ballad of Davey Crockett," 1955), and a growing interest in folk music ("Jimmy Brown the Newsboy," 1959). It was this kind of serendipity, flexibility, and well-tuned business instincts that assured Wiseman's durable appeal over seven decades. And let us not forget his amazing vocal instrument, so pleasing and affecting that he was lastingly branded "The Voice with a Heart" by Don Owens at WARL in the early 1950s.

"It was very nomadical or gypsy-like because other than the few lucky ones that were on the two or three recording labels at the time, nobody had any records out. So you depended entirely on the local stations to get you a couple of daily radio shows, and build up as quickly as possible, and play the local theaters and schools within commuting distance. It was survival of the fittest – you worked hard at it and if you had a few breaks you could build."

– Quoted in Doug Green, "Mac Wiseman: Remembering," *Muleskinner News*, July 1972.

The hamlet of Crimora lies eight miles north of Waynesboro, in the bucolic Valley of Virginia, 260 miles northeast of the Stanley Brothers' Clinch Mountain birthplace in the Virginia coalfields, and 550 miles east of Bill Monroe's childhood home of Rosine in Western Kentucky. Despite the distance in geography and culture,

Born: May 23, 1925, Crimora, VA

Primary instrument:- Guitar

"I probably would not have learned to play the guitar if it hadn't been for a couple of corrective surgeries [for polio contracted as an infant]... When I reached my maximum growth at thirteen... I really had time to work on the guitar, and that's when I mastered it, so to speak. I think most things are God's plan."

– Quoted by Charles Wolfe and Eddie Stubbs in liner notes to *'Tis Sweet To Be Remembered*, Bear Family Records, 2003.

Composed:

BMI's database credits Mac Wiseman with 39 published compositions, co-compositions, and arrangements, including:

"Are You Coming Back To Me"

"Bluebirds Singing for Me"

Photo: W.T. Helfrich, mid-1970s

"I'm a Stranger"

"Let Me Borrow Your Heart Just for Tonight"

"Remembering"

"'Tis Sweet To Be Remembered"

"When I Get the Money Made"

Early influences:

Charlie Poole

The Skillet Lickers (Gid Tanner, Riley Puckett)

The Carter Family

Mainer's Mountaineers

Bradley Kincaid

Karl and Harty

Leary Family (Wilma Lee Cooper)

Lee Moore

Came to fame with:

Mac Wiseman and the Country Boys, 1949-1956

Performed with:

The Hungry Five, New Hope, Virginia, 1940-1943

Buddy Starcher, Harrisonburg, Virginia, 1944-1945

Lee Moore and Juanita, Harrisonburg, Virginia, 1945-1946

Molly O'Day and the Cumberland Mountain Folks, Knoxville, Tennessee, 1946-1947

Lester Flatt, Earl Scruggs and the Foggy Mountain Boys, 1948

Bill Monroe and the Blue Grass Boys, 1949

Mac Wiseman and the Country Boys, 1949-1956

Mac Wiseman, 1957-present

Led the way:

- Brought a sweet tenor solo voice to bluegrass, interpreting folk, Victorian sentimental

Mac Wiseman shared with other bluegrass pioneers a musical heritage conveyed through church, family, hand-cranked phonographs, and battery powered radios.

As a frail child, suffering from the after-effects of infantile paralysis, Wiseman had ample opportunity to learn songs and accompany himself on the guitar. An accommodating mother took him to schoolhouse concerts and transcribed lyrics that appealed to him from the radio into hand-written notebooks. Mac sang on WSVA in nearby Harrisonburg, and in a high school combo, but never contemplated a professional career in music.

After graduating in 1943, he worked in a laboratory at a manganese mine. There, the March of Dimes offered to pay half the cost of a higher education. Mac enrolled in a broadcasting program at the Shenandoah Conservatory of Music and was soon employed as an announcer at WSVA in Harrisonburg. It didn't take long for him to realize that the money in the entertainment industry is not in announcing. As World War II drew to a close, Wiseman began a succession of performing stints at mid-Atlantic and southern radio stations on bass and guitar, but primarily as a featured vocalist and commercial pitchman.

"Overall I feel fortunate to have been accepted for myself over the years. [In bluegrass] I don't have to look for a gimmick and that's one thing that's different from any other phase of the music business. This is a segment of the public you don't hard sell to. They might not even be able to explain why they like you, but they like you period."

– Quoted in Doug Green, "Mac Wiseman: Remembering," *Muleskinner News*, July 1972.

In 1946 he was recruited to play bass and open shows for Molly O'Day and the Cumberland Mountain Folks, based in Knoxville. Wiseman participated in their first Columbia sessions, and learned valuable lessons about the big-time music industry. Next came a band in Bristol, from which he was called in 1948 to join an early edition of Lester Flatt, Earl Scruggs and the Foggy Mountain Boys. Bill Monroe, a guest on their radio show, offered Mac a job while on the air, much to Flatt's consternation. A stint with the Blue Grass Boys followed, in which Mac recorded "Traveling This Lonesome Road" and "Can't You Hear Me Calling" as lead vocalist.

By now a seasoned veteran, Mac Wiseman was disappointed that he had been unable to leverage his visibility into a Nashville recording contract. He contemplated leaving the business, but returned to WCYB, Bristol, until he was able to land a berth on the *Louisiana Hayride* at KWKH, Shreveport, second only to the *Grand Ole Opry* in listenership.

"There is a quality, an essence in Jim and Jesse's music that has always set them apart as something very special. It is a kind of earnestness and near naivete, a kind of youthful, openhearted sincerity."
– "Ranger Doug" Green, music writer, historian, and member of Riders in the Sky, in the liner notes to *Jim & Jesse: Bluegrass and More*, Bear Family Records, 1993.

Photo: Alan Whitman

influenced by the new sounds being made by Bill Monroe, Flatt and Scruggs, their neighbors the Stanley Brothers, and early alumni of those bands. Over the next fourteen years, the brothers migrated to more than a dozen radio stations in at least ten states. Whenever they could get a three-finger five-string banjo player, they incorporated that instrument into their band and recordings.

In idle moments during 1949, Jesse experimented with using a flat pick to imitate Hoke Jenkins's backward bluegrass banjo roll on his mandolin. The style quickly evolved into the first full-blown alternative to Bill Monroe's mandolin technique. Jesse's "crosspicking," the brothers' distinctive smooth vocal duet (influenced by a brief foray into cowboy music), and a propulsive and dynamic band rhythm immediately distinguished the McReynolds' sound from all others.

"I like for a song to have more than the regular three chords… I try to do something different about every time I play."

- Quoted by Thomas Goldsmith in liner notes to *In the Tradition*, Rounder Records, 1987.

A contract with Capitol Records came in 1952, and the group was retitled "Jim and Jesse and the Virginia Boys" (although few of the accompanying musicians who appeared under that name in the next five decades hailed from the Old Dominion). A third and fourth session were squeezed into Jesse's two-week furlough between Army basic training and departure for the Korean conflict. Jesse drove a jeep in the war zone and played in a five-piece band that also included Charlie Louvin (one of the Louvin Brothers, composers of Jim and Jesse's 1952 release, "Are You Missing Me").

[Jesse still practices daily in his pursuit] "to be the best mandolin player in the world and that's something I'll be working on all my life… I learn something every time I pick up the instrument."

- Quoted by Barry R. Willis in *America's Music: Bluegrass*, 1989.

Starting up again in 1954, Jim and Jesse found a musical landscape greatly changed by rock 'n' roll. They survived by promoting their records directly to establishments with jukeboxes, building new audiences in the rural Deep South, pioneering bluegrass music on regional television, and lining up sponsors like Ford Tractors, Pet Milk, and Martha White Mills. A dry spell for recording ended with sessions for Starday in 1958 and 1959, then with Columbia and its subsidiary Epic throughout the sixties.

Jesse's creativity and broad musical awareness led the group in many interesting directions. In addition to a core strength in bluegrass, the

"Pardon Me"
"Stoney Creek"
"Too Many Tears"

Early influences:
Claude and Charles McReynolds (father and grandfather, banjoist and fiddler)
Savannah McReynolds (mother, guitarist)
Oakley Greear (brother-in-law, fiddler)
Carter Family
Blue Sky Boys
Monroe Brothers
Delmore Brothers
Bailes Brothers
Sons of the Pioneers
Louvin Brothers

"Our brother-in-law Oakley Greear (who was a good fiddle player) suggested that we try singing, since everyone else was only playing instrumental music."

- Quoted in liner notes to *Songs from the Homeplace*, Pinecastle Records, 1998.

Came to fame with:
Jim and Jesse and the Virginia Boys, 1952-2002

Performed with:
The McReynolds Brothers, Jesse and James, and the Cumberland Mountain Boys, 1947-1949, 1950-1952
Hoke Jenkins's Smoky Mountaineers, Augusta, GA, 1949
The Virginia Trio, Middletown, OH, 1951
Jim and Jesse and the Virginia Boys, 1952-2002
Jesse McReynolds and the Virginia Boys and Girls, 2002-present

Bluegrass Hall of Fame Inductee Biographies

JIM AND JESSE

Jesse Lester McReynolds \ 1993

Soft-spoken and generously warm-hearted, Jesse McReynolds is the younger and lower-voiced of two brothers who were separated as musical partners only by military service and death. Jim and Jesse performed together, composed together, married sisters (Jesse's first marriage), and lived in adjoining residences – the Double J Ranch in Gallatin, near Nashville, Tennessee. Jesse's mandolin virtuosity, strong lead vocals, and gentlemanly demeanor have endeared him to millions of fans over seven decades.

Jesse McReynolds grew up in a mining and farming community among the mountains of southwestern Virginia. Seriously injured in an auto accident at the age of fourteen, he used the time away from lessons and farm chores to develop his musical skills. A new radio station opened in nearby Norton in 1946 just as Jim was mustered out of the Army and Jesse graduated from high school. The brothers formed a group to play a fifteen-minute daily program, and vowed to pursue a career as entertainers.

"We grew up in a coal mine section in southwest Virginia... The entertainment we had back then was all live. My father's brothers all played. My grandfather, Charlie McReynolds, was the fiddle player in the community... You'd walk down through the valley where he lived and you'd hear his fiddle playing."

- Quoted by Dale Vinicur in liner notes to *Jim & Jesse: 1952-1955*, Bear Family Records, 1992.

With fiddle, mandolin, guitar, and bass, the style they played was known as "mountain" or "hillbilly" music. The term "bluegrass" had not yet arisen, but Jesse and Jim McReynolds were impressed and

Born: July 9, 1929, Carfax, VA

Primary instrument: Mandolin

"Very early in his career, Jesse developed a 'McReynolds style' technique on the mandolin, combining his invention of 'crosspicking' and split-string playing, which distinguished his picking from others."

- From biography at www.jimandjesse.com.

Composed:
BMI's database credits Jesse McReynolds with 115 published compositions, co-compositions (many with brother Jim McReynolds), and arrangements. A few of his original songs and collaborations are:

"Border Ride"

"Drifting and Dreaming of You"

"Hard Hearted"

"I Will Always Be Waiting for You"

"Just Wondering Why"

The fledgling Dot label offered to record him there, and the resulting first single, "'Tis Sweet To Be Remembered," became a regional best-seller and Mac's lifelong theme.

"Bluegrass musicians are serious musicians and shouldn't be presented in a manner that demeans their artistry."

– Quoted by J. Wesley Clark and J. Michael Hosford in "Mac Wiseman: Once More with Feeling," *Bluegrass Unlimited*, August 1987

A string of enduring hits followed, including "Little White Church," "I Still Write Your Name In the Sand," "Four Walls Around Me," "I Wonder How the Old Folks Are At Home," "Shackles and Chains," "Don't Let Your Sweet Love Die," and "Love Letters in the Sand." From 1953 to 1957, Mac Wiseman starred on the *Old Dominion Barn Dance* at WRVA, Richmond, Virginia.

Rock 'n' roll hit in the middle 1950s, challenging the commercial marketplace for bluegrass and traditional country artists. Wiseman responded by disbanding The Country Boys and moving in 1957 to California, as head of artists and repertoire and the country department for Dot Records. He still performed and recorded, but did everything he could to escape the bluegrass stereotype which country format radio was increasingly avoiding. Much to his surprise, it was that very style that attracted folk audiences to his earlier recordings. Soon Mac's performing career was revitalized as college concerts, folk festivals, and the emerging bluegrass festivals sought him as a headlining artist.

Now back in the mid-south and appearing as a solo artist, Mac maintained other business interests in the slow season for performing appearances, including management of the Wheeling Jamboree, his own Wise record label, a mail-order record business, a festival at Renfro Valley, Kentucky, and a stint as secretary of the Nashville local of the American Federation of Musicians. While both were on RCA, Mac and his former bandmate Lester Flatt recorded three successful albums together. Similar collaborations followed with the Osborne Brothers on the RCA and CMH labels.

Since the 1990s, Mac Wiseman has been a visible spokesperson for the bluegrass music industry, narrating the video series *Grassroots to Bluegrass* and the movie *High Lonesome: The Story of Bluegrass Music*. Still a musical innovator, he can be heard with a bluegrass/hip hop fusion group, The Groove Grass Boyz, and on a duet album with John Prine. With Jesse McReynolds, he engaged in a project to record hundreds of songs from the early repertoire that influenced their musical careers. Slowed by health issues, Mac still performs at increasingly rare and treasured concert appearances.

— FRED BARTENSTEIN

ballads, pop standards, and early country music repertoire for generations of listeners.
- The first bluegrass artist to have a parallel music business career, as a label executive, producer, and mail order record entrepreneur.
- From the mid '50s to the present, experimented in a wide variety of recording genres, from Dixieland jazz, to rock 'n' roll, to hip hop.
- Bluegrass Hall of Fame, 1993.
- Country Music Hall of Fame, 2014.

By the way:
- Worked as a chemist before he studied broadcasting, worked as a radio announcer, and became a professional musician.
- Was embarrassed to admit, after joining Bill Monroe, that he hadn't learned any of his songs.
- While an executive with Dot Records in California, suggested that Pat Boone record an old standard that had been successful for Mac, "Love Letters in the Sand." It became a smash hit for Boone in the pop field.
- Co-founded the Country Music Association in Nashville and served as its first secretary, 1958, and served two years on the board of the International Bluegrass Music Association.
- Convinced that his solo voice was the key to his artistic identity, performed very little vocal harmony, and never recorded an instrumental.

Led the way:

- Inventor of "McReynolds style" mandolin playing, which few other players have attempted and none have fully mastered.
- Introduced a smooth vocal harmony to bluegrass, bridging the brother duet and modern country styles.
- Joined the *Grand Ole Opry*, 1964.
- Most Promising Vocal Duo, *Record World*, 1967.
- Bluegrass Hall of Fame, 1993.
- National Heritage Fellowship Award, 1997.

By the way:

- The longest active professional brother duet in country music history – 55 years.
- Grandfather, fiddler Charles McReynolds, recorded at the historic 1927 Bristol sessions as a member of the Bull Mountain Moonshiners.
- At first, Jim played mandolin and Jesse guitar. When neither was making much progress, the brothers exchanged instruments.
- A 1954 Capitol Records promotion booklet listed the following details about Jesse: height: 5'8", black hair, grey eyes, weight: 145 lbs., single, favorite food: fried potatoes, favorite color: blue, favorite sports: fishing, hunting.
- Played mandolin on The Doors' album *The Soft Parade*.
- Toured and recorded as a member of The Masters, a quartet of "superpickers" that included fiddler Kenny Baker, Dobroist Josh Graves and banjoist/guitarist Eddie Adcock.

brothers experimented with electric country, Latin, pop, gospel, and an entire album of Chuck Berry songs backed by acoustic instruments – *Berry Picking in the Country* (1965). During the folk music boom, the act played the prestigious Newport festival and college campuses. A worldwide audience was built through appearances in the British Isles, Europe, and the Far East. When bluegrass festivals grew to a reliable performance circuit, Jim and Jesse dropped electric instruments and drums and built their own recording label, Old Dominion. In the CD era, they also recorded for CMH, Rounder, and Pinecastle.

> *"A country artist can make more money in three or four years with some hits than a bluegrass player can make in a lifetime, but it's a living. It's a volume-type thing; we have to work a lot."*
>
> – Quoted by Barry R. Willis in *America's Music: Bluegrass*, 1989.

Jesse's son and bass player, Keith McReynolds, contracted multiple sclerosis and died at the age of forty-four in 2000. In 2002, both McReynolds brothers were diagnosed with different strains of cancer. Jesse recovered but Jim passed away on the last day of that year. Jesse has carried on the Jim and Jesse tradition and continues to play with the Virginia Boys and Girls. He has recently opened a music park on his family farm in Gallatin, Tennessee, called "The Pick Inn" where he hosts many special events. Jesse's present band lineup includes grandson Garrett McReynolds as tenor singer/rhythm guitarist. Garrett's older sister Amanda sings third-part harmony. Sometimes Jesse grabs the historic fiddle his grandfather played on the Bristol Sessions, and lets grandson Luke McKnight do the crosspicking that Jesse invented and made famous. With his musical family Jesse McReynolds continues on, entertaining fans all over the world.

— FRED BARTENSTEIN

JIM AND JESSE

James Monroe "Jim" McReynolds | 1993

Jim McReynolds was the elder of two brothers who were separated as musical partners only by military service and death. Jim and Jesse performed together, composed together, married sisters, and lived in adjoining residences – the Double J Ranch in Gallatin, near Nashville, Tennessee.

So much has been made of the duet that Jim's remarkable voice seldom received the praise it deserved. A tenor with effortless range, Jim sang high harmonies and the occasional lead vocal with gossamer beauty, far from the strident intensity of most rural singers from the southwestern Virginia and eastern Kentucky coalfields.

Remembered as a neatly dressed, quiet-spoken, and polite gentleman, Jim McReynolds seldom drew attention to himself. He managed the business of the band, while Jesse was the more visible public spokesman, predominant lead singer, and featured instrumentalist. Jim's personality showed its strength when the group was treated in a less than dignified fashion or when he bickered with Jesse – as brothers will – about some insignificant matter.

"Poise, professionalism, dignity, and class are four words that you'll never hear used to describe a current act in today's country music. Jim & Jesse, however, embodied these traits both musically and professionally, on stage and off. Jesse ran the band, while Jim took care of the business end of the operation. As a business agent, he was superb. He was always fair with promoters, and was as honest as the day is long with everyone."

– Eddie Stubbs' eulogy, *Bluegrass Unlimited*, February, 2003.

Born February 13, 1927, Carfax, VA

Died December 31, 2002, Gallatin, TN

Primary instrument: Guitar

"Even into his early seventies, after a more than fifty-year career, Jim never lost a thing musically or vocally. His solid rhythm guitar coupled with his pure clear tenor voice, whether singing harmony or as a soloist, was always right on."

– Eddie Stubbs' eulogy, *Bluegrass Unlimited*, February, 2003.

Composed:

BMI's database credits Jim McReynolds with 56 published compositions, co-compositions (many with brother Jesse McReynolds), and arrangements. A few of his original songs and collaborations are:

"Border Ride"

"Drifting and Dreaming of You"

"Hard Hearted"

"I Will Always Be Waiting for You"
"Just Wondering Why"
"Pardon Me"
"Stoney Creek"
"Too Many Tears"

Early influences:

Claude and Charles McReynolds (father and grandfather, banjoist and fiddler)

Savannah McReynolds (mother, guitarist)

Oakley Greear (brother-in-law, fiddler)

Carter Family

Roy Acuff

Blue Sky Boys

Mainer's Mountaineers

Monroe Brothers

Delmore Brothers

Chuck Wagon Gang

Sons of the Pioneers

Louvin Brothers

Came to fame with:

Jim and Jesse and the Virginia Boys, 1952-2002

Performed with:

The McReynolds Brothers, Jesse and James, and the Cumberland Mountain Boys, 1947-1949, 1950-1952

Hoke Jenkins' Smoky Mountaineers, Augusta, GA, 1949

The Virginia Trio, Middletown, OH, 1951

Jim and Jesse and the Virginia Boys, 1952-2002

Led the way:

- Brought a smooth duet style to bluegrass, bridging the brother duet and modern country styles.
- Member of the *Grand Ole Opry*, 1964-2002.
- Most Promising Vocal Duo, *Record World*, 1967.

The family was musical on both sides, but eked a living from farming, coal mining, and during the Great Depression, the WPA. As a teenager, Jim followed his father into the mines but never returned after the senior McReynolds was almost killed in a mining accident. Jim learned guitar and gospel music from his mother. As World War II ended, he spent a two-year hitch in the Army. He returned home with a mandolin and soon joined his younger brother and his sister's husband in a local dance and radio band.

"One thing about the early days of this business, you had to believe in it and enjoy it because sometimes all the payoff was the enjoyment you got out of it."

– Quoted in Julie Knight, "Hoke Jenkins, Pioneer Banjo Man," *Bluegrass Unlimited*, September, 1985.

Like all regional acts of the era, The McReynolds Brothers and the Cumberland Mountain Boys moved from city to city, angling for higher-wattage stations and playing out the local territory. When the mines were busy, they found their most lucrative bookings in coal country. During an economic lull there, they accompanied Curly Seckler to Augusta, Georgia, for a short hitch with Hoke Jenkins and his Smoky Mountaineers. A year later, the two brothers tried something uncharacteristic of Appalachian bluegrass musicians – they moved to Iowa and Kansas as singing radio cowboys.

The McReynolds' first television and recording work came in 1951 and 1952 in southwestern Ohio – Middletown, Dayton, and Cincinnati. Ten gospel songs were cut for the Kentucky label as the Virginia Trio. It was in Cincinnati that they auditioned unsuccessfully for King. Then, in one of those unexpected quirks of fate, they ran into Capitol Records' Ken Nelson at the Jimmie Skinner Music Center, played a few songs for him, and were invited to record in Nashville. Nelson suggested a new name for the act: Jim and Jesse and the Virginia Boys.

Capitol sessions in 1952, 1953, and 1955 resulted in twenty tracks, sixteen of which were released as 78 and 45 rpm singles. The most enduring were the Louvin Brothers'-penned "Are You Missing Me," and the McReynolds' own "I Will Always Be Waiting for You" and "Just Wondering Why." The brothers were working at WCYB in Bristol when Jesse was drafted for service in Korea. Jim farmed from 1953 to 1954. Jesse returned to a changed musical landscape; Elvis had hit and even the most prominent bluegrass acts had trouble keeping a major label contract.

In the late fifties and early sixties, Jim and Jesse established their base of broadcasting and touring operations in Danville, Virginia; Burlington, North Carolina; Wheeling, West Virginia; Knoxville, Tennessee; and Live Oak, Florida. In the Deep South, they worked a circuit of television shows for Ford Tractors and Martha White Mills. Jim and Jesse built a tight and powerful performing ensemble with fiddlers such as Vassar Clements, Jimmy Buchanan, and Jim Brock; banjoists Bobby Thompson and Allen Shelton; and utility men Don McHan, Chick Stripling, and David Sutherland. In 1958 and 1959, Jim and Jesse self-produced three sessions in Jacksonville, Florida for Starday Records, including "Hard Hearted," "Border Ride," and "I'm Changing the Words To My Love Song."

In 1960, when the folk boom was attracting urban and college audiences for bluegrass acts, Don Law signed the brothers to Columbia Records. On that label and its subsidiary Epic, Jim and Jesse achieved their first top-100 country chart hits: "Cotton Mill Man" (1964), "Better Times a-Coming" (1964), "Diesel on My Tail" (1967), "Ballad of Thunder Road" (1967), "Greenwich Village Folk Song Salesman" (1968), "Yonder Comes a Freight Train" (1968), and "The Golden Rocket" (1970).

"When we first moved to Nashville, bluegrass wasn't doing that well. We had to get something on the record charts before we could get any work. And the only way we could get on the record charts was to get booked country. So that's where we went."

- Quoted in Robert K. Oermann, "Jim & Jesse: Testing the Boundaries of Bluegrass Music – With a Little Help from Charlie Louvin," *Bluegrass Unlimited*, September, 1982.

In 1964, Jim and Jesse became members of WSM's *Grand Ole Opry* and moved to Nashville. With folk audiences shrinking and the bluegrass festival circuit still on the horizon, the act experienced strong economic pressures to record and perform with electric instruments and drums in a mainstream country format. Nine years later, in 1973, they formed their own record label, Old Dominion, and returned almost entirely to bluegrass for the remainder of their career.

Successful international tours, *Opry* appearances, and a steady stream of headline appearances at bluegrass festivals allowed Jim and Jesse to continue as full-time musicians through the eighties and nineties. Jim encountered voice problems at the dawn of the new millennium and was diagnosed with cancer in early 2002. Despite surgeries and chemotherapy, he continued to perform whenever he was able. On December 19, 2002, Jim's wife Arreta died of a massive heart attack. Jim entered hospice care on December 20 and died December 31. He was buried on a mountain overlooking his childhood home in Carfax, Virginia.

— FRED BARTENSTEIN

- Bluegrass Hall of Fame, 1993.
- National Heritage Fellowship Award, 1997.

"To really entertain an audience, you make 'em feel sad one minute and then the next one you get into, you get 'em hollerin' and laughin' with you and that sort of rounds out the show."

- Quoted in Julie Knight, "Hoke Jenkins, Pioneer Banjo Man," *Bluegrass Unlimited*, September, 1985.

By the Way

- The longest active professional brother duet in country music history – 55 years.
- Jim's grandfather, fiddler Charles McReynolds, recorded at the historic 1927 Bristol sessions as a member of the Bull Mountain Moonshiners.
- At first, Jim played mandolin and Jesse guitar. When neither was making much progress, the brothers exchanged instruments.
- A 1954 Capitol Records promotion booklet listed the following details about Jim: height: 5'11," black hair, brown eyes, weight: 145 lbs., single, favorite food: chicken, favorite color: green, favorite sports: fishing, hunting.
- The classic edition of the Virginia Boys consisted of four North Carolinians: Don McHan, Allen Shelton, Jimmy Buchanan, and David Sutherland.

THE OSBORNE BROTHERS

Robert "Bobby" Van Osborne, Jr. | 1994

Bobby Osborne was born to a schoolteacher/grocer in Depression-era eastern Kentucky. Like so many from that region, the family migrated to industrial areas in the early 1940s, winding up in Dayton, Ohio. Robert Osborne, Sr. blended a job at NCR Corporation with part-time farming. In free moments, he enjoyed singing, yodeling, and playing guitar in the styles of the Carter Family and Jimmie Rodgers. He taught rudimentary chords to his namesake and oldest son, who preferred the popular *Grand Ole Opry* artists of the day, particularly Ernest Tubb.

All three children (Bobby, Louise, and Sonny) were musical. In 1947 they were bitten by the bluegrass bug after attending a sold-out Dayton performance by Bill Monroe's classic band. Bobby got a thumb pick and a Martin guitar like Lester Flatt's, but found that his emerging adult voice was as high – or higher – than Bill Monroe's.

"Without Bobby's voice, we'd come across like just another good group."
- Sonny Osborne, quoted by Jack Tottle in "The Osborne Brothers: Breaking Ground," *Muleskinner News*, July 1973.

Still underage, he began performing with like-minded neighbors at a bar. In 1949, a small-time talent scout took him to WPFB in Middletown, Ohio, where Bobby's first broadcast produced quite a local stir. Larry Richardson, a hot young banjo player from Galax, Virginia, came to Middletown, teaming with Bobby in several groups, culminating in several years with the Lonesome Pine Fiddlers. Larry and Bobby converted the group from a style similar to the Delmore Brothers to the increasingly popular (but as yet unnamed) bluegrass sound. Their song, "Pain in My

Born: December 7, 1931, Hyden, KY

Primary instrument: Mandolin

Composed:
BMI's database credits Bobby Osborne with 83 published compositions, co-compositions, and arrangements. A few of his original songs and collaborations are:

"Son of a Sawmill Man (*Billboard* peak at #58, 1968)

"Big Spike Hammer"

"Bluegrass Express"

"Ho Honey Ho"

"I'll Be All Right Tomorrow"

"Midnight Angel"

"Pain In My Heart"

"Sure Fire"

"This Heart Of Mine Can Never Say Goodbye"

Early influences:
Ernest Tubb
Bill Monroe
Flatt and Scruggs

Came to fame with:
The Osborne Brothers, 1956-2004

Photo: Doc Hamilton, mid-1970s

42 | Bluegrass Hall of Fame Inductee Biographies

Heart," recorded for Cozy Records in 1950, was covered by Flatt and Scruggs later in the year, during their final sessions for Mercury.

Jimmy Martin, fresh from his first stint as guitarist/lead singer with Bill Monroe, joined the Lonesome Pine Fiddlers in June of 1951. Bobby switched from guitar to mandolin, and soon arranged to record four songs with Jimmy under their own names for the King label in Cincinnati. After Jimmy left for Knoxville, Bobby played three weeks with the Stanley Brothers before joining the Marines for combat duty in the Korean con-

Performed with:
Miami Valley Playboys, Middletown OH, 1947-1948
Silver Saddle Boys, Welch, WV, 1949
Rex and Eleanor Parker, Bluefield, WV, 1949
Lonesome Pine Fiddlers, Bluefield, WV, 1949-1951

Jimmy Martin and Bob Osborne, Bristol, VA/TN, 1951

Stanley Brothers, 1951

Jimmy Martin and the Osborne Brothers, 1953-1955

Charlie Bailey, Wheeling, WV, 1955

The Osborne Brothers and Red Allen, 1956-1958

The Osborne Brothers, 1958-2004

Bobby Osborne and the Rocky Top X-press, 2004-present

Led the way:

- Bridged the gap between bluegrass and mainstream country music, headlining in both genres.
- Introduced the high-lead vocal trio with the song "Once More" (1956). Using this arrangement Bobby could sing lead on both verses and choruses, where he was joined by two lower voices.
- First bluegrass group to play a college campus, Antioch College, Yellow Springs, Ohio, March, 1960.
- Joined the *Grand Ole Opry*, 1964.
- Vocal Group of the Year, Country Music Association, 1971.
- First bluegrass act to play at the White House, 1973.
- Bluegrass Hall of Fame, 1994.
- National Heritage Fellowship Award, 1997.

flict. Wounded in Panmunjon, he returned to the front until his discharge in late 1953.

By the time Bobby returned to Dayton, his younger brother Sonny had developed into a teenaged banjo prodigy, including a stint touring and recording with Bill Monroe. Bobby appeared as an uncredited guest on Sonny's later sessions for Gateway in Cincinnati. Jimmy Martin came to southwestern Ohio and joined with Bobby and Sunny as Jimmy Martin and the Osborne Brothers. They started at WPFB in Middletown, then moved to WJR radio in Detroit and CKLW television in nearby Windsor, Ontario. A recording contract with RCA Victor produced "20-20 Vision" and five other scorching bluegrass classics.

By early 1956, the brothers were back in Dayton, where they met and formed an act with lead singer/guitarist and fellow Kentuckian Red Allen. A local DJ got them an audition with MGM and "Once More" broke out as a #13 country single. As good as they were – and their playing and harmony singing were truly unique – all bluegrass and classic country artists were facing increasing competition from the rock 'n' roll music preferred by emerging baby boomers. By 1958, Red Allen was gone. Bob's voice became the center of the act, which was henceforth known as the Osborne Brothers.

"I quit [music] twice, and the last time I got into it I said, 'I ain't gonna quit anymore. It's something I want to do and I'm gonna go broke – or whatever – tryin.'"

– Quoted in Barry Willis, *America's Music: Bluegrass*, 1989.

"Sonny and me never laid that mandolin and banjo down and we got a lot of airplay that folks in bluegrass never did get and haven't got until this day."

– Quoted in Barry Willis, *America's Music: Bluegrass*, 1989.

They kept the banjo, mandolin, and the high lead trio, but increasingly experimented with material and backup instrumentation that could penetrate rockabilly, folk, and modern country markets. The Wilburn Brothers became the Osborne Brothers' business mentors, and by 1964 Bobby and Sonny had moved to Nashville, joined the *Grand Ole Opry*, and signed with Decca (later MCA) records.

The career hit "Rocky Top" came in 1968. Written by Felice and Boudleaux Bryant, it was recorded over the objection of the Wilburn Brothers and considered at the time by the Osborne Brothers to be "just another bluegrass song." Within 10 days it had sold 85,000 copies and it stayed in the *Billboard* charts for 10 weeks. Twelve more top-100 country hits – five of them penned by the Bryants – followed in as many years. Mass-market radio play, a rarity for bluegrass artists, opened the door to lucrative package tours. But the brothers found that the PA systems of the time failed to project their acoustic instruments. With pickups, electric bass, and eventually drums, they were able to hold their own against the louder acts with which they shared the stage.

After five years playing through pickups, Bob and Sonny removed them in 1974. By 1991, the last vestige of amplification was gone from the group. In other ways, the band returned to the classic approach with which they had begun. As country and folk audiences turned elsewhere, the bluegrass market was increasingly able to offer a sustainable if modest living, through its own festival and performance circuit, record labels, radio programs, and publications.

"Bobby Osborne made a major contribution to bluegrass mandolin lead playing. I don't know if anyone has properly described the style he initiated in early recordings, with long flurries of single-note arpeggios built around the melody and chords. Today most bluegrass mandolin players play breaks like Bobby pioneered in the '50s."

– Neil Rosenberg, bluegrass historian, 2009

The Osborne Brothers' career hardly stagnated as the second millennium reached its end. Bluegrass was spreading worldwide, and the Osbornes made several international tours. In 1982, "Rocky Top" was named an official song of Tennessee. In 1992, the Osbornes' arrangement of "Kentucky" led to a similar honor from the state of their birth. Bobby and Sonny mentored young musicians (notably the Grascals and Dale Ann Bradley), and produced and recorded with others – including the bluegrass/hip hop fusion GrooveGrass Boyz. Bobby's duet mandolin performance of "Ashokan Farewell" was on the 2000 IBMA Instrumental Album and Recorded Event of the Year.

"It's freeing to be out on my own, but it's hard too. There's a lot of pressure. You get used to looking over your shoulder and seeing another guy there – but now it's all up to me: what songs to do, when we start, when we go, and such.... Most people my age are ready to hang it up, but I'm going full speed ahead!"

– Quoted in Rounder Records promo sheet for the album *Bobby Osborne: Try a Little Kindness*, 2006.

A half-century musical partnership between the brothers came to an end in 2004 when Sonny Osborne's rotator cuff surgery forced him to stop playing the banjo and leave the road. Bobby continued by forming his own band, the Rocky Top X-Press. With son Bobby Osborne, Jr. on guitar, Bobby maintains an extensive schedule of performances, *Grand Ole Opry* appearances, and recordings on the Rounder label.

— FRED BARTENSTEIN

By the way:

- At the age of sixteen, had his mother photograph him in front of a homemade "WSM" sign. Sixteen years later, he was a regular member of WSM's *Grand Ole Opry*.
- After debuting on WPFB, Middletown, OH (1949), was told not to sing "Ruby, Are You Mad" again, because the staff grew tired of answering telephone requests for it.
- Bought his F-5 Gibson mandolin from Charlie Bailey of the Bailey Brothers.
- Bill Monroe once said that there were only three great tenors in country music: himself, Ira Louvin, and Bobby Osborne.
- Sons Robby, Wynn, and Bobby Osborne, Jr. have also performed as professional bluegrass artists.
- "Rocky Top," the Osborne Brothers' biggest hit, charted higher in re-release (#2, 1996) than it did in 1968 (#33).

Bluegrass Hall of Fame Inductee Biographies

THE OSBORNE BROTHERS

Roland "Sonny" Osborne ⟨ 1994

Sonny Osborne was born in the coalfields of eastern Kentucky. Like so many others from that region, the family migrated to industrial areas in the early 1940s, winding up in Dayton, Ohio. His father, Robert Osborne, Sr., blended a job at NCR Corporation with part-time farming. He loved country music and transmitted that love to three children: Bobby, Louise, and Sonny.

By 1949 brother Bobby was a professional musician, performing with the Lonesome Pine Fiddlers in West Virginia. In the sixth grade, Sonny became interested in the banjo and convinced his father to purchase an inexpensive starter instrument. Before it arrived, Sonny visualized how to play two pieces: the Stanley Brothers' "We'll Be Sweethearts in Heaven" and "Cripple Creek." He surprised himself and his family by playing them the day the package arrived. As he later described in the autobiographical song "Me and My Old Banjo," Sonny became obsessed, practicing eight to fifteen hours a day until he felt ready to perform in public.

Ott Ginter, a neighbor, took the banjo prodigy to the *WPFB Jamboree* in nearby Middletown, Ohio, and released four home recordings on the Kitty label under the name "Lou and Sonny Osborne." These included Louise's composition, "New Freedom Bell." Also performing were

> *"I don't believe in sitting and rehearsing a thing over and over again. Playing something isn't what's hard, it's thinking it out. People work on their instruments too much… they should be thinking about the instrument and what it can do, and listening to what it has to say."*

– Quoted in Jack Tottle, "The Osborne Brothers: Breaking Ground," *Muleskinner News*, July 1973.

Born: October 29, 1937, Hyden, KY

Primary instrument: Banjo

Composed:
BMI's database credits Sonny Osborne with 31 published compositions, co-compositions, and arrangements. A few of his original songs and instrumentals are:

"Banjo Boy Chimes"
"Bluegrass Concerto"
"Charlie Cotton"
"Me and My Old Banjo"
"Old Hickory"
"Siempre"
"Sledd Ridin'"

Early influences:
Larry Richardson
Earl Scruggs
Bill Monroe

Came to fame with:
The Osborne Brothers, 1956-2004

Photo: Doc Hamilton, mid-1970s

Bluegrass Hall of Fame Inductee Biographies

"We're on the line between bluegrass and country, and as long as we can put the banjo, mandolin, guitar, and bass on a record and get country fans and bluegrass fans to buy and like it, we are doing what all of us should be doing, promoting bluegrass, modern as it may be."

– Letter to the editor from Sonny Osborne, *Bluegrass Unlimited*, June 1967.

Performed with:

Siblings Bobby and Louise, Dayton, OH, 1949-1952

Bill Monroe and the Blue Grass Boys, 1952-1953

Sonny Osborne and the Sunny Mountain Boys, 1952-1953

Jimmy Martin and the Osborne Brothers, 1953-1955

Charlie Bailey, Wheeling, WV, 1955

The Osborne Brothers and Red Allen, 1956-1958

The Osborne Brothers, 1958-2004

Led the way:

- An endlessly innovative instrumentalist, Sonny was the first to popularize double banjos, the six-string banjo, and instruments combining various elements of the banjo, Spanish and resonator guitars.

- Helped to introduce the high-lead vocal trio (Sonny sang baritone, the second-highest part) and complex vocal arrangements that echoed pedal steel guitar harmonies.

Bluegrass Hall of Fame Inductee Biographies | 47

- Bridged the gap between bluegrass and mainstream country music, headlining in both genres.
- First bluegrass group to play a college campus: Antioch College, Yellow Springs, Ohio, March, 1960.
- Joined the *Grand Ole Opry*, 1964.
- Vocal Group of the Year, Country Music Association, 1971.
- First bluegrass act to play at the White House, 1973.
- An active member of the International Bluegrass Music Association from the beginning, spearheaded the idea of a Bluegrass Trust Fund to help members of the bluegrass community in emergency need.
- Bluegrass Hall of Fame, 1994.
- National Heritage Fellowship Award, 1997.

By the way
- Guested on recordings with Carl Smith, Charlie Pride, Conway Twitty, Wade Ray and Jethro Burns, Gary Burton, Mac Wiseman, and the GrooveGrass Boyz, among others.
- Shortly after a zealot cut the cord of his amplified banjo the first time he played it at a bluegrass festival, Sonny padlocked the resonator and refused to disclose his electronic solution for preserving its quality tone.
- The Osborne Brothers' hit "Rocky Top," named a Tennessee State song in 1984, is played every time the University of Tennessee Vols score a touchdown.

brother Bobby and Jimmy Martin, who had joined the Lonesome Pine Fiddlers in 1951.

Sonny was a talented athlete. He played varsity football in high school, but music remained his first interest. During Sonny's summer vacation before the tenth grade, Jimmy Martin took him to see Bill Monroe at Bean Blossom, Indiana. There, Jimmy decided to return to the Blue Grass Boys and convinced Bill to take the fourteen-year-old banjo player as well. In July of 1952, they recorded nine songs and instrumentals for Decca, including Bill's "Memories of Mother and Dad," "The Little Girl and the Dreadful Snake," and "Pike County Breakdown."

The next school year was tumultuous for Sonny. Bobby was fighting in Korea with the Marines. The family moved from the farm back to Dayton, where Sonny met Judy, the girl from across the street who later became his wife. He recorded three sessions under his own name for the Gateway label in Cincinnati, including "Sunny Mountain Breakdown," which sold some 67,000 copies. And when Bill Monroe came through Toledo in need of a banjo player, Sonny left school to pursue music full-time.

[Of his professional debut with Bill Monroe at age 14] "I'll tell you, this is the truth. I had no business being there… I didn't know any time; I didn't know any good licks."

– Quoted in Neil Rosenberg, "The Osborne Brothers," *Bluegrass Unlimited*, September 1971.

When Bobby left the military, the brothers first played together in Knoxville, Tennessee, on November 6, 1953. Unable at first to sustain an act on their own, Sonny and Bobby teamed with Jimmy Martin for a year, Charlie Bailey for a few months, and Red Allen from early 1956 to mid-1958. During this period, they gained valuable performing and business experience, radio and television exposure, and recorded for nationally distributed labels RCA and MGM. Sonny became famous as a cutting-edge banjo player and harmony singer, but the Osborne Brothers' ace in the hole was Bobby's stunningly high and clear voice.

Devotedly loyal to his elder brother, Sonny worked tirelessly to build the act as a commercially viable package. Interested in a wide variety of music, it was Sonny who brought to their sound elements of rock 'n' roll, rhythm and blues, modern country, pop, folk, and jazz. As each Osborne Brothers record was released, banjo fans would delight in discovering the new licks Sonny had adapted from horn, keyboard, lead and steel guitar, and even percussion players. Sonny was also principal architect of some of the most complex and effective trio vocal arrangements ever recorded in bluegrass or country music.

In 1963, after a decade of effort to carve a niche in the music business, the brothers were still driving and maintaining taxicabs in Dayton to make ends meet. Sonny found Doyle Wilburn's business card and called him from a motel in Chester, Pennsylvania. Within days, Doyle had arranged a guest spot on the *Grand Ole Opry*. In the next year, under the tutelage of the Wilburn Brothers, the Osborne Brothers had a contract with Decca, a permanent berth on the *Opry*, radio airplay, a publishing contract, and bookings in more upscale settings.

Some of the Osborne Brothers' most popular songs as country/bluegrass artists included "Ruby Are You Mad," "Once More," "Rocky Top," "Making Plans," "Up This Hill and Down," "Midnight Flyer," "Muddy Bottom," "Tennessee Hound Dog," "Georgia Pineywoods," and "I Can Hear Kentucky Calling Me." They played major country package shows and bluegrass festivals, bringing to both the same brand of high-powered, crowd-pleasing entertainment: Sonny's banjo, Bobby's mandolin, perfect vocal harmony and – for a time – amplified instruments, electric bass, and drums.

A changing country marketplace and the brothers' lifelong preference for bluegrass brought them back to an all-acoustic act by the 1990s. Audiences at festivals and concert appearances welcomed the more traditional sounds. A string of Osborne Brothers albums for niche labels CMH, Sugar Hill, and Pinecastle exposed primal bluegrass to those who weren't alive for the classic bands of the 1940s and early 1950s.

Sonny Osborne found a side career in producing recording sessions for emerging artists, including the Pinnacle Boys, the Virginia Squires, Terry Eldredge, and Dale Ann Bradley. A half-century musical partnership between the brothers came to an end when Sonny Osborne's rotator cuff surgery forced him to stop playing the banjo and leave the road in 2004. Sonny remains active in musical affairs, distributing a line of banjos branded with his nickname, "Chief." Always outspoken, Sonny continues to advocate for high standards in bluegrass and respect for the founding pioneers, who struggled, with little reward, to create an art form and industry with worldwide impact.

"When they booked you [at the Flame Club in Minneapolis], they booked you for a week. It was a big place, and we just didn't go over at all there. That's where we figured, 'Well, what have we got to lose? We'll go out and get us some amps and pickups, and we'll peel those people off the wall…' They had to shut up and listen, at least."
- Interview with Eddie Stubbs, quoted by Marty Godbey in liner notes to *The Osborne Brothers: Decca/MCA Recordings, 1968-1974*, Bear Family Records, 1995

— FRED BARTENSTEIN

"['Rocky Top'] opened the door that has allowed us to go into the part of the business where no one in bluegrass has been, before or since."
- Quoted by Glenna H. Fisher in "The Osborne Brothers," *Bluegrass Unlimited*, July 1984.

- Catalyst for recognition of the Pioneers of Bluegrass (pre-1954 professional performers) at the International Bluegrass Music Museum.
- A section of Route 421 in Kentucky was named "Osborne Brothers Way" in 2000.

James Henry "Jimmy" Martin | 1995

Jimmy Martin was a true original in any field of endeavor. A talented singer and guitar player, he was a musical perfectionist with a clear and unswerving vision of what would sound good and please the public. He led some of the tightest performing and recording ensembles in the history of bluegrass music. He was also profoundly insecure, compensating with a brash and overbearing personality that derailed many personal and professional opportunities. For good or ill, no one who ever saw Jimmy Martin ever forgot him.

"He didn't have sense enough to tone it down – thank God... When he hits the stage, it's like cannons going off... I think he's uncontrollable. He dared to be different, and he's paid the price for it."

- Marty Stuart, quoted in Edward Morris, "'King of Bluegrass' Jimmy Martin Dead at 77," *CMT.com*, May 14, 2005.

Born in the East Tennessee farming community of Sneedville, Jimmy Martin was the middle child of seven, two of whom died in infancy. When he was four and his father succumbed to pneumonia, Jimmy and his siblings assumed much of the farm work, under the cruel direction of stepfather Ellis Johnson. Johnson sang gospel music in a quartet and took the aspiring vocalist with him to performances, but discouraged Jimmy's interest in instruments because of his religious beliefs.

Martin dropped out of school in the eighth grade and left home for work as a painter and factory hand, playing music on the side. Hearing that lead singer and guitarist Mac Wiseman would be leaving Bill Monroe in 1949, the twenty-two-year-old took a bus to Nashville and insinuated

Born August 10, 1927, Sneedville, TN

Died May 14, 2005, Nashville, TN

Primary instrument
Guitar

"I learned the basic chords from an old hillbilly named Reuben Gibson, who lived in the hills around Sneedville, and I taught myself how to play. I heard Lester Flatt and Charlie Monroe both play runs, but I didn't try to top them."

- Quoted in *The Big Book of Bluegrass*, 1984.

Composed:
BMI's database credits Jimmy Martin with 92 published compositions, co-compositions, and arrangements. A few of his original songs and collaborations are:

"Night" (*Billboard* peak at #26, 1959)

"Tennessee" (*Billboard* peak at #72, 1968)

"Bear Tracks"

"Hit Parade Of Love"

"Hold Whatcha Got"

Photo: Alan Whitman

"Last Song"
"Losing You (Might Be the Best Thing Yet)"
"My Walking Shoes"
"Prayer Bells of Heaven"
"Run Pete Run"
"She's Left Me Again"
"Stormy Waters"

Early influences:
Roy Acuff
Bill Monroe

Came to fame with:
Bill Monroe and the Blue Grass Boys. 1949-1954

Performed with:
Tex Climer and the Blue Band Coffee Boys, Morristown, TN, 1949

Bill Monroe and the Blue Grass Boys, 1949-1951, 1952-1954

Lonesome Pine Fiddlers, 1951

Jimmy Martin and the Osborne Brothers, 1953-1955

Jimmy Martin and the Sunny Mountain Boys, 1955-2005

> *"I was paintin' machinery in a factory in Morristown, Tennessee, and I was playin' on WCPK from 4:30 to 5:00 every evening. I got fired on my job for singin' too much, and I cussed out the foreman for firin' me. When I went back after my clothes, I seen him on the street, and told him, 'Listen in on Saturday night, 'cause I'm singin' with Bill Monroe on the Grand Ole Opry.'"*

– Interview with Wayne Winkler, "Jimmy Martin: Too Wild for the *Grand Ole Opry*," *Now & Then*, East Tennessee State University, fall, 2008.

Led the way:
- Sang and recorded memorable duets with Bill Monroe that led to the description of bluegrass music as the "high lonesome sound."
- Built enthusiastic audiences for bluegrass from radio and concert appearances in Detroit, Michigan; Shreveport, Louisiana; and Wheeling, West Virginia.
- Pioneered the propulsive "Good 'n Country" beat, in which a snare drum accentuates the mandolin rhythm.
- One of the first bluegrass bandleaders to include a female voice in harmony arrangements.
- Placed six songs in the *Billboard* top-100 country charts between 1958 and 1973.
- Appeared with the Nitty Gritty Dirt Band on all three of the "Will the Circle Be Unbroken" recording projects: 1972, 1989, and 2002.
- Bluegrass Hall of Fame, 1995.

his way backstage at the *Grand Ole Opry*. Monroe's banjo player Rudy Lyle heard him sing and arranged an on-the-spot audition. A week later, Jimmy was traveling the road as a Blue Grass Boy.

During several stints with the band, Jimmy Martin participated in eleven Decca sessions during 1950, 1951, 1952, 1953, and 1954. Martin's high voice and vocal stamina contributed to an intense and harder-edged sound for the style (which had not yet been named bluegrass). The Monroe-Martin harmonies are revered as some of the best and most affecting ever recorded, including "Memories of You," "I'm On My Way to the Old Home," "I'm Blue, I'm Lonesome," "Uncle Pen," "Lord Protect My Soul," "Letter from My Darling," "Memories of Mother and Dad," "The Little Girl and the Dreadful Snake," and "On and On."

Money was tight in those days, and Jimmy Martin tried several times to find a better-paying musical niche. In 1951, he joined the Lonesome Pine Fiddlers and recorded four sides for King with bandmate Bobby Osborne under their own names. After Bobby's stint with the Marines in Korea, they formed Jimmy Martin and the Osborne Brothers at WJR-AM in Detroit and CKLW-TV in nearby Windsor, Ontario. RCA liked the sound and released three singles, including "Save It! Save It!" and "20/20 Vision." When the Osbornes left for Wheeling in 1955, Jimmy decided to stay in Detroit as the head of a group he called the Sunny Mountain Boys.

> *"Martin's high, reedy voice, and subtle intonations complemented Monroe's singing extremely well, and his strong rhythm guitar playing, punctuated frequently with dynamic bass runs, gave the Blue Grass Boys a surging, supercharged sound that not even the Lester Flatt years had witnessed.... Martin and Monroe evoked images of that lonesome, rural life that had originally been the context for bluegrass music's emergence. It was 'white soul singing' at its best."*

– Bill C. Malone, *Country Music U.S.A.*, 1968.

Decca had been interested in recording Jimmy as a solo act since he was a Blue Grass Boy on that label. In 1956, he began eighteen years with Decca by recording "Hit Parade of Love," "You'll Be a Lost Ball," and six others. By the next year, he had assembled his classic band, with brother-in-law Paul Williams on round-hole mandolin and tenor vocals and J.D. Crowe on banjo and baritone vocals. The act rehearsed diligently and was hard to beat in any field of music. From 1958 to 1960 they starred at the *Louisiana Hayride* in Shreveport, and from 1960 to 1962 at the *Wheeling Jamboree* in West Virginia. KWKH and WWVA were both clear-channel 50,000-watt powerhouses that exposed the Sunny Mountain Boys to millions. In

1962, Martin returned to Tennessee and established his base of operations just outside Nashville, where WSM's *Grand Ole Opry* proved an elusive goal.

During the Decca/MCA years, some of Jimmy Martin's most popular songs were "Sunny Side Of The Mountain," "Widow Maker," "Ocean Of Diamonds," "Freeborn Man," and "You Don't Know My Mind." A few of the other musicians who passed through the band were Bill Emerson, Paul Craft, Doyle Lawson, Vic Jordan, and Alan Munde on banjo; Earl Taylor, Vernon Derrick, and Ronnie Prevette on mandolin; Bill Yates on bass; Tater Tate on fiddle; and Lois Johnson, Penny Jay, and Gloria Belle as high harmony singers and instrumentalists. Jimmy's MCA contract – as well as those of country music icons Ernest Tubb and Loretta Lynn – ended in 1974.

Jimmy continued recording with Gusto Records and performed in country and bluegrass settings, including outdoor music parks and a growing circuit of festivals. He drew national attention among new audiences as a featured guest on the Nitty Gritty Dirt Band's three *Will the Circle Be Unbroken* albums, and as the subject of a book (*True Adventures with the King of Bluegrass*, 1999) and a movie (*King of Bluegrass: The Life and Times of Jimmy Martin*, 2003). Feisty to the end, Jimmy served as ambassador for the Bean Blossom Bluegrass Festival and held court each year in the lobby of the International Bluegrass Music Association's annual convention. After he was diagnosed with bladder cancer in 2004, a steady stream of fans and interviewers passed through his home in Hermitage Hills until the end came on May 14, 2005, at the age of seventy-seven.

— FRED BARTENSTEIN

"I love bluegrass. It's the only kind of music I ever will love. When I sing those songs it hits me deep, and when I'm at the microphone I give it all I've got. I want to see bluegrass stay up so bad, and do something for it however I can."

- Quoted in *The Big Book of Bluegrass*, 1984.

By the way:
- Kept a stable of coondogs, most of them named for country music stars.
- Received a "Distinguished Citizenship Award" for pulling a mother and three children from a burning car in Nashville, 1964.
- Designed his own tombstone, six feet tall, and had it installed six years before his death at Spring Hill Cemetery, Madison, Tennessee.

"Freddie, you would make a good hunter but I believe my son Ray could give you some good pointers: first, Freddie, you ain't a good shot without you can shoot 'em in the head every time, and the reason why, Freddie, is because the groundhog is no good to eat if you hit him anywheres else, because you'll mess him up. And second, Freddie, if you miss him he just goes back to his hole."

- Photo caption composed by Jimmy to accompany a photo of Ray Martin, Fred Bartenstein, and Jimmy Martin holding guns in "*Muleskinner News* Visits Jimmy Martin," *Muleskinner News*, September, 1971.

Peter Van Kuykendall ⟩ 1996

Pete Kuykendall grew up in Arlington, Virginia, a suburb of Washington, D.C. During the 1950s a variety of music types and styles was available to him. His mother's career as a piano instructor made lessons on that instrument his first musical endeavor but, Pete says, "She got frustrated pretty early." During junior high and high school, he also played the clarinet in the concert band.

"He was determined to take his passion for bluegrass and make it his life, which he did. He didn't really want to travel in a band, having a young family, but he wanted to stay as close to the music as he could. What better way than to take a newsletter and turn it into a full-scale magazine?"

- Ginger "Sam" Kuykendall Allred, daughter, 2009.

While in his early teens, he discovered boogie-woogie and what is now called bluegrass music. During his years at Washington and Lee High School, Pete became interested in the guitar and the five-string banjo. "I was one of the early ones that Earl Scruggs influenced. He caught my ear. I heard it on the radio, probably from Don Owens on WGAY. I did a lot of [radio] band-scanning at night." Kuykendall eventually learned to play bass, mandolin, fiddle, guitar, and banjo.

An avid record collector, he began writing a bluegrass column in *Disc Collector* magazine. His record collection started with boogie-piano and then, "I started to hear some blues, what they now call country blues. It seems like I've always been a 'roots music' person. I might hear something played in a polished professional way, but I'll usually dig back to find where it came from."

Born: January 15, 1938, Washington, DC

Primary Instrument: Banjo

"Benny and Vallie Cain had me switch from fiddle to banjo when we were playing at a little dive in D.C. called the B&J Tavern. I was about seventeen. I had learned to play banjo but didn't have one. Vallie said, 'Your instrument is the banjo.' Donnie Bryant left shortly thereafter, so it might have been a set-up to replace him in the group."

- Interview with George McCeney for the Video Oral History Project, International Bluegrass Music Museum, 2006.

Composed:
BMI's database credits Peter Kuykendall with 22 published compositions, co-compositions, and arrangements. A few of his original songs and collaborations are:

"Down Where The Still Waters Flow"

Photo: Frank and Marty Godbey, 1972

After graduation from high school, with his sights set on a radio career, Pete enrolled in the Capitol Radio and Electronics Institute (CREI) in Washington, D.C. In those days, a disc jockey either doubled as ad salesman and DJ or as an engineer and DJ. "I was not a very good salesman, so I opted to go the engineering route."

Pete left school, short of his degree, in 1957 and took his first full-time radio position at WKIK in Leonardtown, Maryland. "I was also playing with Benny and Vallie Cain, a little with Buzz Busby, and this was about the time the Country Gentlemen formed."

The Country Gentlemen were originally assembled as a fill-in group for Buzz Busby who, along with Eddie Adcock, his guitarist at the time, had been injured in an auto accident. "It doesn't make much difference

"I Am Weary (Let Me Rest)" – used in the soundtrack of the movie *O Brother, Where Art Thou?*
"Journey's End"
"No Blind Ones There"
"Out On The Ocean"
"Remembrance Of You"
"Rollin' Stone"

Early influences:
Don Owens
Smitty Irvin
Donnie Bryant

Came to fame with:

Bluegrass Unlimited Magazine

"When the magazine started publishing, bluegrass was pretty much at a low point. The magazine spread the word and highlighted the artistic aspect of the music, which helped to bring it out of the bars where it was in the 1950s. Without him I don't know where the bluegrass industry would be today."

– David Freeman, Rebel Records owner, quoted by Connie Sprague in "Bluegrass Ambassador: Magazine Publisher Has Helped Nourish the Music for 30 Years," *The Fauquier Citizen*, November 1, 1996.

Performed with:

Log Cabin Boys, Washington, D.C., mid-1950s

Benny and Vallie Cain and the Country Clan, mid-1950s

The Country Gentlemen, 1958-1959

Red Allen, Frank Wakefield and the Kentuckians, 1962

Led the way:

- One of the founders of *Bluegrass Unlimited* magazine in 1966, and editor since 1970.
- An important figure in developing the career of the Country Gentlemen as an early member, recording engineer, source of song material, artistic and business advisor.
- Published bluegrass and blues songs as a partner in Wynwood Music Company.

---

now, but I distinctly remember playing bass with Charlie Waller, John Duffey, and Bill Emerson at the Admiral Grill, and I think it may have been the first night."

When he left WKIK, Pete returned to Arlington and CREI to finish his degree. Bill Emerson had left the Country Gentlemen, so, while continuing his education, Pete played banjo regularly with them.

After graduation from CREI, Pete married and went to work at the Library of Congress, which required working Friday nights, so he had to give up the band job. While employed at the Library, one of Pete's primary duties was dubbing music from the fragile discs and cylinders to tape; this provided access to a vast array of recorded music. Pete would find old gems and present them to the Country Gentlemen.

In 1960, hours for his job at the Library were reduced. Since Pete had a family a part-time job wouldn't suffice, so he accepted a chief engineer position at WKCW in Warrenton, Virginia. He left there after about six months and took a job with an electronics distributor, Electronic Wholesalers. There Pete began assembling the components for Wynwood Recording Studio. He also played banjo for a while with Red Allen and Frank Wakefield.

"Pete used to constantly urge John Duffey to take advantage of opportunities to promote their band, the Country Gentlemen. Pete grew frustrated, calling Duffey 'Booger Mule' for his stubbornness. Even after John was in the new band, the Seldom Scene, Pete would try to help John, usually getting nowhere. I thought Pete had gone crazy, expecting to make a profit out of a starving non-profit magazine. He proved me wrong."

– Tom Gray, former member of the Country Gentlemen and Seldom Scene, 2009.

Mike Seeger had been working at Capitol Transcriptions in Washington and engineered the first Country Gentlemen Folkways Records session. After Mike moved to another job, the band called on Pete to engineer its next sessions for the label. "That was where I got my feet wet, actually recording a band. 'Cause I didn't have any better sense, I put together a recording studio. We had bought a house, so I put it in the basement."

Wynwood Studio was quite active for several years, doing not only bluegrass but also country and blues sessions. Rebel Records released a four-record set of seventy songs for mail-order, and much of it was done in Pete's basement. In 1963, Mississippi John Hurt recorded there. Wynwood was also the chosen name for a music publishing company that Pete has operated since the early 1960s.

By the mid-1960s, the number of bluegrass fans in the D.C./Balti-

Bluegrass Hall of Fame Inductee Biographies

more/Philadelphia region had grown significantly, due in large part to the migration from Appalachia after World War II. As a result, locally based bands, as well as nationally touring bands, were frequently playing in the area. A problem, however, was that many times the fans wouldn't know about these performances. On one occasion, the Stanley Brothers appeared in Waldorf, Maryland. Radio personality Gary Henderson got a call from a listener who had missed the show and who suggested that a newsletter be put together to advise people of these performances in advance. The listener had an old mimeograph machine, and volunteered to type the stencils if the information could be collected.

One spring evening in 1966, Henderson, Kuykendall, Dick Freeland (then, of Rebel Records), Dick Spottswood (then of Melodeon Records), and Dianne and Vince Sims (the radio listeners) met at the Kuykendalls. *Bluegrass Unlimited* was born. As the discussion proceeded, it was decided that articles and record reviews would be included in addition to the performance schedule. Over the next four years, the fledgling enterprise made several moves as it outgrew its residence in various volunteers' homes.

By mid-1970, the journal was too much for a volunteer effort, yet not enough for a full-time job. Enter serendipity. The rock band Cream had recorded an old Skip James song, "I'm So Glad," published by Wynwood Music. The royalties gave the proverbial 'kick in the pants' to Pete, enough for him to say to his late wife Marion, "Hon, I'm gonna quit my job and go into doing *Bluegrass Unlimited* full-time." That year, with visits to several major bluegrass festivals and making nearly the whole process a do-it-yourself operation, a period of rapid growth began.

From 1972 through 1980, *Bluegrass Unlimited* produced seventeen major bluegrass festivals at a campground near Hagerstown, Maryland. The Indian Springs Bluegrass Festival is remembered for several firsts, including Bill Clifton's first U.S. appearance after several years abroad, and the only festival appearance by Clarence White before his untimely death.

Since 1985, Pete Kuykendall has been involved with the International Bluegrass Music Association as one of its founding members and as a board member. He and his current wife, Kitsy, have been staunch supporters of the young organization and served in several capacities on committees for many of IBMA's endeavors.

Kuykendall has been integral to the success of bluegrass music over the past five decades. He has been a performer, a songwriter, a magazine and music publisher, an event promoter, a disc jockey, a record producer, booking agent, and one of the best baritone singers. Moreover, his endeavors have all met with a very high level of success.

– STEVE SPENCE

- Played a leading role in making Washington, D.C., the most prominent center for bluegrass music from the late 1950s through the 1970s.
- Instrumental in the formation of the International Bluegrass Music Association (1985) and International Bluegrass Music Museum (1991).
- Bluegrass Hall of Fame, 1996.

By the way:
- His mother was from Brown County, Indiana, so Pete probably knew where Bean Blossom was before Bill Monroe did.
- Played Flatt and Scruggs's 1949 recording of "Foggy Mountain Breakdown" for high school classmate Warren Beatty, who later used it in the 1967 film *Bonnie and Clyde*.
- Won the banjo contest at the National Country Music Contest, Warrenton, Virginia, 1956.
- Sang tenor to John Duffey on the Country Gentlemen's "The Church Back Home" (1958).
- Helped entertainment lawyers to establish that the 1958 monster hit "Tom Dooley" had a provenance older than the Kingston Trio's arrangement.
- Recorded blues masters – including Mississippi John Hurt – and got their songs copyrighted.

For more information on the early history of the Country Gentlemen, see profiles of Eddie Adcock, John Duffey, Tom Gray, and Charlie Waller.

THE CLASSIC COUNTRY GENTLEMEN

Edward Windsor "Eddie" Adcock ⟨ 1996

Born: June 21, 1938, Scottsville, VA

Primary instrument: Banjo

"My brother brought instruments home and I'd try them. Thank you, Bill, for giving me a life of poverty."

- Oral history video, International Bluegrass Music Museum

Composed:

BMI's database credits Eddie Adcock with 134 published compositions, co-compositions, and arrangements, including:

"Another Lonesome Morning"

"El Dedo"

"Turkey Knob"

"Nightwalk"

"Let's"

Early influences:

Merle Travis

Ralph Stanley

Les Paul

Jimmy Bryant and Speedy West

Don Reno

Andres Segovia

Eddie Adcock was born at home in Scottsville, Virginia, a tiny, historic town located twenty miles south of Charlottesville. Eddie, who is primarily known for his banjo playing, was first exposed to the instrument when his brother Bill brought instruments into the family home, including a tenor banjo. However, it was the guitar and mandolin that Eddie favored when he first began to learn to play music. Music, he says, gave him a chance to get off the farm where he was "throwing hay bales five bales high on the downhill side of a wagon. Playing banjo is easier than that."

Eddie left home at age fourteen. From age fifteen to twenty-two, he boxed semi-professionally. During this period he joined Smokey Graves, a quasi-bluegrass entertainer who toured the eastern seaboard and was on the radio in a number of cities, including Crewe, Virginia. Eddie noted, "I played mandolin, and guitar and a little bit of tenor banjo. When he said he needed a five-string banjo player, I sold my calf and bought a Gibson RB-100 banjo. I said I could be there in probably two or three weeks. In that time, I had to learn to play the five-string banjo. I had no idea they used a three-finger roll!" (quoted by Marty Godbey in *Crowe on the Banjo: The Music Life of J.D. Crowe*, University of Illinois Press, 2011.)

"There's a river of notes going by at all times; I'm a fisherman – I just throw the hook in. The secret is not to dislike [any form of] music whatsoever – I love everything, and I listen to everything. I love Van Halen; I love Bill Monroe."

- Quoted by Bill Vernon in "Eddie Adcock and Talk of the Town: Band on the Cutting Edge," *Bluegrass Unlimited*, January 1987.

Photo: Ron Petronko, 1966

Came to fame with:
The Country Gentlemen, 1959-1970

Performed with:
James River Playboys, 1948 or 9-1953

Smokey Graves and His Blue Star Boys, 1954-1955

Mac Wiseman and the Country Boys, 1956

Bill Harrell and the Rocky Mountain Boys, 1956-1957

Buzz Busby and the Bayou Boys, 1957

The Stoneman Family, 1957

Bill Monroe and the Blue Grass Boys, 1958

The Country Gentlemen, 1958-1970

The Clinton Special, 1970

II Generation, 1971-1980

Eddie and Martha Adcock, 1976 to present

Adcock (country-rock band), 1978-1984

David Allan Coe, 1984-1985

Talk Of The Town, 1985-1993

The Masters, 1990

Adcock, Gaudreau, Waller & Gray (Country Gentlemen Reunion Band), 2008

Led the way:
- One of the first musicians to introduce rock, jazz, blues, gospel, rockabilly and folk elements into bluegrass.
- One of the few truly original banjo stylists, incorporating a self-invented single-string, a pedal-steel style, string-bending, a rhythmic thumb style, an energetic bounce, and unlimited improvisation.

Bluegrass Hall of Fame Inductee Biographies \ 59

- Acknowledged by Bill Monroe as the Blue Grass Boys' best baritone singer.
- Invented a number of items of musical and sound equipment, including the Gitbo, a double-necked instrument incorporating an electric guitar and electrified acoustic banjo, 1978.
- Multi-Grammy nominee.
- *Muleskinner News* Entertainer of the Year, 1974.
- Virginia Country Music Hall of Fame, 1987.
- IBMA Instrumental Recorded Performance of the Year for *The Masters*, CMH Records, 1990.
- IBMA Recorded Event of the Year for *Classic Country Gents Reunion*, Sugar Hill Records, 1990.
- MIRL Instrumentalist of the Year, 1991.
- SPBGMA Preservation Hall of Greats, 1993.
- Bluegrass Hall of Fame, 1996.
- America's Old-Time Country Music Hall of Fame, 1996.
- Bill Monroe Hall of Fame, 2005.
- Washington Monument Award, 2012.
- Served on boards of IBMA and the Kentucky Center for Traditional Music.

By the way:
- Set two track records at the Manassas, Virginia, drag-racing track.

The road looms large in a musician's life, and the freeway system was in its infancy when Eddie started his career. He recalls traveling U.S. Highway 40 when it was too narrow for two vehicles to pass. Hotels were just in cities. There were a few bed and breakfast places, but you could go 200 miles without seeing one. There was a lot of sleeping in the car. Thank God for Vienna sausages. They kept us going."

Following his tenure in the Blue Star Boys, Eddie worked in a succession of different groups, starting with Mac Wiseman in about 1956 (he was recommended for that job by Don Reno). His next stop was in the Rocky Mountain Boys, headed by Bill Harrell, on WARL radio in Arlington, Virginia. Eddie's stay lasted until the early part of 1957, when Bill was drafted and the group broke up. Eddie then played with various groups, including the Stonemans, and won numerous music contests.

Eddie next found musical employment with Buzz Busby and the Bayou Boys, another group from the Washington, D.C. area. Busby was known for his wildly erratic mandolin playing and achingly poignant high-pitched vocals. The group was on an upward trajectory when Buzz and several other band members – including Eddie – were involved in a serious automobile accident on July 4, 1957. While Adcock spent several weeks in the hospital, uninjured fellow band member Bill Emerson contacted Charlie Waller and John Duffey and organized a band to fill in for the recovering Bayou Boys. Soon they were calling themselves the Country Gentlemen.

Following the crash, Eddie opted for less glamorous but safer work as a custodian in a high school in Annandale, Virginia. His detour from music was short-lived. Bill Monroe came calling, looking for a banjo player. "I was with Bill for about six months, at a time when he wasn't drawing flies. That's not to say anything bad about him, because all of bluegrass music was rough then. We worked some places that didn't even have floors. Sometimes, I went two or three days without food. I helped Bill on his farm also. We would work six to eight hours during a day, and then we would go do a show that night."

A bus trip from Nashville took Eddie back to Virginia where he landed a job as a sheet-metal mechanic. Again, his intention to get away from full-time music was sidelined when the Country Gentlemen lured Eddie into the group in the early spring of 1959. With that band he gained his greatest fame. He was a member of what has come to be known as the "Classic" Country Gentlemen, who took their brand of bluegrass music all the way to Carnegie Hall. Adcock stayed with the band for twelve years, adding his memorable baritone vocals, improvisational banjo work, and a keen knack for selecting and arranging great material.

Eddie appeared on numerous LP and single recordings with the

Country Gentlemen, cutting for such labels as Starday, Folkways, Mercury, Design, Rebel, and Rome. Eddie's first "solo" outing came in 1968 when he and Don Reno teamed up for an album on Rebel called *Sensational Twin Banjos*.

By the early part of 1970, Eddie was ready for a change. He headed to the West Coast for a brief flirtation with country rock. He played electric guitar and performed under the stage name of Clinton Codack. Back East, he assembled a progressive bluegrass outfit with Jimmy Gaudreau, Bob White, and Wendy Thatcher called II Generation. The group and its subsequent configurations recorded for Rome, Starday, Rebel and CMH.

Eddie gained his longest-lasting partner when Martha Hearon joined II Generation in 1973. The couple married in 1976 and have been together ever since. They shared a high profile gig in 1984-1985 when they toured with "outlaw country" musician David Allan Coe. Various recording projects marked milestones and changes in Eddie's career. CMH albums from the couple included an instrumental outing called *Guitar Echoes* and a release called *Love Games*. 1989 brought Eddie back together with Charlie Waller, John Duffey and Tom Gray for an album on Sugar Hill called *Classic Country Gents Reunion*, which garnered IBMA's Recorded Event of the Year. Also in 1990, Eddie teamed with Kenny Baker, Josh Graves, Jesse McReynolds, Martha Adcock, and Missy Raines to record for CMH Records as The Masters.

Eddie and Martha signed with Pinecastle Records from 1996-2003 and released three recordings. In 2008, he teamed up with ex-Country Gentlemen Jimmy Gaudreau and Tom Gray as well as Randy Waller, son of the late Charlie Waller, to record an album as the Country Gentlemen Reunion Band. Eddie, Martha, and Tom Gray recorded a Country Gentlemen retrospective on the Patuxent label called *Many a Mile* in 2011.

In 2008 a right-hand tremor that had begun threatening Eddie's ability to continue to play banjo and guitar was alleviated by an operation performed at Vanderbilt University Medical Center in Nashville. The procedure placed electrodes in Eddie's brain that allowed him to regain full use of his picking abilities. He had to remain awake, with banjo in hand, while surgeons worked to correct the problem. Several follow-up surgeries were required to fine-tune the procedure. The operations were a success and Eddie and Martha remain vibrant performers on the bluegrass and acoustic music scene, continuing to write, record, produce, instruct, appear on radio and television, and tour the USA, Canada, Europe and Japan. Martha is currently working to finish a book on Eddie's life and times.

— GABRIELLE GRAY, GARY REID & MARTHA ADCOCK

- Held a variety of jobs while pursuing his musical quest, including auto mechanic, heating and air conditioning repairman, sheet-metal mechanic, laundry deliverer, dump truck driver, auto parts salesman, and gas station owner.
- Pursued a successful side career providing sound amplification for bluegrass festivals as Adcock Audio, 1970s-2006.
- Played banjo while undergoing groundbreaking brain surgery (seen in video and print worldwide) at Vanderbilt University Medical Center in 2008 and 2011, earning him the title "The Bionic Banjo Man."
- Hosts numerous good-works benefit concerts, including an annual event for the homeless of Nashville, TN, since 2000.

"I love bluegrass, and I love bluegrass people, but they aggravate me to think that they can go out and have them a good job and make big money and put money in the bank and drive a fine car around... but tell me that I can't do what they're doing. I'm not allowed to have any money. I've got to play bluegrass or else. They just don't understand that I like bluegrass, but I've got to eat, too."

- Quoted by Robert Kyle in *Blueprint* (date unknown); reprinted in Don Rhodes, "Finding Their Place in Bluegrass Music: Eddie and Martha Adcock," *Bluegrass Unlimited*, April 1982.

THE CLASSIC COUNTRY GENTLEMEN

John Humbird Duffey 1996

Listening to the radio while a student at Bethesda-Chevy Chase High School in Washington's Maryland suburbs in the late 1940s, John Duffey was exposed to and became interested in the music of Appalachian migrants to the capitol region. His father, a professional tenor who performed for a time with the Metropolitan Opera chorus, disliked country music but taught his son breathing and vocal techniques that could increase his power and clarity in performing what was then called "hillbilly music." Starting with the guitar, in 1957, John took up the mandolin and Dobro and soon developed a reputation for competence that overcame his cultural distance from the mountain-born Southerners with whom he played.

Duffey performed and recorded with several amateur and semi-professional groups after graduating from high school, but made his primary living as a printer, instrument repairman, and driver of a surgical supply truck. Bill Emerson, a younger neighbor in suburban Bethesda, Maryland, was also getting interested in bluegrass. In July of 1957, Emerson was playing banjo with Buzz Busby and the Bayou Boys. The mandolin-playing bandleader, guitar player (Eddie Adcock), and bassist were injured in a serious auto accident. It fell to Emerson to recruit fill-in musicians for a weekend job at the Admiral Grill in Bailey's Crossroads, Virginia. Bill knew that John Duffey was driving almost fifty miles to Frederick,

> "What people love about him is that you know he's one of these guys stuck in the '50s, but he's so happy with himself, so confident, and he's also nuts."
>
> - Mike Auldridge, quoted in Bart Barnes, John Duffey obituary, *Washington Post*, December 11, 1996.

Born: March 4, 1934, Washington, DC

Died: December 10, 1996, Arlington, VA

Primary instrument: Mandolin

> "His approach to the mandolin sometimes appeared to be aimed at seeing how many different and unexpected sounds could be coaxed, squeezed, or beaten out of his instrument. In addition to his own impressive high-energy variations on Monroe-style mandolin playing, John did such unheard-of things as playing breaks on three or four strings simultaneously instead of the usual one or two. He twisted the strings, he played jazz chords, played breaks alternating between first and fourth strings, and sometimes he'd use fingerpicks instead of a flat pick."
>
> - Jack Tottle in "Bluegrass Mandolin 1/3 Century Later," *Bluegrass Unlimited*, March 1972.

Composed:

BMI's database credits John Duffey with 107 published compositions, co-compositions, and arrangements, including:

"Bringing Mary Home" (*Billboard* peak at #43, 1965)

"Along the Way"

"Border Incident"

"A Cold Wind A' Blowin'"

"Christmas Time Back Home"

"Don't Bother with White Satin"

"Hills and Home"

"This World's No Place to Live (But It's Home)"

"Travelin' Dobro"

"Victim to the Tomb"

Early influences:

Bill Monroe

Flatt and Scruggs

Stanley Brothers

The Osborne Brothers and Red Allen

Bill Clifton

"He told me that he had heard my music before and that my recording of 'Mary Dear' [1957] was one of the reasons he had decided that he wanted to play music. John told me that after he had heard the mandolin, he went to the local music store and looked at the instruments and said: 'I'll take that one!' He bought it, took it home, and just hoped that he could figure out what to do with it."

– Bill Clifton, quoted in Rienk Janssen's liner notes to *Bill Clifton: Around the World To Poor Valley*, Bear Family Records, 2001.

Came to fame with:

The Country Gentlemen, 1957-1969

> "We're not mountain boys. We're gentlemen."
>
> – Quoted in Richard Harrington, John Duffey obituary, *Washington Post*, December 11, 1996.

Performed with:

David Swan and the Rainbow Mountain Boys, 1953-1957

Lucky Chatman's Ozark Mountain Boys, 1957

The Country Gentlemen, 1957-1969

Bill Clifton and the Dixie Mountain Boys, late 1950s – early 1960s

The Seldom Scene, 1971-1996

> "When I first met him in 1958, he wouldn't talk on stage, he wouldn't say a word – he couldn't do the MC work or anything. Charlie [Waller] and I did that the first year or so, but slowly, a word here and a word there came, until we couldn't control him any more."
>
> – Eddie Adcock, quoted by Jon Weisberger in liner notes to *John Duffey: Always in Style*, Sugar Hill Records, 2000.

Led the way:

- Prominent vocalist (lead, tenor) and instrumentalist (mandolin, Dobro, guitar) with two of the most popular and influential groups in bluegrass history: the Country Gentlemen and the Seldom Scene.
- One of the earliest to challenge the accepted way of doing things in bluegrass, broadening its audience appeal and fan base.
- One of the first suburban and northern-born artists to make a career in bluegrass.

Maryland, to play mandolin and sing tenor with Lucky Chatman and the Ozark Mountain Boys, and thought he might appreciate a closer gig. Guitarist Charlie Waller, a former member of the Bayou Boys, and bassist Larry Leahey were brought in to complete the ensemble.

The sound clicked, and the members soon dubbed themselves the Country Gentlemen. Country music historian Bill Malone perceptively observed that this band made its reputation by heightening every aspect of bluegrass – they played faster, sang higher, and performed with a dynamism that made other groups look stodgy. WARL's Don Owens got the Gentlemen a morning show on that Arlington, Virginia, station. Independent producer Ben Adelman recorded them in Washington and sold the masters to Nashville-based Starday Records. In 1958, John Duffey decided to leave his day job and play bluegrass full-time.

The bluegrass performance circuit provided scant economic rewards. At first Duffey had to moonlight to make ends meet, filling in on various sessions arranged by Adelman and Rebel Records producer Dick Freeland, and on recordings and live appearances with Bill Clifton and Mike Seeger. For ten years starting in 1960, the Country Gentlemen appeared on Tuesday and Thursday nights at the Shamrock Club on M Street in Washington's Georgetown. There they developed a following from the burgeoning folk music audience.

Instrumentally, the Gentlemen could play rings around popular folk artists such as the Kingston Trio and the Limelighters. John Duffey was especially quick to see in folk music an opportunity to break free of bluegrass and traditional country music's dead-end orbit. Making only minor changes to their singing and playing, the group found that John's spontaneous and at times sophomoric wit was their best magnet for college-educated audiences.

One barrier to folk music acceptance at the time was the band's commercial country and newly composed material. John Duffey and his companions began to haunt the Library of Congress and area collections of old 78 rpm records in search of traditional tunes and lyrics. Through Mike Seeger, the Country Gentlemen arranged to record for New York-based Folkways Records.

In the first half of the 1960s, the Country Gentlemen maintained dual brands. South of the Mason-Dixon line they were a hot bluegrass band, with Starday singles on truck-stop and beer-joint jukeboxes. Outside the South, they were a hip and progressive folk/comedy act, bringing banjo, mandolin, guitar, string bass, and thrilling vocal harmonies to familiar songs of singer-songwriter composers such as Bob Dylan and Tom Paxton.

It is ironic that, as the folk audience relaxed its demand for traditionalism, the bluegrass world began to self-consciously define its boundaries.

The Country Gentlemen weren't invited to the first multi-day bluegrass festival in 1965, and the next year they were presented as a novelty act. John Duffey lashed out verbally and in print, reminding critics of the risks of recycling even the best music without innovation, entertainment, and cultivating new audiences. Tired of the struggle, he left the Country Gentlemen in early 1969. For two years he worked as an instrument repairman, jamming and recording occasionally as a guest musician, happy to be off the road.

In January of 1972, a pick-up band that included John Duffey began appearing weekly at the Red Fox Inn in Bethesda, Maryland. All had day jobs and expected their music to be an occasional thing – they jokingly called the group "the Seldom Scene" to celebrate this intention. Once again, the chemistry was magical. The sound of the Scene fit an emerging culture, in which bluegrass, country, rock 'n' roll, and folk influences could blend in an appealing and entertaining package. Recordings for Rebel and concert appearances, infrequent as they were, propelled the group to headline status. By 1974, they were named the top band in bluegrass in the *Muleskinner News* reader poll.

John Duffey's powerful tenor voice, muscular mandolin stylings, and outrageous stage antics endeared him to new generations of fans and fellow artists. For the next two decades, Duffey enjoyed the prestige and financial success which had previously eluded him. John's canny business mind and self-confidence helped the Seldom Scene to realize that, as a commodity in short supply and hot demand, they could ask and receive both top dollar and respectful treatment.

Eight albums on Rebel and nine on Sugar Hill included star-studded live concerts at the fifteenth and twentieth anniversaries of the band. Membership of the Seldom Scene changed over time, but the innovative formula and spotlight on Duffey remained constants.

In September of 1996, John Duffey was inducted into the Bluegrass Hall of Fame, together with other members of the classic edition of the Country Gentlemen. The second weekend of December, he performed with the Seldom Scene in Englewood, New Jersey. Upon returning home, he experienced difficulty breathing and went to Arlington Hospital. Later that morning, he died of a sudden heart attack, still at the peak of his powers at age sixty-two. Already reeling from Bill Monroe's death three months earlier, the bluegrass community was numb with shock. A theme of all the writers of obituaries and memorial messages was that they couldn't believe the big man was gone. He was such a larger-than-life presence – and such an anomaly – that his important role in the development of bluegrass music has taken more than a decade to come into focus.

– FRED BARTENSTEIN

- From the 1950s through the 1990s, played a leading role in making Washington, D.C. the most prominent capitol for bluegrass music.
- Bluegrass Hall of Fame, 1996.

"When you can make the snobs think you're one of them, pretty soon they are on your side. And they will take notice of what you are doing. This makes it easier for the next group who comes along."

- John Duffey, "So You Don't Like the Way We Do It," *Bluegrass Unlimited*, April 1967.

By the way:
- Never left the Washington, D.C. area as his base of operations.
- A gifted instrument craftsman, he designed an unusual mandolin known as "The Duck," which he played onstage until the return of his stolen F-12 Gibson.
- Found inspiration in entertainers like Johnny Carson, studying what they did to gain and hold an audience's attention.
- His outrageous sense of style was legendary. Duffey never gave up his flat-top buzz-cut hairdo, his bowling shirts, or multicolored body-builder pants.

THE CLASSIC COUNTRY GENTLEMEN

Thomas L. "Tom" Gray | 1996

If the Country Gentlemen are to be credited with popularizing bluegrass to college and northern audiences, Tom Gray was arguably their first and most passionate convert. While in high school (class of 1958) and a university undergraduate in Washington, D.C., Gray was a regular at the Gentlemen's gigs and occasionally sat in. When the bass chair opened in September of 1960, he was invited to fill it and did so for four years, at the same time finishing his studies and starting work as a cartographer for the National Geographic Society.

Born in Chicago, Gray moved to Washington at the age of seven, when his father took a job with a trade association in 1948. There he was exposed by a babysitter to the sounds of the *Grand Ole Opry*, before country music was considered respectable in educated circles. At twelve, he started playing guitar and then the mandolin. Attracted to the lowest notes in music, he began playing what eventually became his primary instrument when Tom Morgan left a string bass in Gray's basement after a jam session. His primary role models were the

"I was lucky when I joined the Country Gentlemen, because they were an ideal group to improvise in just as freely as I liked.... The thing that made it good for the walking style I played was that the lead instrument players were singing in the trios, and that left nobody with a lead instrument to play back-up. That left a clear path for me to use the bass as a back-up instrument, playing a bit of counter-melody along with the usual rhythm functions."

– Quoted by Jon Hartley Fox in liner notes to *The Country Gentlemen: Going Back to the Blue Ridge Mountains*, Smithsonian Folkways Records, 2007.

Born: February 1, 1941, Chicago, IL

Primary Instrument: String bass

"No one plays more bass and seems less willing to take credit for his own genius than Tom Gray. He invariably plays interesting notes in just the right places."

– Bill Vernon, "Part-Time Professionals: The Seldom Scene," *Muleskinner News*, March 1973.

Composed:
Composed and arranged several songs and instrumentals that were recorded by the Country Gentlemen, the Seldom Scene, and others, including:

"Silence or Tears" (melody; words were borrowed from a Lord Byron poem)

"Walking the Blues"

"You Left Me Alone"

"(I Know You) Rider" (co-arranger)

Early influences:
George and John Shuffler
Keeter Betts
Bill Monroe
Flatt and Scruggs
Stanley Brothers

Came to fame with:
The Classic Country Gentlemen, 1960-1964

Performed with:
Rocky Ridge Ramblers, 1958
Bill Clifton and the Dixie Mountain Boys, 1959
Buzz Busby, Pete Pike and the Bayou Boys 1959-1960, 1967
The Country Gentlemen, 1960-1964
Benny and Vallie Cain and the Country Clan, 1965-1967, 1970
Bill Emerson, Cliff Waldron and the New Shades of Grass 1968-1969
The Seldom Scene, 1971-1987
Paul Adkins's Borderline Band, 1988-1989
Gary Ferguson Band, 1990-1999
Federal Jazz Commission, 1994-2008
(Tom) Gray, (Roger) Green, and (Fred) Travers Trio, 1994-1996
Hazel Dickens Band, 1998-2003
Randy Barrett and the Barretones, 2000-present
Jay Armsworthy and Eastern Tradition, 2004-present
John Starling and Carolina Star, 2004-present
Emmylou Harris with Carolina Star, 2006-2007
Eddie and Martha Adcock with Tom Gray, 2005-present

inordinately flashy Shuffler Brothers, George and John, of Valdese, North Carolina, who began playing bass on Stanley Brothers Columbia and Mercury 78s in 1952. Tom ardently collected these discs, and the older mountain music that preceded them. He was also influenced by Keeter Betts, a jazz bassist who played with guitarist Charlie Byrd.

As a student at Western High School and George Washington University, Tom Gray found kindred musical spirits at the dawn of the folk music craze. Jerry Stuart and Gray (playing guitar) joined Pete Kuykendall and Smiley Hobbs on Stuart's mandolin instrumental "Rocky Run" for the 1959 Folkways album *Mountain Music Bluegrass Style*, produced by Mike Seeger.

The Country Gentlemen welcomed innovation and virtuosity. When he joined that group, Gray was encouraged to play flashy walking 4/4 bass lines and to solo. John Duffey instructed engineer Pete Kuykendall to raise Tom Gray's levels for their Folkways recordings, as Starday had used such inferior vinyl that the bass was virtually inaudible.

> *"He's the only one of us who always knows exactly where he is."*
> – John Duffey on Tom Gray, quoted by Eugene Chadbourne in artist biography, *AllMusic.com*.

Paradoxically, Tom Gray, who had the least rural background of any member, was the most devoted to tradition and the least comfortable with stylistic accommodations to the folk audience. A florid bassist, his vocals – most often duets with John Duffey or on gospel quartets – were decorous and thoroughly within the bluegrass tradition. Surrounded by the constant stage antics and outbursts of John Duffey, Eddie Adcock, and Charlie Waller, Tom Gray was the dapper and unflappable straight man.

In September, 1961, the Country Gentlemen appeared on a multi-artist bill at New York City's Carnegie Hall, sponsored by *Sing Out!* magazine. The concert was recorded and six tracks were subsequently released in a reissue of the Folkways live album, *On the Road*. Starday released an album of studio recordings titled *The Country Gentlemen at Carnegie Hall* featuring Tom Gray on bass.

Folk Session Inside was a nationally distributed Mercury album, released in 1963. It was well received and helped the group to increase its booking rates and radius. A second Mercury album was recorded and network television appearances were under discussion in 1964 but, when label personnel and the folk music market changed, the industry didn't seem to know what to do with the Country Gentlemen – and so it did nothing.

By this time, Tom had married Sally Govers Gray, and begun to father a growing family. His career was musically rewarding but the unpredictability, scarce financial rewards, and constant traveling were aggravating even to a man in his early twenties. In July, 1964, Tom Gray left the Country Gentlemen and was replaced by Ed Ferris.

For the next two decades he compiled and edited maps for the National Geographic Society. Several times a week, he would play bass in the Washington area with local and touring acts.

When Tom Gray and John Duffey got together with John Starling, Ben Eldridge, and Mike Auldridge in 1969, it was for a basement jam session at Eldridge's house in Bethesda, Maryland. Their first public performance was at a Georgetown rock club in late 1971. All had day jobs, so the group named itself the Seldom Scene. Their weekly gig at Bethesda's Red Fox Inn (moving to the Birchmere in Alexandria, Virginia, after five years) continued to be packed, and the demand for concert, festival, and recording appearances was irresistible.

Through John Duffey's death in 1996, the act was consistently in the top ranks of the bluegrass world, winning numerous group, individual artist, song, and album awards. As had the Country Gentlemen in an earlier era, the Seldom Scene supercharged bluegrass, adding elements of country, folk, and rock, in the context of a spontaneous and entertaining stage show.

At the end of 1975, the Seldom Scene released a double live album. It was an audacious venture in bluegrass at the time, but became a classic, and has since been reissued twice on CD. It features Tom Gray's bass solo tour de force, "Grandfather's Clock." Tom also performed on the group's fifteenth and twentieth anniversary live albums, the latter as a returning alumnus four years after leaving the group.

Bluegrass music cooled off a bit in the eighties. Anxious to broaden their appeal and attract new markets, members of the Seldom Scene sought to modernize the band's sound. This didn't go over well with Tom Gray, the most traditionally oriented member of his band. "To avoid becoming an obstacle to progress" (in his own words), Tom left in October of 1987, replaced by T. Michael Coleman on electric bass.

Retiring from full-time band work for the second time, Tom Gray hardly let his instrument gather dust. He was in demand for recording sessions, performed on Country Gentlemen and Seldom Scene reunion albums, and accompanied old friend Bill Clifton on four international tours. Especially as he began to wind down his career as a cartographer, Gray found himself saying "yes" to more and more part-time band work. Most were bluegrass and folk oriented, but Tom also enjoyed a regular Dixieland gig with a group called the Federal Jazz Commission. The youngest member of bluegrass music's pioneers, Tom Gray continues to be a welcome and familiar presence onstage.

— FRED BARTENSTEIN

Country Gentlemen Reunion Band, 2007-2008

Darren Beachley and Legends of the Potomac, 2009-present

Led the way:
- A member of the "classic" edition of the Country Gentlemen, one of the first bands to introduce bluegrass to urban and college audiences, and a founding member of the Seldom Scene, perhaps the most influential bluegrass act of the 1970s and 1980s.
- Played a leading role in making Washington, D.C. the most prominent center for bluegrass music from the late 1950s through the 1970s.
- Voted best bluegrass bass player eight times while a member of the Seldom Scene.
- Bluegrass Hall of Fame, 1996 – the first bassist to be inducted.

By the way:
- Played accordion and piano before discovering bluegrass in the early 1950s.
- Played on more than 100 albums
- Calls his bass "Bessie" in honor of Bessie Lee Mauldin, Bill Monroe's long-time bassist and muse.
- Currently plays in seven Washington-based bands in several genres, and occasionally edits maps for the National Geographic Society's Book Division.
- Tom's late wife Sally edited *Bluegrass Unlimited* magazine in the 1960s.

THE CLASSIC COUNTRY GENTLEMEN

Charles Otis "Charlie" Waller | 1996

Charlie Waller was born in a now-tiny East Texas town named for Columbus Joiner, who drilled the first oil well there in 1930. Waller's family must have experienced the bust, leaving Joinerville shortly after Charlie's birth during the Great Depression. The Wallers moved to a farm in northern Louisiana, where Charlie remembered picking cotton.

At the age of ten, he purchased his first guitar – a Stella – for fifteen dollars and decided to make his career in entertainment. His mother, who had taken a job with Potomac Electric Power Company and ran a rooming house in Washington, D.C., sent for Charlie to join her. He left school in the eighth grade and landed his first professional music job in 1948 at the age of thirteen, with Richard Decker and Jack Jackson. Also working by day in a gas station and body shop, Waller picked up musical and performance skills from the slightly older Scott Stoneman.

"The thing we had going for us was we didn't care to sound like the rest. We mixed in a few older country songs and folk songs; we did some jazz and movie themes."

- Quoted in obituary, *Washington Post*, August 19, 2004.

In the early 1950s, Charlie played with Earl Taylor and the Stoney Mountain Boys in the bars of Baltimore until switching to Buzz Busby and the Bayou Boys. Buzz had also migrated from northern Louisiana, and the band (which included Don Stover on banjo) decided to try out for the *Louisiana Hayride* in Shreveport. There they appeared alongside Elvis Presley, Johnny Cash, George Jones, the Browns, Johnny Horton, and Jimmie C. Newman and recorded classics such as "Lost" and "Me

Born: January 19, 1935, Joinerville, TX

Died: August 18, 2004, Gordonsville, VA

Primary instrument:- Guitar

"One of the things that caught my attention early on was the way he held his guitar on stage.... With his feet planted wide, he would lean into that Martin with his right hand balled up and turned in toward the sound-hole as his arm stroked out the rhythm."

- Walt Saunders in liner notes to *Joe's Last Train*, Rebel Records, 2004.

Composed:

BMI's database credits him as an arranger or co-arranger of 35 songs and instrumentals, including:

"Calling My Children Home"

"Little Bessie"

"One Wide River To Cross"

"Two Little Boys"

"Under The Double Eagle"

Bluegrass Hall of Fame Inductee Biographies

Photo: W.T. Helfrich, mid-1970s

Early influences:
Hank Snow
Mac Wiseman
Don Reno
Bill Monroe
Flatt and Scruggs

Came to fame with:
The Country Gentlemen, 1957-2004

"Really we were kind of crazy on stage. You know, just by itself we were that way, but we figured it was more fun and especially if people are watching you. If you're having a good time, they're having a better time."
- Quoted in Tom Henderson, "Charlie Waller: the Original Country Gentleman," *Muleskinner News*, December 1973.

Performed with:
Earl Taylor and the Stoney Mountain Boys, 1954-1955
Buzz Busby and the Bayou Boys, 1955-1957
The Country Gentlemen, 1957-2004

Led the way:
- During six decades, prominent vocalist and rhythm guitarist (and since 1992, leader) of the Country Gentlemen.
- Member of the first band to incorporate a large share of repertoire from other genres, an essential link between the early pioneers of bluegrass and the newgrass movement.
- Played a leading role in making Washington, D.C. the most prominent

and the Jukebox."

The Bayou Boys had returned to Washington, and Eddie Adcock had replaced Charlie on guitar, by the time an auto wreck hospitalized Busby and Adcock. Banjo player Bill Emerson hastily assembled Charlie Waller, John Duffey, and Larry Leahy to fill in at the Admiral Grill in Bailey's Crossroads, Virginia, on July 4, 1957. Waller and Duffey had never met, but were pleased by the blend of their voices and musical interests. The group adopted the name the Country Gentlemen and self-produced Carter Stanley's song "Going to the Races" and Duffey's "Heavenward Bound" on the Dixie label before beginning to lease tracks to the Starday label later in 1957.

For almost fifteen years, the Country Gentlemen appeared two nights a week at the Shamrock Club in Washington's Georgetown district. It wasn't a fancy place, but the informal atmosphere and audience of southern migrant country music fans, college students, and government workers created an environment in which a variety of musical tastes, experimentation, and onstage rehearsal could forge a distinctive and appealing act.

"With a straight face he would convulse audiences with witty off-the-cuff remarks. Once at the Shamrock Restaurant in Georgetown, D.C., the Gents were on stage when the door opened and an elegantly attired woman walked in – clearly overdressed for her surroundings. Charlie took one look at her and barked, 'I thought I told you to stay in the truck!'"
- Walt Saunders in liner notes to *Joe's Last Train*, Rebel Records, 2004.

"I've always loved Charlie's voice, and it's still wonderful. If I had to describe it I'd say, 'Take Hank Snow and Bing Crosby, put them together, and you have a little bit of Charlie Waller.' There are many excellent singers out there – some with terrific voices, some with great technique and phrasing, and others with lots of soul… but Charlie has it all."
- Eddie Adcock, liner notes to *Charlie Waller and the Country Gentlemen, Songs of the American Spirit*, Pinecastle Records, 2004.

By 1964, the Country Gentlemen's recordings were nationally distributed on the Folkways and Mercury labels. Ruggedly handsome, sincere, and baritone-voiced Charlie Waller contrasted with the wiry and volatile wiseacre John Duffey, the flashy and aggressive banjo star Eddie Adcock, and the quiet and collegiate bassman Tom Gray – members of the "classic" edition of the band. Some of Charlie's most popular solos from the early days included "Two Little Boys," "Copper Kettle," and "Matterhorn."

The group took a new lease on life with a quite-different-sounding ensemble in 1971: Bill Emerson in his second stint on banjo, Doyle Lawson on mandolin, and Bill Yates on bass. Waller was the constant and increasingly the "star" vocalist, a role he had previously shared with John Duffey. Songs such as "Fox on the Run," "Teach Your Children," and "Legend of the Rebel Soldier" won awards and became perennial bluegrass standards. Opposite from the experience of other country and bluegrass acts of the time, the Country Gentlemen's popularity grew from a northern fanbase into the south, midwest, and southwest, as outdoor festivals proliferated. This edition of the Country Gentlemen toured Japan and recorded a live album in Tokyo.

"Music is an emotional thing. If you can't sing a song from the heart, you haven't sung it."
- Quoted in Tom Henderson, "Charlie Waller... the Original Country Gentleman," *Muleskinner News*, December 1973.

More band changes followed, but the group's Waller-centric sound continued for three more decades. During this era, recordings on Rebel, Vanguard, Sugar Hill, and Pinecastle were best sellers and frequent visitors to the bluegrass charts.

Charlie Waller faced health challenges as the millennium turned, but he kept up his touring and recording. The end came unexpectedly. At 6:30 p.m. on August 18, 2004, his wife found him dead of a heart attack in the same Gordonsville, Virginia, garden where his mother had died.

— FRED BARTENSTEIN

capital for bluegrass music from the late 1950s through the 1970s.
- Bluegrass Hall of Fame, 1996.

By the way:
- As a teenager, parked cars in Washington near where Roy Clark worked. The two would jam while Charlie waited for customers.
- While his most resonant range was lower than most bluegrass vocalists, sang lead, baritone, bass, tenor, frog, duck, and girl parts (the last three on *Ain't Got No Home*).
- Loved being on the water and even lived on his motorboat for a while.
- According to Tom Gray, suggested that two ex-bandmates name their new group "The Seldom Scene."
- Mentored scores of young musicians who passed in and out of the Country Gentlemen, while Charlie remained the only constant – and therefore the defining – element of the band's sound.
- Son Randy Waller (born in 1959) saw little of his traveling father during his childhood, but began touring with the Country Gentlemen in 2003 and continues to lead the band today.

Burkett Howard "Josh" or "Buck" Graves | 1997

Born: September 27, 1927, Tellico Plains, TN

Died: September 30, 2006, Nashville, TN

Primary Instrument: Dobro

"I met Cliff Carlisle – he played the Dobro on some of Jimmie Rodgers's records. I remember he and his brother Bill Carlisle came in to Knoxville, Tennessee, in '38, '39... somewhere in there. I was just a little feller, and they played my little home community."

- Interview with Barry Willis, 1994.

Composed:

BMI's database credits Josh Graves with 55 published compositions, co-compositions, and arrangements, including:

"Backin' To Birmingham"

"Come Walk With Me" (BMI Award Winning Song)

"Evelina"

"Fireball"

"Flatt Lonesome"

In 1955 Burkett Howard "Buck" Graves changed the sound of bluegrass music when he added a new instrumental voice, that of the Dobro, to the five instruments – fiddle, guitar, mandolin, bass, and banjo – first heard together in Bill Monroe's Blue Grass Boys of the mid-1940s.

Graves's Dobro became part of bluegrass music when he joined Lester Flatt and Earl Scruggs's band, the Foggy Mountain Boys. Subsequently he participated in all of their Columbia recording sessions except one, more than any other Foggy Mountain Boy.

Lester and Earl hired him to work as bassist, and as comedian in the role of "Uncle Josh." At first he played Dobro only at their recording sessions and on a few pieces in

"[Bill Monroe] was quoted as saying the Dobro wasn't a bluegrass instrument. He came to me and told me he was misquoted. That he'd said it wasn't bluegrass unless Josh played it... Bill loved those blues licks."

- Interview with Bobby Wolfe, "Josh Graves: Father of the Bluegrass Dobro," *Bluegrass Unlimited*, October, 1990

shows. But Uncle Josh's picking was so well received that Lester and Earl quickly moved him to Dobro full-time and hired a second comedian, E.P. "Cousin Jake" Tullock, to play bass. Thereafter, Josh and Jake's wonderful comedy routines and singing were part of every Flatt and Scruggs show.

Josh's Dobro became an integral part of the instrumental signature of bluegrass music's most successful band – not just on their chart-topping records, but on radio and television and in personal appearances as well. Soon other bands began adding the Dobro to their sound.

"Foggy Mountain Rock"

"The Good Things Outweigh The Bad"

"If You're Ever Going To Love Me"

"Just Joshing"

"Roust A Bout"

"Sure Wanna Keep My Wine" ("Great Big Woman")

Early influences:

Cliff Carlisle

Clell "Cousin Jody" Summey

Lightnin' Hopkins

Earl Scruggs

Speedy Krise

Bob Wills

Came to fame with:

Lester Flatt, Earl Scruggs and the Foggy Mountain Boys

Performed with:

Pierce Brothers, Gatlinburg, TN, 1942

Esco Hankins, Knoxville, TN, 1943-1947 and Lexington, KY, 1949-1951

Wilma Lee and Stoney Cooper and the Clinch Mountain Clan, 1951-1954

Toby Stroud and the Blue Mountain Boys, 1954

Mac Wiseman and the Country Boys, 1954-1955

Lester Flatt, Earl Scruggs and the Foggy Mountain Boys, 1955-1969

Lester Flatt and the Nashville Grass, 1969-1972

Earl Scruggs Revue, 1972-1974

Josh Graves (solo and studio work), 1974-1984

Josh Graves and Kenny Baker, 1984-2006

The Masters, 1989-1997

Graves not only introduced a new voice to this music, he also developed a multifaceted musical vocabulary for it. He had studied the sounds and techniques introduced by the masters of early country music steel guitar – players like Brother Oswald of Roy Acuff's Smoky Mountain Boys, and Cliff Carlisle, who recorded with Jimmie Rodgers. To this he added his own upbeat bluegrass-style picking developed from Earl Scruggs's right-hand banjo technique, which Scruggs personally taught him when they were both working at WVLK near Lexington, Kentucky.

"Josh put the Dobro in bluegrass music. He also took the Dobro far beyond bluegrass. He was extremely versatile and a real trouper. Josh was, and will continue to be, an inspiration to many."

- Earl Scruggs in *Bluegrass Unlimited* obituary, December 2006.

Josh grew up listening to African American musicians in his home community in East Tennessee as well as through radio and records. Still, in those segregated times it was not always easy to meet with, listen to, or play with musicians across color lines. To do this took determination and social grace, and Josh had those qualities. Throughout his life he sang and played the blues, collected blues recordings, and counted famous bluesmen like Lightnin' Hopkins among his personal friends. His signal contribution came as he added the rhythms and licks of this music he loved and believed in to the bluegrass sound.

Starting in the mid-1950s, each new Flatt and Scruggs single had Josh's picking front and center. Pieces like "Big Black Train," with its bluesy Dobro opening, drew even teenage fans with a taste for rhythm and blues and the era's new rockabilly sounds into this new music. His blues feeling transformed the Foggy Mountain Boys sound. This can be heard clearly by comparing their 1952 recording of "If I Should Wander Back Tonight" (made before he joined the band) with their 1961 version. There are other examples of this kind of transformation with Josh in the band: compare Flatt and Scruggs's 1950 Columbia recording of "I'm Head Over Heels in Love" with Lester's 1971 version on RCA.

"Carl Smith once told me that if they ever figured out all that junk, blues and jazz, that [I was playing] they would fire me in a minute."

- Interview with Bobby Wolfe, "Josh Graves: Father of the Bluegrass Dobro," *Bluegrass Unlimited,* October 1990.

Graves worked with other top acts besides Flatt and Scruggs. Before joining them he'd played with Esco Hankins, Wilma Lee and Stoney Cooper, and Mac Wiseman. After Lester and Earl split up in 1969, Josh was a member in each of their bands. In 1974 he began performing and

> *"It makes me feel awful good that, when I'm gone, I'll leave something that someone else can go on with."*
>
> – Interview with Stacy Phillips in *Complete Dobro Player*, Mel Bay Publications, 1996.

recording as a featured soloist. He collaborated with many other leading performers, like long-time partner Kenny Baker, the Masters (Eddie and Martha Adcock, Kenny Baker, Jesse McReynolds and Missy Raines) and Red Taylor, to name but a few.

Josh inspired hundreds of musicians to pick up the steel bar and slide it over the strings of the Dobro. Befriending many of them, he encouraged Dobroists to develop their own music, and sometimes even graciously performed with them on their recordings and at their personal appearances.

Josh Graves died on September 30, 2006, three days after his seventy-ninth birthday. It's good and fitting that the story of this talented and influential musician has been preserved in *Bluegrass Bluesman*, a posthumous autobiography.

— NEIL V. ROSENBERG

Led the way:
- Brought the Dobro guitar into bluegrass music with pathbreaking techniques which influenced generations of Dobro players and induced hundreds to take up the instrument.
- One of the most important links between the blues and bluegrass music.
- A prominent instrumentalist and vocalist with Flatt and Scruggs, the most successful bluegrass-style act of the 1950s and 1960s.
- Bluegrass Hall of Fame, 1997.

By the Way
- Also a master at finger-picking the steel-string guitar, although that skill was seldom recorded.
- He borrowed the "Uncle Josh" comedy character from turn-of-the-century entertainer Cal Stewart while with Esco Hankins, but was known as "Buck" in the Wilma Lee and Stoney Cooper band.
- The primary cook for the Flatt and Scruggs band in the early days, while on the road.
- Guested on recordings with artists like Charlie McCoy, J.J. Cale, Steve Young, and Kris Kristofferson.
- Sons Josh Jr., Billy Troy and Bryan also pursued musical careers.

For more information on the history of the Foggy Mountain Boys, see profiles of Lester Flatt, Earl Scruggs, Louise Scruggs, Curly Seckler, and Paul Warren.

Robert Russell "Chubby" Wise (birth name Dees) \ 1998

Chubby Wise began a long, colorful, and varied career in show business backing his adoptive father, Robert Wise – a fiddler – on banjo and guitar in Lake City, Florida. After dropping out of school in the seventh grade, Chubby took up the fiddle himself at the age of twelve or thirteen.

At eighteen he married Geneva Kirby – the daughter of a prominent neighboring farmer, drove taxis in Jacksonville by day, and made music by night. It was here that he encountered the Rouse Brothers and Ervin Rouse's classic "Orange Blossom Special," which became one of Chubby's most-featured numbers. Wise broke into full-time work as a professional musician on WRUF-AM in Gainesville at the age of twenty-two. With the Jubilee Hillbillies, who nicknamed him "Chubby," he played a mixture of country, swing, blues, and pop music. These influences can be clearly heard in Chubby's distinctive fiddling.

"Hank [Snow] liked Chubby's ability to play twin fiddle parts, and Chubby's exceptionally smooth, rich tone, with more vibrato than many country fiddlers use."

- Charles Wolfe in liner notes to *Hank Snow: the Singing Ranger, Volume 2*, Bear Family Records, 1990.

At the height of World War II, Chubby heard on the radio that the fiddler in Bill Monroe's Blue Grass Boys – either Howdy Forrester or Carl Story (sources disagree) – was leaving for the Navy. Some time afterwards (sources disagree on the month and year), Wise grabbed a train (some sources say he drove or took a bus) to Nashville, auditioned, and joined a band that included Clyde Moody, David "Stringbean" Akeman, and "Cousin Wilbur" Wesbrooks. Chubby's style evolved

Born: October 2, 1915, Lake City, FL

Died: January 6, 1996, Bowie, MD

Primary Instrument: Fiddle

"The fiddle bow fit my hand a lot better than them plow handles did."

- Quoted in Paul Wadey, "Obituary: Chubby Wise," *The Independent*, February 5, 1996.

Composed:
BMI's database credits Chubby Wise with 93 published songs and tunes, mostly arrangements of traditional or older material. His best-known co-composition is "Shenandoah Waltz."

Early influences:
Bryan Purcell
Fiddlin' Arthur Smith
Curly Fox
Clayton McMichen

Came to fame with:
Bill Monroe and the Blue Grass Boys

Photo: courtesy of Pinecastle Records, c.1943

from swing to bluegrass under Monroe's tutelage. Fiddlers Carl Story and Floyd Ethridge were also carried with the band until Monroe was satisfied that Chubby Wise would work out.

Wise was still in the group when Howard Watts joined in 1944, followed by Lester Flatt in March of 1945. Shortly thereafter, Chubby left for almost a year when Howdy Forrester returned from the service to claim his job. Forrester soon left and Jim Shumate played with Monroe for a few months. By the time Wise returned in March of 1946, Earl Scruggs had joined. This ensemble is considered the classic bluegrass band. Together for just three years, they influenced generations with their WSM broadcasts, Columbia recordings, and personal appearances. Tunes such as "Blue Moon of Kentucky," "Will You Be Loving Another Man," "Wicked Path of Sin," "Little Cabin Home on the Hill," "Blue Grass

"It was Bill Monroe who taught me to play the long, blues notes. You don't get that feel in country [music]."

– Quoted in Sam Hodges, "True Bluegrass," *Orlando Sentinel*, April 30, 1989.

Performed with:

Jubilee Hillbillies, Gainesville, FL, 1938-1942

Bill Monroe and the Blue Grass Boys, 1943-1948, 1949-1950

Clyde Moody, Chubby Wise and the Radio Ranch Men, 1948-1949

Lester Flatt, Earl Scruggs and the Foggy Mountain Boys, 1951

Elton Britt, early 1950s

Hank Snow and the Rainbow Ranch Boys, 1954-1970

Chubby Wise (solo artist), 1970-1996

"Now I'm living in Texas... I have an agent down there and I work 90 percent in clubs, doing dance work. I go to San Anton' and within a radius of 300 miles of Houston and play different clubs, one nighters."

- Quoted in Tex Logan, "A Conversation with Chubby Wise," *Muleskinner News*, September 1972.

Led the way:

- A member of the classic 1945-1948 edition of the Blue Grass Boys, Wise helped to establish the essential form of the bluegrass style and became the pattern for generations of bluegrass fiddlers.
- "Shenandoah Waltz," which he co-wrote with Clyde Moody, was a hit for Moody and sold 150,000 in the pop field for Sammy Kaye.
- Starred as a fiddler in bluegrass, country, and western swing during a musical career that spanned seven decades.
- SPBGMA Preservation Hall of Greats, 1991.
- Bluegrass Hall of Fame, 1998.

Breakdown," and "Sweetheart You Done Me Wrong" are cornerstones of the bluegrass legacy.

While with Monroe, Wise also recorded two sessions with Hank Williams in 1947, including "I Can't Get You Off Of My Mind," "My Sweet Love Ain't Around," and "A Mansion on the Hill."

In 1948, Chubby moved to Washington, D.C. to perform with Clyde Moody, with whom he had co-written "Shenandoah Waltz" – a sizable hit on King the previous year. Country music entrepreneur Connie B. Gay showcased them in capital-region radio, TV, and concert appearances during two stints, punctuated by a sojourn in Durham, North Carolina.

After this, Wise freelanced for several years, appearing briefly with the York Brothers, Bill Monroe again, Flatt and Scruggs, with Elton Britt, and as a session musician in Nashville. With Monroe and Mac Wiseman as lead singer, Chubby recorded "Can't You Hear Me Callin'," and "Travelin' This Lonesome Road." With Flatt and Scruggs, he recorded "Somehow Tonight" and "Don't Get Above Your Raising."

In 1954 he joined Hank Snow and the Rainbow Ranch Boys on the *Grand Ole Opry* and RCA Victor records. He was a prominent member of that recording and touring band for the next 16 years. By 1954, Snow had made 200 recordings, scored 17 top-10 country hits, and was represented by Colonel Tom Parker, with whom he co-owned a booking agency. On personal appearances, Chubby Wise and Hank Snow often performed hot fiddle-guitar duets in the manner of Hugh and Karl Farr (best known for their work with the Sons of the Pioneers).

In 1967, promoter Carlton Haney prevailed upon Chubby Wise to appear at the Berryville, Virginia, Labor Day weekend festival, to participate in the Sunday afternoon "Story of Bluegrass" concert with Bill Monroe. This triggered a number of subsequent appearances at bluegrass events.

After leaving the Rainbow Ranch Boys in 1970, Wise moved to Hous-

"Chubby's a little more a lonesome type of fiddler, and he plays some blues in it... Chubby could beat Howdy [Forrester] on a song, but Howdy would have beat Chubby on a fiddle piece like 'Cotton-Eyed Joe.'"

- Bill Monroe, quoted in Charles K. Wolfe, "Bluegrass Touches: an Interview with Bill Monroe," *Old Time Music*, Spring 1975.

"Chubby makes the fiddle sing like a singer sings. He told me that once you start a break, you should never take the bow off the strings. It should just be like a sea gull flying over the ocean waves. He said that's how smooth you have to get it."

- Tommy Cordell, quoted by Barry Willis in *America's Music: Bluegrass*, 1989.

"Neighbors, I hate to say this, but this is my final show for a while. I'm gonna, kinda, semi-retire. I'm not gonna completely quit – I love this old fiddle too good. I love you people too good to give it up completely. I've been in this business forty-six years, and forty years of it, I guarantee, I've lived out of a suitcase, on the road. So I'm getting a little tired. I'm not as young as I used to be. I'm very grateful that I can still saw a little bit on the fiddle at sixty-three. [applause] All right, here we go, let's make the old rooster crow [on 'Chubby's Cacklin' Hen']."

- from *The Tennessee Mountain Bluegrass Festival*, August, 1978, CMH Records.

ton, where he recorded extensively with Stoneway Records in a variety of genres, and toured as a solo act at nightclubs and bluegrass festivals. In 1971, he was featured in the film *Bluegrass: Country Soul*, backing Jimmy Martin, playing in the fiddle jam session, and on "Orange Blossom Special," backed by Mac Wiseman and Sonny Osborne.

In 1984, his health in decline, Chubby Wise returned to his childhood home of Lake City, Florida. The bluegrass community produced several benefit concerts to help with his medical bills. Chubby Wise died at the age of eighty in January, 1996, while visiting relatives of his second wife Rossi in the Washington, D.C. area, shortly after being hospitalized for double pneumonia. His last recordings, made in 1994, were released shortly after his death as *An American Original*.

— FRED BARTENSTEIN

By the Way:

- Learned banjo at age eight, while recovering from a leg injury which later made him ineligible for the military during World War II, when Bill Monroe's fiddlers were leaving for the service.

- Played guitar with a flat pick on Bill Monroe gospel numbers, while guitar thumb-picker Lester Flatt sang in the quartet.

- According to a mid-1950s Hank Snow Fan Club profile, "When he is not playing fiddle you can find him on the bank with a fishing pole in his hand… His favorite food is fried chicken and his favorite color is blue. His favorite sport is baseball… Chubby is one of the friendliest persons you could hope to meet."

- His first album, oddly titled "*The Tennessee Fiddler*," was produced by Hank Snow at Snow's home studio in 1961 for the Starday label. He made seventeen more LPs for Stoneway between 1970 and 1979, and two CDs for Pinecastle in the mid-90s.

- Profiled in *Orange Blossom Boys: The Untold Story of Ervin T. Rouse, Chubby Wise and the World's Most Famous Fiddle Tune*, Randy Noles, 2002.

- Recorded sessions with Hank Williams, Red Foley, Ernest Tubb, Eddy Arnold, Merle Haggard, Hylo Brown, Jimmy Martin, Mac Wiseman, Red Allen, Hazel and Alice, Charlie Moore, Larry Sparks, the Good Old Boys, the Bass Mountain Boys, and others.

Lawrence Carlton Haney | 1998

Carlton Haney was a larger-than-life character. His verifiably significant accomplishments are sometimes hard to disentangle from legends – his own and those of others. Between the early 1950s and the late 1970s, Haney played major roles in the popularization, preservation, and business development of bluegrass and country music. His contributions helped mightily in reversing bluegrass music's decline in the rock 'n' roll years.

"Haney was not only an intellectual, he was a home-grown mystic who expressed his belief in the strength of Bill Monroe's music in terms of 'vibrations.'"

- Neil Rosenberg in *Bluegrass: a History*, 1985.

Carlton Haney grew up in Reidsville, a town in the North Carolina Piedmont dominated by the American Tobacco Company. In high school, he was a baseball catcher and earned spending money by outfitting bashful farmers in downtown clothing stores. The family listened to the *Grand Ole Opry* on Saturday nights. His brother Charles played country music with friends, but Carlton didn't particularly enjoy or follow any style of music. He took a job in a Reidsville battery plant and was about to be promoted to a supervisory position when destiny intervened.

Probably in 1953 (the chronology is uncertain), Bill Monroe's sixteen-year-old daughter Melissa was sent to live temporarily with former Blue Grass Boy Clyde Moody and his wife in nearby Danville, Virginia. Perhaps it was hard feelings boiling over between Melissa and her father's lady friend Bessie Lee Mauldin. Perhaps it was to separate the teenager from twenty-five-year-old Blue Grass Boy Jimmy Martin, for whom she had developed an attraction. In any case, Haney had come to know

Born: September 19, 1928, Rockingham County, NC

Died: March 16, 2011, Greensboro, NC

Primary Involvement in Bluegrass Music:
Festival Promoter, Booking Agent

Composed:
Wrote or co-wrote several memorable songs in Reno and Smiley's repertoire, including:

"He Will Forgive You"

"Jimmy Caught the Dickens (Pushing Ernest in the Tub)"

"Kneel Down"

"Never Get To Hold You in My Arms Anymore"

Wrote or co-wrote several songs recorded by Conway Twitty, including the 1969 #1 country hit, "To See An Angel Cry"

Photo: Ron Petronko

Left to right: Don Reno, Fred Bartenstein, Carlton Haney, unidentified and John U. Miller, Berryville, VA, 1969.

the Moodys, met Melissa while visiting them, and asked the high-spirited girl for a date. Catching wind of the burgeoning relationship, Bill Monroe called Haney and asked him to book some show dates in the Piedmont. When these turned out well – and probably to keep a closer eye on the young man courting his daughter – Monroe offered Haney a job promoting bookings and traveling on his show dates to manage advance publicity.

In the summer of 1955, Monroe sent Haney to Bean Blossom, Indiana, to help with his Brown County Jamboree. This arrangement and Haney's audacious ideas didn't please Bill's older brother Birch, the resident manager. In September, Haney was sent home to Reidsville in a car with bald tires, with little to show for his efforts.

Back in North Carolina, Haney began booking for a band called the Farm Hands: Allen Shelton, Curly Howard, Roy Russell, and Bill

Associated with:
Bill Monroe and the Blue Grass Boys, 1953-1955 (booking agent)

Don Reno, Red Smiley and the Tennessee Cut-Ups, 1955-1964 (booking agent and manager)

Led the way:

- Promoted notable early bluegrass festivals in the 1960s and 1970s, including events in Fincastle (Roanoke), Virginia; Berryville, Virginia; Camp Springs, North Carolina; Gettysburg, Pennsylvania; and Escoheag, Rhode Island.
- Publisher of *Muleskinner News*, the second prominent monthly bluegrass magazine, 1969-late 1970s.
- IBMA Award of Merit (Distinguished Achievement Award), 1990
- Bluegrass Hall of Fame, 1998.

[Recalling the Sunday afternoon "Bluegrass Story" at the first multi-day bluegrass festival, Labor Day weekend, 1965] "Carlton asked for complete silence from the audience. 'We don't want to hear a sound,' he said, 'just the wind in the trees.' Then Bill played his famous mandolin introduction to 'Mule Skinner Blues,' and they were off!"

– Phil Zimmerman, www.bluegrasstime.com.

By the Way:

- Interest in music started with a crush on Bill Monroe's teenaged daughter Melissa.
- Believed that bluegrass should be printed as two words, as a derivation of the band name the Blue Grass Boys.
- Got North Carolina fiddler Bobby Hicks a job with Bill Monroe in 1954, initially as a bass player.

Phillips (they later became the core of Jim Eanes's Shenandoah Valley Boys). At the *Old Dominion Barn Dance* in Richmond, Virginia, Carlton was introduced to Don Reno, Red Smiley and the Tennessee Cut-Ups, who asked him to book shows for them. Haney did so successfully, and a business relationship ensued from January, 1956, until the group's break-up in November, 1964.

During his years with Reno and Smiley, Haney made astute suggestions and contacts, including the initiation of a daily television show, *Top 'o the Morning*, on WDBJ, Roanoke. He helped the group pick material for their frequent King single and album releases and wrote a few songs.

According to Haney, his interest in Bill Monroe's music stemmed from a backstage jam session at the *Grand Ole Opry* in October of 1957. Twice, Jimmy Martin started "Live and Let Live," and twice Bill Monroe stopped it. When Bill started the song, Haney could hear a distinct difference in the timing and began to seriously study Monroe and his recordings. He developed the idea of a stage performance where Monroe would perform in successive reunion with former members of his band, many of whom had gone on to their own prominent careers.

The *Old Dominion Barn Dance* ended in 1957 after eleven years, a victim of changing public tastes. Carlton Haney was recruited to revive the show as the *New Dominion Barn Dance* through 1964. There Haney learned how to book combinations of popular country artists that would sell tickets. Bluegrass music was also a significant part of the program, including rare (at the time) joint appearances by multiple bluegrass-type acts. Carlton Haney observed or participated in a number of events that led up to the multi-day bluegrass festivals, including Watermelon Park, Berryville, Virginia (1960); Oak Leaf Park, Luray, Virginia (1961); indoor winter concerts in Richmond (1962) and Roanoke, Virginia (1963); and the Newport Folk Festival (1964).

After Reno and Smiley's break-up, Carlton Haney booked shows for Red Smiley and the Bluegrass Cut-Ups and conceived of a series of "Country Shindigs," package shows in huge venues in multiple markets. At his peak, Haney promoted more than 100 major shows a year in 30-

> "I believe Bill Monroe's the only man you can learn bluegrass from... You can sing off-key until you go to singing with him for about a year and a half and you'll sing just as true as a dollar and you'll play an instrument just true as a dollar. He's the only man in the world can make you do that. What Bill Monroe plays is bluegrass, and what everybody else plays is just a copy of him."
>
> – Quoted in Fred Bartenstein, "The Carlton Haney Story," *Muleskinner News*, September 1971.

some cities, from Philadelphia to Oklahoma City, generating handsome profits. He played important roles in building the careers of a number of country artists, including Porter Wagoner, Loretta Lynn, Merle Haggard, Conway Twitty, and the Osborne Brothers.

Haney's financial success, contacts, and credibility in the country music field helped him to take a risk on a concept he had nurtured for almost a decade. On Labor Day Weekend, 1965, Carlton Haney booked what he called the "Blue Grass Festival" at Cantrell's Horse Farm, twelve miles north of Roanoke, Virginia, at Fincastle. Present were Bill Monroe and the Blue Grass Boys, Jimmy Martin and the Sunny Mountain Boys, Clyde Moody, Don Reno and the Tennessee Cut-Ups, Red Smiley and the Bluegrass Cut-Ups, the Stanley Brothers and the Clinch Mountain Boys, Mac Wiseman, and Doc Watson. The highlight for everyone was "The Story of Bluegrass Music," emceed by Haney and assisted backstage by Bill Monroe's former manager Ralph Rinzler. For a glorious Sunday afternoon, Monroe held the spotlight as musician after musician joined him to recreate their musical triumphs from earlier decades.

The format of the Labor Day Weekend festival was repeated in 1966 at Fincastle; in 1967 and 1968 at Berryville, Virginia; and from 1969 at Camp Springs, North Carolina, near Haney's hometown of Reidsville. Others promoted similar events in other states and very soon thereafter in hundreds of locations each year throughout the world.

Carlton Haney initiated *Muleskinner News* magazine in 1969, and *Grassound* (aimed at a younger, more progressive, demographic) in 1974. He was prominently featured in the movie *Bluegrass: Country Soul* (1971, reissued on DVD in 2006). He began an annual Newgrass Music Festival at Camp Springs in 1972. He continued to generate ambitious ideas (for example, a bluegrass hall of fame, library, and archives, to be located in North Carolina), but by the end of the 1970s, fewer of these projects were coming to fruition. Much of his capital and energy seemed to be drained by extended litigation with the American Federation of Musicians, with whose Unfair List tactics he took particular exception.

By 1980 Haney was for all practical purposes out of the music business. For a while he operated grocery stores with family members. In his later years, Carlton loved to talk about music and a surprising number of other topics. He was known for extensive, late-night, telephone conversations and occasionally made appearances at bluegrass events; the early 1990s video series *Grass Roots to Bluegrass*, and a celebration of the fortieth anniversary of the Fincastle Bluegrass Festival in 2005. He died on March 16, 2011, following an earlier stroke, at Moses H. Cone Hospital in Greensboro, North Carolina.

— FRED BARTENSTEIN

- Introduced Merle Haggard on two live albums: *Okie from Muskogee* (1969) and *The Fightin' Side of Me* (1970), and performed a recitation with Conway Twitty on "Papa Sing Me a Song" (1969).

"One day I understand they were all sittin' around sayin' that I couldn't pull it off when Lucky Moeller [a banker turned ballroom owner in Oklahoma who moved to Nashville to help manage Webb Pierce and operate a talent agency] said, 'You know, we're all sittin' here tellin' each other Haney can't do it. But has anybody told Haney he can't do it?"

- Quoted in John Pugh, "Carlton Haney: the P.T. Barnum of Country Music," *Hustler*, November 1977.

Kenneth Clayton "Kenny" Baker | 1999

Kenny Baker was the son and grandson of old-time fiddlers. Family roots trace back to England, North Carolina, and the coal-mining region of southwestern Virginia. By the mid-1920s his parents had settled on the Kentucky side of the state line. Kenny's first instrument was the guitar. He learned to play a unique four-finger style in open G tuning, influenced by Ernest Johnson, a blind African-American musician who sold peanuts in Jenkins, Kentucky.

For most of his working life starting at age fourteen, Baker was a deep-pit coal miner for Consolidated Coal Company (later Bethlehem Steel) in Jenkins, taking occasional breaks to play music as a semi-professional and professional. During World War II, he volunteered for the Navy and was stationed in the South Pacific. When a USO show came through, Kenny sat in on guitar and spent the next eighteen months playing lead guitar and entertaining troops. He knew enough fiddle to play square dances for the Red Cross in Okinawa. Returning home, he concentrated almost exclusively on the fiddle.

In his early days as a fiddler, though surrounded by bluegrass and the music that preceded it, Kenny preferred the jazz style of French violinist Stéphane Grappelli and Bob Wills's Western Swing. From such influences, he drew lifelong habits of listening intently to fellow musicians,

"Bluegrass, of all the styles of music, is the most difficult – to get in every note you hear, the time and syncopation. Bluegrass is countryman's jazz. It's not mechanical, but heartfelt, and there's really no written music to get you started."

- Quoted by Maria Gajda in "Kenny Baker: Country Jazz Fiddler," *Muleskinner News*, October, 1972.

Born June 26, 1926, Burdine, Kentucky
Died July 8, 2011, Nashville, Tennessee
Primary Instrument: Fiddle

"The only way to catch up with and understand Bill Monroe's own feeling that Kenny Baker is the 'greatest bluegrass fiddler in the world' is to listen to Kenny's playing – to his power, his control, his intonation and articulation, and most of all to his artistic intentions."

- Thomas Adler, in liner notes to *Kenny Baker Country*, County Records, 1976.

Composed:
BMI's database credits Kenny Baker with 82 compositions, co-compositions, and arrangements, including:
"Baker's Breakdown"
"Big Sandy River"
"Doc Harris The Fisherman"
"Farmyard Swing"
"First Day In Town"

"Frost On The Pumpkin"
"High Country"
"Washington County"
"Windy City Rag"

Early influences:
Thaddeus Earl Baker (father)
Richard Baker (grandfather)
Marion Sumner
Stéphane Grappelli
Bob Wills
Chubby Wise

Came to fame with:
Bill Monroe and the Blue Grass Boys

"Baker and Monroe are both artistic superheroes in their own right. Plainly, this sort of leader-sideman relationship is almost without precedent or parallel in the world of American music."

- Thomas Adler, in liner notes to *Kenny Baker Country*, County Records, 1976.

Performed with:
Don Gibson, 1953-1957

Bill Monroe and the Blue Grass Boys, 1957-1958, 1962-1963, 1968-1984

Josh Graves and Kenny Baker, 1984-2006

The Masters, 1989-1997

"I've never heard a fiddler I couldn't learn something from."
Quoted by Joe Wilson in liner notes to *Kenny Baker: Master Fiddler,* County Records, 1993.

Led the way:
- Played longer than anyone else with Bill Monroe and the Blue Grass Boys, at the heart of one of the band's best-remembered sounds.
- A mentor to many well-known fiddlers, including James Bryan, Blaine Sprouse, and Aubrey Haynie.
- National Heritage Award, 1993.
- Bluegrass Hall of Fame, 1999.

By the Way:
- Recorded sessions with Estil Stewart and the 7 Flat Mountain Boys (1954), Hobo Jack Adkins (1958), Red Rector and Fred Smith (1969), Jimmy Martin (1971), the Down Homers (the Whites, 1972), Bill Clifton (1974), Charlie McCoy (1975), Tom T. Hall (1976), the Osborne Brothers (1978), Wayne Lewis (1980), Dry Branch Fire Squad (1981), Ron Mesing (1990), Mac Wiseman (1990), Mark O'Connor (1993), and Carroll Best (2001).

responding to the emotional tone of the moment, and constantly building upon and varying his approach to a tune or break.

Following in the footsteps of mentor and swing fiddler Marion Sumner of nearby Hazard, Kentucky, in the 1950s Baker played fiddle and sang tenor with Don Gibson's country band. They were based at the time mostly at WNOX in Knoxville, Tennessee.

Bill Monroe enjoyed Baker's work with Gibson and offered him a job should he ever need one. Baker joined the Blue Grass Boys for the first time in 1957, recording the classics "Panhandle Country" and "Scotland." When he came back in 1962, he sang baritone on the gospel album *I Saw the Light* and was the featured fiddler on tunes such as "Big Sandy River," "Baker's Breakdown," "Shenandoah Breakdown," and "Santa Claus." Leaving the mines after his two sons were grown, Baker rejoined the Blue Grass Boys and accompanied Bill Monroe on almost every recording he made – an astounding 237 cuts – from November, 1968, to December, 1983.

"I've never heard a fiddler I couldn't learn something from."
Quoted by Joe Wilson in liner notes to *Kenny Baker: Master Fiddler,* County Records, 1993.

Throughout his life, Kenny Baker listened to fiddlers and fiddle tunes, in jam sessions, on the radio, and on recordings. A musician's musician, he was highly regarded and often found in the company of predecessors, contemporaries, and disciples. Early festival-goers recall close bonds between Kenny Baker, the North Carolina legend Tommy Jarrell, young Jimmy Arnold, duet partner Joe Greene, and pre-teen James Bryan. In earlier years, Baker had a prodigious musical memory and was able to remember a tune from one hearing. As he worked, in the mines or on his Tennessee farm, he continually reviewed tunes in his mind and thought of ways to improve, combine, or spin an existing melody into another of his own creation.

Kenny Baker contributed mightily to the bluegrass fiddle repertoire. His twelve County-label LPs (some recorded in motel rooms between festival sets) received wide circulation. Although his original material and arrangements were rarely played onstage with Bill Monroe, fiddlers young and old learned them from the albums and late-night festival jam sessions. Extensive travel as a musician exposed Baker to a wealth of material – from British Isles to Missouri, Canada, Texas, and southeastern states – which he further propagated.

Hundreds of musicians passed through the Blue Grass Boys between 1939 and Bill Monroe's death in 1996. Although Monroe built upon many of their ideas, his musical relationship with Kenny Baker was by far the deepest and most collaborative. Bill considered Kenny the first worthy heir to tunes he had learned from his Uncle Pen Vandiver in the second two decades of the twentieth century. One of Monroe and Baker's lasting contributions was the *Uncle Pen* album, recorded in 1969 and 1970. Another was Kenny Baker's own *Kenny Baker Plays Bill Monroe* from 1976, in which Bill unexpectedly and uncharacteristically appeared at the recording studio and played mandolin. In private moments, Bill played for Kenny his previously unrecorded and unfinished compositions. Many of these, such as "Jerusalem Ridge" and "Land of Lincoln," came to reflect the ideas of both men.

Kenny functioned as section boss and wrangler for Bill Monroe's band during his last and longest stay. Retired from a more physically demanding and remunerative career, Baker was resigned to the low wages and constant low-amenity travel of the Blue Grass Boys; selling his fiddle LPs on the road became an important supplement. He trained and oriented each new man, communicating expectations and feedback in a way that the taciturn bandleader was unable to manage. Live recordings from the period evidence an amazing reliance on Baker's rich, long-bowed fiddling, often doubling Monroe's vocal lines.

Both Monroe and Baker were headstrong and stubborn. It was perhaps inevitable, but nevertheless tragic, that their ways parted over a clash of wills. In the fall of 1984, with his brother in the hospital, Kenny was miffed when Bill neglected his request for a touring schedule. On October 12, he walked off the stage permanently after Bill instructed him to play "Jerusalem Ridge" in response to a loud and drunken audience member's request. In 1994, near the end of Bill's life, intermediaries arranged a meeting of reconciliation and an onstage reunion at the Bean Blossom, Indiana, festival.

After leaving the Blue Grass Boys, Baker teamed with Dobro innovator Josh Graves until shortly before Graves's death in late 2006 (the two had earlier recorded a pair of guitar/Dobro albums in the 1970s, before a knife accident in 1977 ended Baker's guitar career). The fiddle/Dobro duo recorded CDs for Ridge Runner in 1986 and Montana in 1987. Baker and Graves made three albums and toured a bit with Jesse McReynolds, Eddie and Martha Adcock, and Missy Raines as the Masters, beginning in 1989. In the 1990s, Baker toured with fiddlers of many genres in *Masters of the Folk Violin* for the National Council for the Traditional Arts. Kenny made two fiddle CDs for OMS in 2000 and 2002. In his eighties, Kenny Baker seldom played publicly, but was a frequent and welcome guest at bluegrass events. He died in a Nashville convalescent home, a few days after suffering a stroke at the age of eighty-five, on July 8, 2011.

— FRED BARTENSTEIN

- Although he moved close to Nashville in 1968, Kenny Baker always lived in country settings and engaged in farming and animal husbandry.
- Son Johnny Baker played guitar and sang tenor with the Dry Branch Fire Squad in the late 1970s and early 1980s.
- Other famous Kenny Bakers include a singer/actor who appeared on Jack Benny's radio show in the 1930s, a British jazz trumpeter of the 1940s, and the diminutive British actor who played R2D2 in the Star Wars film series.

"Ornery and irascible, cheerful and charming, demanding musically yet frequently found jamming all night with sleepy, mediocre musicians, stubborn and bullheaded, witty and warm, Kenny Baker, like bluegrass music itself, is complex, contradictory, and deep."

- Doug Green in liner notes to *Kenny Baker Plays Bill Monroe*, County Records, 1976.

Lansing B. ("Lance") LeRoy, Jr. ⦚ 2000

Born: May 26, 1930, Tignall, GA

Primary Involvement in Bluegrass Music:
Agent and manager

Came to fame with:
Lester Flatt and the Nashville Grass (booking agent and manager), 1969-1979

Composed:
Copyright records list Lance LeRoy as a co-writer of the music for two instrumentals in Flatt and Scruggs's 1968 album, *The Story of Bonnie and Clyde*: "Reunion" and "Get Away." He also composed the gospel number "Sailing for Glory," recorded by the Bluegrass Cardinals in 1980.

Led the way:
- Pioneering agent and manager for major bluegrass acts, including Lester Flatt, the Bluegrass Cardinals, Jimmy Martin, Johnson Mountain Boys, Del McCoury, and others.

Lance LeRoy is a living repository of bluegrass lore and traditions. He has known and worked alongside legends, and spent the second half of his life totally immersed in bluegrass music. Today he is a highly visible spokesman for the industry, generous to all comers with his time and knowledge.

LeRoy started life in upper Georgia in the town of Tignall (2000 population: 653). Wilkes County is an area steeped in Revolutionary and Civil War history. His father, a mail carrier by profession, had a strong interest in country music and radio. The family owned the first receiver in the community. Neighbors would gather by the score on Saturday nights to listen to the *Grand Ole Opry* from the LeRoys' open window.

Tignall was a fortunate location for someone interested in early bluegrass and the music which preceded it – central to Atlanta, Augusta, and the South Carolina cities of Columbia, Spartanburg, and Greenville. (The Lewis Family's base in Lincolnton, Georgia, is only twelve miles away.) Regular country shows were held at the Wilkes County High School gym, and Lance was always there. He remembers seeing Bill Monroe and the Blue Grass Boys several times. On one occasion, Monroe, Lester Flatt, Earl Scruggs, Chubby Wise, and Howard Watts played, in

> *"Lance used to live in Georgia and when we were working through there he would drive for miles to see the shows. He'd always be there and we always looked forward to Lance coming around to the shows. He's been a fan of bluegrass for many years before getting into the business end of it."*
>
> – Earl Scruggs, quoted by Traci Todd in "Lance LeRoy, part 1," *Bluegrass Unlimited*, February 1993.

their uniform of riding boots and jodhpurs. That band, together from 1945 to 1948, is considered the template for all subsequent bluegrass music.

Lance wanted to play fiddle like his country music heroes, and began violin lessons in the eighth grade. Formal training soon gave way to learning by ear. He played well enough to appear with Buster and Lawrence Simmons and the Georgia Mountain Boys for square dances and on three 1,000-watt radio stations (1959-1962). Although he hasn't played since, LeRoy developed a deep appreciation for music and especially the fiddle.

Lance studied accounting in college and worked in financial positions

- Produced and contributed photographs and liner notes for numerous bluegrass albums, and wrote many magazine articles on bluegrass artists and topics.
- In 1985 initiated and organized meetings of industry leaders, resulting in the establishment of the International Bluegrass Music Association.

Lester Flatt and Lance LeRoy, c.1971.

Bluegrass Hall of Fame Inductee Biographies

- IBMA Award of Merit (Distinguished Achievement Award), 1994.
- Bluegrass Hall of Fame, 2000.

By the Way:
- In 1968, exposed future Rider in the Sky "Ranger Doug" Green to a recording of Elton Britt, which Green cites as his "yodeling epiphany."
- Arranged for fourteen-year-old Marty Stuart to complete his high school diploma by mail, when the ninth grader moved to Nashville in 1972 to join Lester Flatt and the Nashville Grass.
- Got Rhonda Vincent her first festival bookings in the early 1980s, when she was a young member of the family band the Sally Mountain Show.
- Produced his close friend Paul Warren's only fiddle album – after Warren died – from tapes of live and radio shows.
- Can be heard on various CMH-label recordings introducing Lester Flatt, the Bluegrass Cardinals, and talking about Josh Graves.
- Wrote for *Bluegrass Unlimited* magazine under the pseudonym Brett F. Devan. Says LeRoy, "I made that name up purely out of the air to sound like a British blighter, so I could say whatever I wanted without making my friends mad."

in Asheville, North Carolina (1952-1966), and Nashville, Tennessee. In both locations, the self-described "Flatt and Scruggs groupie" was able to take in many of his favorite group's performances and come to know all of its members personally. Shortly after arriving in Tennessee in 1966 to work as an internal auditor with a finance company, he began to moonlight for Lester Flatt, doing his accounting and taxes. In that role LeRoy came to appreciate the business skills of Earl Scruggs's wife Louise, who was agent and manager for the Flatt and Scruggs enterprise.

> *Through Lance LeRoy I learned a lot about country music, especially bluegrass music. When I first moved to Nashville, Roland [White] would take me out to Lance's house and we would play records into the wee hours."*
> – Marty Stuart, quoted by Traci Todd in "Lance LeRoy, part 2," *Bluegrass Unlimited*, March 1993.

Flatt and Scruggs's legendary partnership of two decades ended in early 1969 over artistic and business differences. Lance LeRoy, involved in the sensitive task of dividing the partners' joint assets, was appreciated by both for his acumen and diplomacy. When Lester Flatt decided to continue on his own with a band – eventually dubbed the Nashville Grass – he asked LeRoy to serve as agent and manager. Notably disinterested in business details, Flatt was glad to have a trusted associate along on the road. Lance's duties included the 4:00 a.m. stretch "riding shotgun" – keeping the bus driver awake – a challenge for even such a loquacious communicator.

During Lance LeRoy's decade with the Flatt association, he was involved in label contracts with RCA and CMH, several bluegrass festivals, and a booking agency. Flatt and LeRoy founded Allied Artists with Bobby and Sonny Osborne in 1975. After the Osbornes bought their shares in 1977, Lance and Lester combined their names to form the Lancer Agency, which LeRoy continues to operate.

Lester Flatt's health and spirits declined as the 1970s wore on. Despite a bypass operation and several hospitalizations, he continued to tour and record almost to the end, leaning ever more on Lance for key decisions and leadership. Shortly after a much-appreciated visit from his estranged former partner Earl Scruggs, Lester died May 11, 1979. LeRoy was named co-executor with a Nashville bank, and continues to protect Flatt's legacy and the family's business interests.

Lance LeRoy was impressed by the Bluegrass Cardinals, a young bluegrass group which had moved from the Los Angeles area to Virginia in 1976. He used them on Lester Flatt's festivals and signed on as their booking agent at the beginning of the 1978 season. With his virtually full-time support, the Cardinals became headliners for almost two decades before disbanding in 1997.

LeRoy credits the Bluegrass Cardinals for the growth and success of the Lancer Agency in the years following Lester Flatt's death. Other acts previously represented by the organization include Jimmy Martin, the Johnson Mountain Boys, the New Coon Creek Girls, Lonesome Standard Time, the (Vincent family's) Sally Mountain Show, and Del McCoury. In the close-knit and financially constrained bluegrass community, LeRoy found his roles expanding from agent to personal manager, business advisor, publicist, advertising coordinator, photographer, and record producer.

Over many years, Lance developed thousands of contacts in all corners of the nation and the music industry. At bluegrass events, he is constantly engaged in conversation, and the telephone lines in his home-based office support an amazing network of business connections.

Perhaps inevitable for someone reared in an area rich with history, and for someone whose listening career dated back to the very dawn of bluegrass, Lance became a reputable historian of the music and its related forms. A facile writer and dogged researcher (drawing upon his skills as an auditor), he was in demand as a writer of album notes and magazine articles. LeRoy amassed a huge collection of recordings, which he generously shared with musicians both learning and searching for repertoire before transferring the collection to the Kentucky School of Bluegrass and Traditional Music in Hyden, Kentucky.

Discussions about creating a trade organization for bluegrass music began to circulate in the 1970s, but factionalism, regional pride and mistrust seemed to thwart every initiative. In the summer of 1985, Lance LeRoy used his stature and positive relationships to call a meeting at BMI in Nashville at which the International Bluegrass Music Association was established. Others present included Bill and James Monroe, Peter Kuykendall, Allen Mills, Sonny Osborne, Milton Harkey, Jim and Jesse McReynolds, Mac Wiseman, Doyle Lawson, Randall Hylton, Larry Jones, Ray Hicks, John Hartin, Joe Carr, Len Holsclaw, and the organization's first executive, Art Menius.

"When asked if a certain act would be on this year's show, [Lester] Flatt replied, 'To tell you the truth, I leave that up to Lance LeRoy. I don't even know if I'm going to be on it. Lance has been my right arm for eight years. He's a good, honest man. You don't find anybody like him everyday.'"

– Don Rhodes in "Marty Stuart and Lester Flatt," *Bluegrass Unlimited*, September 1978.

In the new millennium, Lance LeRoy and the Lancer Agency continued to represent great artists and promote the legacy and future of bluegrass music.

— FRED BARTENSTEIN

"From my earliest days in the business… I strove to enhance the image of this music by things such as having printed the best possible quality stationery, buying an $850 IBM Selectric typewriter (in 1969 dollars), and getting a multi-line telephone system, even though there was no one but myself answering it. I also bought a Code-A-Phone answering machine that surely must have been a prototype, as well as securing a Pitney-Bowes postal meter. All of these tools I felt were necessary to project a professional image for my agency…

"With that mindset, it seemed to me that all of bluegrass needed a similar representation. So I sat at my typewriter and pounded out a form letter that February, 1985, morning, outlining my thoughts and suggesting—no, urging—that some of us get together and discuss starting a bluegrass association, by whatever name, with a top-of-the-line awards show. I mailed copies of that letter out to some prominent artists and a few others who were influential in our business. Of course the import of that letter or its future significance never entered my mind."

– Quoted in Nancy Cardwell, "IBMA Marks 20th Anniversary June 2005, Leaders Reflect," *International Bluegrass*.

Arthel Lane "Doc" Watson | 2000

Because Doc came to fame in the 1960s, after he had turned forty, it is easy to forget that he was born earlier (1923) than any of the other pioneers of bluegrass lead guitar: Earl Scruggs (1924), George Shuffler (1925), Don Reno (1927), Dan Crary (1939), Clarence White (1944), or Tony Rice (1951). Doc's childhood musical influences pre-dated bluegrass. Indeed, the young man listened to the very same 78 rpm records, radio broadcasts, and local live performances that shaped the founders of bluegrass.

Deep Gap is a pass in western North Carolina's Blue Ridge mountains, named by Daniel Boone. Doc was born and spent his entire life there. Watauga County has a rich musical tradition (birthplace of country recording pioneer Al Hopkins) and is near to other old-time music heartlands in Virginia, West Virginia, Tennessee, and Kentucky.

In his first year of life, Watson lost his eyesight to an infection. The sixth of nine siblings, he never lacked for companionship and was expected to pull his weight around the home and farm. The Watsons were a singing family. His mother sang ballads around the house and to lull the children to sleep. His father led shape-note hymns at the Mt. Patron Baptist Church.

Given a harmonica at age six, the boy devised a single-string accompaniment using a steel wire stretched across the woodshed door. When he was seven, the family acquired a wind-up record player and a large stack of old records. His father made him a banjo at age eleven. By then, Watson had entered the Governor Morehead School for the Blind at Raleigh. There he was exposed to classical and jazz music, including recordings by guitarists Django Reinhardt and Nick Lucas.

Born: March 3, 1923, Stoney Fork Township, near Deep Gap, NC

Died: May 29, 2012, Winston-Salem, NC

Primary Instrument:
Guitar

"The banjo was something I really liked, but when the guitar came along, to me that was my first love in music."

– Quoted in *Dirty Linen* magazine, June/July 1995.

Composed:
BMI's database credits Doc Watson with 136 published compositions, co-compositions, and arrangements, including:
"Doc's Guitar"
"Southbound"
"Your Lone Journey"

Early influences:
Delmore Brothers
Jimmie Rodgers
Carter Family
Merle Travis
Chet Atkins

Doc Watson and Jack Williams, Grandfather Mountain, NC, 1953.

Came to fame with:

Clarence Ashley, on folk tours and recordings, 1960-1962

Performed with:

Jack Williams and the Country Gentlemen (North Carolina), 1953-1962

Clarence Ashley and Friends, 1960-1962

Doc Watson, 1962-1970

Doc and Merle Watson, 1970-1985

Doc Watson, 1985-2012

Led the way:

- The most significant influence on lead guitar in bluegrass music. Most famous for his flat-picked arrangements of fiddle tunes, Doc is also widely appreciated for his guitar finger-picking, old-time banjo playing, harmonica, and rich vocals.
- Released more than 40 albums.
- Received seven Grammy awards in 1973, 1974, 1979, 1986, 1990, 2002, and 2006, and the Grammy Lifetime Achievement Award in 2004.
- National Heritage Fellowship, National Endowment for the Arts, 1988.
- National Medal of Arts, 1997.
- Bluegrass Hall of Fame, 2000.

"The late Ralph Rinzler, the wonderful guy who helped me get started, said, 'Doc, play the old-time things till you get your foot in the door, and then you can expand.'"

– Quoted by Barry Mazor in *Meeting Jimmie Rodgers*, 2009.

A friend at school taught him a few guitar chords. Not knowing this, Watson's father offered to help buy his son a guitar if he could learn to accompany himself on one song. Doc's first guitar was a twelve-dollar Stella, which he acquired at age thirteen. About five years later, he financed his first Martin instrument by playing on the street for tips. At a station in Lenoir, NC, an announcer mentioned that Arthel wasn't a good radio name and a member of the studio audience shouted, "Call him Doc!" The nickname stuck.

After his marriage to a neighboring fiddler's daughter at twenty-four (Rosa Lee was sixteen), Watson tuned pianos to support his growing family. Eddy Merle was born in 1949 and Nancy Ellen in 1951. In 1953, Doc got a job playing electric guitar in a local country band. Unable to afford two instruments, he traded his Martin for a Gibson Les Paul. The group often lacked a fiddler and Watson taught himself fiddle tunes on the electric instrument, in addition to the popular finger-style music of Merle Travis and Chet Atkins.

Folklorist/musician Ralph Rinzler came to the Union Grove, North Carolina, Fiddler's Convention in April, 1960. There he rediscovered pioneer recording artist Clarence Ashley playing under the name "Tom" with a pick-up band that included Doc Watson. Rinzler arranged for Ashley to record for Folkways.

"Doc has picked the fiddle tunes when the fiddler didn't show and played rock 'n' roll for the drunks at the VFW because, by God, ten dollars was a lot of money and he had a family to feed and clothe."

– Joe Wilson in "Doc Watson: Just One of Us," *Muleskinner News*, June 1974.

Doc made several northern tours with Ashley. Most folk venues lacked the budget for a full group, so in 1961 he began playing as a solo artist. He traveled with Ralph Rinzler or by inter-city bus, performing at first with borrowed guitars. He mined the song repertoires of his family, in-laws and neighbors for material that would be considered traditional, fresh, and interesting. He went back into the old-time and blues records he had heard as a child and – for a time, at least – packed away the jazz, rock, and modern country for which he was best known locally.

Sensitive, complex, and capable in a range of fields (from rockabilly to electronics), Watson knew that the young, disoriented generation that came to his concerts and bought his records most warmed to that side of his personality that was fatherly, calm, and perfectly straightforward. They loved the mountain man who could teach them about country ways in terms that were simple but clever, who could play with lightning speed and stunning precision, and who could educate them about his music and the people and places from which it arose.

Folk music artists at the time consisted mostly of elderly pioneers, revered but exotic and difficult to approach, and young urban revivalists. Doc Watson stood out, an authentic folk musician who could entertain and relate to them as others – and their own fathers – couldn't. Doc was the hit of the 1963 Newport Folk Festival and quickly became a star, but in cities, at campuses and on Folkways, then Vanguard, records. This was a very different path from that of rural contemporaries who worked the *Grand Ole Opry* and the bluegrass circuit.

In the 1960s, Ralph Rinzler managed both Doc Watson and Bill Monroe, booking them into the same colleges, festivals, and folk clubs. When Doc and Bill appeared together, they enjoyed recreating 1930s Monroe Brothers songs that Watson had memorized from 78 rpm records, and soon added this feature to their stage show.

In December of 1966 Lester Flatt and Earl Scruggs invited Doc Watson to Nashville to add his widely popular flatpicking guitar to a Columbia album called *Strictly Instrumental*, issued under all three of their names. Five years later, Watson was a participant with Scruggs, Jimmy Martin, Vassar Clements, his guitar hero Merle Travis, and other country music pioneers on the Nitty Gritty Dirt Band's first *Will the Circle Be Unbroken* album.

Folk music faded as a commercial phenomenon, but Doc Watson was just hitting his stride as a performer and recording artist. Freed from the pressures to make only traditional music, Doc brought modern elements back to his sound. He also added other members to his ensemble, including T. Michael Coleman on electric bass and, after son Merle's death in 1985, Jack Lawrence, Marty Stuart, and grandson Richard on second guitar.

In his eighth decade Doc Watson reduced his touring but was still a revered figure in American music. Although he never represented himself as a bluegrass artist, he was a favorite with bluegrass fans, cited as a primary influence by all of the increasingly prominent flatpicking lead guitarists in the genre. Just as he mined the repertoire of his predecessors, young artists are introducing Doc's music to their generation. Alison Krauss brought "Down in the Valley to Pray" to the 2000 movie *O Brother, Where Art Thou?* and "Your Lone Journey" to the Grammy-winning *Raising Sand* she recorded in 2008 with Robert Plant, an original member of Led Zeppelin.

Doc underwent colon surgery after a fall at his home in May, 2012. He died a few days later at the Wake Forest Medical Center in Winston-Salem, NC, at the age of eighty-nine.

– FRED BARTENSTEIN

"As we discussed the events and changes in Doc's life during the past fifteen years, I asked if any particular one thing stood out as the most important. Doc thought for a moment, smiling… 'One day I came home from a trip, sat down, and wrote to the people with the State, and told them I wouldn't be needing their help anymore.'"

- Joe Wilson in "Doc Watson: Just One of Us," *Muleskinner News*, June 1974.

By the Way:

- Doc's widow Rosa Lee (1931-2012) was the daughter of Gaither Carlton, a neighbor and old-time fiddler. Married in 1947, Rosa Lee and Doc composed "Your Lone Journey" about their separations during Doc's early 1960s travels as a performer.

- Son Eddy Merle (named for Eddy Arnold and Merle Travis, and the namesake of Merlefest) was Doc's musical and touring partner from his middle teens until his death at thirty-six in a farming accident.

- Appeared at the first multi-day bluegrass festival, Fincastle, Virginia, 1965.

- Bill Monroe loved an introductory run Doc played with him on an instrumental version of "You'll Find Her Name Written There" and renamed it "Watson Blues."

- Doc's first Gallagher guitar, which he named "Old Hoss," is on display at the Country Music Hall of Fame in Nashville, Tennessee.

THE CARTER FAMILY

Alvin Pleasant Delaney "A.P." Carter \ 2001

A.P. Carter was born at the foot of Clinch Mountain, where his southwestern Virginia family had lived since the late eighteenth century. He was the first of eight children born to a ballad-singing mother and gospel-singing father (who gave up the banjo in deference to his wife's religious beliefs). His mother attributed his slight palsy to a near lightning strike two months before he was born. As a boy, A.P. sang in church, in a quartet with two uncles and a sister, and played a bit on the fiddle and guitar.

"There was always a professional air to the shows themselves, with A.P. announcing each number and introducing the members of the group. Sara and Maybelle sat down to play their instruments, while A.P., always nervous, wandered around the stage... After the show they would often stay the night with friends, sometimes learning new songs if their friends were musical."

– John Atkins in "The Carter Family," *Stars of Country Music*, 1975.

At the age of twenty, he traveled to Richmond, Indiana, for a railroad job. There he first tried composing songs to channel his homesickness for Virginia. Returning after a year, he tried his hand at selling fruit trees. On a sales trip to the other side of Clinch Mountain, he heard a teenaged Sara Dougherty singing and playing the autoharp. In 1915, the awkward young man somehow convinced her to marry.

The couple – who were joined by children Gladys (1919), Janette (1923), and Joe (1927) – sang together at their Maces Spring home and in local churches. Their primary sources of income included black-

Born: December 15, 1891, Little Valley, Scott County, VA

Died: November 7, 1960, Kingsport, TN

Primary Musical Accomplishments:
Vocalist, Song Collector

"Since he never sang to any set pattern, on the trios his voice appears and vanishes with alarming regularity, often joining in on the middle of lines; apparently at recording sessions he would walk around the studio just singing whenever his excursions brought him 'on mike.' He suffered from palsy and a lot from sheer nerves, which could explain some of the exaggerated tremor in his voice. Remember, though, that Carter was no ordinary man, so that we should not justifiably expect him to sing like anyone else."

– John Atkins in "The Carter Family," *Stars of Country Music*, 1975.

smithing, carpentry, nursery sales, and logging. Sara had two younger cousins, Maybelle and Madge Addington, who enjoyed making music with her. After Maybelle married A.P.'s brother Ezra and moved to their side of the mountain, A.P. and Sara asked her to join in on guitar and vocal harmony.

Shortly after Maybelle's arrival, A.P. learned that Victor Talking Machine Company executive Ralph Peer would be auditioning talent in nearby Bristol. The trio overcame all manner of personal, natural, and mechanical obstacles to make the trip in a borrowed auto. Peer loved the group – Sara's singing in particular – and recorded six sides on August 1 and 2, 1927. Peer also loved A.P.'s extensive collection of unrecorded material, which he offered to publish under his new company, Southern Music, if A.P. would claim authorship. On November 4 the first of approximately 300 Carter Family records was issued.

> "In A.P. [the Carter Family] had one of the greatest creative song doctors in country music history."
>
> – Charles Wolfe in *The Encyclopedia of Country Music*, 1998.

A.P. was hard-pressed to fill the demand for fresh material. He systematically mined and re-arranged, to Carter Family style, chestnuts from the era of Victorian parlor song, sacred material from white and black traditions, American and British Isles folk ballads, the recordings of contemporary and earlier country and blues artists, pop songs, and new compositions from family and friends. The disabled African-American musician Lesley Riddle, who accompanied A.P. Carter on song hunting trips, was especially adept at remembering melodies. Riddle lived with the Carters for a time and taught his finger-picking blues guitar style to Maybelle.

The Carter Family recorded for Victor and budget subsidiary Bluebird until 1934, then – still managed by Ralph Peer – American Record Corporation (later part of Columbia) in 1935, Decca from 1936 to 1938, Okeh in 1940, and back to Victor's Bluebird in 1941. In 1952 and 1956, the A.P. Carter Family (A.P., Sara, and their children Janette and Joe) recorded for Acme. None of their recording, performing, or publishing ventures were particularly lucrative except for three winters (1938-1941) spent in Del Rio, Texas, broadcasting on Mexican border stations that blanketed North America with powerful signals that circumvented the 50,000-watt U.S. limit.

When record sales fell abruptly at the onset of the Great Depression in 1929 and 1930, A.P. spent six months seeking work in the automobile industry in Detroit. Maybelle followed her husband E.J.'s railroad career to Bluefield, West Virginia, and Washington, D.C. The greatest imped-

Composed:

Tony Russell and Richard Weize's discography of commercial recordings by the Carter Family (*In the Shadow of Clinch Mountain*, Bear Family Records, 2000) credits A.P. Carter with scores of arrangements and copyright credits, including these staples:

"Bury Me Under the Weeping Willow"
"Carter's Blues"
"Darling Little Joe"
"East Virginia Blues"
"Foggy Mountain Top"
"Hello Stranger"
"Homestead on the Farm"
"Honey in the Rock"
"I'm Thinking Tonight of My Blue Eyes"
"I'm Working on a Building"
"Jimmie Brown the Newsboy"
"John Hardy Was a Desperate Little Man"
"Keep on the Sunny Side"
"Little Darling, Pal of Mine"
"My Little Home in Tennessee"
"Sad and Lonesome Day"
"Storms are on the Ocean"
"Wabash Cannonball"
"Wandering Boy"
"Wildwood Flower"
"Will the Circle Be Unbroken"
"Will You Miss Me When I'm Gone"
"You are My Flower"

Came to fame with:

The Carter Family, 1926-1943

"The Carters never had spectacular financial success like that of Jimmie Rodgers or Gene Autry. They never really 'crossed over' to the huge popular audiences of network radio, Hollywood films, and big-time vaudeville. They kept returning to their beloved Clinch Valley, disgusted or puzzled by the show business world."

– Charles Wolfe in "The Carter Family," *The Encyclopedia of Country Music*, 1998.

Left to right: Sara, Maybelle and A.P. Carter, Del Rio, Texas, 1938.

Performed with:

The Carter Family, 1926-1943

The A.P. Carter Family (A.P., Sara, and their children Janette and Joe), 1952, 1956

Led the way:

- Organized and propelled into a professional music career the original Carter Family, which consisted of A.P., his then-wife, Sara, and his sister-in-law and wife's cousin Maybelle.
- Recorded at the Victor Bristol sessions of July and August, 1927, considered the "big bang" of commercial country music.
- Collected, helped to arrange, sometimes composed, and recorded scores of songs which are now at the core of the bluegrass repertoire.
- Country Music Hall of Fame, 1970.
- Bluegrass Hall of Fame, 2001 (induction presented by Bill Clifton).

By the Way:

- In 1927, before Maybelle joined the group, A.P. and Sara auditioned for Brunswick Records in Norton, Virginia.
- A.P.'s offer to clear a patch of weeds convinced brother Ezra to let his seven-months-pregnant wife Maybelle attend the Bristol sessions.
- Appeared just once on WSM's *Grand Ole Opry* in Nashville.
- Virginia Route 614, which passes through Maces Spring, is now called the A.P. Carter Highway.

iment to the group's career, however, must have been A.P. and Sara's separation in 1933 and eventual divorce in 1939. After Sara's move to California, the original Carter Family ended its performing life in 1943.

A.P. never remarried and spent the remainder of his life in Maces Spring. He opened a marginal grocery store; promoted small concerts by artists such as the Stanley Brothers; and occasionally pitched songbooks, pictures and Bible pamphlets on regional radio stations. A number of the early bluegrass artists spoke of encountering him at WCYB in Bristol, where he would gladly reminisce about the glory years of the Carter Family.

A.P.'s heart weakened, and after a year of steady decline he died at the age of seventy at Holston Valley Community Hospital. He lived to see one of his arrangements, "Worried Man Blues," make

"You know Bill, when you're not working it's a good idea if you're somewhere where people do not know you're not working."

– A.P. Carter, quoted by Bill Clifton in *Rienk Janssen, Bill Clifton: Around the World to Poor Valley*, Bear Family Records, 2001.

the charts in 1959 as the Kingston Trio's "A Worried Man," but LP reissues of the Carter Family's recordings didn't begin until 1961. Worldwide fame and recognition as a foundational act in folk, country, and bluegrass music followed within a decade of A.P. Carter's little-noted passing.

A.P. Carter's legacy lives on at the Carter Family Fold, a nonprofit performance venue established by his daughter Janette on the Maces Spring family homestead. A.P.'s grocery is now a museum, packed with artifacts from the careers of three generations of musical Carters. In 2004, the cabin in which he was born 113 years earlier was moved from its inaccessible location to the complex.

— FRED BARTENSTEIN

THE CARTER FAMILY

Sara Dougherty Carter \ 2001

Sara Carter was born two years before the close of the nineteenth century at Flatwoods, on the north side of Virginia's 150-mile Clinch Mountain ridge, not far from the Kentucky and Tennessee borders. After her mother's death in 1901, the child and her sister moved in with an aunt and uncle. Neighbors owned autoharps, and a preteen Sara acquired her first from the Sears catalog by selling greeting cards. This instrument, held on the lap, provided a singer with chordal accompaniment. Its limitations required that a song be arranged in simple and regular form. Sara also learned to accompany herself on guitar and banjo, but it was her striking, strong, and expressive singing voice that attracted the most local attention.

> *"The only noticeable difference between their first and last recording sessions was the fact that that they had improved in every direction within that style.... Even when Sara recorded with Jimmie Rodgers, it was in the Carter Family style."*
>
> – John Atkins in "The Carter Family," *Stars of Country Music*, 1975.

A.P. Carter, a fruit tree salesman from the other side of Clinch Mountain, came to call. He heard Sara singing (family legend says the song was "Engine 143") and started to court the young lady. Although she professed not to like him, they married a month before her seventeenth birthday.

The couple – who were joined by children Gladys (1919), Janette (1923), and Joe (1927) – moved to Maces Spring (near Hiltons), where they sang together at home and in local churches. A.P. was restless by nature and often away from home. Their primary sources of income included blacksmithing, carpentry, nursery sales, and logging. On a trip to

Born: July 21, 1898, Flatwoods, Coeburn, Wise County, VA

Died: January 8, 1979, Lodi, CA

Primary Musical Accomplishments:
Vocalist, guitar and autoharp accompanist

"Sara's voice... was the major element in their continued success and certainly the prime factor in securing their initial recording contract.... Over the years Sara's voice took on a deep, almost masculine tone and... seemed to improve almost from one recording session to the next."

- John Atkins in "The Carter Family," *Stars of Country Music*, 1975.

Composed:
Sara Carter is credited as the writer, co-writer, or arranger of:

"Farther On"

"Fifty Miles of Elbow Room"

"Goin' Home"

"The Hand that Rocks the Cradle"

"Keep on the Firing Line"

"A Lad from Old Virginia"

"Lonesome Pine Special"

"Railroading on the Great Divide"

"The Ship that Never Returned"

"Three Little Strangers"

"While the Band is Playing Dixie"

Came to fame with:
The Carter Family, 1926-1943

Performed with:
The Carter Family, 1926-1943

The A.P. Carter Family (A.P., Sara, and their children Janette and Joe), 1952, 1956

Led the way:
- The first major female vocalist in commercial country music, and a participant in the famous Victor Bristol sessions of July/August, 1927.
- Recorded approximately 300 songs, scores of them still in today's bluegrass repertoire.
- Country Music Hall of Fame, 1970.
- Bluegrass Hall of Fame, 2001 (induction presentation by Bill Clifton).

By the Way:
- Sara recorded "Wabash Cannonball" in 1929, seven years before it was covered by Roy Acuff and the Crazy Tennesseans. Acuff also employed the Carters' tune to "I'm Thinking Tonight of My Blue Eyes" for his version of "The Great Speckled Bird."

visit relatives in a borrowed car, the couple had a breakdown and no money. Asked what they should do, Sara suggested they arrange a performance at a local schoolhouse – their first attempt at professional singing.

"Aunt Sara was a woman hard to explain. She was tall, buxom, black-eyed, and always beautiful. She was a thoroughbred."
– June Carter, quoted by Charles Wolfe in liner notes to *In the Shadow of Clinch Mountain*, Bear Family Records, 2000.

A.P. heard that the Brunswick Record Company was seeking talent and arranged an audition, where the couple performed "Log Cabin By the Sea," "Poor Orphan Boy" and several fiddle tunes. Brunswick was looking for a singing fiddler rather than a family act, so that audition came to naught.

Sara had two younger cousins in Copper Creek, Maybelle and Madge Addington, who enjoyed making music with her. After Maybelle married A.P.'s brother Ezra and moved to their side of the mountain, A.P. and Sara asked her to join in on guitar and vocal harmony.

A more successful recording audition involved the trio in Bristol, Virginia/Tennessee, on August 1 and 2, 1927. Sara's singing on "Single Girl, Married Girl," "The Storms Are On the Ocean," "The Poor Orphan Child," and "The Wandering Boy" so impressed the Victor Talking Machine Company's Ralph Peer that those became the first of an amazing 144 songs released by that company and its subsidiaries over the next seven years. An equal number of recordings were made for other labels between 1935 and 1940.

Sara separated from A.P. in 1933 and moved back to Copper Creek, on the other side of the mountain. At the urging of Ralph Peer's wife Anita – who reminded Sara that Hollywood movie couples continue to perform together after splitting – she remained a member of the performing and recording ensemble. According to family and friends, distance improved her and A.P.'s relationship and they remained cordial thereafter, despite an eventual divorce in 1939 and Sara's marriage to A.P.'s first cousin, Coy Bayes.

After several winters spent performing on Mexican border radio and one wartime year on WBT in Charlotte, North Carolina, the original Carter Family disbanded in 1943 after sixteen years together. Sara and Coy moved to California, Maybelle and her daughters established their own country act, and A.P. opened a grocery store in Maces Spring.

Clifford Spurlock, a Kentucky preacher, approached A.P. about making records for his Acme label. Sara was convinced to come back and record fifty-eight tracks in 1952 and 1956 with her ex-husband

and their children Janette and Joe. The recordings (reissued on CD in 2008) made little impact on a market that was at the time spawning rock 'n' roll. Folkways included a handful of Carter Family songs on the influential compilation *Anthology of American Folk Music* in 1952. Further reissues post-dated A.P.'s death in 1960 and Joan Baez's popularization of the Carter repertoire.

Sara maintained contact with her Virginia and Tennessee family members. In 1965, she sent Maybelle a tape of home recordings for Christmas. In a wry comment about how low her voice had become, she suggested Maybelle play it for her soon-to-be son-in-law Johnny Cash (Johnny and June Carter were married in 1968). Cash arranged a recording session for Columbia, and the album *An Historic Reunion* was released in 1966. A year later, Mike Seeger and Bill Clifton arranged for Sara and Maybelle to appear at the Newport Folk Festival (they were included in the documentary film *Festival!*).

Sara and Maybelle were both present to accept the Carter Family's induction into the Country Music Hall of Fame in 1970. Their last performance together was in floor-length, high-necked gold dresses at daughter/niece Janette's Carter Family Fold at Maces Spring in 1977. By December of the following year Maybelle was dead. Soon after, Sara was hospitalized for circulatory and respiratory problems and died January 8, 1979. After a funeral at the Carter Fold, she was laid to rest two rows from A.P.'s grave at the nearby Mount Vernon Methodist Church Cemetery.

Beginning with the Monroe Brothers (Bill and Charlie), in 1936, bluegrass artists in all generations have made extensive use of the Carter Family's recorded repertoire. It is fitting that the Carters were the first inductees to the Bluegrass Hall of Fame selected entirely for their influence upon, rather than direct participation in, bluegrass music.

— FRED BARTENSTEIN

> "She grew up before World War I, and carried herself in the aristocratic manner of women at that time. She did not defer to anyone musically; the timing was dead on, and the voice had an arresting power even at age sixty. [Sara's husband] Coy told with glee of the time in a bar when a country bandleader offered Sara his big Martin guitar and suggested a singing contest with his 'girl singer.' At Coy's urging, Sara accepted the guitar, carefully tuned it, and sang 'Sweet Sunny South.' Afterwards the 'girl singer' could not be found, and Coy said she never came back to the band."
>
> – Joe Wilson, personal communication, 2013.

- In 1931, recorded a duet yodel with Jimmie Rodgers on "Why There's A Tear In My Eye."
- Woody Guthrie borrowed Carter Family tunes – among them "Wildwood Flower" for "The Sinking of the Reuben James" and "When The World's On Fire" for "This Land Is Your Land."
- After retiring at the age of 44 from her career as a musical performer, Sara Carter raised peacocks in Angel's Camp, California.
- Bluegrass tribute albums to the Carter Family include Flatt and Scruggs (1961), Bill Clifton (1962), the Stanley Brothers (2004, a compilation of older recordings), and Ralph Stanley (2006).

THE CARTER FAMILY

Maybelle Addington Carter | 2001

Maybelle Addington's sister Madge (eight years older) and her cousin Sara Dougherty (eleven years older) were neighborhood singing partners in rural southwestern Virginia as young Maybelle first grew interested in music. She took up the autoharp and the banjo before acquiring, at age thirteen, an instrument with which she would inspire generations of country and folk musicians – the guitar. By then Sara had married fruit-tree salesman A.P. Carter and moved to Poor Valley, on the other side of Clinch Mountain. Guitars were just beginning to penetrate the area in the 1920s. On her inexpensive Stella, Maybelle taught herself a unique way to play melodies and strum accompaniment at the same time.

A.P. and Sara were beginning to perform in surrounding churches and schools, and had even auditioned for the Brunswick Record Company. In March of 1926, fate brought sixteen-year-old Maybelle even closer as she married A.P.'s younger brother Ezra "Eck" (also known as "E. J.") Carter and moved to their side of the mountain. A year later, the duo had become a trio, with Sara singing lead, Maybelle a higher harmony, and A.P. the bass part. Maybelle's guitar was the sole lead instrument, accompanied by Sara on guitar or autoharp. The Carter Family's repertoire included material all three of its members had collected from various family and community sources, both secular and sacred.

Maybelle was seven months pregnant with her first child when A.P. promised to weed a corn patch for Ezra if he would let his wife accompany A.P. and Sara on a trip to Bristol. In late July and early August of 1927, Ralph Peer was seeking rural talent for the Victor Talking Machine Company of Camden, New Jersey. "Must I take my guitar?" Maybelle asked.

Born: May 10, 1909, near Nickelsville, Scott County, VA

Died: October 23, 1978, Nashville, TN

Primary Instrument: Guitar

"Perhaps the most remarkable of Maybelle's many talents was her skill as a guitarist. She revolutionized the instrument's role by developing a style in which she played melody lines on the bass strings with her thumb while rhythmically strumming with her fingers. Her innovative technique, to this day known as the Carter Scratch, influenced the guitar's shift from rhythm to lead instrument."

– Holly George-Warren, "Hillbilly Fillies: The Trailblazers of C&W," quoted in *Helen Reddington, The Lost Women of Rock Music,* 2007.

Bluegrass Hall of Fame Inductee Biographies

The audition was successful, resulting the following fall in the first of some 150 Carter Family releases on 78 rpm discs. Ralph Peer owned the publishing company Southern Music; he arranged for otherwise uncopyrighted material to be registered under A.P.'s name (A.P. divided royalty checks three ways for the rest of his life). Peer also managed the group's recording and performing career. The Carter Family's concert dates and revenues were limited by quickly growing families, Ezra's railroad work, the Depression, A.P. and Sara's 1933 separation, and the inaccessibility of their Poor Valley home. But their 78 rpm records traveled all over the world, generating fan loyalty and musical disciples wherever they were heard.

After several winters spent performing on Mexican border radio and one wartime year on WBT in Charlotte, North Carolina, the original Carter Family disbanded in 1943, after sixteen years together. Sara and her new husband moved to California. A.P. opened a grocery store adjacent to his home in Maces Spring (near Hiltons). Maybelle and her daughters – Helen, Anita, and June – lost no time in establishing their own country act, with encouragement and tour support from Ezra.

Mother Maybelle and the Carter Sisters' repertoire included Carter Family favorites, but also expanded into popular sounds of the day. Maybelle's iconic f-hole L-5 Gibson guitar (purchased in 1928 for $275) was but one of the group's lead instruments. Ever the innovator, Maybelle devised a method for cradling the autoharp (typically a lap instrument) in her arms and playing both melodies and accompaniment with thumb and fingerpicks. Helen played the accordion, an instrument frequently used in country music at that time. In 1949 a skinny Tennessee mountain boy, Chester "Chet" Atkins, became the first non-family member of the group, on fiddle and finger-style electric guitar. Breaking the laconic and dour mood of the predecessor act, June added energetic comedy while her mother and sisters sparkled, smiled, and sang sweet trio harmonies.

Starting with three years at tiny WRNL in Richmond, Virginia, the

> *"She is short, but she casts a long shadow – long and a half-century wide. Her voice is shy and unassuming, but it was boomed over the loudest airwaves of her time and made her a household sound. She is so modest that digging facts out of her is like digging clams on a rocky, clammed-out Maine shore at high tide, because many of these facts would sound like compliments to herself and she is not, and never has been, on an ego trip."*
>
> Billy Edd Wheeler, "Mother Maybelle Carter: Her Career Spans a Half-Century," *Country Music Magazine*, December 1973.

Composed:
BMI's database credits Maybelle Carter with 64 published compositions, co-compositions, and arrangements, including:
"Charlie Brooks"
"Chinese Breakdown"
"Drunkard's Hell"
"East Virginia Blues"
"Fair And Tender Ladies"
"False Hearted Lover"
"Loafer's Glory"
"Lonesome For You Darling"
"Troublesome Waters"

"Because they used autoharp and guitar, most of the old ballads had to be taken out of their modal keys to lend themselves to instrumental band accompaniment."

Billy Edd Wheeler, "Mother Maybelle Carter: Her Career Spans a Half-Century," *Country Music Magazine*, December 1973.

Came to fame with:
The Carter Family, 1926-1943

Performed with:
The Carter Family, 1926-1943
Mother Maybelle and the Carter Sisters (daughters Helen, Anita, and June), 1943-1975

Led the way:
- The first prominent female instrumentalist in commercial country music, and a participant in the famous Victor Bristol sessions of July/August, 1927.
- Recorded hundreds of songs and tunes, scores of them still in today's bluegrass repertoire.
- Member of the *Grand Ole Opry*, 1950-1967.

- Played autoharp on Lester Flatt and Earl Scruggs's album, *Songs of the Famous Carter Family*, 1961.
- Country Music Hall of Fame, 1970.
- Featured performer on the Nitty Gritty Dirt Band's historic *Will the Circle Be Unbroken* three-album set, 1971.
- Her image appeared on a U.S. postage stamp honoring the Carter Family, 1993.
- Bluegrass Hall of Fame, 2001 (induction presentation by Bill Clifton).

By the Way:
- Enjoyed classical music and riding her Indian-model motorcycle.
- Hired Chet Atkins as a fiddler and electric guitarist, late 1940s.
- Toured with Elvis Presley in 1955.
- Johnny Cash's mother-in-law (Cash married her daughter June, 1968).
- Her Gibson L-5 guitar was purchased on behalf of the Country Music Hall of Fame and Museum for $575,000 in 2004.
- Portrayed by Sandra Ellis Lafferty in the movie *Walk the Line*, 2005.
- The Maybelle Carter Retirement Life Community in Madison, Tennessee, was built by Johnny Cash and June Carter Cash in her memory.

act moved up to 50,000-watt WRVA and the *Old Dominion Barn Dance* in Richmond, then on to WNOX and the *Mid-Day Merry-Go-Round* and *Tennessee Barn Dance* in Knoxville, and then Springfield, Missouri's KWTO, RadiOzark's syndicated program, and the *Ozark Jubilee*. The big step to Nashville, WSM, and the *Grand Ole Opry* came in 1950, shortly followed by national label contracts on RCA and Columbia.

Raised on a hard-work ethic in Virginia, Maybelle was quite the road warrior. She drove long shifts in the group's touring cars and managed wardrobes and musical issues, while Ezra took care of most business decisions and chaperoned the daughters' solo ventures until all three were married.

As the swinging sixties began, Maybelle found her style out of favor and her daughters preoccupied with other musical and family activities. She took work as a part-time practical nurse, caring for the elderly, while still performing weekends on the *Grand Ole Opry*. Then, after A.P.'s death in 1960, a new generation discovered the historic recordings and classic style of the Carter Family. This time, they were calling it "folk music." Maybelle found herself being interviewed for national publications and demonstrating her guitar and autoharp styles for adoring disciples at places like the Newport Folk Festival and early bluegrass festivals. Sara was even convinced to come out of retirement for a Columbia album and a few joint appearances with Maybelle.

But the biggest opportunity, a combination of Maybelle's country and folk fame and Johnny Cash's growing interest in daughter June, was a long-term contract for Mother Maybelle and the Carter Sisters to appear on the self-contained Johnny Cash touring package, and eventually his network TV show. From the mid-1960s to the early 1970s, they sang back-up to Johnny and performed their own set. Feeling the pain of arthritis in her fingers, Maybelle turned lead guitar playing over to daughter Helen and stuck mostly to autoharp.

Shortly before Ezra's death in 1975, Maybelle decided to retire from music, despite the protests of her daughters, Johnny Cash, and Chet Atkins. She spent more time at a second home in Florida, enjoying an active social life with friends, bingo, cards and low-stakes gambling. Her health seriously deteriorated in 1978, and she died peacefully in her sleep on October 23 of that year. Her passing was nationally noted, but it is likely that the soft-spoken, hard-working, and well-loved Maybelle Carter never fully understood the extent of her impact upon the world's musical heritage.

— FRED BARTENSTEIN

THE LILLY BROTHERS AND DON STOVER

The Lilly Brothers \ 2002

Michael Burt "Bea" Lilly
Born: December 5, 1921, Clear Creek community, Raleigh County, WV
Died: September 19, 2005, Plymouth, MA
Primary Instrument: Guitar

"Bea played fine rhythm guitar in an earlier style, utilizing a thumb and index finger technique."
- Traci Thomas, "Bluegrass Hall of Honor to Induct the Lilly Brothers and Don Stover," press release, August 15, 2002.

Charley Edwin ("Everett") Lilly
Born: July 1, 1924, Clear Creek community, Raleigh County, WV
Died: May 8, 2012, Clear Creek community, Raleigh County, WV
Primary Instrument: Mandolin

Driving through the mountains of West Virginia, a visitor can't help but notice how many mailboxes display the names Lilly and Stover (a popular bumper sticker reads: "West Virginia: 1 million people and 15 last names"). Bea and Everett Lilly began life in the beautiful but remote community of Clear Creek, twenty miles and across Spruce Mountain from Beckley, in a landscape dominated by a railroad trestle.

Known throughout his life as "Bea," Michael Burt Lilly was born in 1921. In later life, he sometimes signed his first name "Mitchell" and legally changed his middle name to "Bea." In 1924, tow-headed brother Everett joined the family of three brothers and four sisters. The newest member of the Lilly family was known from the beginning as Everett. Later in life, he sometimes spelled his name "Everette" and found that his birth certificate actually read "Charley Edwin." Bea and Everett loved the singing at Clear Creek Methodist Church as well as the mountain music they heard on a neighbor's battery radio and wind-up Victrola.

"[During their 15-minute segment on WWVA radio in 1948] Bea would list the songs to be performed. Everett did not concern himself with Bea's selection. Without warm-up, rehearsal, or discussion, they went on the air, and their music was dynamic."
- Mac Martin in liner notes to *The Lilly Brothers and Don Stover: Live at the Hillbilly Ranch*, Hay Holler Records, 1996.

As children, both learned guitar and mandolin and the two vocal parts of the brother duet style then popular on radio and records. Eventually, Everett became the sole mandolin player, the predominant tenor, and the

Bluegrass Hall of Fame Inductee Biographies \ 109

110 | Bluegrass Hall of Fame Inductee Biographies

The Lilly Brothers at the Hillbilly Ranch, Boston, MA, 1978.

"[Everett] cloned Bill Monroe's mandolin style from his pre-bluegrass Monroe Brothers days, and even improved it with a great rhythm snap at the end of phrases."

- Joe Wilson, personal communication, 2004.

Composed or Co-Composed:

"Beneath the Old Southern Skies" (Everett)

"Over the Hills to the Poorhouse" (Everett)

"Your Love Is Like a Flower" (Bea)

Early influences:

Carter Family

Monroe Brothers

Blue Sky Boys

Callahan Brothers

Paul Buskirk

Came to fame with:

The Lilly Brothers and Don Stover, 1952-1996

"The Lilly Brothers sing with the sturdy implicit honesty of the old-time singing greats, and with a supple fluency that characterizes bluegrass singing at its best."

- Bill Vernon in liner notes to *The Lilly Brothers and Don Stover: Early Recordings*, County Records, 1991.

Performed with:

The Lonesome Holler Boys, 1938

Molly O'Day and the Cumberland Mountain Folks, 1945

The Smiling Mountain Boys, Knoxville, TN, 1940s

Red Belcher's Kentucky Ridgerunners, 1948-1950

Lester Flatt, Earl Scruggs and the Foggy Mountain Boys, 1951-1952, 1958 (Everett)

leader of their group (he continued to play lead guitar and later took up the fiddle as well). They listened to 78s by a variety of early country acts, but the Monroe Brothers – Charlie and Bill – became their particular favorites. The year is in question, but a family story recalls that one Christmas Eve Everett and Bea left their families to join up with Bill and Charlie Monroe. When a heavy snowstorm blocked their progress, they went back home and gave up that adventure. Bea could copy Charlie Monroe's vocal parts and guitar style almost perfectly (later in life he was thrilled to perform onstage, with Bill, the Monroe Brothers' hit "What Would You Give In Exchange for Your Soul," after which Bill remarked, "That'll put Everett in his place. We don't want to hear no more out of him!").

"Bea, with his quietness and stubborn sincerity, is a good counter to Everett's impulsiveness. He spent a year carving a guitar out of a piece of wood with a penknife and sandpaper, put strings on it, and uses it every night at the club, without feeling any necessity to tell anybody about it."

- Sam Charters, "The Lilly Brothers of Hillbilly Ranch," *Sing Out!*, July 1965.

As they noted when interviewed in the movie *Bluegrass Country Soul*, the brothers didn't have bicycles or the other things that modern kids enjoy, so they had to entertain themselves. Both left formal education at a young age and struggled to make a living in the West Virginia coal mines. Everett sustained burns to his hands in an electrical accident. During a slate fall, the workers ran out of the mine. With the top continuing to fall and black coal dust everywhere, Everett and an African-American miner headed back for Bea while other miners yelled for them to come back. Together they pulled Bea from a large piece of slate that lay on his hip.

Music was a safer and more pleasurable – if not more remunerative – outlet for their talents. While still in their teens, Bea and Everett performed with neighbor and old-time banjo player Paul Taylor on radio shows and small performances in the local area. With families to feed, staying in their beloved hills was not an option. So they began an odyssey typical for country bands of the time – moving from town to town and radio station to radio station – trying to build an audience and hoping for a lucky break.

Known for their vocal harmony and instrumental accompaniment, the Lillys became popular on WJLS, Beckley, "The Voice of the Smokeless Coal Fields." There, during 1939 and the early 1940s, they met Molly O'Day and in 1945 went with her Cumberland Mountain Folks to Knoxville, Tennessee.

Early in 1948, the brothers' biggest break came when they joined clear-channel WWVA in Wheeling, West Virginia. Its Saturday night *Jamboree* reached millions throughout the northern states and Canada.

As featured members of banjo-playing comedian Red Belcher's troupe, the Kentucky Ridgerunners, Bea and Everett made their first records for the Page label. As the Lilly Brothers, they recorded "They Sleep Together Now At Rest" and "What Are They Doing in Heaven." Under Red Belcher's name — and with Coahoma County, Texas, native Tex Logan on fiddle — Bea sang the solo "Kentucky is Only a Dream." Bea also backed Logan, who was taking a break from his graduate engineering studies, on "Old Gray Goose." Everett refused to participate on the latter recordings, vowing to record only under the Lilly name.

A disagreement between the Lillys and Belcher broke up the Kentucky Ridgerunners in 1950. After a short interlude at WMMN, Fairmont, Bea went home to Clear Creek and worked in Beckley. Everett couldn't resist the offer of a steady job playing mandolin and singing tenor with increasingly the most successful act in the genre – Lester Flatt, Earl Scruggs and the Foggy Mountain Boys. His wife and children stayed in Clear Creek as Everett hit the road in the fall of 1950. During his tenure, which lasted until September, 1952, the group was based in Versailles, Kentucky; Roanoke, Virginia; and Raleigh, North Carolina.

Although Everett soloed effectively on the mandolin with Flatt and Scruggs, it was his wonderful voice that attracted their attention and that of countless listeners since. Everett was unerringly on key, his powerful tenor head tones blended well with both related and unrelated harmony partners, and, most distinctively, he was achingly sincere in his delivery. When Everett sang a number – although a listener may have heard it before by other singers – it became forever associated with Everett Lilly, imprinted with the call of the West Virginia backwoods.

Everett recorded fourteen sides with Flatt and Scruggs on Columbia. His contributions were particularly notable on "I'm Workin' on a Road (to Glory Land)," "Somehow Tonight," "He Took Your Place," "'Tis Sweet to Be Remembered," and "Over the Hills to the Poorhouse." In 1953, after Everett had left the band, Flatt and Scruggs recorded Bea's composition, "Your Love Is Like a Flower," which he wrote while sitting on a big rock by Clear Creek (according to nephew Everett Alan Lilly).

> *"Tex speaks fervently of the many times Everett's strength of character would come to the fore in times of crisis – one icy night, the car in which the band was riding skidded out of control; Everett rose from the back seat and literally seized the wheel, skillfully bringing the car back under control, at a time when lesser men might have joined the driver in terrified immobility."*
>
> – Bill Vernon, "Tex Logan Remembers the Lilly Brothers," *Muleskinner News*, November-December 1970.

The Confederate Mountaineers, Boston, MA, 1952-1956

The Lilly Brothers and Don Stover, 1957-1996

The Lilly Brothers and the Lilly Mountaineers, 2001-2002

Clear Creek Crossin' or Everett Lilly and the Lilly Mountaineers, 1970-2012 (Everett)

Led the way:
- Bridged the brother duet style of the 1930s into the emerging bluegrass genre of the 1940s and 1950s. A kind of "living encyclopedia," the Lilly Brothers evoked for modern audiences the sounds and performance techniques of earlier decades.
- Influenced numerous country, bluegrass, and folk artists in New England and West Virginia, and played a major role in popularizing bluegrass in Japan.
- Appeared in the movies *Festival!* (1967) and *Bluegrass Country Soul* (1971) and the West Virginia Public Television documentary *True Facts in a Country Song* (1979).
- Massachusetts Country Music Hall of Fame, 1986.
- Bluegrass Hall of Fame, 2002.
- West Virginia Music Hall of Fame, 2008.
- IBMA Recorded Event of the Year for *Everett Lilly and Everybody and Their Brother*, 2008.

By the Way:
- Everett was the only sideman in the Foggy Mountain Boys ever separately credited on a record label.

- Nicknamed "the Colonel" by Tex Logan probably because, in his Confederate Mountaineers uniform and being the boss of the outfit, Everett came across as a colonel type.
- When asked to spell his first name at the U.S./Canadian border, Bea reportedly responded, "Jist a big ol' B."
- Everett accused his older brother of "going modern" when he added a few Lefty Frizzell and Hank Snow songs to the group's otherwise-well-aged repertoire.
- Performed in 1959 with Merle Travis in the first all-country program at Boston's prestigious Jordan Hall.
- Everett's six sons – Everett Alan, Tennis, Jiles, Charles, Mark, and Daniel – also performed and recorded with bluegrass and country acts, including the Charles River Valley Boys, Billy Walker, Stonewall Jackson, Stella Parton, Jim and Jesse, Joe Diffie, Johnny Russell, the Nashville Pickers, and the Lilly Mountaineers.
- Everett was vice president of Towa Kikaku and Company, which booked the Lilly Brothers and Don Stover, Bill Monroe, Jim and Jesse, and J.D. Crowe on tours of Japan and issued commercial recordings from some of those performances.

Meanwhile, fiddler/mathematician Tex Logan left to finish a master's program at Massachusetts Institute of Technology. In Boston, Tex found a burgeoning country music scene. On a trip through the south looking to find a guitarist for his band, he stopped in Raleigh to see his old friend Everett Lilly. Shortly after that, the brothers joined Tex in the Confederate Mountaineers, together with three-finger and drop-thumb banjo prodigy Don Stover, who had been performing with Bea in West Virginia. Thus was bluegrass music (although it would not be so named for another few years) introduced to New England.

The Confederate Mountaineers aired a daily radio show on Boston's WCOP and performed every Saturday night on that station's *Hayloft Jamboree*. They also found work at the Plaza Bar and the Mohawk Ranch before (minus Tex) settling into a seven-night-a-week gig at the Hillbilly Ranch, next to the Trailways Bus Station. The area became known as the "Combat Zone" for the frequent scuffles involving sailors, soldiers, and other

"Not long after my Dad went with Flatt and Scruggs he showed up at my grandparents' house all excited. He had a copy of their first Columbia recordings, which included 'Over the Hills to the Poorhouse,' which Dad had taken to Lester. My grandparents never did have a record player but Dad managed to borrow one from someone. Soon we gathered around and heard my Dad playing mandolin and singing tenor.

– Everett Alan Lilly (son), personal communication, 2009

denizens of its X-rated businesses and bars. Owners of the establishment later confided that dancers found the quick pace of the band's music exhausting – and thus drank more – a key to the group's longevity there.

Bea, Everett, and Don continued year after year at the Hillbilly Ranch as the Lilly Brothers and Don Stover. The brothers were fish out of water in the urbane, fast-moving, and fast-talking northeast. Seemingly unchanged by the entire experience, their wonderfully droll characters and expressions (they sang "Down on the banks of the old Hio" and spoke of the "Silver War") are fondly remembered by hundreds of bluegrass pilgrims who made their way to the unlikely shrine at Carver and Stuart Streets. Everett was loquacious and given to sermons on both biblical and musical subjects. Bea was quiet, and he developed a streak of stubborn resistance to his younger brother's assertive manner.

In their early days in Boston, Everett, Bea, and Don lived by themselves in triple-decker apartments in East Cambridge, making yearly visits to their families in West Virginia. Everett rejoined Flatt and Scruggs briefly late in the 1950s, but Boston provided a more stable and remunerative base of operations than the group could find in the South at the time. This was particularly true as the folk music boom swept America. Boston was one of its epicenters, and the Lillys were viewed as among the most authentic and appealing acts in the southern mountain tradition. Able to add recording, college, and folk festival dates to their steady nightclub revenue, the three were finally able to send for their wives and children and move to the suburb of North Billerica.

During two decades spent in Boston, the Lilly Brothers and Don Stover recorded two singles for Event (re-released with additional tracks on the County label), an album for Folkways, and two albums for Prestige. The albums sold primarily to the folk music market, and the group was booked by Manuel Greenhill (Joan Baez and Doc Watson's manager) into Newport, other folk festivals, and several colleges. Radio, television, and concert appearances in the late 1960s were shadowed by Bea's occasional last-minute failure to appear. Another generation of Lillys was primed to fill in on lead vocal and guitar.

In January of 1970, Everett's sixteen-year-old son Jiles – one of Bea's stand-ins – was killed in an auto accident. In their grief and realization that the city was not where they belonged, Everett, his wife, and the three children who were still in school moved back to Clear Creek. Bea briefly joined Everett there on a local television show, but soon returned to Boston.

The Lilly Brothers and Don Stover reunited a number of times for appearances at bluegrass festivals (sometimes with Tex Logan), a gospel album on County, and two tours of Japan that produced three live LPs. Bea made little other music in his last years, slowly declining into the Alzheimer's Disease which took his life in September of 2005.

Everett formed another family band for appearances and recordings, mostly in the West Virginia market. At first called Clear Creek Crossin', and then Everett Lilly and the Lilly Mountaineers, it included sons Mark, Charles, and Daniel, occasionally their older brother Everett Alan (a professor of social work), and an assortment of grandchildren and friends. The act was a fast-moving conglomeration of modern country music, traditional folk material, bluegrass, and comedy. In a sad echo of the earlier tragedy, Everett's son Charles was killed in a van accident while on tour with *Grand Ole Opry* star Billy Walker in 2006. Facing various health challenges, Everett Lilly continued to enjoy performing, riding his four-wheeler through the woods, and preaching the gospels of Jesus and mountain music until his peaceful death at home in 2012 at the age of eighty-seven.

— FRED BARTENSTEIN

"I remember asking Everett when I visited Boston while in high school why he did not write more songs. He lectured me on the beauty of the old songs and noted that if the Lilly Brothers did not do them audiences would not get a chance to hear them."

– Michael Toney (nephew), personal communication, 2009

THE LILLY BROTHERS AND DON STOVER

Don Stover | 2002

Don Stover was born in the coal mining company town of Ameagle, six miles northwest of the Lilly Brothers' homeplace of Clear Creek, West Virginia. Three years younger than Everett and six years younger than Bea, Don's path and family relationships undoubtedly crossed theirs before the three lifelong partners became involved in music.

The Stover family had a banjo at home, with which both father and mother entertained the family. Don wasn't allowed to touch it but – at seven years of age – he would secretly play while his parents were outside. In early 1941, he heard five-string banjo players Wade Mainer and Emory Martin and became seriously interested in mastering the instrument. By 1945 he had developed his own three-finger style of picking, which was heavily influenced by that of Earl Scruggs (Earl joined Bill Monroe on the *Grand Ole Opry* in 1945).

Don was earning a living as a coal miner when the Lilly Brothers convinced him to pull up stakes and move with them to Massachusetts.

> *"I remember the mountains where I left home, back where I was born, down at the end of a hollow... I remember walking to church on a Sunday when I was a youngster, and I had to walk the old dirt road when it was raining and there were mudholes you had to step in. I'd listen to somebody sitting in their cabin up on the hillside playing guitar or fiddle or banjo. The music was just ringing down those hollows and over that mountainside. It was a beautiful sound."*
>
> – In liner notes to *Don Stover and Friends*, White Oak Records, 1989.

Born: March 6, 1928, Ameagle, Raleigh County, WV

Died: November 11, 1996, Brandywine, MD

Primary Instrument: Banjo

Composed:
BMI's database credits Don Stover with 30 published compositions, co-compositions, and arrangements, including:
"Black Diamond"
"My Blue Ridge Memories"
"The Old Coon Dog"
"Things in Life"
"West Virginia Coal Miner's Blues"

Early influences:
J. V. Williams
Paul Taylor
Monroe Brothers
Earl Scruggs
Rudy Lyle
Don Reno

Photo: © Henry Horenstein, 1972

116 | Bluegrass Hall of Fame Inductee Biographies

Came to fame with:
The Lilly Brothers and Don Stover, 1952-1996

Performed with:
Coal River Boys, Artie, WV, late 1940s

The Confederate Mountaineers, Boston, MA, 1952-1954

Buzz Busby and the Bayou Boys, 1954-1956

Bill Monroe and the Blue Grass Boys, 1957

The Lilly Brothers and Don Stover, 1957-1996

Bill Harrell and the Virginians, 1965-1966

Don Stover and the White Oak Mountain Boys, 1970-1996

First Generation, 1978-1995

"Whenever I catch sight of a lonely hero of bluegrass, twisting on his pedestal, I summon up a vision of Don Stover, with a gleam in his eye, to stand just in back of him and to festoon an empty place in whatever is happening with a Chuck Berry lick or perhaps a surf music arpeggio. Don winks to the audience as if to say, 'You got that, didn't you?'"

– Joe Wilson, personal communication, 2004.

Led the way:
- One of the earliest and most-skilled exponents of the Scruggs style of three-finger banjo picking, as well as the older clawhammer style (Don could switch effortlessly from one to the other), an outgoing entertainer, and a preserver of Appalachian musical tradition.

Bluegrass Hall of Fame Inductee Biographies

- Influenced two generations of bluegrass artists in the northeast, including Bob French, Bill Keith, Tony Trischka, and Béla Fleck. The Grateful Dead's Jerry Garcia credited Don as an inspiration, and his recordings continue to inspire banjo players everywhere.
- Appeared in the movies *Festival* (1967) and *Bluegrass Country Soul* (1971).
- SPBGMA Preservation Hall of Greats, 1993.
- Massachusetts Country Music Hall of Fame, 1987.
- Bluegrass Hall of Fame, 2002.
- West Virginia Music Hall of Fame, 2008.

By the Way:
- A traveling salesman coming through town in 1945 explained that Earl Scruggs was using metal picks; Don made his first ones from a Prince Albert Tobacco tin.
- Bill Keith credits the genesis of his melodic banjo style to a lick Don played on "Bring Back My Blue-Eyed Boy to Me" (Event Records 1957).
- "Black Diamond," the title of one of Don's banjo instrumentals, refers to a nickname for coal, not the brand of banjo strings.
- Don's varied life is reflected in three names he gave to the same banjo tune: "Rockwood Mountain Deer Chase" (referring to a favorite hunting spot in Maine), "Boston After Dark," and "The Nashville Express."

There they linked up with Tex Logan (their friend and a former bandmate of the Lillys at Wheeling's WWVA) who was in graduate school and moonlighting in Boston's lively country music scene. Starting in late 1952, the four worked every day on WCOP radio and in a string of nightclubs. The Lilly Brothers and Don Stover eventually landed a sixteen-year, seven-night-a-week, booking at the rough-and-tumble Hillbilly Ranch in downtown Boston. A stream of homesick southerners, servicemen, college students, and bluegrass aficionados from throughout the world found their way to the door of that mountain music nirvana.

Everett Lilly dubbed Don (whose birth-certificate name is actually Don Stover) "Little Don Stover," an apt description of his stature at the time. Thinking it sounded good from the stage, Tex Logan called him "Donald Eugene" or "Eugene." Don liked that name, and later named one of his nine children Donald Eugene.

At WCOP's *Hayloft Jamboree*, Don met Buzz Busby, Scotty Stoneman, and Jack Clement, who were performing there as the Bayou Boys. When Busby headed for Washington, D.C., and later the *Louisiana Hayride* in Shreveport between 1954 and 1956, he took Don with him. With the Bayou Boys, Don recorded the original versions of "Lost" and "Just Me and the Jukebox."

Don Stover played banjo with Bill Monroe for about six months in 1957, recording eleven tracks with him. His playing is heard to particular effect on the Decca records: "I'm Sittin' on Top of the World," "Out in the Cold World," "Goodbye Old Pal," "Molly and Tenbrooks," and "In Despair" (which also features Don's strong lead vocal on the trio).

In those years, rock 'n' roll had bluegrass and traditional country music in retreat. Don recalled that a call to work from Monroe might as likely involve plowing with a mule or loading hay bales as it would heading out on a show date. For a family man, the security of the Hillbilly Ranch was a better choice than the fleeting glory of the *Grand Ole Opry*. For a time, in 1958-1959, Stover co-led the band at Hillbilly Ranch with Bea Lilly and Chubby Anthony, while Everett Lilly went to Nashville for a second tour of duty with Flatt and Scruggs.

In 1965, Stover moved to Washington/Baltimore to appear with Bill Harrell and the Virginians, but in less than a year he returned to Boston, where the folk music boom was opening new doors for the Lilly Brothers and Don Stover in recordings and concert appearances. The boom also motivated a stream of paying banjo students, who added to Don's still-marginal income as a working bluegrass musician. In 1968, Don was invited to accompany Doc Watson, Tex Logan, and Bukka White for appearances at the Summer Olympics in Mexico City. This led to his participation on the Vanguard album *Good Deal! Doc Watson in Nashville* later the same year.

At smaller venues Don would go way out on the limb with creative and humorous banjo experiments, which meant that things didn't turn out perfectly every time. But on the big shows, like the Newport Folk Festival, he bore down and put everything together in ways that revealed his greatness. On the first Lilly Brothers, Don Stover, and Tex Logan appearance there, as the show opened with a fast instrumental, Don whistled through his teeth like a man at the plow whistling to his horse to start a tough row. The enthusiastic audience response prompted the band to a new height of energy and excellence.

In early 1970, the Hillbilly Ranch era came to an end. Don continued teaching banjo and organized his own White Oak Mountain Boys. In the 1970s, the Lilly Brothers and Don Stover reunited for occasional festival appearances (sometimes with Tex Logan), a gospel album on County, and two tours of Japan that produced three live LPs. Don recorded an album on the Towa label with Everett Alan Lilly and three long-overdue albums under his own name, two for Rounder and one for Old Homestead. The title song from one of these – Don's autobiographical "Things in Life" – has since become a bluegrass standard.

"He is the possessor of an instantly recognizable style that is at once unique and thoroughly rooted in tradition. While many 'contemporary' banjo-pickers sound like students preparing apprehensively for an examination, Don Stover's picking always sounds as if school had just let out."

- Bill Vernon in liner notes to *Don Stover and the White Oak Mountain Boys*, Rounder Records, 1974.

From 1978 until the mid-1990s, Don teamed with Bill Clifton and Red Rector (and after Red's death, Jimmy Gaudreau) in the First Generation, which made a series of international tours and recordings on the Elf label. In 1990, Don underwent fourteen hours of brain surgery, was out of intensive care on September 17, and was back playing on stage at Harper's Ferry, West Virginia, on September 19.

Struggling with health and resulting financial issues, Don relocated from Boston to his West Virginia childhood home in White Oak, a hollow adjoining the "town" of Artie, and then to the Maryland suburbs of Washington, where he could receive needed support from family and friends. In the latter years, Hank Edenborn's White Oak Records produced cassette tapes, LPs, and CDs of Don Stover's playing, supplementing his income and recorded legacy. Don told Hank that he planned to write a book – tentatively titled "BIG" for "Bluegrass in General" – but said he wouldn't do it while Bill Monroe was living. Monroe died in September of 1996. Two months later, Don followed him to the heavenly bluegrass band.

— FRED BARTENSTEIN

"Don's soul was exuberant, motivated, determined, and full of mountain experiences. He never stopped developing and refining his skills. On stage, you never knew what Don was going to do. While my father, Everett Lilly, was the acknowledged leader of the group and emcee, Don often took the microphone and joked with the audience. He had complete faith in his instincts and trusted them completely. I think Don belonged with the Lilly Brothers, because they shared such intensity and passion for the music. It would have been difficult to imagine them without each other."

- Everett Alan Lilly, personal communication, 2009.

For more information on the Lilly Brothers and Don Stover, see profiles of the Lilly Brothers.

David Freeman | 2002

Born: May 22, 1939, New York, NY

Primary Involvement in Bluegrass Music:
Record Label Owner

"I started with $500 and I never looked back. When I took a leave of absence from the post office, I was fully expecting I'd have to go back. But it just worked out – it just kept expanding and I never had to go back."

– Quoted by Marshall Wyatt in "Every County Has Its Own Personality," *The Old-Time Herald*, Volume 7 Number 2 (1999).

Associated with:

County Records, 1964 - present

County Sales (mail-order outlet), 1965 - present

Record Depot (wholesale distributorship), 1978 - 2003

Sugar Hill Records, 1978 - 1980

Rebel Records, 1979 - present

Markyle Music (publishing company), 1984 - present

I was in high school and still too young to drive when I bought my first County record: *Larry Richardson and Red Barker and the Blue Ridge Boys*. It was in September of 1965, at the first multi-day bluegrass festival in Fincastle, Virginia. The album, David Freeman's very first bluegrass release, had just been issued. Several months later, I found my way to the world headquarters of County Records, a small room tucked into David's father's art business on East 37th Street, near the United Nations in New York City.

In this unlikely circumstance, I came to know a soft-spoken New Yorker who had instantly fallen in love with country and blues music on the radio during a family driving trip to Florida in 1953. David always wore work shirts and pants of matching colors (mostly green or blue). Until recently, he had been employed by the Railway Mail Service sorting U.S. mail on trains, but he spent every free moment pursuing his musical interests. Whenever a southern artist appeared within reasonable distance of the city, Freeman was there. Since the late 1950s, he had been traveling to the South in search of records, listening to the radio, and attending concerts and fiddle conventions along the way.

What started as a record-collecting hobby began to evolve into a group of related businesses. First came casual selling and trading of duplicates and less-desired records to make space for others. This grew

"County has had a considerable impact on the way a couple of generations of fans have perceived the music, and on the way a lot of younger musicians have learned styles and repertoires."

– Charles Wolfe, "Dave Freeman and County Records," *Bluegrass Unlimited*, December 1980.

Bluegrass Hall of Fame Inductee Biographies \ **121**

> "Freeman was attracted to the music because of its rural nature, and believes very little of that is left in most of the acoustic music coming out today. According to Freeman, this 'is to be expected, because every aspect of our lives has become so homogenized by TV and the media... I feel that even though the rural edge is gone, there still can be great acoustic music today, based on the music and traditions of yesterday.'"

– Scott Perry, "David Freeman and County Sales," *"Don't Start Me to Talkin', I'll Tell Everything I Know"* Blog, Floyd, Virginia, April 6, 2008.

Led the way:
- A pioneer in reissuing country string band recordings of the 1920s and 1930s and new recordings of tradition-oriented bluegrass and old-time musicians.
- Created and built distribution channels through which bluegrass and old-time music reached new audiences outside the American South and throughout the world.
- Set high standards for recording, documenting, and producing artists, raising the bar for the entire industry.
- Mentored others who made notable contributions to the recording field, including Charles Faurot, Richard Nevins, Barry Poss, Chet Rhodes, Gary Reid, and Chris King.
- Produced hundreds

into mail-order auctions and relationships with enough customers to attempt – in 1964 – a reissue LP, *A Collection of Mountain Fiddle Music*, County 501. Freeman pressed less than 500 copies, designing and printing the jackets with the help of his father, a commercial artist. He thought the name "County" would connote the rural associations and geographic distinctions of his favorite music.

David Freeman shared a warehouse in Weehawken, New Jersey, with another Bluegrass Hall of Fame member – the late Bill Vernon – who introduced him to New Yorkers with a shared interest in traditional country music. These included Charlie Faurot, a traveling representative for a bank, and Tom Whitmore, a classical radio station's chief engineer. In 1964, Faurot and Whitmore made field recordings of Wade Ward, Kyle Creed, Fred Cockerham, and George Stoneman in Galax, Virginia. They approached Freeman about releasing them, and so was born *Clawhammer Banjo*, County 701, the first in a series of new recordings by traditional artists.

More historical and newly recorded albums followed, some produced by friends and others by Freeman himself – including *Red Allen* and Joe and Janette Carter's *Carter Family Favorites*. The limited-edition releases took years to recoup their expenses and would not have been a viable business model on their own.

Freeman found that by selling and distributing the often-obscure releases of other labels – by mail order, and to specialty record shops – he could build enough volume to devote his full-time energies to rural music, and earn a modest living. His first customers were in the British Isles, readers of the magazine *Country News and Views*. The *County Sales Newsletter* (more than 300 editions have been published), sent to a growing list of North American and international buyers, became known for its comprehensive coverage and pull-no-punches reviews of available recordings. By the end of his first decade of operations, buyers in rural and small-town areas had replaced Freeman's original big-city markets. Speedy service, reasonable prices, knowledgeable advice, and a comprehensive stock of

> *"When my first re-issues were on the market, most of my sales were to the folk-oriented college age groups, selling primarily through stores in the larger cities… This market has fallen off almost entirely, so that I sell very few LPs in the big cities anymore. Fortunately, this drop-off has been more than made up for by a large number of scattered rural customers throughout the country who have learned of County in one way or another."*

– Quoted by Robert Carlin, "The Small Specialty Record Company in the United States," *John Edwards Memorial Foundation Quarterly*, Summer 1976.

Bluegrass Hall of Fame Inductee Biographies

recordings and related merchandise built *County Sales* into the dominant mail-order outlet for old-time and bluegrass music buyers worldwide.

The Blue Ridge region – a mountain music mecca – called to the native New Yorker. When he saw a Floyd, Virginia, farmhouse advertised for sale, David Freeman began the process of moving his family and business operations to a county of less than 15,000 residents (but perhaps the world's highest ratio of fiddles and banjos). In nearby Roanoke, he soon added Record Depot, a warehousing and distribution operation serving Virginia and adjoining states for 35 labels. The Floyd mail-order operation continues today; it is even an attraction on the Crooked Road: Virginia's Music Heritage Trail. The Freemans have since relocated to university towns: Charlottesville, Virginia (where label offices remain), and Chapel Hill, North Carolina.

The County label continues its original vision of releasing reissues and the most tradition-oriented of new recordings, including twelve albums by master fiddler Kenny Baker. In 1978, as major labels continued to move away from bluegrass headliners, David Freeman helped Barry Poss to found Sugar Hill Records for acts with the greatest touring and commercial potential. In 1979, Rebel Records founder Richard Freeland decided to retire and sold his pioneering bluegrass label to David Freeman.

The Freeman enterprises have consolidated over the years. In 1980, David sold his interest in Sugar Hill Records to Barry Poss. In 2003, he sold Record Depot to an employee, Chet Rhodes. Son Mark Freeman grew up in the business and today manages most of the operations of County and Rebel Records. Web-based purchases and digital downloads account for a growing share of transactions. David Freeman continues to be involved, but can often be found at the pursuits that originally engaged him: collecting and auctioning rare artifacts from the early days of southern rural music.

Bluegrass and traditionally oriented country music have gone through countless changes – as have technology, media, finance, and marketing – in the five decades of David Freeman's business career. Unique among his early peers, he has managed to weather the changes and evolve to changed conditions while never losing sight of his original vision: to produce and sell music he believes in.

— FRED BARTENSTEIN

of influential bluegrass releases by artists including Ralph Stanley, Ricky Skaggs, Kenny Baker, Charlie Waller, Larry Sparks, Red Allen, Rhonda Vincent, Lonesome River Band, IIIrd Tyme Out, Blue Highway, Ronnie Bowman, Lost and Found, the Forbes Family, Claire Lynch, and Del McCoury.
- IBMA Award of Merit (Distinguished Achievement Award), 1989.
- Bluegrass Hall of Fame, 2002.

By the Way:
- Holds a degree in Classics from Columbia University.
- Played mandolin and sang baritone with Southern Express in New York/New Jersey and backed fiddlers on several albums.
- Sold and/or produced recordings in every technological format introduced during the fast-changing twentieth and early twenty-first centuries.
- His personal passion continues to be collecting the 78 and 45 rpm recordings and song and picture books sold by early country artists.
- Son Mark Freeman has taken on many of the day-to-day operations of County and Rebel Records.

James Dee "J.D." Crowe | 2003

J.D. Crowe had a musical conversion experience at the age of twelve, on September 17, 1949, when he first heard Lester Flatt, Earl Scruggs and the Foggy Mountain Boys play at WVLK's *Kentucky Mountain Barn Dance* in Lexington, Kentucky. There are photos showing the youngster sitting in the aisle, his eyes intently fixed on Scruggs's banjo.

The next year, Crowe won a radio appearance with Esco Hankins in a talent competition, which led to other stage and radio work in the local area. Jimmy Martin, driving through Lexington, heard the young banjo player on the radio. Martin convinced J.D.'s parents to let him come to Middletown, Ohio, and play with his group on radio station WPFB. Crowe credits his emerging style — hard and constantly driving — as the way Jimmy Martin wanted to hear the banjo played. But there are blues licks in J.D.'s music that derive from a different source — his teen-aged interest in blues and rock 'n' roll guitar.

> *"My best time was playing [with Jimmy Martin at the* Louisiana Hayride*]. Everyone couldn't wait for Saturday night. It was a good atmosphere."*
>
> - Quoted by Chris Skinker in liner notes to *Jimmy Martin and the Sunny Mountain Boys*, Bear Family Records, 1994.

Having promised his parents he would, Crowe left the band in the fall of 1954 to return to school. Shortly thereafter, Jimmy Martin moved to Detroit, teaming with Bob and Sonny Osborne. The Osbornes and Martin split in 1955 and Martin stayed in Detroit, where Sam "Porky" Hutchins (on banjo) and Earl Taylor (on mandolin) joined the band. J.D. Crowe played the summer of 1955 with Mac Wiseman and returned to

Born: August 27, 1937, Lexington, KY

Primary Instrument:
Banjo

Composed:
BMI's database credits J.D. Crowe with six published compositions, co-compositions, and arrangements, including:
"Bear Tracks"
"Black Jack"
"Crow on the Banjo" (an arrangement of "Bugle Call Rag")

Early influences:
Ernest Tubb, Esco Hankins, and other country artists of the late 1940s
Lester Flatt, Earl Scruggs and the Foggy Mountain Boys
Scotty Moore (Elvis Presley's guitarist)

Came to fame with:
Jimmy Martin and the Sunny Mountain Boys, 1956-1961

Photo: Ron Petronko, 1970

Bluegrass Hall of Fame Inductee Biographies

Performed with:

Jimmy Martin and the Sunny Mountain Boys, summer 1954, 1956-1961

Mac Wiseman and the Country Boys, summer 1955

J.D. Crowe and the Kentucky Mountain Boys, 1961-1972

J.D. Crowe and the New South, 1972-present

Bluegrass Album Band, 1980-1996 (six albums and occasional performances)

"If [my band members] want to go out on their own, then that's their privilege. Anybody that does that, I hope they have a lot of success. I feel it looks good to me, or the group, to have some guy out of the group leave and do well."

– Quoted in "J.D. Crowe and the New South: An Interview by Fred Bartenstein," *Muleskinner News*, July 1975.

Led the way:

• One of the first disciples of Earl Scruggs to make a lasting impression on bluegrass banjo playing.

• A member of the classic edition of Jimmy Martin's Sunny Mountain Boys while still a teenager, J.D. Crowe was held up by Martin as the model for all his subsequent banjoists.

• An exemplary bandleader who fostered the talents of many successful artists, including Doyle Lawson, Tony Rice, Ricky Skaggs, Jerry Douglas, and Keith Whitley.

---

school again that fall. When banjoist Sam Hutchins returned to Baltimore in 1956, Crowe joined Martin full time in Detroit.

In 1958, former Lonesome Pine Fiddlers' guitarist Paul Williams was discharged from service and joined Martin and Crowe on mandolin. From 1958 to early 1961, this crack ensemble built a huge following on KWKH's *Louisiana Hayride*, WWVA's *Wheeling Jamboree*, and Decca Records. The trio's performances of songs such as "Ocean of Diamonds," "Sophronie," "Rock Hearts," "She's Left Me Again," "Home Run Man," "Who'll Sing for Me," "My Walking Shoes," and "Undo What's Been Done" left a permanent legacy in the bluegrass canon. J.D.'s crackling banjo and impeccable timing propelled instrumentals such as "Bear Tracks," "Cripple Creek," "Big Country," and "Crow on the Banjo."

"Southern California and the rock scene have provided them with some of their most requested numbers: 'Sin City,' and 'Devil in Disguise'… Their fresh and novel approach comes as a relief to bluegrass fans, who've survived a long time just on the original greats and their imitators."

– Fred Bartenstein, from "A New Wind Blowing: J.D. Crowe and the Kentucky Mountain Boys," *Muleskinner News*, November-December 1970.

Although he enjoyed his time with Martin, during which he recalls playing banjo in the touring car for 400 miles without stopping, Crowe left the band in 1961 to return to Lexington and work a "day job," behind a counter at a distributor and rental center for heavy equipment. In Kentucky, J.D. teamed with other local part-time musicians to work weekends in several local taverns. They took the name The Kentucky Mountain Boys, and soon included Doyle Lawson on guitar and mandolin, and Bobby Slone on bass and fiddle.

In 1968 J.D. was asked to take his band to the Red Slipper Lounge at Lexington's Holiday Inn North for five-night-a-week performances. This was one of the first times a bluegrass group had played in an upscale environment. Crowds lined up in the parking lot to wait for vacant seats. With Doyle Lawson and Bobby Slone still in the band, Crowe recruited Red Allen to play guitar and sing lead vocals. This group of seasoned, full-time bluegrass professionals recorded the album *Bluegrass Holiday* on the Lemco label (later reissued on Rebel) before Red left the band in 1969.

Doyle Lawson briefly rejoined Jimmy Martin, then came back with J.D., this time on guitar, after Larry Rice moved from California to play mandolin and sing lead with the band. The Kentucky Mountain Boys became a headline act on the early summer bluegrass festivals, while maintaining nightly appearances at several different clubs in Lexington, Louisville, and southern Indiana.

When Lawson joined the Country Gentlemen in the late summer of 1971, Larry Rice's brother Tony came to the band on guitar. Retitled The New South, the band experimented with an electrified bluegrass/country/folk synthesis.

One of the most brilliant ensembles in the history of bluegrass music came together in late 1974, after Larry Rice left to tour with a Dickey Betts-led spinoff of the Allman Brothers. Ricky Skaggs moved over from the Country Gentlemen, adding a strong tenor voice to the trio, and the band quickly "unplugged." Now appearing five nights a week at the Lexington Sheraton Inn, the group perfected an acoustic sound and vocal trio renowned for its technical perfection, sparkle and originality. Jerry Douglas guested on Dobro for the legendary Rounder debut album *J.D. Crowe and the New South* (widely known as simply "0044") in January, 1975, then joined the band for that summer's festival season and an August tour of Japan. At the end of that tour, Tony Rice went to California to join the first iteration of the David Grisman Quartet. Skaggs and Douglas left to found Boone Creek.

J.D. continued to explore new musical ground with a succession of talented musicians. These included Jimmy Gaudreau, Harley Allen, Glenn Lawson, Gene Johnson, Steve Bryant, Paul Adkins, Wendy Miller, and Tony King. Bobby Slone was a constant, staying with the band through the mid-1980s. When Keith Whitley left Ralph Stanley and the Clinch Mountain Boys in 1978, he shared with J.D. his lifelong dream to perform country music. With Crowe's encouragement, Whitley prepared for his subsequent solo career as a featured vocalist on the New South's Rounder albums *My Home Ain't in the Hall of Fame* (1979) and *Somewhere Between* (1982). Both included steel, electric bass, and drums.

Beginning in 1981, J.D. Crowe balanced the progressive sounds of his own band with those of a recording (and occasionally performing) traditional bluegrass supergroup. The Bluegrass Album Band was conceived as a vehicle for introducing to new generations the classic repertoire, mostly out of print in the early CD era. Six best-selling albums were released (the last in 1996) featuring Crowe, Tony Rice, Doyle Lawson, Jerry Douglas, Bobby Hicks, Vassar Clements, Todd Phillips, and Mark Schatz.

After a hiatus from touring with the New South, J.D. was back in 1993 with yet another generation of New South members. *Lefty's Old Guitar* tied for Album of the Year in 2007. In his seventh decade as a professional musician, a living legend still at the top of his game, J.D. Crowe no longer carries a band on the road but makes occasional personal and recording appearances.

— FRED BARTENSTEIN

- Helped to revitalize the bluegrass genre with songs and styles adapted from rock, rhythm and blues, country, and folk music sources.
- Banjo player of the year in 1971, 1994, and 2004.
- Grammy winner for "Fireball," 1983.
- Bluegrass Hall of Fame, 2003.

"I'm not sure they realize how much it takes and what you have to sacrifice, the frustrations you go through. A lot of people won't do it, and in this day and time you can hardly afford to do it. But the groups that work for that 'band sound' will be the ones that are remembered."

- Quoted by Leon Smith in "Talking With the Stars: Two Interviews from a 'Bluegrass Hornbook,'" *Bluegrass Unlimited*, July 1981.

By the Way:
- Based for most of his more than half-century career in the city of his birth: Lexington, Kentucky.
- Initially aspired to be an electric guitarist with Ernest Tubb's Texas Troubadours.
- J.D.'s baritone voice blends so well with other singers that it adds strong notes without standing out.
- While starring with Jimmy Martin on the *Louisiana Hayride*, J.D. worked in a gas station to supplement his income.
- Crowe's rare vocal solos, never recorded, included occasional Little Richard covers on Sunny Mountain Boys concerts in the late 1950s.

John Ray "Curly" Sechler (Seckler) \ 2004

Curly Seckler embarked on a music career more than seventy-five years ago to escape the hard life of picking cotton on the family farm in China Grove, North Carolina. With a neighbor, Murray Belk, Curly and his brothers (Marvin "Slim," George, and Duard "Lucky") formed a band known as the Yodeling Rangers. The group secured a spot on radio station WSTP in Salisbury, North Carolina. The show was simulcast on several other stations, including WSJS in Winston-Salem and WPTF in Raleigh.

"...singing high ain't everything. It's harmony singing. Lester and I worked awful hard on that, and I don't believe there was a duo anywhere, in our style, that could hardly beat what we did."

– Quoted by Penny Parsons in "Curly Seckler: Bluegrass Pioneer," *Bluegrass Unlimited*, June 2004.

Curly's first big break came in 1939 when he came to the attention of Charlie Monroe. The Monroe Brothers, one of the most popular country music acts of the 1930s, had recently disbanded and the older Monroe was looking for someone to replace his younger brother. After much persuasion, Curly agreed to sign on as banjo player and tenor singer for Charlie Monroe's Kentucky Pardners. At the age of nineteen, Curly found himself with that band in West Virginia, appearing on WWVA and the *Wheeling Jamboree*. He received an unheard of (to him) salary of twenty dollars a week.

Curly next teamed up with Tommy Scott, another Charlie Monroe alumnus. The two worked as a duo under the sponsorship of Vim Herb Products. World War II put Curly's musical career on hold. Although he worked briefly with Leonard Stokes, in a duo known as the Melody

Born: December 25, 1919, China Grove, NC

Primary Instrument: Mandolin

Composed:
BMI's database credits John Ray Sechler with 43 published compositions, co-compositions, and arrangements, including:
"A Purple Heart"
"That Old Book of Mine"
"No Mother or Dad"

Early influences:
The Monroe Brothers with Byron Parker
The Morris Brothers
The Briarhoppers

Came to fame with:
Lester Flatt, Earl Scruggs and the Foggy Mountain Boys, 1949-1962

Performed with:
Yodeling Rangers, c. 1935-1939
Charlie Monroe and the Kentucky Pardners, 1939-1940, 1945-1946, 1948
Trail Riders, 1940-1941

Boys, Curly stayed put in Columbus, Ohio, working for the post office. Near the War's end, he found work in Nashville with the Bailey Brothers as a stand-in for Charlie Bailey, who had been drafted.

The late 1940s were busy years for Curly. In 1945, he rejoined Charlie Monroe in Winston-Salem, North Carolina, and moved with that band to Charlotte and then WNOX in Knoxville, Tennessee. During this stint, he recorded four songs with the group, including some of the Kentucky Pardners' best-known recordings: "Who's Calling You Sweetheart Tonight," "There's No Depression in Heaven," and "Mother's Not Dead, She's Only Sleeping." The following year, he teamed up with Mac Wiseman in Bristol, Virginia/Tennessee. When Mac left to join Flatt and Scruggs's new group in the spring of 1948, Curly worked briefly in Knoxville with his own band and then rejoined Charlie Monroe in Bristol. By year's end, he was in Augusta, Georgia, with a group that included Jim and Jesse McReynolds, Hoke Jenkins, and Wiley Morris.

Curly Seckler and Tommy Scott, 1941-1942

The Melody Boys (with Leonard Stokes), 1942

Danny Bailey and the Happy Valley Boys, 1945

Mac Wiseman, 1947

Smoky Mountaineers, 1948-1949

Lester Flatt, Earl Scruggs and the Foggy Mountain Boys, 1949-1951, 1952-1958, 1958-1962

The Sauceman Brothers, 1951

The Stanley Brothers and the Clinch Mountain Boys, 1951-1952

Jim and Jesse, 1952

Photo: Alan Whitman, courtesy of County Records, 1970

Bluegrass Hall of Fame Inductee Biographies

Carl Sauceman, 1958

Lester Flatt and the Nashville Grass, 1973-1979

Nashville Grass, 1979-1994

Occasional solo work, 1994-present

Led the way:

- One of the premier tenor singers in bluegrass, with an instantly recognizable style.

- A member of six integral bluegrass and country music groups: Charlie Monroe, Flatt and Scruggs, Sauceman Brothers, Stanley Brothers, Jim and Jesse, and the Nashville Grass.

- An integral part of the most popular bluegrass band of the 1950s, Flatt and Scruggs.

- Bluegrass Hall of Fame, 2004.

By the Way:

- Although known primarily for his singing and mandolin work, Curly started as a four-string banjo player. Curly likes to recall Lester Flatt's observation, "You're not the greatest mandolin player in the world, but I always liked the way you hold it."

- Known as "Smilin' Bill" while working with Charlie Monroe.

- During the busiest days of working on the road with Flatt and Scruggs, Curly would shave with water from a soda bottle.

- Exempted from military service during World War II because of bronchial asthma, but served briefly in the Army reserves.

The act billed itself as the Smoky Mountaineers. The next year, 1949, Curly joined up with Flatt and Scruggs, the group with which he would become most associated.

It wasn't long before Curly was in the recording studio with Flatt and Scruggs, making the first of what would amount to 138 recordings with that group. He appeared on 24 of the 28 sides the group recorded for Mercury Records, including classics such as "Roll in My Sweet Baby's Arms," "Old Salty Dog Blues," "Preachin', Prayin', Singin'," and "Foggy Mountain Breakdown," as well as one of his own compositions, "No Mother or Dad." When the group moved to Columbia in November of 1950, Curly was there for the debut session, with such memorable cuts as "Come Back Darling," "I'm Waiting to Hear You Call Me Darling," "The Old Home Town," and the Flatt-Seckler composition "We Can't Be Darlings Anymore."

In the early part of 1951, Curly left the Foggy Mountain Boys and joined the Sauceman Brothers in Bristol. He worked with them for eight or nine months and appeared on their *Farm and Fun Time* broadcasts. Although he never recorded with the group, he can be heard on a series of radio broadcasts released as *On WCYB Bristol*. By the end of the year, Curly was working with another WCYB band, the Stanley Brothers. He engineered that band's move to WVLK in Lexington, Kentucky. His stay with the Stanleys was rather brief and by the early part of 1952, he was working with Jim and Jesse, also in Lexington. One of Curly's most enduring compositions, the Korean War lament "A Purple Heart," was recorded with Jim and Jesse.

> *"We used to always open the show for Lester and he'd come walking out on stage after three or four numbers. You still expect to see Lester come strolling out."*
>
> - Quoted by Joe Edwards in "Flatt's Nashville Grass Carries On," *Associated Press*, January 28, 1980.

Curly rejoined Flatt and Scruggs in the late summer of 1952, moving with them from Raleigh, North Carolina, to Knoxville, and eventually to Nashville. The impetus for moving to Music City was the group's sponsorship by Martha White Mills. The flour company placed Flatt and Scruggs on powerful WSM for daily live early morning radio broadcasts. Eventually, these programs were pre-recorded, allowing the group to tour more extensively.

In 1954, Curly went with Flatt and Scruggs to Virginia once again. They appeared on WSVS in Crewe and were cast members of Richmond's *Old Dominion Barn Dance*. They started off 1955 back in Nashville, with a new television program that was also sponsored by Martha White.

With the exception of a brief time-out in 1958, when Curly performed with Carl Sauceman in Alabama, Curly appeared with one of the most celebrated versions of the Foggy Mountain Boys, which included Paul Warren on fiddle, Jake Tullock on bass, and Josh Graves on Dobro. When vocalist Hylo Brown was added to the mix in the early part of 1962, Curly made his final departure from the band. For the next decade, he contracted as an independent truck driver. He kept a hand in bluegrass, often times coordinating his trucking runs with newly flourishing bluegrass festivals where he appeared as a solo and/or master of ceremonies. Curly's part-time presence on the music scene led to his debut solo recording for County Records in 1971. Ably assisted by the ultra-traditional Shenandoah Cut-Ups, *Curly Seckler Sings Again* foreshadowed his full-time return to music.

In 1973, Curly was reunited with his old boss and singing partner, Lester Flatt. He stayed with Flatt's Nashville Grass for the next six years, picking up many of the performance duties as Lester's health began to deteriorate.

Following Flatt's passing in May of 1979, Curly assumed leadership of the band and continued to operate it for the next fifteen years. In 1981 Curly added Willis Spears, an excellent singer and rhythm guitarist. Very reminiscent of Flatt from his best days of the early 1950s, Spears's addition to the group allowed Curly to recreate a lot of musical magic from the past. Eventually, Spears was made a partner in the organization.

In 1994, Curly retired the Nashville Grass and gave up full-time touring. He has by no means been inactive since then. He has recorded three new albums (*60 Years of Bluegrass With My Friends*, *Down in Caroline*, and *Bluegrass Don't You Know*) and has seen his 1971 solo album reissued on CD, with several additional tracks. He has been the subject of two cover articles in *Bluegrass Unlimited* magazine, and is having his life story chronicled in a biography by noted journalist Penny Parsons. He was elected to the Bluegrass Hall of Fame in 2004 and to the North Carolina Music Hall of Fame in 2010. Despite significant health challenges, Seckler continues to bless audiences with his positive and genial personality and frequent stage appearances.

— GARY REID

"It was a solid group back then. With Scruggs in there with that different banjo style, they were solid as a rock. Lester Flatt could lead a song to water."

- Quoted by Randall Franks in "His Voice Soars Out Above the Pines," *The Catoosa County News*, July 28, 2004.

- Rejoined Lester Flatt in the Nashville Grass, and led the ensemble after Flatt's death.

"Leading the Nashville Grass was the best time of my career."

- Quoted by Randall Franks in "Sitting on Top of the World," *The Chattooga Press*, July 21, 2004.

Bill Vernon \ 2004

If anyone seemed an unlikely candidate for inclusion in the Bluegrass Hall of Fame, it would be Bill Vernon. Born and reared in Brooklyn, New York, he was the son of a "self-made" corporate tax attorney. His father very much wanted to see young William follow in his footsteps. To that end, as a young teen, he was shipped off to Kent School, an Episcopal prep/boarding school in Connecticut. The Vernons' plans began to unravel in 1951 when Bill, at age thirteen or fourteen, had a chance encounter on the radio with the music of Flatt and Scruggs, in the form of "We Can't Be Darlings Anymore."

Vernon later attended Chicago's Northwestern University and the Ivy League's Brown University in Providence, Rhode Island. He never graduated from either institution and actually flunked out of Brown. By 1959, he was married to first wife Mary T. Vernon (he often reflected that his first love of bluegrass music cost him three marriages), was employed as a margin clerk on Wall Street, and was living in Columbia Heights, overlooking the East River. But, more importantly, by this time he had developed a passion for collecting bluegrass music recordings, mostly on 78s but later in other formats as well. And he was enthusiastically sharing his passion with anyone who would listen. In those days, the New York City metro had a small but active and influential bluegrass community, including fellow Hall of Fame members

"With all the Ivy League education to which I've been exposed, the wisest, sagest people that I've run across have been people like Charlie Monroe, Lester Flatt and some of the old people."

- Quote by Brenda McDaniel in "Profiles - High on Bluegrass," *The Roanoker*, December 1981.

Born: July 4, 1937, New York, NY

Died: November 20, 1996, Rocky Mount, VA

Primary Involvement in Bluegrass Music:
Radio Personality and Writer

"When I feel the best, I want to hear bluegrass, and when I feel the worst, I have to hear bluegrass."

- Quoted by Brenda McDaniel in "Profiles – High on Bluegrass," *The Roanoker*, December 1981.

"That's part of why I flunked out of college: I was always working on radio!"

- Quoted by Penny Parsons in "Bluegrass with Bill Vernon," *Bluegrass Unlimited*, August, 1983.

Mentors:
Ray Davis
Fred Bartenstein
Carlton Haney
Jim Eanes

Photo: Alan Whitman

Associated with:
WBAI Radio, New York, NY, 1964-1972

WDHA Radio, Dover, NJ, 1969-1972

Muleskinner News magazine, 1970-1977

Rebel Records, 1972-1973

WYTI Radio, Rocky Mount, VA, 1973-1976, 1977-1996

WVWR/WVTF Radio, Roanoke, VA, 1975-1990

WNLB Radio, Rocky Mount, VA, 1976-1977

WTJU Radio, Charlottesville, VA, 1992-1996

Led the way:
- Wrote liner notes for approximately 100 bluegrass and old-time music albums and CDs.
- Set high standards of professionalism for broadcasting, writing, and emceeing within the bluegrass community.
- Served as a mentor to other broadcasters and presenters.

- Documented the careers of early bluegrass pioneers with informative and insightful articles for *Muleskinner News*.
- IBMA Award of Merit (Distinguished Achievement Award), 1988.
- Two-time recipient of IBMA award for Best Liner Notes, 1994 and 1998.
- Bluegrass Hall of Fame, 2004.

"I knew Bill from the many festivals, the late nights talking in the funniest ways possible about things I never heard anyone else in bluegrass mention, let alone know so eloquently. He was a first-rate intellect who always had great jokes to tell. I admired his mind... always coming away from a conversation with an acute sense of cortex envy."

Tim Stafford, post to *bgrass-l*, November 20, 1996.

By the Way:
- Worked as a margin clerk on Wall Street and compiler of country music charts for *Billboard* magazine before becoming a full-time radio personality. Both of these occupations required a quick mind and the capacity to manage massive amounts of detail.
- Loved the dobro (especially Josh Graves) and played a little.

David Freeman and Ralph Rinzler, as well as Tex Logan, Peter Wernick, Fred Bartenstein, Joe Wilson, Kathy Kaplan, and Doug Tuchman.

Bill Vernon's day job in New York lasted for twelve years, until 1970. It was never a career, but only a means to enable his bluegrass addiction. In 1962, Vernon began writing a music column for a British publication, *Country News and Views*. In 1964, he launched *Country Music*, a weekly radio program on New York City's WBAI-FM, playing primarily bluegrass. It was also during this time that Bill had a position at *Billboard* magazine, helping to compile their weekly charts of popular country music recordings. Thus by the middle 1960s, he was perfecting the two talents for which he would become best known: writing about and broadcasting bluegrass music.

1970 was a watershed year for Bill. He left Wall Street and found radio employment – part-time at first – in Dover, New Jersey, on WDHA. He also became the record review editor for *Muleskinner News*, one of the leading bluegrass publications of the early 1970s. He became the editor of *Muleskinner News* in 1976 and 1977. During this time, he began adding yet another dimension to his entertainment profession: master of ceremonies. Among his early engagements were Bill Monroe's festival at Bean Blossom, Indiana; Ralph Stanley's festival in McClure, Virginia; Carlton Haney's festivals in Berryville, Virginia, Camp Springs, North Carolina, Gettysburg, Pennsylvania, and Escoheag, Rhode Island; and the Berkshire Mountains festival in Ancramdale, New York.

In addition to doing reviews, Bill also wrote a number of articles for *Muleskinner News*. A number of these extensively documented the careers of bluegrass pioneers such as Don Reno, Lester Flatt, Tex Logan, and Curly Seckler. There were also articles on new acts just beginning to tour the bluegrass circuit, such as Cliff Waldron, Del McCoury, and the Seldom Scene. Bill Vernon was the co-recipient (with Gary Reid) in 1994 of the organization's first award for Best Liner Notes (*Don Reno and Red Smiley, The Early King Years 1951–1959*), and posthumous beneficiary of the 1998 award for Best Liner Notes (*Rebel 35th Anniversary Collection*).

In February of 1972, Bill sought to expand his experience in the music industry by relocating to the Washington, D.C. area and working for Dick Freeland's Rebel Records. He was hired as director of promotion and public relations.

In December of 1973, Bill made a move to the area that would be his home for the next 23 years, the small town of Rocky Mount (population 4,000) in southwestern Virginia. Bluegrass balladeer Jim Eanes made Bill aware of an opening at a local AM station, WYTI. The station, 20 miles south of Roanoke, afforded Bill the chance to play two hours of bluegrass daily, in addition to the country fare of the day, local news, and – much to his disdain – the reading of advertisements for regional grocery stores.

Although he was airing to a tiny audience with his radio work, Bill was establishing a national presence with his festival appearances, mail-order sales of collectible records, and writing of album liner notes. These were mostly for independent labels that specialized in bluegrass, but he landed a few assignments for some of the majors as well.

In October of 1975 Bill started a one-hour program of bluegrass that aired on Sunday evenings on Roanoke's public radio station, WVWR (later WVTF). The program was called *Bluegrass with Bill Vernon*. As the nature of the music continued to evolve, the name of the program was changed to *In and Around Bluegrass*. Eventually, the show was expanded to three hours. The program was cancelled – just short of its fifteenth anniversary – by a station manager who wanted to make the NPR station "more talk and less music," provoking considerable upset among the local listening audience and national bluegrass community.

He didn't just write and talk about the performers. He became their friend, confidante and, at times, supportive critic. He befriended and assisted Charlie Monroe and Lester Flatt in their latter years. When Jim Eanes's health began to fail, Bill moved in with him to become his caretaker. Beyond the compassion, there was Bill's comedic wit and his ability to launch immediately and endlessly into side-splitting tales – as only he could tell them – of his many encounters on the bluegrass trail. As someone once observed, only Bill Vernon could insert the phrase "Chernobylian" into a record review!

1996 was shaping up to be a good year for Bill. His beloved *In and Around Bluegrass* show – after a six year absence – was about to go back on the air on a different Roanoke radio station. He was working diligently on one of the most prestigious writing assignments of his career: the massive booklet for Rebel Records' four-CD boxed set, *35 Years of the Best in Bluegrass, 1960 - 1995* and notes for the long-awaited VHS reissue of the 1971 movie *Bluegrass: Country Soul* (that reissue attempt failed but Vernon can be seen in the 2006 Time/Life DVD release). In November, he served as a co-emcee for the gala fiftieth anniversary celebration for Ralph Stanley at the Country Music Hall of Fame in Nashville. Tragically, one week later, Bill Vernon was dead, the victim of an asthma-induced heart attack, at the age of fifty-nine.

Following Vernon's death, the International Bluegrass Music Museum negotiated purchase of Vernon's vast store of recordings and correspondence, where it is available to visitors and researchers as the Bill Vernon Collection. An extensive number of Bill Vernon's radio broadcasts are archived at the Blue Ridge Institute in Ferrum, Virginia.

– GARY REID

- Interviewed numerous artists on his *Bluegrass with Bill Vernon* program including Ricky Skaggs, Larry Sparks, the Country Gentlemen, Charlie Moore, Mike Auldridge, John Starling, J.D. Crowe, Curley Lambert, and Wilma Lee Cooper.

- Amassed a collection of 70,000 recordings, including 78s, 45s, LPs, and CDs. As a natural offshoot of his collecting, Vernon also sold bluegrass, country, and jazz recordings by auction, set sale, and at flea markets and record shows. With an almost photographic memory, Vernon could quote not only the artist, title, and release number of a record, but usually its master number.

- Was a pall bearer at the funeral of Charlie Monroe and an honorary pall bearer for Lester Flatt.

Harley "Red" Allen \ 2005

Born: February 12, 1930, Pigeon Roost, KY

Died: April 3, 1993, Dayton, OH

Primary Instrument:
Guitar

Composed:
BMI's database credits Red Allen with 24 published compositions, co-compositions, and arrangements, including:

"It Hurts to Know"

"Keep On Going"

"Troubles Around My Door"

Early influences:
The Monroe Brothers

Bill Monroe, with Lester Flatt and Earl Scruggs

Lester Flatt and Earl Scruggs, with Curly Seckler

Came to fame with:
The Osborne Brothers and Red Allen, 1956-1958

Performed with:
Blue Mountain Boys (with Frank Wakefield and Noah Crase), 1952-1954

Eastern Kentucky native Harley "Red" Allen learned of country music, as did countless other Depression era youth, by listening to the *Grand Ole Opry* on a battery powered radio. Other jamboree type programs, such as Knoxville's *Mid-Day Merry-Go-Round* with Mother Maybelle and the Carter Sisters and Charlie Monroe, also informed his early musical development.

Red got his first guitar at age seventeen, when he was hearing Bill Monroe, with Lester Flatt and Earl Scruggs, on the *Opry*. By the latter part of 1951, he had progressed to the point that he was appearing on the *Kentucky Barn Dance* in Lexington as a guest with established artists such as the Stanley Brothers, Flatt and Scruggs, and Jim and Jesse.

In 1952, Red relocated to Dayton, Ohio, and formed a trio with Frank Wakefield on mandolin and Noah Crase on banjo. This group, the Blue Mountain Boys, appeared at various bars in the area, working four nights a week for eight dollars apiece. Red made his first recordings for the Kentucky label, in Cincinnati. These were mostly covers of recently popular gospel songs such as "The White Dove" and "The Boat of Love." Also included was his rendering of "Paul and Silas," a spiritual that was later recorded by Carl Story, the Stanley Brothers, and Flatt and Scruggs.

When Noah Crase left the band to play with Bill Monroe in 1954, one of his replacements was a sixteen-year-old Sonny Osborne. Due to his

"We'd work four nights a week, eight dollars a night for each man, and some places it would be so rough you would have a couple or three shootings or cuttings a night."

— Quoted by Tom Teepen in "Allen Grass: A Family Affair," *Muleskinner News*, February 1973.

Photo: Carl Fleischhauer

age, Sonny wasn't able to play in the bars, but he did help out with radio shows and some show dates. His stay was brief, but it foreshadowed one of the most important phases of Red's career, his later pairing with Bob and Sonny Osborne. Less than two years later, the three were playing together – along with fiddler Art Stamper – at a Dayton nightspot called the Friendly Inn.

In 1956, the group signed a recording contract with MGM as the Osborne Brothers and Red Allen. Over the next two years, they recorded sixteen songs for the label. Bob Artis, in his book *Bluegrass*, noted of Red's singing at this time: "Red had more power and range to his voice than anyone, and his trios with the Osborne Brothers were some of the best ever… Almost overnight the Osborne Brothers and Red Allen shifted the bluegrass vocal emphasis from the duet to the trio." Several of the later MGM selections featured an innovative trio style that sported Bobby's high lead vocals, with Sonny's baritone directly under it. Red supplied

The Osborne Brothers and Red Allen, 1956-1958

Red Allen and the Kentuckians, 1959 (with Frank Wakefield -1964) -1967

Lester Flatt, Earl Scruggs and the Foggy Mountain Boys, 1967

Red Allen (solo), 1967, 1973-1993

The Kentucky Mountain Boys, 1968

Red Allen and the Allen Brothers, 1971-1973

Left to right: John Hickman, Red Allen, Sid Campbell, Columbus, OH, 1968.

Bluegrass Hall of Fame Inductee Biographies \ 137

Led the way:

- Popularized innovative high-lead vocal harmony arrangements with the Osborne Brothers.
- One of the premier bluegrass vocalists of the 1950s and 1960s, with a unique style influenced by the blues.
- Made classic recordings for for MGM, Rebel, County, Melodeon, and Folkways.
- Bluegrass Hall of Fame, 2005.

"I can't play and sing with any person I don't like, I don't care how good they are. I've got to like a man first. Being a good man is as important as being a good picker and singer."

- Quoted by Marty Godbey in "A Conversation with Red Allen," *Bluegrass Unlimited*, June 1979.

By the Way:

- Walked eight miles, at age nine or ten, to see his first live country music show, featuring Charlie Monroe and the Kentucky Pardners.
- Got his start as a performer in 1951 on the *Kentucky Barn Dance* in Lexington, Kentucky.
- Appeared at Carnegie Hall on September 21, 1963.
- Had planned to record an album of trio arrangements with the Louvin Brothers.
- Sang lead and played guitar with the Flatt and Scruggs show in 1967 when Lester Flatt was recovering from a heart attack.

an even lower harmony part. The recordings led to the group's joining the *WWVA Jamboree* in Wheeling, West Virginia. Their broadcasts did much to popularize the group throughout the Northeast and inspired a host of young players, most notably the fledgling Country Gentlemen.

Red parted with the Osborne Brothers in the middle of 1958. The next year and a half was a period of relative musical inactivity. In 1959, Red and his first wife divorced and not long afterwards he relocated to the Washington, D.C. area. In 1960, he teamed again with Frank Wakefield and formed the Kentuckians. Performance highlights during this era included regular appearances on the *WWVA Jamboree* and a September 21, 1963, show at Carnegie Hall.

Red recorded some of the best music of his career in the early and middle 1960s, during his years in Washington. A six-song session for Starday, in November of 1962, featured him and Frank Wakefield with Don Reno

"Allen was about to embark on an astonishing four-year burst of creativity and recording activity that would forever anchor his reputation as one of the most intense, hard-edged and soulful lead singers in the annals of bluegrass."

- Jon Hartley Fox, in liner notes to *Red Allen: Keep on Going, The Rebel and Melodeon Recordings*, Rebel Records, 2004.

on banjo, Chubby Wise on fiddle, and Tommy Hill on bass. There were several sessions for Rebel, one of which included a memorable arrangement of "Little Birdie." Another contained classics such as a cover of Bill Monroe's "Close By" and "Keep On Going," with some fiery fiddle by Scotty Stoneman.

In addition to the singles, four albums were released during this period. The first, on Folkways, was the excellent Allen-Wakefield collection called simply *Bluegrass*. Recorded in the fall of 1963 and spring of 1964, it included banjoists Bill Keith and Pete Kuykendall and bass players Tom Morgan and Fred Weisz. By January of 1965, Frank Wakefield had moved on to the Greenbriar Boys, and a new group, consisting of banjoist Bill Emerson, mandolin player Wayne Yates, and bass player Bill Yates, recorded an album with Red for Dick Spottswood's Melodeon label. The album was titled, much to Allen's chagrin (his name was absent from the album title), *The Solid Bluegrass Sounds of the Kentuckians*. In December of 1965 and September of 1966, two albums were recorded for the County label, *Bluegrass Country* and *Red Allen and the Kentuckians*. Both were produced by up-and-coming New York City mandolin player David Grisman. Personnel for the two sessions included Porter Church on banjo, Richard Greene on fiddle, Wayne Yates and David Grisman on mandolin, Bill Yates and Jerry McCoury on bass, and Craig Wingfield on dobro.

Not only was Red Allen a consummate bluegrass vocalist, he was an engaging master of ceremonies who kept his performances lively and entertaining. Fred Bartenstein noted, "Red's legendary sense of humor and tendency to say the most outrageous things onstage and on the air caused not a few broadcasters to ride the 'bleep button' when Red was at the mic!"

Red ended his tenure in the Washington area and moved to Nashville in 1967 to substitute for Lester Flatt, who was convalescing from a heart attack. When Lester returned, Red went on to work as a solo, appearing on various bluegrass festivals. His last significant work of the 1960s was a stint in 1968 with J.D. Crowe, Doyle Lawson, and Bobby Slone as the Kentucky Mountain Boys at the Holiday Inn in Lexington, Kentucky. They recorded one album together, *Bluegrass Holiday*, for Lemco, later reissued by Rebel under J.D. Crowe's name.

In the early 1970s, Red began working with his sons – Neal, Ronnie, Greg, and Harley – in a combination that was labeled Allen Grass. An album under that title was recorded for the Lemco label. Several additional LPs were done under Red's name, over a two-year period, for King Bluegrass. With this group, Red renewed his association with the *WWVA Jamboree*. Working with his sons – long hair and all – pushed him in new directions, and bluegrass classics gave way to more contemporary fare such as Creedence Clearwater Revival's "Proud Mary." This era of Red's career was cut short by Neal's untimely passing in 1973 from pneumonia. This tragedy, coupled with Red's open heart surgery in 1976, greatly curtailed his musical activities.

Red continued to make occasional recordings, mostly for the Folkways label. One noteworthy release from this era was the Grammy-nominated *Bluegrass Reunion*, featuring Red, Jim Buchanan, Herb Pedersen, Jerry Garcia and others on David Grisman's ACD label. Aside from recording, he spent his last few years out of the entertainment spotlight except for occasional appearances at clubs in Dayton. A heart condition that he had since a child was taking its toll.

It was complications from lung cancer that forever silenced one of the greatest voices in bluegrass in 1993. Despite the length of his service and his immeasurable talent, Red Allen has never achieved the acclaim of other pioneering pickers and singers. Happily, much of his best recorded work has been reissued in recent years in a series of meticulously produced CDs, affording old fans and new converts alike a chance to enjoy and appreciate his artistry.

— GARY REID

- Worked as a bluegrass DJ on WDXL-FM in Dayton, Ohio, 1979.
- Red's late son Harley was a successful songwriter in Nashville with over 350 songs to his credit.

"My whole world changed when I lost my son, when Neal went away. That changed my whole outlook on life, and all of a sudden, music... You miss your kids when you're out on the road. You just don't live a normal life. But when we lost Neal, there was other things more important to me than picking, singing, and making a dollar."

- Quoted by Glenna H. Fisher in "Red Allen: Bluegrass From the Man Who's Been There," *Bluegrass Unlimited*, January 1984

Benjamin Edward "Benny" Martin | 2005

Benny Martin was born in Sparta, Tennessee, the hometown of legendary bluegrass singer Lester Flatt. He came from a musical family and received a fiddle at age six or seven. Several early teachers/mentors included local fiddlers Carl Orvison and Louis Armstrong (an African-American, not the famous trumpeter). By 1936, he was performing in the family's band, the Martin Family, on radio station WHUB in Cookeville, Tennessee, and making Saturday evening appearances at the *Upper Cumberland Jamboree*.

"I always liked the sound of a fiddle. I would lie down at night and I could visualize myself really playing that fiddle."

- Quoted by Earl V. Spielman, in liner notes to *Benny Martin, The Fiddle Collection*, CMH Records, 1976.

In the early 1940s, Martin would hitchhike to Knoxville to be near the radio powerhouse WNOX, home to notable artists such as Molly O'Day, Chet Atkins, Charlie Monroe, Jethro Burns, and Bill Carlisle. While there, he was employed by gospel singer Wally Fowler. A year or so later, Jeff Bess took Benny to Nashville to appear with Big Jeff and the Radio Playboys on WLAC.

While in Nashville, he worked with several *Grand Ole Opry* acts, including Robert Lunn, Curly Fox, and the blackface comedy duo of Jam Up and Honey, with whom he made his first *Opry* appearance in 1946. In 1946 Benny released his first record, on the Pioneer label: "Me and My Fiddle," backed with "So Blue to Cry."

The *Opry* continued to be an important connection for Martin. In 1947, he performed and recorded with Red Foley. Later in the year he joined Bill Monroe and the Blue Grass Boys (which included Lester

Born: May 8, 1928, Sparta, TN

Died: March 13, 2001, Nashville, TN

Primary Instrument: Fiddle

Composed:
BMI's database credits Benny E. Martin with 134 published compositions, co-compositions, and arrangements, including:
"Me and My Fiddle"
"Ice Cold Love"
"Two O'Clock"

"When Benny Martin is right there is no one better for driving bluegrass fiddle or delicate backup work."

- Frank J. Godbey, record review, *Bluegrass Unlimited*, February 1980.

Early influences:
Jimmie Rodgers
The Carter Family
Clayton McMichen

Photo: Nobuharu Komoriya, 1976

Came to fame with:

Lester Flatt, Earl Scruggs and the Foggy Mountain Boys, 1952-1954

Performed with:

Wally Fowler and the Oak Ridge Boys, 1944-1945

Big Jeff and the Radio Playboys, 1945-1946

Bill Monroe and the Blue Grass Boys, 1947-1948

Roy Acuff and the Smoky Mountain Boys, 1949-1951

Lester Flatt, Earl Scruggs and the Foggy Mountain Boys, 1952-1954

Johnnie and Jack and the Tennessee Mountain Boys, 1954-1955

Solo artist and with the Benny Martin Band, 1955-2000

Don Reno, Benny Martin and the Tennessee Cut-Ups, 1965

Pat Boone, 1973-1974

Lester Flatt and the Nashville Grass, 1977

Led the way:

- Recognized as one of the premier fiddlers from the golden age of bluegrass and country music, with a flamboyant and dynamic approach that captivated audiences.

- Performed and/or recorded with a number of seminal first-generation bands including Bill Monroe, Flatt and Scruggs, the Stanley Brothers, and Don Reno, as well as country legend Roy Acuff, and the duo of Johnnie and Jack.

- Invented the eight-string fiddle.

Flatt, Earl Scruggs and Cedric Rainwater). He stayed with Monroe into 1948 and was part of Monroe's next classic group, with Don Reno and Jackie Phelps.

Benny's next move was to Roy Acuff and the Smoky Mountain Boys where he recorded for Columbia. While working for Acuff, in February of 1951, Martin signed with MGM as a solo artist. Two discs were released on that label.

By the middle of 1952, Benny was reunited with Lester Flatt and Earl Scruggs as fiddler and bass singer with the Foggy Mountain Boys, while they were working at WNOX in Knoxville. He recorded two sets of sessions with that group in 1952 and 1953, including "Why Did

Bluegrass Hall of Fame Inductee Biographies \ **141**

- Enjoyed a successful solo career in country music and recorded for a variety of labels including MGM, Mercury, RCA, Decca, Starday, and CMH. "Rosebuds and You" (1963) and "Soldier's Prayer in Viet Nam" (1966, with Don Reno) made the country music charts.
- An accomplished songwriter who had his songs recorded by Kitty Wells, Roy Acuff, and others.
- International Bluegrass Music Association Distinguished Achievement Award, 1997.
- Bluegrass Hall of Fame, 2005.

"In Knoxville, I slept in cars or the bus station; basically anywhere I could find. I was just a kid, and I was scared to death, but also happy to be playing music and on my own."

- Benny Martin, in liner notes to *The "Big Tiger" Roars Again, Part 1*, OMS Records, 1999.

By the Way:
- Friends since childhood with bluegrass legend Lester Flatt, also from Sparta.
- Skipped school to play fiddle but was usually located by the local truant officer who followed the sound of his music.
- Hitchhiked to Knoxville, Tennessee, as a young teen to appear on WNOX's *Mid-Day Merry-Go-Round*.
- Nicknamed "Big Tiger" by Hank Williams.

You Wander," "Flint Hill Special," "If I Should Wander Back," "Dim Lights, Thick Smoke," "Dear Old Dixie," "Reunion in Heaven," "I'll Go Stepping Too," "I'd Rather Be Alone," "Foggy Mountain Chimes," "Someone Took My Place," and "Your Love is Like a Flower."

It was Benny's playing on the Flatt and Scruggs recordings that endeared him to generations of bluegrass fans. His playing was loud and aggressive, favoring double stops (multiple notes). John Hartford observed that Benny put "as much emotion as I have ever heard any one human being put into music... His bow licks, timing and syncopations are the key to what he's doing... His accenting and slides are very important, his way of pushing the beat ever so slightly for energy." ("Benny Martin: The Genius of Music City, USA," *Fiddler Magazine*, Fall 1999)

Benny was always very candid about his struggles with alcohol, and readily admitted that this was the reason for his termination with the group. He went next to the duo of Johnnie and Jack. In essence, the two groups traded fiddlers – Benny Martin for Paul Warren. From February of 1954 through July of 1955, Benny recorded seven sessions and seventeen songs with Johnnie and Jack, among them "Goodnight, Sweetheart, Goodnight," "Sincerely," "Carry On," and "Look Out." As Johnnie Wright was married to Kitty Wells, Benny recorded two sessions with her on Decca including her hit, "Makin' Believe."

While working for Johnnie and Jack, Benny signed a two-year recording contract with Mercury Records. Twenty-one songs were released on that label. He played guitar and sang on all the selections (except for a remake of "Me and My Fiddle") leaving the fiddle chores to Nashville session players Dale Potter, Grover "Shorty" Lavender or Howdy Forrester.

Benny embarked on a solo career after leaving Johnnie and Jack, signing a management agreement first with Hal Smith and then Col. Tom Parker, the promoter who oversaw Elvis Presley's early rise to fame. Benny appeared as an opening act for Elvis on about fifty show dates in 1955 and early 1956. During that period Benny became a member of the *Grand Ole Opry* and appeared on a number of *Opry* package tours.

In 1957, Benny switched from Mercury to RCA and recorded several singles which failed to attract much attention. He continued with touring and did a considerable amount of Nashville session work. In November of that year he and Howdy Forrester played twin fiddles on a Stanley Brothers session for Mercury, including the classic instrumental "Daybreak in Dixie."

Benny signed with Starday in 1960 and recorded about forty songs and tunes for that label and its budget subsidiary, Nashville. In addition to one album – *Country Music's Sensational Entertainer* – his tracks were included on at least thirty various artists' compilations.

By 1965 Benny Martin, done with touring in *Opry* package shows, returned to his bluegrass roots, teaming up with Don Reno for a short-lived duo. They reunited while appearing separately at the first multi-day bluegrass festival, on Labor Day weekend in 1965, later recording a pair of singles for Monument and an album of gospel songs for the Cabin Creek label.

For the next three-and-a-half decades Benny didn't tour much and admitted that his drinking and no-show reputation hurt him professionally. He recorded bluegrass albums with Earl Taylor, the Barrier Brothers, the Osborne Brothers, and Porter Wagoner, and toured briefly with Lester Flatt in 1977, filling in for Paul Warren. With the help of Alcoholics Anonymous, he finally got his drinking under control and cited November 14, 1978, as the day he took his last drink.

When John Hartford moved back to Nashville in the 1970s he befriended his childhood idol. John was a major patron for Benny in the last decades of his life, arranging and producing recording sessions for him and promoting his legacy and prodigious talents, within a community and industry that looked upon Martin as a has-been.

The 1970s were witness to a number of fine recordings. In contrast to his solo vocals of the 1950s, Martin's new efforts saw his return to the fiddle. One of the first and best was a 1975 collection on Flying Fish called *Tennessee Jubilee*, with guest artists including Lester Flatt, John Hartford, and Curly Seckler. A series of albums and double-album sets followed on the CMH label, and one additional release for Flying Fish.

In 1980, Benny was diagnosed with spasmodic dysphonia, a voice disorder characterized by involuntary movements of speech muscles and gradual paralysis of the larynx. The condition likely accounts for the dearth of new recordings from 1980 until 1999. When the disorder spread to his eyes, he wore a bandana tied tightly around his head to hold his eyelids open.

Benny ended his recording career with a pair of CDs issued in 1999 and 2001. Titled *The "Big Tiger" Roars Again, Parts 1 and 2*, these discs were star-studded events that recalled several of his musical triumphs of the past and paired them with new material. Benny won an IBMA award for Best Liner Notes for *Part 1*.

Benny died in 2001 of congestive heart failure. He was inducted posthumously into the Bluegrass Hall of Fame in 2005. Today Benny Martin's legacy is well established among generations of bluegrass fiddlers who cite him as an influence, including, notably, Michael Cleveland and Jason Carter.

— GARY REID

- Appeared as an opening act for Elvis Presley on fifty show dates in 1955 and 1956.
- Successfully sued Dolly Parton for plagiarizing the melody of his signature song "Me and My Fiddle" in her 1980 hit "Nine to Five."

"I first heard Benny Martin with Lester Flatt and Earl Scruggs in the early fifties and his playing opened up a whole new world to me of how the fiddle should go… [He] played these lush beautiful chords and slides that just hugged and danced and got up all around me and before the music was over I was bouncing off the walls."

- John Hartford, "Benny Martin: The Genius of Music City, USA," *Fiddler Magazine*, Fall 1999.

The Lewis Family | 2006

James Roy "Pop" Lewis
Born: September 22, 1905, Pickens, SC
Died: March 23, 2004, Washington, GA
Primary instrument: Bass

Blanche Pauline "Mom" Lewis
Born: June 20, 1910, Washington, GA
Died: February 8, 2003, Washington, GA
Primary involvement: Tour support

Nannie Omega "Miggie" Lewis
Born: May 22, 1926, Augusta, GA
Primary involvement: Vocalist

James Wallace Lewis
Born: July 6, 1928, Lincolnton, GA
Died: May 16, 2007, Washington, GA
Primary instrument: Guitar

Talmadge Lewis
Born: December 31, 1934, Lincolnton, GA

The Lewis Family – known to their many fans as "The First Family of Bluegrass Gospel" – hailed from Lincolnton, a small community of 1,500 residents on the northeast edge of the state of Georgia, not far from South Carolina. Named for Revolutionary War general Benjamin Lincoln, the town did much to infuse the group's show with a genuine country charm as well as the members' thick Southern accents.

In its classic configuration, the band consisted of family patriarch Roy "Pop" Lewis on bass and his children: Wallace on guitar, Talmadge on fiddle and mandolin, Roy M. "Little Roy" on banjo, and daughters Miggie, Polly, and Janis on vocals.

> *"Bill [Monroe] is one of the main reasons why our gospel music has a bluegrass sound. I've said several times that if we're on the wrong road with bluegrass gospel then Bill is responsible for it."*
>
> – Pop Lewis, quoted in liner notes to Bill Monroe's *Road of Life*, MCA Records, 1974.

The group got its start in 1947 as the Lewis Brothers and featured yet another brother, Esley, on bass. This ensemble played country music and fiddle tunes at square dances. When the rest of the family came on board in 1951, they switched to all gospel music and remained that way throughout their career.

The Lewis Family made its first recordings in 1953. A session was held in the studio of radio station WJAT in Swainsboro, Georgia, and the songs' intended destination was the Bibletone label. That label ceased operation before the records could be released, and they found a new home with Sullivan Records of Greenwood, South Carolina. Two 78 rpm discs were released in 1954: "He's the Only One," backed with "Lights in the Valley" and "Did You Do What the Lord Said To Do?," backed with "Wait a Little Longer, Please Jesus."

The label's owner, Hoyt Sullivan, figured prominently in the next phase of the group's career. In April of 1954, he was the initial sponsor of the Lewis Family's television show, on station WJBF in Augusta, Georgia. The program aired live every Sunday from noon until 1:00 pm and continued, with different sponsors, for the next thirty-eight years.

The group released three additional singles on Hollywood, a subsidiary of King Records, before landing at Starday in 1958. Initially, the Starday material appeared as a series of extended play 45 rpm discs, with two songs on each side of the records. Those singles were grouped together to form their first album, *Singing Time Down South*. From 1960 to 1969, the Lewis Family released thirteen albums on Starday, including a banjo album by Little Roy and a release that joined them with another popular Starday gospel artist, Carl Story. Several notable songs included included Pop Lewis's perennial favorite, "Just One Rose Will Do," and "The Gospel Ship."

"Flatt and Scruggs played Augusta the night Hank Williams died. That was the first time I saw them in person. We used to go sit in our car under a chinaberry tree everyday at 1:00 p.m. to listen to them over the car radio when they had a program in Raleigh, North Carolina."

- Little Roy Lewis, quoted by Don Rhodes, from "On The Hallelujah Turnpike With the Lewis Family," *Bluegrass Unlimited*, June 1980.

As their popularity increased, the Lewis Family performed farther away from their Georgia base of operations. Typical venues included high school auditoriums, civic centers, fairs, and churches. To accommodate their travel needs, they purchased a 1948 GM Silverside bus, making them one of the first bluegrass bands to use this mode of transportation.

It was also during this time, in the early 1960s, that the various family members quit their day jobs to devote themselves full-time to music. Things intensified in 1963-1964 when their television show, which had been done live, began to be videotaped and syndicated to approximately twenty-five different markets.

By the time they played their first bluegrass festival – in 1969 at Hugo, Oklahoma – the Lewis Family had perfected their stage show. Working within the confines of gospel music, they presented an entertaining and well-paced program. There were instrumentals featuring Little Roy's hard-driving banjo, trio selections featuring the three sisters, spirituals, popular gospel songs of the day, originals, and a healthy dose of comedy by Little Roy… usually at the expense of other family members. Keeping

Primary instrument:
Fiddle

Polly Lewis Williamson Copsey
Born: January 23, 1937, Lincolnton, GA
Primary instrument:
Piano

Janis Lewis Phillips
Born: February 13, 1939, Lincolnton, GA
Primary involvement:
Vocalist

Roy M. "Little Roy" Lewis
Born: February 24, 1942, Lincolnton, GA
Primary instrument:
Banjo

Travis Lewis
Born: December 26, 1958, Greenwood, SC
Primary instrument:
Bass

Lewis Phillips
Born: April 5, 1972, Washington, GA
Primary instrument:
Banjo

Composed:
BMI's database credits Wallace and Polly with 84 published compositions, co-compositions, and arrangements, including:
"A Beautiful City"
"I'm Not Alone"
"Joshua"
"Just One Rose"
"Nearer Home"

Early influences:
Masters Family
Johnson Family
Chuck Wagon Gang
Bill Monroe
Lester Flatt, Earl Scruggs and the Foggy Mountain Boys
The Stanley Brothers

Left to right: Pop, Miggie, Janis, Polly, Litle Roy, Talmadge, Wallace. McClure, VA, 1972.

Came to fame with:
The Lewis Family, 1951-2009

Performed with:
The Lewis Family, 1951-2009

Led the way:
- One of the first family bands devoted exclusively to bluegrass gospel music.
- One of the first bluegrass bands to utilize television on a regular basis; their program was syndicated to twenty-five markets.
- One of the first bluegrass bands to effectively market merchandise to fans at personal appearances.
- One of the first bluegrass bands to utilize custom bus coaches to travel to performances.
- Released more than 80 LPs, CDs, videos, and DVDs.
- Georgia Music Hall of Fame, 1992.
- IBMA Distinguished Achievement Award, 1992.
- Bluegrass Hall of Fame, 2006.

By the Way:
- At age eight in 1950, "Little Roy" Lewis won a banjo contest at the Lincolnton, GA, High School. At a slightly older age, he recalls walking to the highway to watch Flatt and Scruggs's bus go by on the way to weekly television tapings.
- "Mom" and "Pop" Lewis were married for 77 years.

the program on an even keel was the genial MC work of Pop and Polly. The group was visually striking on stage, the men in matching suits and the women in matching dresses, many hand-sewn by Mom Lewis.

Immediately noticeable was the group's savvy salesmanship. Unlike most bands of the time, which might have sold two or three albums from a folding card table, the Lewis Family came prepared for business. They displayed an array of merchandise (albums, songbooks, photos, etc.) on custom-made racks. Their sales area was usually mobbed as soon as the group finished their sets on stage. It's a safe bet that the group grossed as much from merchandise sales as they did from performance fees.

In 1970, the Lewis Family moved from Starday to Canaan Records of Waco, Texas, then a leading independent gospel label. Over a fourteen-year period, they released a total of twenty-three albums – roughly one every seven months! The group must have been selling a lot of product to justify such a frenetic schedule of releases. Memorable songs from this era included "Honey in the Rock," "Joshua," "Slippers With Wings," "Baptism of Jesse Taylor," "Me and Jesus," "I'm Just an Old Chunk of Coal," and "Hallelujah Turnpike."

As children in the family's next generation began to come of age, they too joined

> *"What's amazing to me is that younger people come up to us and they can't believe we worked with people like Lester Flatt and Earl Scruggs, Carter and Ralph Stanley, and Albert Brumley."*
>
> – Little Roy Lewis, quoted by Lance LeRoy in the Lewis Family's history/picture book, *45 Years on the Stages of America – A Retrospective*, 1996.

the performing ensemble. These included Wallace's son Travis on bass, and Janis's son Lewis Phillips on banjo and lead guitar. Travis, who performed double duty as the bus driver, was voted Best Bluegrass Bass Player for five years in a row by the Society for the Preservation of Bluegrass Music in America (SPBGMA). Lewis Phillips made his recording debut at age five in 1977, on *Lester Flatt's Bluegrass Festival*, CMH Records. The following year, he appeared with Dolly Parton and Carol Burnett on their Nashville television special *Dolly and Carol*. He has one solo CD, *Empty Fields*, and has received two Gospel Music Association Dove awards. Polly's daughter Sherri and her husband Jeff Easter also performed briefly with the group before launching their own highly successful duo act.

In recent years, the Lewis Family recorded for the Riversong and Daywind labels. Since 1999 the group's recordings have won eleven Dove awards for Best Bluegrass Song or Best Bluegrass Album. Other awards and honors have included the Lewis Family's induction into the Georgia Music Hall of Fame in 1992, Pop Lewis's induction into the Southern

"I don't care where we go. Home looks good to me when we drive into Lincolnton."

– Mom Lewis, quoted by Don Rhodes, from "On The Hallelujah Turnpike With the Lewis Family," *Bluegrass Unlimited*, June 1980.

Gospel Music Hall of Fame in 2000, a Lifetime Achievement Award in 2003 from the digital magazine *SGN Scoops*, the family's induction into the Gospel Music Association's Hall of Fame in 2005, four awards from SPBGMA, and two IBMA awards: a Distinguished Achievement Award in 2002 and induction into the Bluegrass Hall of Fame in 2006.

The Lewis Family disbanded in 2009 after original members passed on (Mom Lewis in 2003, Pop in 2004, and Wallace Lewis in 2007) or retired due to illness (Polly was diagnosed with Parkinson's disease in 2005). Several offshoots quickly developed to keep the legacy alive. Little Roy and Lizzy Long have formed a duo known as the Little Roy and Lizzy Show. The Lewis Tradition features three former members of the Lewis Family: Janis and her son Lewis, Wallace's son Travis, as well as Travis's son, Jameson.

– GARY REID

- Had a weekly television show on WJBF in Augusta, GA for 38 years that was syndicated in later years. Among their fans in the Memphis market was Elvis Presley.
- Due to the long-running popularity of "Pop" Lewis's signature song, "Just One Rose Will Do," he received 100 red roses on his 89th birthday in 1994 from the "Godfather of Soul," James Brown.
- One of the Lewis Family's touring busses once belonged to country music star Conway Twitty.
- A portion of Georgia Highway 378 in Lincoln County was dedicated in memory of "Pop" Lewis.

Sydney "Syd" Nathan | 2006

Syd Nathan, recognized as one of the true innovators in the independent record business, led King Records for twenty-five years. He scored successes with hillbilly artists such as the Delmore Brothers, Cowboy Copas, and Grandpa Jones, and also with a host of rhythm and blues performers. His greatest claim to fame was his association with James Brown, including the groundbreaking album *Live at the Apollo* (1963). To bluegrass fans, Nathan is best known for recording such seminal acts as Reno and Smiley, the Stanley Brothers, Charlie Moore and Bill Napier, and Jimmy Martin and Bob Osborne.

Nathan was born in Cincinnati, Ohio, in 1904. From birth, he had problems with asthma and poor eyesight, problems that would plague him throughout his life. Music was an important part of his childhood and he learned to play both drums and piano. His poor eyesight hampered his ability to keep pace with fellow students and he dropped out of high school after the ninth grade.

Over the next fifteen years, Nathan held a variety of jobs that included working in a pawn shop, jewelry sales, operating a park concession, managing a shooting gallery, bucking rivets, bussing tables at a men's club, and promoting wrestling matches. His early entrepreneurial enterprises included a photo finishing lab and – most important to his future – a Cincinnati record shop. Nathan was quick to notice two distinct sets of record buyers: rural whites in search of hillbilly recordings and

"Syd was gruff, crude, an eccentric and a true pioneer. He will never be given the credit he deserves."
– Shad O'Shay, a former DJ and friend of Nathan's, quoted by Greg Evans in "The Cincinnati Sound," *Cincinnati* magazine, June 1986.

Born: April 27, 1904, Cincinnati, OH

Died: March 5, 1968, Miami, FL

Primary Involvement in Bluegrass Music:
Record Label Owner

Mentors:
Max Frank
Earl Herzog

Associated with:
King Records, 1943-1968
Queen Records, 1945-1947
Federal Records, 1950-early 1960s
Deluxe Records, 1947-1968
Lois Publishing, c. 1945-1968
Royal Plastics, 1945-1968

Led the way:
- Launched one of the first and largest independent record labels in the United States.
- Ran a racially integrated company before it was ever mandated by law.

Photo: courtesy of Brian Powers

African-Americans who came to buy "race records," as they were called at the time. These two segments were the primary targets of Nathan's marketing strategies for the remainder of his career.

Syd Nathan's record shop opened in the middle of World War II and was quickly followed by King Records. He hired country music talent that was popular on local radio stations and, in November of 1943, issued his first releases. In August of 1944, he incorporated the business, raised $25,000 in capital, and purchased a building at 1540 Brewster Avenue in Cincinnati – King's home for the next 25 years.

- Produced recordings for significant early bluegrass acts (Reno and Smiley, Stanley Brothers, Moore and Napier).
- Managed one of the few recording companies to make a record from start to finish, all under one roof.
- Unlike other labels, that tended to be genre-

specific, King Records covered a variety of styles including country, blues, R&B, black gospel, bluegrass, and more.

- Rock and Roll Hall of Fame, 1997.
- Bluegrass Hall of Fame, 2006.

"The Stanley Brothers have done really well for us and, who knows, you might do better."

- Quote by Syd Nathan, as told by Ralph Stanley in Ralph Rinzler, "Ralph Stanley: Tradition From the Mountains," *Bluegrass Unlimited*, March 1974.

By the Way:

- Wore glasses that were as thick as the bottoms of soft drink bottles.
- Reportedly hated fiddle music and encouraged his groups to discontinue using the instrument on recordings.
- Noted for a volatile temper and colorful language, but fondly remembered by most associates.
- Took advantage of major label disputes with the American Federation of Musicians to release records while others were on the sidelines during 1940s recording bans.
- Genre-bending experiments included having the Stanley Brothers record Hank Ballard's R&B hit, "Finger Poppin' Time," and using James Brown's drummer on the Stanleys' "How Bad I Do Feel."

Nathan didn't like being at the mercy of other suppliers. When the shellac used to manufacture records was diverted to wartime use, he began acquiring equipment to manufacture his own discs. By 1946, he was manufacturing and shipping 100,000 records per week. In time, King Records became a fully in-house operation. King had its own recording studio, mastering facilities, record pressing machines, and presses to print and fabricate album jackets.

Nathan was quick to take advantage of trends taking place in the music industry. If he saw that a song was getting good coverage by one of his rivals, he had one of his artists record the same song and could have the cover version available for shipping the next day.

King Records flourished during turbulent times in American history. Cincinnati, on the border between northern and southern states, was hardly a progressive city in race relations during Nathan's era. While much of the nation had to be forced into desegregation through court orders, Nathan embraced the idea of an integrated work force. African-Americans worked alongside whites in all aspects of the company and one of Syd's key producers and right hand man, Henry Glover, was black. A newspaper article from 1949 noted that everyone attended company social functions with no problems.

"[Syd] was a pioneer. He was smart, too. Some people said he was gruff and mean, and he smoked those foul-smelling-cigars. But, I tell you this: if Syd Nathan were alive today, I'd probably still be working for him. He had insight, a special way of seeing talent in people."

- Ray Pennington, former producer at King Records, as quoted by Larry Nager in "Seymour Stein Learned the Ropes at King," *Cincinnati Enquirer*, January 17, 1990.

Nathan made overtures to bluegrass artists in the late 1940s when he unsuccessfully tried to hire Flatt and Scruggs and the McReynolds Brothers (Jim and Jesse). Several early King artists skirted close to the sounds of bluegrass, most notably J.E. and Wade Mainer and The Maddox Brothers and Rose. It was not until August of 1951 that the label recorded its first unadulterated bluegrass – four songs by the duo of Jimmy Martin, Bob Osborne, and the Sunny Mountain Boys. In January of 1952 the label signed another duo, Don Reno and Red Smiley. With the exception of a brief excursion to Dot Records in 1957 and 1958, Reno and Smiley's entire recorded output was for King – about 250 songs in all. Their first hit was "I'm Using My Bible For a Roadmap" and they had chart success with other songs such as "I Know You're Married (But I Love You Still)," "Please Remember That I Love You," and "Love, Please Come Home."

The other big bluegrass addition to the roster came when the Stanley

"In many ways, he was a remarkably open-minded man. He perceived this wonderful notion of American music as not being segregated into different styles, but one big cross-ethnic whole. He did that because it was a way to make money."

- Henry Glover, former producer at King Records, as quoted by Rick Kennedy and Randy McNutt in *Little Labels – Big Sound: Small Record Companies and the Rise of American Music*, Indiana University Press, Bloomington, 1999.

Brothers were signed, in 1958. The Stanleys first and self-titled album for the label was one of the best of their career. Over the next seven years the group recorded fourteen albums for King. Nathan took a personal interest in a number of the sessions and sought to introduce changes in their sound that he felt would boost sales. Most notably, he sought to soften the hard bluegrass edges by dropping mandolin, fiddle, and banjo and replacing them with the lead guitar. Purists winced, but the lead guitar has been a standard element of the Stanley sound ever since. Nathan also had the Stanley Brothers recycle material for which he owned publishing rights. Usually this took the form of covering old country classics from King artists like Cowboy Copas or the Mainers. In one instance, he had the group record a cover version of a recent King R&B hit called "Finger Poppin' Time," an experiment that wasn't repeated.

Nathan added several other bluegrass groups to his roster over the years: Leon Jackson, Johnny Bryant and the White Oak Mountain Boys; the Green Valley Quartet (Easter Brothers); Bill Duncan; Charlie Moore and Bill Napier; the New Grass Revival; and Larry Sparks among them. After the passing of Carter Stanley in 1966, King kept Ralph Stanley as a solo artist. After the splitting up of Reno and Smiley, Nathan signed the new Don Reno and Bill Harrell partnership.

In addition to his poor eyesight and asthma, Syd Nathan developed heart problems in later years. On one of his frequent trips to Miami for rest and relaxation, he had a fatal heart attack. The family kept the label for several months before selling it to Nathan's friendly rival, Don Pierce of Starday Records. Since the middle 1970s, the catalog has been owned and operated by Moe Lytle of the International Marketing Group in Nashville.

— GARY REID

- So anxious to bring to market a King-label cover of Hack Johnson's 1955 single "Home Sweet Home" that he sent Don Reno into a Charlotte studio to record all the parts without waiting for the rest of the Tennessee Cut-Ups.

Howard Staton Watts (stage name: "Cedric Rainwater")) 2007

Born: February 19, 1913, Monticello, FL

Died: January 21, 1970, Nashville, TN

Primary Instrument: Bass

Composed:
"Remember the Cross"
"I'll be Going to Heaven Sometime"

Early influences:
Jim Boyd
Dock Williams
Paul Howard

Came to fame with:
Bill Monroe and the Blue Grass Boys, 1943-1948

"It was this group [of Bill Monroe's Blue Grass Boys], including Chubby Wise on fiddle and Howard Watts ("Cedric Rainwater") on bass, that refined bluegrass style and instrumental techniques."

- Ralph Rinzler, "Bill Monroe," in Bill C. Malone and Judith McCulloh, eds., *Stars of Country Music*, 1975.

Florida native Howard Watts embarked on his musical career in the early days of the Great Depression as a singer and guitarist. During this era, he formed his own Howard Watts Trio, won a talent contest, and appeared on his first radio broadcast. As the 1930s progressed, Watts added to his performing capabilities by teaching himself to tap dance and by working up comedy routines. With a friend, he joined a group known as Jim Boyd and the Melody Boys and toured throughout Florida, Georgia, and Alabama.

"His metronomic playing serves as a rhythmic reference for everyone in the band, freeing them from any worries whatsoever concerning the location of the beat."

- Tom Ewing, "Howard Watts: Better Known as Cedric Rainwater," *Bluegrass Unlimited*, May 2002.

In 1938, he adopted the stage name of "Arizona Slim" and teamed up with Tex Willis to form Tex and Slim and the Sunset Ramblers. The group, heavily steeped in western music, wore ten-gallon hats and bandanas. Even with the addition of Howard's crowd-pleasing fire-eating stunts, the band was unable to make a go of it. The duo found musical employment with Jacksonville-based Dock Williams (not the same performer as Wheeling-based Doc Williams) and the Santa Fe Trailriders. It was while working in Jacksonville that Watts met and became friends with Florida fiddler Chubby Wise.

In 1941, Watts moved to Nashville in hopes of hooking up with an established group. His friend Tex Willis was working in a western swing outfit, Paul Howard and his Arkansas Cotton Pickers, and before year's end Howard was signed on to play guitar. While working with

Photo: courtesy of Bear Family Records

Left to right: Bill Monroe, Earl Scruggs, Howard Watts, Chubby Wise in the mid-1940s.

the Cotton Pickers, Watts developed an interest in the bass fiddle. Two years later, with the assistance of Chubby Wise, he joined Bill Monroe's Blue Grass Boys playing bass. It was a post he would hold, off and on, for the next five years.

As soon as he joined Monroe's group, Watts adopted a new comedic stage name, C. Cedric Rainwater. Eventually, the "C." was dropped and he was known simply as Cedric Rainwater. His comic persona dressed in "baggy pants, suspenders, and a funny-looking hat" while he would "play bass with the band, interjecting comments that tickled band and audience," according to Tom Ewing's May 2002 biography in *Bluegrass Unlimited*. Other band members included Dave "Stringbean" Akeman on banjo, Sally Ann Forrester on accordion, Chubby Wise on fiddle, and Clyde Moody on guitar.

Working with Monroe wasn't easy. The recording and radio star had a traveling tent show that usually worked five nights a week and then

Performed with:

Howard Watts and His Trio, c. 1932-1933

Jim Boyd and the Melody Boys, 1937-1938

Tex and Slim and the Sunset Ramblers, 1938

Dock Williams and the Santa Fe Trailriders, 1939

Paul Howard and his Arkansas Cotton Pickers, 1941

Bill Monroe and the Blue Grass Boys, 1943-1945, 1946, 1947-1948

Lester Flatt, Earl Scruggs and the Foggy Mountain Boys, 1948-1950

Hank Williams's Drifting Cowboys, 1950-1952

Hank Snow and the Rainbow Ranch Boys, 1953

Bill Carlisle and the Carlisles, 1953

Ferlin Husky and the Hush Puppies, 1954, 1957-1958

Hawkshaw Hawkins, 1956

Patsy Cline, Cowboy Copas, Lefty Frizzell, Johnnie and Jack, 1958-1963

Hank Williams, Jr. and the Drifting Cowboys, 1968-1970

"All gussied up in the usual silly suit, telling corny stories, and serving as the butt of the other boys' [Drifting Cowboys'] jokes, he quickly became a favorite with Hank's Williams audiences."

- Roger M. Williams, *Sing A Sad Song: The Life of Hank Williams*, 1970.

Led the way:
- A member of the classic edition of Bill Monroe's Blue Grass Boys, with Lester Flatt, Earl Scruggs, and Chubby Wise.
- Refined the 4/4 walking style of bass playing that has been a popular feature of bluegrass.
- A charter member of Flatt and Scruggs and the Foggy Mountain Boys.
- A key member of Hank Williams's Drifting Cowboys.
- Bluegrass Hall of Fame, 2007.

By the Way:
- Better known to the public by his comedic stage name of Cedric Rainwater.

journeyed back to Nashville for the Saturday evening *Grand Ole Opry*. In addition to performing, traveling, and assisting with the set up and tear down of the tent, the Blue Grass Boys competed against local baseball teams prior to their performances.

Watts's recording debut came in February of 1945 when he journeyed to Chicago to record eight sides with the Blue Grass Boys for Columbia. Monroe had yet to solidify the definitive bluegrass sound. and this session included elements that later disappeared from the music, most notably two-finger style banjo and accordion. Although Watts had only been playing bass for a year or so, Tom Ewing's biography noted his "great tone and style throughout the session."

"I had made up my mind to quit [Monroe]... I turned in my notice then and before my notice was up, fellows like Cedric Rainwater said, 'Let me join with you and we'll form a band.'"

- Lester Flatt, quoted by Pete Kuykendall in "Lester Flatt and the Nashville Grass," *Bluegrass Unlimited*, January 1971.

Reflecting the influence of western swing, Howard Watts played walking bass (a quick four beats to the measure) on about half the recordings on his initial session. Others had used the technique sporadically during a song, but he was the first to do so from start to finish. Examples include the bluesy vocal, "Rocky Road Blues," and the swingy instrumental, "Blue Grass Special."

A turnover in personnel resulted in what has come to be termed the "original bluegrass band," including Bill Monroe on mandolin, Lester Flatt on guitar, Earl Scruggs on banjo, Chubby Wise on fiddle, and Howard Watts on bass. No time was wasted in getting this classic ensemble into the recording studio. Over a two-day period, September 16 and 17, 1946, a dozen songs were cut. Again, Howard walked his bass through a number of songs and tunes such as "Heavy Traffic Ahead," "Blue Yodel No. 4," "Will You Be Loving Another Man," and "How Will I Explain About You." He also contributed baritone harmony to "Summertime is Past and Gone."

This group recorded together one more time, again over a two-day period. On October 27 and 28, 1947, a marathon session produced a total of sixteen masters. Howard walked the bass on four songs: "Little Cabin Home on the Hill," "Sweetheart, You Done Me Wrong," "When You Are Lonely," and "Along About Daybreak." On one song, "I Hear a Sweet Voice Calling," he played bass on the verses and instrumental breaks but ceased playing on the verses to concentrate on singing baritone harmony. He also sang bass on five gospel quartet selections, which included only guitar and mandolin backing. One of these, "Remember the Cross," was written by Howard Watts and his wife Alice.

In the spring of 1948, Lester Flatt, Earl Scruggs, and Howard Watts left Monroe and shortly afterwards organized their own group, the Foggy Mountain Boys. Watts stayed with that band for nearly two years, working with them on radio in Danville, Virginia; Hickory, North Carolina; Bristol, Virginia; Knoxville, Tennessee; and Lexington, Kentucky. He participated in Flatt and Scruggs's first four recording sessions for Mercury, cutting a total of sixteen songs. Among the standouts were "My Cabin in Caroline," "Foggy Mountain Breakdown," "Baby Blue Eyes," as well as a gospel composition Watts co-wrote with his wife, "I'll Be Going to Heaven Sometime."

A growing family prompted Howard to leave the road in order to have a more stable home life. Instead of securing steady local employment, Howard soon found himself working in one of the busiest outfits of the day, Hank Williams and the Drifting Cowboys. With Hank he toured, played the *Opry*, did radio work – including shows for Mother's Best Flour which were recently issued by Time Life – and most likely assisted with Hank's MGM recordings. Williams's untimely passing on January 1, 1953, left Howard without steady employment.

For a brief period Watts found work with Hank Snow's Rainbow Ranch Boys. The Drifting Cowboys reunited to help up-and-coming country star Ray Price on one of his early Columbia sessions. For the balance of the decade, and into the early 1960s, Howard often worked as a bass player and featured soloist in his comic persona Cedric Rainwater for a variety of entertainers such as Marty Robbins, Carl Smith, Ernest Tubb, Hawkshaw Hawkins, Ferlin Husky, Patsy Cline, Cowboy Copas, Lefty Frizzell, and Johnnie and Jack. He also did session work in Nashville. Of interest to bluegrass fans are recordings he helped make with Bill Monroe – featuring Carter Stanley – in 1951; six songs by Jimmy Martin and the Osborne Brothers for RCA in the middle 1950s; several of Jimmy Martin's first solo recordings for Decca, also in the middle 1950s; and a Flatt and Scruggs session in 1957.

In the early 1960s, Watts left performing and recording to take a job with the Aud-Lee booking agency, a firm set up by Hank Williams's widow Audrey and talent agent Buddy Lee. A subsequent foray into the restaurant business was cut short when Hank Williams, Jr. resurrected the original Drifting Cowboys. Howard Watts worked in this capacity for about two years until his untimely passing from a fatal heart attack in 1970. He was fifty-six.

– GARY REID

- Composer of Bill Monroe's early gospel classic, "Remember the Cross."
- A medical condition exempted him from service during World War II, at a time when the war led to a scarcity of working musicians.
- Performed in the bands of both Hank Williams, Sr. and Hank Williams, Jr.
- After Watts left the Foggy Mountain Boys in 1950, his replacement, Chuck Johnson, assumed the comedy role of his "brother," Jody Rainwater.

Carl Moore Story | 2007

Carl Story came by his love of old-time and country music naturally, having been exposed to it as a youth at home in western North Carolina. His father was an old-time fiddle player who enjoyed collecting recordings of Charlie Poole, Grayson and Whitter, and others. Carl took up the fiddle at age nine and eventually learned guitar and clawhammer banjo.

He organized the first iteration of his band, the Rambling Mountaineers, on October 13, 1934. In the middle 1930s he signed on with J.E. Clark and the Lonesome Mountaineers; his stay was short-lived and he soon left to re-organize his own group. Members of that band included Carl on fiddle, guitarists Ed McMahan and Dudley "Uncle Dud" Watson, and banjoist Johnnie Whisnant. Whisnant had by this time developed his own version of the three-finger banjo style later popularized by contemporaries Earl Scruggs and Don Reno. This band, which Story said made commercial recordings for OKeh that were never released, operated in various configurations from 1935 until 1942, when World War II and the draft made it increasingly difficult to keep a group together.

A chance meeting with fellow North Carolina musician Clyde Moody led to Carl's joining Bill Monroe's Blue Grass Boys. He played fiddle for Monroe from the waning days of 1942 until October of 1943, at which time he was called to join the Navy.

Following his discharge from the Navy in 1945, Carl again re-assembled the Rambling Mountaineers. Members included brothers Jack and Curley Shelton, banjoist Hoke Jenkins, and Claude Boone on bass. It wasn't long until the group secured a spot on WNOX radio in Knoxville, Tennessee, where they played on its popular *Mid-Day Merry-Go-Round*.

Born: May 29, 1916, Lenoir, NC

Died: March 31, 1995, Greenville, SC

Primary Instrument:
Guitar

Composed:
BMI's database credits Carl Story with 178 published compositions, co-compositions, and arrangements, including:

"I Overlooked an Orchid While Searching For a Rose"

"Always Be Kind To Mother"

"I Heard My Mother Weeping"

"I Love The Hymns They Sang At Mother's Grave"

"The release "Light at the River" / "Mocking Banjo" is probably the most important single in Carl Story's recording history."

- Ivan Tribe, from "Carl Story: The Father of Bluegrass Gospel," Precious Memories, *Journal of Gospel Music*, September-October 1988.

Early influences:
Riley Puckett
Charlie Poole and the North Carolina Ramblers
G. B. Grayson and Henry Whitter
Uncle Dave Macon

Came to fame with:
Carl Story and the Rambling Mountaineers, 1945-1995

Performed with:
Rambling Mountaineers, c. 1934, 1935-1942
J.E. Clark and the Lonesome Mountaineers, c. 1935
Bill Monroe and the Blue Grass Boys, 1942-1943
Carl Story and the Rambling Mountaineers, 1945-1995

Led the way:
- The first prominent artist to specialize in bluegrass-style gospel music, he was nicknamed the "Father of Bluegrass Gospel."
- Story's career in traditional country, bluegrass, and gospel music spanned more than six decades.
- Led one of the first bands to utilize the three-finger style of banjo playing.
- Fostered the talents of many band members, including Red Rector, Bud and Willie G. Brewster, Bobby Thompson, and Tater Tate.
- Released the first all-bluegrass gospel album on a major label (*Gospel Quartet Favorites*, 1958, Mercury Records).

Carl stayed at the station for five years, honing the talents of the band. They sometimes teamed up for show dates with other performers from the station such as Molly O'Day and the Cumberland Mountain Folks.

It was in Knoxville that Carl came to the attention of Mercury Records' producer Dee Kilpatrick, who heard the group on radio and approached them about recording. From 1947 until 1953, Story recorded eleven sessions for Mercury, cutting a total of fifty songs. Initially he recorded a mix of secular and gospel songs. Numbers like "I Watched You Walk Away," "Faded Love," and "Tennessee Border" fared well alongside rousing quartet arrangements such as "I've Found a Hiding Place," "Keep on the Firing Line," and "He Will Set Your Fields on Fire."

Knoxville proved a good location for securing new material, especially songs sold by composer Arthur Q. Smith and the prolific pens of Ira and Charlie Louvin. Some early Louvin classics introduced for the first time on record by Carl Story were "God Saved My Soul," "Are You Afraid to Die," and "I'll Live With God (To Die No More)."

> *"It was no trouble at all to sell 20,000 song books a week."*
> - Quoted by Don Rhodes in "Carl Story," *Pickin'*, January 1978.

It was a common practice among rural entertainers in the 1940s and 1950s to move from radio station to radio station, using the exposure of live broadcasts to promote local concert appearances. When artists had been in one location for a while and had "played out the territory," they would move on to a new location. Such was the case with Carl Story. After a five-year stretch at WNOX, he left for WPAQ in Mount Airy, North Carolina, in the summer of 1951. In January of 1952, he set up shop at WCYB in Bristol, Virginia/Tennessee, where he appeared on the legendary *Farm and Fun Time* during a brief stay there. Then it was off to WAYS in Charlotte, North Carolina, where Carl did live radio and also worked as a disc jockey. By the mid 1950s he was back in Knoxville, performing on WNOX or appearing on television for grocery store magnate Cas Walker.

In 1953, Carl changed labels and landed at Columbia. Over the next three years, he recorded a total of eighteen songs which, like his earliest Mercury material, mixed secular and gospel selections. The sessions highlighted the talents of one of Carl's best bands, which included long-time bass player Claude Boone and mandolin player Red Rector. Rector's lead singing graced one of Story's best Columbia sides, the Louvin Brothers' composition "Love and Wealth." Other notable tracks included the Story standard, "My Lord Keeps a Record," and his original composition "I Love the Hymns They Sang at Mother's Grave."

In 1955, Carl returned to Mercury for three years, cutting sixteen more songs. During his second stay at Mercury, Carl solidified his bluegrass sound by adding five-string banjo. For a period of time, his 45 rpm releases featured a gospel song on one side and a hot bluegrass instrumental on the other. The first session with bluegrass banjo had Bud Brewster playing "Mocking Banjo," a cover of the recent Arthur Smith/Don Reno release "Feudin' Banjo," and "Banjo on the Mountain." A subsequent session featured Bobby Thompson, one of the innovators of the melodic style of banjo playing, on "Banjolina" and "Fire on the Banjo." At this session, Carl added several signature numbers to his sacred repertoire with "Light at the River" and "Family Reunion."

For a period of time in the late 1950s, Starday Records supervised Mercury's country and western division. A number of Carl's releases were labeled Mercury-Starday. When the two labels terminated their partnership in 1958, Carl went with Starday. Over the next ten years, Carl released a dozen albums, making him one of the most-recorded artists on the label. One release paired him with another powerhouse Starday act, the Lewis Family. Many of Story's Starday albums featured the talents of the Knoxville-based Brewster brothers, Bud and Willie G., along with Claude Boone. A few of the later albums were augmented with the talents of the Jones Brothers, a duo from North Carolina.

As the bluegrass festival phenomenon caught fire in the 1970s, Carl's performing career and visibility received a strong boost. Sadly, many of his strongest earlier recordings on Mercury and Columbia, many released originally only as singles, never made it to album except in Europe, and were thus unavailable to North American fans during the years that the seminal work of other pioneers shaped the bluegrass repertoire. All have since been reissued by the German label Bear Family.

In the 1970s, Carl recorded for several labels, most notably Atteiram Records of Marietta, Georgia, and the newly founded CMH label of Los Angeles, a joint venture involving Arthur "Guitar Boogie" Smith and former Starday staffer Martin Haerle. Initial releases on CMH usually consisted of lavishly produced two-LP sets that featured re-recorded versions of past hits. Such was the case with Carl's *The Bluegrass Gospel Collection*. Single CMH albums included *Mountain Music* and *A Lonesome Wail From the Hills*.

Carl spent the last thirty years of his life in Greer, South Carolina, where he headquartered the Rambling Mountaineers. As he had done throughout the earlier portions of his career, he supplemented his touring schedule by working during the week as a disc jockey. His last DJ work was a five-year stint on WESC in nearby Greenville, South Carolina. Carl passed away in March of 1995 from complications of heart bypass surgery.

— GARY REID

- Co-wrote "I Overlooked an Orchid," an early country music hit for Carl Smith in 1950, revived by Mickey Gilley in 1974.
- Bluegrass Hall of Fame, 2007.

"During this time [c. 1952-1953] they sponsored a contest giveaway of a TV set and received some 27,000 pieces of mail, reminiscent of the '30s and '40s when country acts received so many thousands of letters in a short time."

- Ivan Tribe, in "Carl Story: Bluegrass Pioneer," *Bluegrass Unlimited*, January 1975.

By the Way:
- A broken leg resulting from a line drive ended his hopes of becoming a professional baseball player.
- Played fiddle for the first decade of his career.
- One of the first to record the instrumental "Feudin' Banjos" (as "Mocking Banjo"), later a hit in the movie *Deliverance* as "Dueling Banjos" (1972).
- Story's cover recording of Johnny Cash's "Daddy Sang Bass" enjoyed brisk sales when it appeared as an alternate selection in the Capitol Record Club.

William August Marburg (stage name: "Bill Clifton") 2008

Born: April 5, 1931, Riderwood, MD

Primary Instrument: Guitar

Composed:
BMI's database credits Bill Clifton with 111 published compositions, co-compositions, and arrangements, including:

"Lonely Heart Blues"

"When Autumn Leaves Begin to Fall"

"My Nights Are So Lonely"

Early influences/mentors:

The Carter Family / A.P. Carter

Carter Stanley

Don Owens

Came to fame with:

Bill Clifton and the Dixie Mountain Boys, 1953-1962

Performed with:

Clifton Brothers, 1950-1952

Bill Clifton and the Dixie Mountain Boys, 1953-1962

In contrast to many early bluegrass performers raised in rural, agricultural backgrounds, Bill Clifton came from a well-to-do family residing ten miles from downtown Baltimore, Maryland. In his teen years, workers from Virginia on his family's farm exposed him to mountain music and the *Old Dominion Barn Dance*, broadcast from Richmond on WRVA. During this time he bought 78 rpm discs by the Carter Family, Eddy Arnold, and Wiley and Zeke Morris, and learned to play the guitar.

By 1949, Bill was enrolled at the University of Virginia in Charlottesville. While there he met folk enthusiast Paul Clayton and the two formed a duo they called the Clifton Brothers. With Clayton, along with banjoists Dave Sadler and/or Johnny Clark and bass player Carl Boehm, Bill made his first recordings. The masters were intended for release on the New York-based Stinson label but finally saw the light of day in the early 1970s on the German Bear Family label.

During his college years in Virginia, Bill met A.P. Carter of the original Carter Family and the two became fast friends. Carter was pleased that his music was still being appreciated by new audiences; Clifton relished the friendship and knowledge imparted by his musical idol. Several years later Bill was one of the first to issue an album in tribute to the First Family of Country Music.

In 1953, Bill took a leave of absence from UVa and assembled the first version of his Dixie Mountain Boys. After brief stints at WMBG and

"I don't think of myself as [a bluegrass artist] at all. I am just a person who sings traditional country music…"

– Quoted by Rienk Janssen in notes to *Bill Clifton - Around the World to Poor Valley*, Bear Family Records, 2001.

Photo: BBC-TV, courtesy of Bill Clifton, 1964

First Generation (with Red Rector and Don Stover), 1978-1990

Pick of the Crop, c. late 1980s-to present

"It is to the early pioneer collectors [A.P. Carter, Bill Bolick, J.E. and Wade Mainer, Bascom Lamar Lunsford, Bradley Kincaid, etc.] that I am forever indebted, for it is through them that I learned most of the songs that I have been singing to audiences around the world for the past fifty years or so."

– Bill Clifton, notes to *Bill Clifton and the Pick of the Crop: Mountain Laurel*, Elf Records, 2004.

Led the way:

- A pioneer in taking the music to people who had never heard it before, including folk music audiences and in England, Europe, Asia, and Africa, during his extended international residencies and tours.

- Compiled one of the first comprehensive bluegrass songbooks.
- An important figure in the early career of the Country Gentlemen (he performed and recorded with several members of that group).
- Organized one of the first all-day bluegrass events, a precursor of the multi-day bluegrass festival.
- Served on the board of the Newport Folk Festival, where he was an advocate for traditional and bluegrass performers.
- IBMA Distinguished Achievement Award, 1992.
- SPBGMA Preservation Hall of Greats, 1993.
- America's Old-Time Country Music Hall of Fame, 2008.
- Bluegrass Hall of Fame, 2008.

{In November 1953... we ended up in Richmond, Viriginia, and contacted A.P. [Carter] and he wrote me this letter in which he says that he was hoping we could do some work together. He had this little house up in the valley that he was aiming to give us for the winter and we could have gotten our food out of his grocery store and that he was gonna get busy and book dates for us in the spring and the summer, and that we would have plenty of work. But the fact that he thought enough of me to make that offer probably is the reason I stayed in the music."

–Bill Clifton, in Rienk Janssen, *Bill Clifton: Around the World to Poor Valley*, Bear Family Records, 2001

WCOD in Richmond, the group headed to West Virginia and WWVA's *Wheeling Jamboree*. Due to the low pay their tenure there was short-lived, from July until November. At A.P. Carter's urging, Bill and Johnny ventured to Kingsport, Tennessee, to secure a spot on radio station WKIN. When this failed to materialize, Bill joined WXGI in Richmond as a DJ. His first recordings were released in 1954 and 1955 on Blue Ridge, a label based in North Wilkesboro, North Carolina.

Shortly after receiving his BA degree, in February of 1954, Bill enlisted for a tour of duty with the Marines. He entered their Officer Training Corps and by April was stationed at Camp Lejeune, North Carolina. The most important use of his spare time during his military training was the assembling of his *Bill Clifton 150 Old-Time Folk and Gospel Songs*. With a foreword from A.P. Carter, the collection made repertoire from the 1930s and 1940s available to bluegrass pickers. The book remained popular over the years and was reprinted several times.

Upon his discharge from the military in 1956, Bill – on the advice of Carter Stanley – contacted Mercury Records, then partnering with Starday Records, to secure a recording contract. Starday label head Don Pierce's elaborate distribution network – reaching Canada, Europe, Asia and Africa – did much to increase Clifton's stature worldwide.

"A.P. [Carter] was most certainly my most important mentor, and I am hard put to come up with anyone who came close to A.P. in importance to me. But… my friendship with Carter Stanley was extremely important to me [as well]."

– Bill Clifton in personal correspondence to Gary Reid, 2011.

Banjoist Johnny Clark was a fixture on most of Clifton's Mercury and Starday recordings, but notable guest sidemen also included Ralph Stanley, Tommy Jackson, Benny Martin, John Duffey, Curley Lambert, Eddie Adcock, and Mike Seeger. Bill's association with Starday lasted for seven years and many of his best recordings were made during this period, including "Little White Washed Chimney," "Mary Dear," and "Springhill Disaster."

In 1961 Bill leased Oak Leaf Park, a country music venue in Luray, Virginia. On July 4, he staged an all-day bluegrass event featuring many of the top names in the business, including Bill Monroe, Mac Wiseman, the Stanley Brothers, the Country Gentlemen, and Jim and Jesse. A significant feature was the reuniting of Bill Monroe with a number of his former sidemen. This was one of the first all-day bluegrass extravaganzas, and the first to acknowledge Monroe as the central figure of the music. The all-day bluegrass show was not repeated in 1962, as Bill accepted a board position with the Newport Folk Festival.

In 1963 Bill moved his family to England for what was to be a six-to-nine-month stay but wound up lasting fifteen years. During that time, Bill became an international "Johnny Appleseed" for American folk music, touring extensively in Austria, France, Germany, Switzerland, and the Netherlands. Later travels included performances in Australia, New Zealand, and Japan, as well as the African countries of Malawi and Rhodesia (now Zimbabwe). Clifton also arranged international tours for such groups as the New Lost City Ramblers and Bill Monroe.

During his first several years abroad Bill was accompanied by the Echo Mountain Boys, a group of schoolboys from Kent, one of the oldest English preparatory schools. A highlight Clifton/Echo appearance was a sell-out at London's Royal Albert Hall, the first time bluegrass had been presented in a major European venue. Another important feature of Bill's time in England was his pairing with American folksinger/activist Hedy West.

In 1978 Bill, with his Dutch-born wife Tineke, moved back to the States and settled in Mendota, in Poor Valley, an area of Virginia rich in physical beauty. An additional bonus was its proximity (less than six miles) to the Carter Family homestead in Maces Spring.

During the 1970s Clifton began an association with County Records with a reissue of recordings made in the late 1950s. This led to studio albums with stellar musicians such as Red Rector, John Duffey, Tom Gray, Kenny Baker, Bill Keith, and Mike Auldridge. Most of Bill's recordings since 1980 have been issued on his own Elf label.

Bill teamed with mandolin wizard Red Rector and ace banjoist Don Stover to form a group called First Generation, active from the late 1970s through much of the 1980s. Sometimes joined by legendary fiddler Art Stamper, they played festivals in the States and made occasional trips to Europe. Jimmy Gaudreau took over on mandolin after Red Rector's untimely passing in 1990. Another void was created in 1996 with the passing of Don Stover. Since that time Bill has continued to duet with Jimmy Gaudreau and perform as a solo, including annual appearances at the Carter Family Fold's festival each August.

In addition to his work as a performer, recording artist, and promoter, Bill is pleased that he has been able to present traditional and bluegrass music to "new ears," especially among socio-economic groups to whom these forms were not previously exposed. Along with friends such as Mike Seeger and Paul Clayton, he used non-bluegrass functions such as birthday parties and anniversaries to expose influential friends to the music. "Many," he noted, "went on to become life-long enthusiasts, promoters, and supporters."

— GARY REID

By the Way:
- Although known primarily for his singing and guitar work, Bill's first instrument was an accordion.
- Born William Marburg, Bill adopted the stage name of Bill Clifton because his father didn't want the family name associated with rural music.
- Performed locally and on radio during his undergraduate years at the University of Virginia, but never on campus.
- Bill's first songbook contained a forward by famed folksinger Woody Guthrie.
- Featured in the Cambridge, England, publications of *Who's Who in Music: Popular.*

"It just so happened that Johnny Clark played a three-finger style banjo. If he had played old-time banjo, we probably would have ended up being called old-time musicians."

- Quoted by Rienk Janssen in notes to *Bill Clifton - Around the World to Poor Valley*, Bear Family Records, 2001.

Charles Keith Wolfe \ 2008

Growing up in central Missouri, Charles Wolfe became enamored with music at an early age and learned to play saxophone, accordion, banjo, and guitar. He later said his best instrument was the typewriter. To that end, he attended Southwest Missouri State University, where he obtained a Bachelor of Arts degree in English in 1965. He went on to receive M.A. (1967) and Ph.D. (1971) degrees in that discipline from the University of Kansas at Lawrence. While a grad student, Wolfe was an instructor in the English department (1967-1970).

In 1970, Dr. Wolfe moved to Murfreesboro, Tennessee, to accept an associate professor position in the English department at Middle Tennessee State University. Becoming a full professor in 1982, he remained affiliated with the school until his retirement in 2005, at which time he was given professor emeritus status.

Shortly after his move to MTSU, Wolfe began a prolific side career of documenting and writing about country music – which included old-time, traditional, blues, gospel, bluegrass, and more. Among his earliest writings were liner notes to albums on the Rounder label for Bashful Brother Oswald (1972) and the duo of Hazel Dickens and Alice Gerrard (1973). His fascination with the early days of the *Grand Ole Opry* led to the publication of a book that documented the first ten years of this leg-

> *"Tennessee has been country music's best environment because Tennessee has been able to maintain both of these cultures, the pop and the traditional... it is this richness and this diversity, and its complex interaction, that justifies a study of country music in Tennessee."*
>
> – Charles Wolfe, *Tennessee Strings*, University of Tennessee Press, 1977.

Born: August 14, 1943, Sedalia, MO

Died: February 9, 2006, Murfreesboro, TN

Primary Involvement in Bluegrass Music:
Historian and Writer

Mentors:
Herman Crook
Sam and Kirk McGee
Deford Bailey
Steve Davis

Associated with:
University of Kansas, Lawrence, 1967-1970
Middle Tennessee State University, 1970-2005
Editor, *Tennessee Folklore Society Bulletin*

Led the way:
- Wrote liner notes for approximately 300 bluegrass and old-time music albums and CDs.
- Set high standards of professionalism for research and writing about country music.

endary radio show (1975). His next book, *Tennessee Strings* (1976), told the story of country music in Tennessee. A year later he served as editor for the Alton Delmore autobiography, *Truth is Stranger Than Publicity*.

Throughout the 1970s, Wolfe was a frequent contributor to the British publication *Old-Time Music*. Starting in 1972, he wrote at least fifteen articles for the magazine, covering a broad range of old-time music topics and artists, such as Ralph Peer and the Bristol sessions, an interview with western swing player Johnnie Lee Wills, Sam McGee, the Powers Family, and his first solidly bluegrass piece, an interview with Bill Monroe. In the late 1970s, he began contributing articles to *Bluegrass Unlimited*, mostly about old-time artists who influenced bluegrass, including Uncle Dave Macon, Clayton McMichen, and Fiddlin' Arthur Smith. Charles Wolfe served as the co-editor of the *Tennessee Folklore Society Bulletin*, the oldest continuously published regional folklore journal in the nation. In the 1970s, he also began writing for *The Devil's Box*, a quarterly journal, initially published by the Tennessee Valley Old Time Fiddlers Association, for the purpose of promoting and preserving fiddling and related

- Served as a mentor to other writers and historians.
- IBMA Award of Merit (Distinguished Achievement Award), 1990.
- Two-time recipient of IBMA award for Best Liner Notes, 1995 and 2004.
- Bluegrass Hall of Fame, 2008.

By the Way:
- An amateur photographer in his youth.
- Became enamored with old-time music by hearing 78 rpm records on the family Victrola.

- His mother loved the music of Elvis Presley.
- Had aspirations of becoming a professional musician, and after graduation from high school spent two years working in local bands including Johnny and the Echoes, Ronnie Self, and Terry Bidell and the Nighthawks.

music. In all, he wrote over fifty articles for that publication.

In the 1980s, Wolfe wrote two more books: *Kentucky Country*, a history of folk and country music in that state, and *Everybody's Grandpa*, a co-authored biography of Grandpa Jones. In this decade, he also wrote liner notes for approximately fifty LPs and CDs. He became a consultant for two series of country music reissues: *Your Hit Parade* (TimeLife) and *Country USA* (Sony Music). In 1984, he wrote the first of a number of excellent booklets to accompany boxed-set reissues for the German Bear Family label. Of interest to bluegrass fans during this period were liner notes he wrote for releases by the Whitstein Brothers, Hazel Dickens, the Nashville Bluegrass Band, and a collection of gospel material by Flatt and Scruggs called *You Can Feel It In Your Soul*.

"From [Bill Monroe's] very first recording session, there was brilliance: breathtaking technical skill, soaring vocals, and a dynamic mixture of tradition and innovation."

– Charles Wolfe in liner notes to *Bill Monroe: Blue Moon of Kentucky 1936-1949*, Bear Family Records, 2002.

The 1990s brought Wolfe's most prolific decade. He published seven books, including *Mahalia Jackson, Civil War Music, DeFord Bailey: A Black Singing Star in Early Country Music, The Life and Legend of Leadbelly, In Close Harmony: The Story of the Louvin Brothers, The Devil's Box: Masters of Southern Fiddling*, and *A Good Natured Riot: The Birth of the* Grand Ole Opry. He wrote notes or served as a consultant for no less than 150 recorded projects, including a number of boxed-set compilations for Bear Family on artists such as Hank Snow, Bill Monroe, Don Gibson, the Louvin Brothers, Carl Smith, and Grandpa Jones. He annotated contemporary recordings by the Johnson Mountain Boys, the Dry Branch Fire Squad, Ralph Stanley, James King, Mark O'Connor, and Paul Williams. Wolfe also contributed more than 25 articles on old-time music to *The Journal*, a publication devoted to traditional country music that was published by *Country Music* magazine.

The 1990s brought well-deserved recognition for Wolfe's life's work. In 1990, he received a Distinguished Achievement Award from the International Bluegrass Music Association (IBMA). In 1997, he received a Lifetime Achievement Award from the Curb Music Business Program at Belmont University in Nashville. In 1998 he received a Belmont Book of the Year Award for *The Devil's Box*. In 1999, he received a Ralph J. Gleason Book Award for *A Good Natured Riot*. Other professional activities included his election to the IBMA Board of Directors and, in the following year, his participation in the Old-Time Radio Conference in Mount Airy, North Carolina, where he and Garrison Keillor were guest speakers.

In the first half of the 2000s, Wolfe authored and co-authored eight books and nearly fifty sets of liner notes. Books released in this period included *Classic Country: Legends of Country Music*, *The Carter Family: In The Shadow of Clinch Mountain*, *Country Music Annual 2002*, *The Women of Country Music*, *Uncle Dave Macon*, *Country Music Goes to War*, *The Bristol Sessions*, and *The Music of Bill Monroe*. Highlights from his liner notes include releases by the Monroe Brothers, Bill Monroe (*1936-1949, Two Days at Newport*, and *My Last Days on Earth*), Mac Wiseman (*'Tis Sweet to be Remembered*), Carl Story (*Lonesome Hearted Blues*), Roy Acuff (*R.C. Cola Shows*), Leroy Troy (*Old Gray Mare*), and several various-artist collections, *Nashville Early String Bands* and *Goodbye Babylon*.

> "The sound [Carl Story] made owed something to bluegrass and something to gospel, but also included early honky tonk country, a taste of rockabilly, and even a nod or two to western music. It was a prime example of what Don Gibson once called 'that old Knoxville sound'."

- Charles Wolfe in liner notes to *Carl Story: Lonesome Hearted Blues*, Bear Family Records, 2005.

The early 2000s saw additional awards and recognition for Charles Wolfe. In 2000 he received an ASCAP/Deems Taylor Award for his book *A Good Natured Riot*, as well as a Lifetime Achievement Award from the Association for Recorded Sound. Other career accolades include three Grammy nominations, two Outstanding Research awards from MTSU, and a Woodrow Wilson Fellowship.

In 2005, with thirty-five years of service and with complications of diabetes taking their toll, Charles retired from MTSU. He continued to research and mentor as time and health permitted. His retirement was short-lived, and he died on February 9, 2006.

— GARY REID

The Lonesome Pine Fiddlers | 2009

Charles "Charlie" Cline
Born: June 26, 1931, Gilbert Creek, WV
Died: November 20, 2004, Jasper, AL
Primary instrument: Banjo

Ezra Cline
Born: January 13, 1907, Gilbert Creek, WV
Died: July 11, 1984, Gilbert Creek, WV
Primary instrument: Bass

Ray "Curly Ray" Cline
Born: January 10, 1923, Gilbert Creek, WV
Died: August 19, 1997, Rockhouse, KY
Primary instrument: Fiddle

Melvin Glen Goins
Born: December 30, 1933, Bramwell, WV
Primary instrument: Guitar

Ray Elwood Goins
Born: January 3, 1936, Bramwell, WV
Died: July 2, 2007, Pikeville, KY

The Lonesome Pine Fiddlers first organized in 1938, basing their style more on the Delmore Brothers than Bill Monroe. The band was headed by West Virginia bass player Ezra Cline. Initial members included his cousins, brothers Ireland "Lazy Ned" (banjo) and Ray "Curly Ray" Cline (fiddle), and a radio announcer by the name of Ordon L. "Gordon" Jennings on guitar. They secured a spot on WHIS radio in Bluefield, West Virginia, but did not record in that configuration.

World War II brought some changes to the group. Ireland Cline joined the military and was later killed in the Normandy invasion on D-Day. A third brother, Charlie, replaced him in the band. Gasoline shortages during the war forced the group to forego the radio program. The group returned to the airwaves in Bluefield in 1945.

More changes occurred in 1949, when Bobby Osborne and Larry Richardson joined the Fiddlers, playing guitar and banjo respectively. Other members at this time included Ezra on bass and fiddle player Ray Morgan. The Fiddlers' first recording session took place during this period for Cozy, a small independent label based in Davis, West Virginia. Releases included "Lonesome, Sad, and Blue," "Don't Forget Me," "Will I Meet Mother in

"I never thought when I left home in 1949 with an old guitar my dad paid $30 dollars for – with no case – that I'd ever amount to a hill of beans. I never dreamed of nothing like this when I joined the Lonesome Pine Fiddlers. It led to many, many things in bluegrass music."

– Bobby Osborne, quoted by Julia Roberts Goad, from "Lonesome Pine Fiddlers Find Home in Hall of Fame," *The Williamson Daily News*, October 9, 2009.

170 | Bluegrass Hall of Fame Inductee Biographies

Heaven?" and "Pain in My Heart," which was picked up and recorded by Flatt and Scruggs the next year.

When Osborne and Richardson left the band in the summer of 1951, Ezra assembled a new group that included Paul Williams on guitar, Charlie Cline on banjo, and Curly Ray Cline on fiddle. Charlie's stay was brief and he was soon replaced by sixteen-year old Ray Goins. The Fiddlers secured a recording contract with RCA and cut their first session in May of 1952. Appearing on those records were Ezra and Curly Ray Cline, Paul Williams, Ray Goins, and West Virginia mandolin player, Charles "Rex" Parker. Williams's singing added greatly to the popularity of the recordings.

Two more sessions were cut, one in October and another in August of 1953, with the same core of musicians: Ezra Cline, Curly Ray Cline, and Paul Williams. Charlie Cline came back and replaced Ray Goins on banjo and an in-law of Ezra's, Albert Punturi, played mandolin. The fourteen recordings of 1953 stand as some of the best in early bluegrass. Among the highlights were "You Broke Your Promise," "Nobody Cares," "My Brown-Eyed Darling," "Honky Tonk Blues,"

"My dad (Ezra Cline) was a showman. Back then, they had to work on radio to get their names out in the public, but that didn't pay too much. [So] they had to improvise and come up with ways to keep the band going."

– Scotty Cline, quoted by Bill Archer, from "On the Trail of the Lonesome Pine Fiddlers," by Bill Archer, *Goldenseal*, Summer 2010.

"Dirty Dishes Blues," and the instrumentals "Lonesome Pine Breakdown" and "Five-String Rag."

In the fall of 1952, the Lonesome Pine Fiddlers (Ezra, Charlie, and Curly Ray Cline plus Paul Williams) moved from Bluefield to Oak Hill, West Virginia. Then, from January to November of 1953, the group was headquartered in Detroit, where they appeared on WJR and the Saturday evening *Big Barn Frolic*. While there, they provided musical backing for one of the early releases by the Davis Sisters (Skeeter Davis went on to enjoy a successful solo career in country music). By November of 1953, the band had relocated to Pikeville, Kentucky, where the Fiddlers appeared on radio station WLSI.

During the next year, more band changes took place. Ray Goins returned on banjo, along with his brother Melvin on guitar. This duo, along with Ezra and Curly Ray Cline and mandolin player James Roberts (who recorded some fabulous gospel tracks in the early 1950s with his wife, Martha Carson), did two more sessions for RCA. These took place in February and September of 1954. Their signature tune, "Windy Mountain," was recorded at the latter date.

Primary instrument:
Banjo

Paul McCoy Humphrey (stage name: "Paul Williams")
Born: March 30, 1935, Wytheville, VA

Primary instrument:
Guitar

Robert "Bobby" Van Osborne, Jr. | 1994
Born: December 7, 1931, Hyden, KY

Primary instrument:
Guitar

Larry Richardson
Born: August 9, 1927, Galax, VA
Died: June 17, 2007, Lake Butler, FL

Primary instrument:
Banjo

Composed:
BMI's database credits various members of the Lonesome Pine Fiddlers with 270 published compositions, co-compositions, and arrangements. A few of their original songs are:
"Windy Mountain"
"No Curb Service"
"Baby You're Cheatin'"

Early influences:
Delmore Brothers
Fiddlin' Arthur Smith
Clayton McMichen and the Georgia Wildcats
Mainer's Mountaineers
Monroe Brothers

Performed as:
The Lonesome Pine Fiddlers, 1938-1968

Led the way:
- Among the first bands to start playing in the bluegrass style, before it was named "bluegrass."

The Lonesome Pine Fiddlers, early 1960s. Left to right: Curly Ray Cline, Ray Goins, Ezra Cline, Melvin Goins.

Bluegrass Hall of Fame Inductee Biographies | 173

- Served as a career launching pad for influential bluegrass and country musicians, including the Goins Brothers, Bobby Osborne, Larry Richardson, Paul Williams, Curly Ray and Charlie Cline, and the Davis Sisters (Skeeter and Betty Jack).
- One of the first bluegrass bands to utilize television.
- One of the first bluegrass bands to record for a major label (RCA).
- Bluegrass Hall of Fame, 2009.

By the Way:
- Sold candy at early shows to generate income for the band. Curly Ray Cline credits this as the start of his salesmanship, which became legendary during his stay with Ralph Stanley.
- Ezra Cline was one of the earliest musicians to play bass fiddle in a mountain music, string band setting.
- Initially known as the Bar-X Buckaroos and the Guyan Valley Boys, they eventually settled on the Lonesome Pine Fiddlers after seeing a road sign for the "Trail of the Lonesome Pine," a byway in the area and the name of a popular 1908 romance novel.
- Meals on the road often consisted of beans, potatoes, or corn from the garden. Oftentimes the band would perform a number or two in exchange for an electric hookup for their hot plate.

By the middle of 1955, Ray and Melvin had departed from the group, replaced by guitarist Udell McPeak, who also played the comedy role of "Jasper," and banjoist Billy Edwards. Paul Williams re-joined the band briefly after his discharge from the military, but soon left to play mandolin and sing tenor with Jimmy Martin. It was during this period that Ezra issued the Lonesome Pine Fiddlers' one and only souvenir song and photo booklet.

During the late 1950s the group consisted of Ezra; Charlie Cline on electric guitar; Charlie's wife, Lee Warren Cline, on vocals; and Curly Ray. The group did radio work in Pikeville as well as a weekly television program on WSAZ in Huntington, West Virginia. Charlie and Lee left the group early in the decade of the 1960s, when Charlie sought a career in the ministry.

Melvin and Ray Goins returned to the Fiddlers one last time in the early and middle 1960s. During this time they cut four albums for Starday, one of which paired the group with fellow Starday artist Hylo Brown. A highlight of this era was a fifteen-month stint on WCYB-TV in Bristol, Virginia. When that show ended in 1964, the grouping of Ezra, Curly Ray, Melvin, and Ray broke up.

Ezra kept a part-time band together for several years while he ran a restaurant in Pikeville. Among his group members was Kentucky Slim (Eddie Branham). That group folded in 1968 and Ezra moved back to West Virginia.

Just as Bill Monroe's Blue Grass Boys were a proving ground for up and coming bluegrass musicians, so too were the Lonesome Pine Fiddlers. Bobby Osborne achieved fame as one half of the Osborne Brothers. Larry Richardson is remembered as one of the finest banjo players from the early days of bluegrass, working with Bill Monroe, the Sauceman Brothers, and appearing on one of the first bluegrass LPs: *American Banjo Scruggs Style*. Charlie Cline became one of Bill Monroe's key sidemen of the early 1950s and also recorded with the Stanley Brothers. In later years, Charlie was an evangelist and toured with the Alabama-based Warrior River Boys. Paul Williams achieved fame as a sideman for Jimmy Martin, appearing on many of Jimmy's great Decca recordings of

> *"A lot of people think that's not the same Curly Ray Cline that plays with Ralph Stanley, but it's the same one. We recorded for RCA for over four years and had some pretty big hits for them. 'Dirty Dishes Blues,' 'My Brown Eyed Darling' and 'I'll Never Make You Blue' were hot numbers for us. We would get forty or fifty pieces of mail every day for 'Dirty Dishes' when it was out."*
>
> – Curly Ray Cline, quoted by Pete Kuykendall, from "Curly Ray Cline," *Bluegrass Unlimited*, May 1981.

the late 1950s and early 1960s. In recent years, Williams has enjoyed a vibrant career singing bluegrass gospel with his group, The Victory Trio. Curly Ray Cline worked briefly with the Stanley Brothers and went on to spend twenty-six years with Ralph Stanley, an indispensible part of his show. Melvin and Ray Goins enjoyed a twenty-five-year partnership as The Goins Brothers. Melvin has had his own solo career for nearly two decades.

The Lonesome Pine Fiddlers were inducted into the Bluegrass Hall of Fame in 2009. Surviving alumni Melvin Goins, Paul Williams, and Bobby Osborne played together on the Awards Show at Nashville's Ryman Auditorium, earning a standing ovation.

— GARY REID

"Curly Ray (Cline), the fiddle player in the band, drove over on a Sunday morning and picked us up at an old train station. Never will forget it. I had $5 in my pocket as we headed out over that 100 miles between Bluefield and Pikeville in Curly Ray's 1947 Plymouth. I won't forget that first show car, either, that the Fiddlers drove to shows in: a 1950 Buick. We tied the bass fiddle on top. We played theaters, schools, drive-ins... wherever we could. There weren't any bluegrass festivals back then."

- Melvin Goins, quoted by Walter Tunis, from "Bluegrass Star Melvin Goins Rose From Hard Times to the Kentucky Music Hall of Fame," The Lexington Herald-Leader, April 3, 2011.

Paul Williams, 2011.

Larry Richardson, 1969.

Charlie Cline, 1986.

The Dillards | 2009

The Dillards, in their classic configuration, were a foursome from Missouri that consisted of brothers Doug (on banjo) and Rodney Dillard (on guitar and lead vocals), mandolin player Dean Webb, and bass player Mitch Jayne. The brothers grew up in a musical household; their father was a fiddler from Tennessee and their mother played guitar. Doug started playing guitar at age five and banjo at age sixteen.

Mitch Jayne, formerly a one-room schoolteacher, worked as a disc jockey and became acquainted with Rodney and Doug when they played live music on his program. Jayne was born in Hammond, Indiana, and attended the University of Missouri before embarking on teaching and radio careers in the Ozarks. He stayed with the Dillards for twelve years playing bass, writing songs, and developing much of the comedy for which the group became known.

> *"I had a bad taste in my mouth from the first time we left Salem, Missouri to play in New York, and all the Monroe freaks and bluegrass heavies gave us a very hard time about what we did."*
>
> – Rodney Dillard, quoted by Richard D. Smith, in "Rodney Dillard: California Hillbilly," *Muleskinner News*, January/February 1975.

When the Dillard brothers and Jayne decided to form a group, they called on Dean Webb, a Missouri native who was exposed to music as a youth through the playing of family members. It was Bill Monroe's 1954 recording of "Blue Moon of Kentucky" that really ignited Dean's passion for bluegrass. By the early 1960s, he was playing mandolin with Lonnie Hoppers and the Ozark Mountain Boys. Their work included regular television appearances in Springfield and Joplin, Missouri. It

---

Douglas Flint "Doug" Dillard
Born: March 6, 1937, East St. Louis, IL
Died: May 16, 2012, Nashville, TN
Primary instrument: Banjo

Rodney Adean Dillard
Born: May 18, 1942, East St. Louis, IL
Primary instrument: Guitar

Roy Dean "Dean" Webb
Born: March 28, 1937, Independence, MO
Primary instrument: Mandolin

Mitchell Franklin "Mitch" Jayne
Born: July 5, 1928, Hammond, IN
Died: August 2, 2010, Eminence, MO
Primary instrument: Bass

was during this period that Dean met and subsequently teamed up with Doug and Rodney Dillard. He worked with various incarnations of the Dillards for thirty years.

Sensing that their potential for growth as a band was limited in Missouri, the foursome journeyed west to California. The day of their arrival in Hollywood, in November of 1962, they headed to the Ash Grove, a trendy folk venue that had previously featured Flatt and Scruggs, the Stanley Brothers, and Maybelle Carter. An impromptu jam session in the lobby of the establishment brought them to the immediate attention of Jim Dickson, a record producer who signed them to a contract with Elektra the next day.

The original group recorded three albums for Elektra: *Back Porch Bluegrass*, *Live… Almost*, and *Pickin' and Fiddlin'*, the latter with guest Byron Berline on fiddle. They introduced a number of original selections written by various band members, including "Dooley," "There is a Time," "Doug's Tune," and "Old Home Place" (revived a decade later when J.D. Crowe included it in his classic album, *J.D. Crowe and the New South*).

> *"It's no exaggeration to say that The Darlings [aka The Dillards] had a lot to do with the spread of bluegrass music overseas. Wherever the TV show was syndicated, which was just about every country, people couldn't get enough bluegrass music."*
>
> - Mitch Jayne, quoted by William Childress in "Bluegrass Branches Out," *The Rotarian*, April 1994.

Publicity generated by the group's affiliation with Elektra led to their being asked to audition for the *Andy Griffith Show*. The Dillards were hired before completing their first song. They appeared in six episodes during 1963 and 1964 as part of the Darling family, headed by family patriarch Briscoe Darling (Denver Pyle). Depicted on the show as socially inept, the boys shone brilliantly on a number of their original musical selections. This led to other television appearances, including guest spots on a Judy Garland special and the *Tennessee Ernie Ford Show*. A further spinoff of the Griffith popularity and Elektra releases was the opportunity to perform at major festivals and venues such as the UCLA Folk Festival, the Newport Folk Festival, and Gerde's Folk City in New York City's Greenwich Village.

By 1966 the brothers began to differ about the direction of their music. After leaving the group that year, Doug helped Gene Clark, a co-founder of the Byrds, with his first solo album. They later formed a duo known as Dillard and Clark. During this time, Doug composed and, with Rodney, recorded music for the soundtrack to the 1967 hit movie *Bonnie and Clyde* (for which Flatt and Scruggs's 1949 "Foggy Mountain Breakdown" was

Composed:
ASCAP's database credits Rodney and Doug Dillard with 129 published compositions, co-compositions, and arrangements. Mitch Jayne shared credits on 22 of these selections, as well as 6 additional songs. Dean Webb shared credits on 14 of these selections. They include:

"Dooley"

"Doug's Tune"

"Old Home Place"

"There is a Time"

Early influences:
Homer E. Dillard, Sr. and Lorene Dillard (Doug and Rodney's parents)

Lester Flatt, Earl Scruggs and the Foggy Mountain Boys

Joe Noel

The Stanley Brothers

Don Reno, Red Smiley and the Tennessee Cut-ups

Came to fame with:
The Dillards, 1962-2012

Performed with:
Howe Teague Band, 1953

Ozark Mountain Boys, 1956-1959

Hawthorne Brothers and Lewis Brothers, 1958-1959

Dixie Ramblers, 1960

Dillards, 1962-2012

Folkswingers (recording act), 1963

Dillard and Clark, 1968-1969

Doug Dillard Band, 1980-c. 1986

Rodney Dillard and the Dillard Band, c. 2010-present

The Missouri Boatride, c. 2000-present

The Dillards, c.1966, left to right: Dean Webb, Doug Dillard, Rodney Dillard, Mitch Jayne.

Photo: courtesy of Diana Jayne

Bluegrass Hall of Fame Inductee Biographies | 179

Led the way:

▪ Exposed bluegrass to a nationwide, and later worldwide, audience through appearances on the *Andy Griffith Show* in 1963-64.

▪ Doug and Rodney Dillard performed most of the soundtrack for the 1967 movie *Bonnie and Clyde*, along with Glen Campbell.

▪ First bluegrass band to release a cover of a Bob Dylan song: "Walking Down the Line" (1964).

▪ One of the first bluegrass bands to use electrified instruments.

▪ Doug Dillard was inducted into the SPBGMA Hall of Greats, 1992.

▪ Doug Dillard Band's album *Heartbreak Hotel* nominated for a Grammy (1988).

▪ Dillards' song "The Darlin' Boys" nominated for a Grammy (1991).

▪ IBMA Distinguished Achievement Award, 1992.

▪ Bluegrass Hall of Fame, 2009

By the Way:

▪ When making their first trek from Missouri to California in 1962, the band ran out of money along the way. They secured a week's work playing at the Buddhi Club in Oklahoma City and earned enough to complete their trip.

▪ Francis Bavier (Aunt Bea) made homemade candy and brought it to the boys when the Dillards were filming the Andy Griffith Show.

used as the main theme). Doug later produced background music for commercials by *7 Up*, Chevrolet, Kentucky Fried Chicken, and Visa.

Rodney kept the name "The Dillards" and replaced Doug with Herb Pedersen. The group recorded two additional albums for Elektra: *Wheatstraw Suite* and *Copperfields*. With electrified instruments, drums, and tunes borrowed from the Beatles, folk singer Tim Hardin and the like, Wheatstraw Suite combined bluegrass with rock and country. It has been cited as one of the origins of folk rock. *Copperfields* followed the same format but its sales at the time were not sufficient to warrant renewal of their Elektra contract.

Separately, Doug and Rodney participated in several high profile tours during the late 1960s and early 1970s. Doug toured Europe as a member of the Byrds while Rodney and the Dillards performed more than thirty dates as part of Elton John's first tour of the United States. The Dillards' most commercially successful album, *Roots and Branches*, was released during this time.

"Doug and I, the original guys who started this, will finish it. For whatever our time is, Douglas and I are going to continue to perform, continue to make records, and continue to enjoy life in a more moderate way."

- Rodney Dillard, quoted by Nancy Cardwell, from "They're Back: Rodney and Douglas Dillard," *Bluegrass Unlimited*, June 2005.

Other well-received recordings surfaced during the 1970s. Among them were *Tribute to the American Duck*; *Dillard-Hartford-Dillard*, a reunion album that paired Rodney and Doug with their old pal John Hartford; and *Duelin' Banjo*, a solo album by Doug that nicely complemented *The Banjo Album*, an earlier solo release.

During the 1980s Rodney toured with Earl Scruggs, performing at a number of major venues. He appeared on Earl's 1983 album, *On Top of the World*, singing lead on the title track and "Carolina Star." Following this, Rodney and his wife, Beverly Cotton Dillard, along with Dean Webb put in a six-year stretch at Silver Dollar City in Missouri. In 1983 Doug reactivated his Doug Dillard Band with Ginger Boatwright, Billy Constable, Roger Rasnake, and David Grier. This band recorded two albums for Flying Fish: *What's That?* and *Heartbreak Hotel*.

Mitch Jayne returned to Missouri in 1974, built a log house in a remote area, and resumed radio work with a program called *Hickory Holler Time*. He wrote several books: *The Forest in the Wind*, *Old Fish Hawk* – which was later made into a movie – and *Fiddler's Ghost*. He also wrote a weekly newspaper column called "Driftwood" and lectured on conservation issues, culture, and history.

1990 marked the 30th anniversary of the *Andy Griffith Show*. What

"Mayberry is my home away from home. It seems like the town that I grew up in."
- Doug Dillard, quoted in *Ken Beck and Jim Clark, Mayberry Memories*, 2005.

started as a modest celebratory tour of four dates – featuring the original Dillards – morphed into 132 shows, with appearances in England and Japan.

The original foursome of Rodney and Doug Dillard, Mitch Jayne, and Dean Webb performed their last musical engagement together on July 15, 2002, at Carnegie Hall, where they shared the stage with Arlo Guthrie and Pete Seeger. Rodney and Doug teamed again in 2004 to play festivals and concerts for the next several years. Today Rodney fronts Rodney Dillard and the Dillard Band; with his wife Beverly he also presents *Mayberry Values*, an "inspirational and entertaining program with singing, testimony and the Word." Dean Webb has been appearing with another Missouri band, the Missouri Boatride.

The Dillards were inducted into the Bluegrass Hall of Fame in 2009. Rodney Dillard said, "Bluegrass has allowed me to make friends all over the world. It's given me a wonderful family, and by the grace of God we got this while we're still alive. We all thought that in order for this to happen, one of us would have to die – but no one wanted to volunteer!" Less than a year later, in 2010, Mitch Jayne passed away at the age of eighty-two. Doug Dillard died in 2012 at seventy-five.

— GARY REID

- A commercial airline pilot was known to route his plane over Salem, Missouri, so his passengers could listen to Mitch Jayne's radio program.
- Doug Dillard sat in with the Blue Grass Boys when Bill Monroe showed up in Los Angeles without a banjo player.
- When Mitch Jayne's cabin home was destroyed by fire in 1981, the Dillards held a reunion/benefit concert to raise money to rebuild the structure.
- The Dillards are recipients of the Outstanding Missourian award.

John Cowan Hartford
(born Harford) 2010

John Hartford was born John Cowan Harford (the "t" in Hartford was added by record producer Chet Atkins) in New York City on December 30, 1937. The son of a medical doctor, he grew up in St. Louis, Missouri, where he acquired a love for music and the Mississippi River.

Hartford's parents loved to square dance. John was playing the fiddle by his early teens, but it was Flatt and Scruggs's 1953 banjo instrumental "Dear Old Dixie" that transformed his life. In June of that year, shortly after hearing the tune on the radio, the fifteen-year-old saw the band in person at Chain of Rocks Amusement Park in St. Louis. He was especially taken by the sounds of the banjo and fiddle as played by Earl Scruggs and Benny Martin. Assisted by local fiddle legend Gene Goforth, Hartford tried to emulate Martin's style of fiddling. With a set of finger picks he also worked at the Scruggs style of banjo playing.

In the 1950s, John Hartford worked with several groups, including the Mississippi Valley Boys, the Missouri Ridgerunners, and the Dixie Ramblers, which also included future Bluegrass Hall of Fame members Doug and Rodney Dillard.

From 1958 until 1963, John worked with Don Brown and the Ozark

> *"I was bad to sit and daydream in school anyway and many times, when I could hear the wind in the trees outside the classroom window, it sounded like fiddles and banjos off in the distance somewhere, and I then couldn't even begin to be able to concentrate on what was happening up on the blackboard."*
>
> – John Hartford, "Benny Martin: The Genius of Music City, USA," *Fiddler Magazine*, Fall 1999.

Born: December 30, 1937, New York, NY

Died: June 4, 2001, Nashville, TN

Primary instruments: Banjo and Fiddle

Composed:

BMI's database credits John Hartford with 214 published compositions, co-compositions, and arrangements, including:

"Gentle on My Mind"

"In Tall Buildings"

"Skippin' In the Mississippi Dew"

"Steam Powered Aereo Plane"

"I wrote 'Gentle on My Mind' after seeing Dr. Zhivago. I was writing all the time then, writing while I tied my shoes, writing while I ate. I had Julie Christie's face in front of me while I was writing those first two lines."

– John Hartford, quoted by Katie Laur in "Oh Captain, My Captain," in *Cincinnati* magazine, October 2001.

Mountain Trio. The band gained quite a bit of prominence locally and had radio shows on several stations, a lot of television work, and even scored an appearance on WSM Nashville's *Ernest Tubb Midnight Jamboree*. With the Trio, John made his first recordings, four songs on a various-artists' gospel album produced for St. Louis radio station KXEN.

In 1963 John left the Trio to work in record distribution, promotion, and as a disc jockey. At WHOW in Clinton, Illinois, he reconnected with Red Cravens and the Bray Brothers, whom he had met at Bill Monroe's Brown County Jamboree Park in the late 1950s. John performed in various configurations with these musicians and Pat Burton. In the 1970s, he produced two albums of their early and classic radio programs.

A move to Nashville in 1965 to take a job at radio station WSIX put Hartford's career on an upward trajectory. Newly in town, he signed as a songwriter with the publishing concern owned by the Glaser Brothers, who in turn landed a deal for him as a recording artist with RCA. From

Early influences:
Lester Flatt and Earl Scruggs
Benny Martin
Gene Goforth

Came to fame with:
Glen Campbell Goodtime Hour (TV show), 1969

Performed with:
Mississippi Valley Boys, mid-1950s
Don Brown and the Ozark Mountain Trio, 1958
Missouri Ridgerunners, late 1950s
Dixie Ramblers, late 1950s

Red Cravens and the Bray Brothers, early 1960s

Solo performer, late 1960s, early 1970s through 2001. Notable backing musicians included the Aereo-plain Band (1971), Jamie Hartford (1991), and Hartford String Band (late 1990s)

"When I'm working by myself, I still work as a band. I'm not a one-man act; I'm a one-man band, because I tune to standard and play in strict meter. So actually I'm a dance band even though I'm by myself on stage."

– John Hartford, quoted by Arthur Menius in "John Hartford: Living His Dreams," *Bluegrass Unlimited*, June 1985.

Led the way:

- Best known for composing the mega hit song "Gentle on My Mind."
- Four-time Grammy winner.
- Contributed music and commentary to Ken Burns's television documentary, *The Civil War*.
- Contributed music to the *O Brother, Where Art Thou?* movie soundtrack and appeared as a headliner on the *Down From the Mountain* tour.
- Americana Music Hall of Fame, 2005.
- Bluegrass Hall of Fame, 2010.
- Folk Alliance Hall of Fame, 2011.

1967 to 1971 – during the folk music boom – he released six albums and several singles for the label, including his composition, "Gentle on My Mind." He also began working as a solo performer. Several of the RCA recordings made it to the Smothers Brothers, who were riding high with their popular comedy/variety TV show. Soon John found himself in Los Angeles as a writer for the program as well as for the show's spin off, *The Glen Campbell Goodtime Hour*.

While John's earlier recording of "Gentle on My Mind" had charted modestly in the *Billboard* country charts and was covered by a few other artists, it was Glen Campbell's release that turned it into a mega-success. It became the most-played country song of 1969 and won four Grammy awards that year, two to Hartford and two to Campbell. The song has since been recorded more than 400 times by artists including Elvis Presley, Aretha Franklin, Frank Sinatra, and Lou Rawls. According to BMI, the song has been played at least six million times on the air. The biography on his website notes, "Hartford often said that 'Gentle on My Mind' bought his freedom."

"The first live bluegrass I had ever seen was Lester and Earl and Benny Martin and Curly Seckler, and boy – I'll tell you what – I stood right in the front row with my mouth open, and I think it had a profound effect on me, 'cause I've never been right since."

– John Hartford, quoted by Doug Green in "John Hartford: I Haven't Been Right Since," *Muleskinner News*, August 1973.

1971 was a busy year for John. He moved from RCA to Warner Brothers, where his first release, *Aereo-Plain*, became an instant classic. Along with Vassar Clements, Norman Blake, and Tut Taylor, the Aereo-Plain Band (which Hartford dubbed the Dobrolic Plectral Society in honor of Taylor's unusual style of flat-picking the Dobro) artfully moved bluegrass in a new direction. Sam Bush noted, "Without Aereo-plain, there would be no 'newgrass' music." The same year saw the publication of the first of John Hartford's two books, *Word Movies*, a collection of his original lyrics and poems.

The following year, John recorded and toured with Norman Blake. Their follow-up LP to *Aereo-Plain*, called *Morning Bugle*, also featured jazz bass master Dave Holland.

While advancing his music career in the late 1960s and early 1970s, John also pursued his other love: the river. Having previously worked as a deckhand on towboats and the Delta Queen, he spent three years earning a pilot's license that would enable him to operate riverboats on inland waterways. Starting in 1973, he worked the Mississippi on the Julia Belle Swain, pulling ten days of duty each month between Memorial Day and Labor Day. His love of the river and experiences as a riverboat pilot inspired his Grammy-winning 1976 release for Flying Fish, *Mark Twang*.

Over the next quarter century John released nearly thirty albums, mostly as a solo artist and on the Chicago-based Flying Fish label. Other outlets included Rounder, his own Small Dog a-Barkin', Acoustic Disc, Dot, Blue Plate, and even the Children's Book-of-the-Month Club.

John's association with Flying Fish extended from 1976 to 1991. Eleven albums released on the label included several reunions: with his old picking buddies from Missouri, Doug and Rodney Dillard (*Glitter Grass from the Nashwood Hollyville Strings* and *Permanent Wave*); with Vassar Clements and Dave Holland (*Vassar Clements, John Hartford, Dave Holland*); and a pairing of John with his son Jamie (*Hartford and Hartford*). During this era John helped to resurrect the career of his fiddling hero Benny Martin, incorporating him on a number of the Flying Fish releases and playing on Martin's own *Tennessee Jubilee*.

The Rounder releases included a coupling with old-time banjoist Bob Carlin (*The Fun of Open Discussion*), two albums with the Hartford String Band (*Good Old Boys* and *Hamilton Ironworks*), and a collection of out-takes and jam sessions from the 1971 *Aereo-Plain* album (*Steam Powered Aereo-Takes*).

During the 1980s, John played 150 to 200 dates per year as a solo, often accompanied by his wife Marie and two drivers. He showcased his fiddle, guitar, and banjo talents and incorporated an additional percussive sound by dancing on a piece of amplified plywood. In 1986, the second of John's books was published, *Steamboat in a Cornfield*. Aimed primarily at young readers, the book documented the grounding, and subsequent re-floating, of the steamboat Virginia in the early 1900s.

John augmented his touring, recording, and writing activities by helping with music and narration for the 1990 *The Civil War* series, produced by Ken Burns for PBS. A year later he wrote and hosted a special for the Nashville Network called *Fiddles, Banjos, Riverboats*. In 1991, John founded his own label, Small Dog a-Barkin', and released six of his own albums as well as three by other artists.

John's last recorded triumph came in 2001 with the release of the *O Brother, Where Art Thou?* soundtrack. He received his fourth Grammy for his part of the soundtrack album and participated in the highly successful *Down From the Mountain* tour. While on this tour he was forced to retire, due to complications from non-Hodgkin's lymphoma. He battled the disease for twenty-one years and succumbed to it on June 4, 2001. At the time of his passing, he was working on the manuscript to a third book, a biography of old-time fiddler Ed Haley.

— GARY REID

"Bill [Monroe] is always talking about looking for the high tones. I think I'll be just the reverse and look for the low tones. It seems I have more success in that direction."

- John Hartford, quoted by Doug Green in "John Hartford: I Haven't Been Right Since," *Muleskinner News*, August 1973.

By the Way:
- Worked as a riverboat deckhand and pilot.
- A television screenwriter for the *Smothers Brothers* and *Glen Campbell Goodtime Hour*.
- Never considered himself to be a good instrumentalist.
- Descendent of Patrick Henry ("Give me liberty, or give me death") and cousin of playwright Tennessee Williams.
- Saved keys from more than 1,500 hotel rooms he occupied throughout his career.

Ann Louise Certain Scruggs \ 2010

Ann Louise Certain was born on February 17, 1927, in the town of Grant, about twelve miles due east of Nashville, Tennessee. She graduated from Watertown High School in 1945, having completed a number of business classes. She moved to Nashville and found employment doing accounting work.

A visit to the *Grand Ole Opry* in 1946 led to a meeting with Earl Scruggs, who was then playing banjo with Bill Monroe. After a courtship of a year and a half, the couple married on April 18, 1948. A few weeks prior to this, the duo of Lester Flatt and Earl Scruggs also got underway.

"Everybody always thought Louise was tough and hard. To me she was one of the finest people you'd ever want to meet. Earl and Louise have been awful good to me. They was business, strictly business. If I borrowed $100 out of that company, I had to sign a note, son. And that ain't nothing but business."

– Josh Graves, in *Bluegrass Bluesman: A Memoir*, 2012.

During the first seven years of the Flatt and Scruggs partnership the business affairs were handled by Earl Scruggs. This changed in 1955 when, offhandedly, Earl asked Louise to return a phone call to a promoter to finalize details for an upcoming show date. She completed the call and promptly asked for more such assignments. Thus began her role as booking agent for Flatt and Scruggs.

In 1956 she became the band's manager, performing such additional chores as publicity, payroll, and accounting. She also came to be the point person for renegotiating their recording contracts.

Among Louise's accomplishments in managing the band was pro-

Born: February 15, 1927, Grant, TN

Died: February 2, 2006, Nashville, TN

Primary involvement in bluegrass music:
Booking Agent and Manager

Early influences:
Grandparents
Watertown High School
Earl Scruggs

Came to fame with:
Lester Flatt, Earl Scruggs and the Foggy Mountain Boys, 1955-1969

"Well, [Earl will] speak with you. He won't do business with you. So, since you'll have to come back to me eventually anyway, we might as well just wrap this up now."

– Quoted by Eddie Stubbs in "Louise Scruggs," *Bluegrass Unlimited*, April 2006.

Associated with:
Lester Flatt, Earl Scruggs and the Foggy Mountain Boys, 1955-1969
The Earl Scruggs Revue, 1970-1980

Bluegrass Hall of Fame Inductee Biographies

Photo: Les Leverett, 1961

Led the way:

- First woman to act as a booking agent or manager in a country music/bluegrass setting.
- Formed Scruggs Music publishing company.
- Brokered contracts for Flatt and Scruggs, including renewals of their Columbia contract and their appearances on *The Beverly Hillbillies* TV show.
- Garnered huge successes for Flatt and Scruggs by pitching them to the booming folk music audience.
- Successfully managed the Earl Scruggs Revue from 1970 to 1980.
- Bluegrass Hall of Fame, 2010.

"Wheeling across a great part of our nation is the freshest, and yet the oldest, sound in folk music. There's a banjo boom and the leaders are Lester Flatt and Earl Scruggs."

- Louise Scruggs, in liner notes to *Lester Flatt and Earl Scruggs: Folk Songs of Our Land*, Columbia Records, 1962.

By the Way:

- A toy typewriter received for Christmas as a child sparked her interest in a business career.
- Her grandfather took her to the *Grand Ole Opry* in her youth.
- Met Earl Scruggs, her future husband, for the first time at Nashville's Ryman Auditorium where he was appearing with Bill Monroe and the Blue Grass Boys.
- In addition to her work as a booking agent and manager Louise was an excellent cook and homemaker.

moting their success in the then-booming folk music market. In a step away from conventional bluegrass record album packaging, she arranged for New York artist Thomas B. Allen to illustrate their covers with oil portraits. Louise initiated the band's *Live at Carnegie Hall* album, only the second live album in country music history. She also conceived the concept for the *Songs of the Famous Carter Family* album, which included a guest appearance by fellow *Grand Ole Opry* member Maybelle Carter.

As a publicist, Louise's writings about Flatt and Scruggs – some signed and some anonymous – began surfacing in a number of places, including album liner notes (*Foggy Mountain Banjo* and *Folk Songs of Our Land*) and the song and picture folios issued by the group. She also had an article published in the *Tennessee Folklore Society Bulletin* called "The History of the Five-String Banjo," which naturally extolled Earl's role in the instrument's revived popularity.

In 1962, Flatt and Scruggs received their biggest dose of publicity when they performed the theme music for a new television program, *The Beverly Hillbillies*. Louise was initially opposed to the idea. She had worked hard to build the band's reputation in the folk music world and was fearful that their affiliation with the sitcom could undermine her efforts. CBS network executives eventually persuaded her otherwise, and soon the duo was making regular guest appearances on the top-rated program. So on board with the show did Louise become that she suggested the group record the show's theme song for release as a single. The song shot to the top of the *Billboard* country music charts; it was the first and only time a bluegrass song has held this distinction.

"I think it's ridiculous when people talk about who's real bluegrass and who's not. Music's music. Enjoy it."

- Louise Scruggs, quoted by Peter Cooper in "The Earl of Banjo," *Nashville Tennessean*, May 14, 2000.

As the band continued to rise in popularity, Louise continued to market the group and look out for its interests. To that end she formed a publishing company and had all of the band's original selections copyrighted and placed with Scruggs Music, thus eliminating a share of the proceeds that would have gone to an outside publisher. She also established a mail order company from which fans could order songbooks, recordings, and copies of Earl Scruggs's banjo instruction book.

The group prospered financially. They were second in sales among country artists at Columbia Records, topped only by Johnny Cash. A *Time* magazine article from 1960 reported that Flatt and Scruggs each cleared $100,000 after expenses. Adjusted for inflation, that figure today would be more than three quarters of a million dollars.

By the mid-sixties there were signs of discontent. Earl embraced the new directions of the band but Lester felt ill at ease. With the addition of several of Earl's children to the band's recordings, Lester began to feel squeezed. In 1969, the duo parted ways.

The Scruggses didn't miss a beat in forming a new group, the Earl Scruggs Revue. The Revue included three of the couple's sons – Gary, Randy and Steve – and combined bluegrass, rock, folk, country, and gospel music. Louise promoted them much as she had the old Flatt and Scruggs group, but opened a lot of new doors as well. The act was booked on college campuses, large nightclubs, and featured on festivals with major rock performers. For two years in a row, the Revue was the number one college act, eventually bumped to the number two spot by Elton John.

The Earl Scruggs Revue disbanded after a decade. Earl spent the balance of his career making select solo appearances and limited-engagement partnerships with Rodney Dillard and with the Three Pickers: Earl, Doc Watson, and Ricky Skaggs. He also continued with his recording career for Sony, Columbia's corporate successor. All of this was of course coordinated and overseen by Louise.

Starting in 1999, Louise began receiving credit for her life's work as a successful agent and manager. In that year she received the Tex Ritter Award from the International Fan Club Organization for "outstanding contributions to the field of country music." In connection with the 2004 Miss Music City/Miss Capital City Scholarship Pageant, Louise was presented with an award at the festivities kickoff event, Diamond Divas: A Tribute to Remarkable Women. The award recognizes women for their "accomplishments, achievements and visions and for providing exemplary role models." In 2005 the SOURCE Foundation's Awards Committee, which honors pioneering women of Music Row, recognized Louise at its annual awards ceremony. Also in 2005, Louise was featured as part of "Banjo Man," an exhibit at the Country Music Hall of Fame in Nashville that honored Earl and Louise Scruggs's accomplishments.

After her 2006 death from a lengthy illness at age seventy-eight, the Country Music Hall of Fame continued to honor Louise. Starting in 2007, they have hosted the Louise Scruggs Memorial Forum. The program "honors industry leaders who follow in the footsteps of Scruggs, who was Nashville's first female booker and manager." Museum Director Kyle Young cited Louise for being considered "the first female manager in country music history, (who) set new managerial and music business standards for both men and women over the course of her illustrious and trailblazing career."

— GARY REID

Photo: Dan Loftin, 1998

- Nicknamed "Tough Cookie" by a prominent Nashville journalist.
- In later years, hosted gala birthday parties for Earl.
- Started a book about her life and role as a driving force behind the Flatt and Scruggs duo.

For more information on the history of Flatt and Scruggs, see profiles of Lester Flatt, Earl Scruggs, Josh Graves, Curly Seckler and Paul Warren.

"The former Music Director for [The Beverly Hillbillies], phoned me three weeks before the show went on the network, and said they would like to have Flatt and Scruggs record the theme for the show... Two days later he was in Nashville, the theme was taped, and he was on his way back to California. Just before the show went on the network I phoned that I thought the theme would make a good record. Two days later he was back in Nashville, the theme was recorded by Columbia Records, and in five weeks in the Top 100 in the trade papers. Flatt and Scruggs had their first 'pop' hit."

- Louise Scruggs, quoted by Dixie Deen (now Dixie Hall) in "The 'Woman' Behind the Man," *Music City News* magazine, November 1965.

Delano Floyd "Del" McCoury | 2011

Born: February 1, 1929, Bakersville, NC

Primary instrument:
Guitar

Composed:
BMI's database credits Del McCoury with 38 published compositions, co-compositions, and arrangements, including:
"Beauty of My Dreams"
"Blue Piece of Paper"
"I Feel the Blues Movin' In"
"Rain Please Go Away"
"Take Me In Chains"
"You've Got the Look of a Perfect Diamond"

Early influences:
Hazel McCoury (mother)
Grover C. "G.C." McCoury (brother)
Flatt and Scruggs
Bill Monroe
Keith Daniels

Came to fame with:
Del McCoury and the Dixie Pals, 1969-1989

Delano Floyd "Del" McCoury was born into a musical family on February 1, 1939, in Bakersville, North Carolina, a small mountain community about an hour's drive from Asheville, North Carolina, and Johnson City, Tennessee. In 1941 the McCourys relocated to York County in southeastern Pennsylvania. Del's mother, Hazel, sang and played the organ, piano, and harmonica. His older brother, G.C., instructed him in playing the guitar and made him aware of bluegrass musicians such as Bill Monroe and Earl Scruggs.

"I heard a lot of music but I never really was enthused about it until I heard Earl Scruggs pick the banjo. It's funny how the music you're raised around, you just take it for granted."
– Quoted in liner notes to *Del McCoury: High on a Mountain*, Rounder Records, 1972.

The sound of Earl Scruggs's banjo prompted Del to learn on an instrument that his father borrowed. Upon graduation from high school, Del purchased a new Gibson banjo and played that for several years. In 1957 he acquired another Gibson previously owned by Baltimore banjoist Walter Hensley. Not long after that, Del got his first job as a musician, playing banjo on the radio with the Stevens Brothers. His next stint was with Keith Daniels and the Blue Ridge Ramblers. That group stayed busy for several years, making numerous appearances on the *New Dominion Barn Dance* in Richmond, Virginia. They recorded an album for the Empire label in 1962.

Del was drafted in 1962 but soon received a medical discharge. He then played with several groups, including Melvin Howell and the Franklin County Boys and Jack Cooke and the Virginia Mountain Boys. It

Photo: Eugenia Snyder, 1982

Performed with:

Stevens Brothers, c.1958

Keith Daniels and the Blue Ridge Ramblers, c.1959-1962

Melvin Howell and the Franklin County Boys, 1962

Jack Cooke and the Virginia Mountain Boys, 1962-1963

Bill Monroe and the Blue Grass Boys, 1963-1964

Golden State Boys, 1964

Shady Valley Boys, 1964

Del McCoury and the Dixie Pals, 1969-1989

Del McCoury Band, 1989-present

"We've recorded things from all different genres of music through the years, and I think that helps bring people to our shows, too... There's so many young people coming into the music, and I think the reason is they see it's a great art form."

- Quoted by Bill Michaels in "O Brother, Is Bluegrass Music Growing," *Bluegrass Unlimited*, June 2005.

Led the way:

- Leading practitioner of the classic bluegrass sound in the post-Bill Monroe era.

- SPBGMA Preservation Hall of Greats, 1989.

- Recipient of multiple IBMA awards including Entertainer of the Year, Male Vocalist of the Year, Instrumental Group of the Year, Album of the Year, Song of the Year, and Recorded Event of the Year.

- Grammy award for Best Bluegrass Album, 2006.

- Bluegrass Hall of Fame, 2011.

> *"I was working with Jack Cooke when Bill stopped to pick him up on the way to New York; he needed a banjo player, so I went with them and played the show, and Bill offered me a job. After a month or so, I decided to go down to Nashville and see about it, but by then, Bill had hired Brad Keith to play banjo, and he asked me if I would play guitar and sing lead. You know, I had sung every part, but mostly tenor up until then, so I knew the words to the choruses but not the verses. Learning all those songs was the hardest part of the job."*
>
> – Quoted by Jon Weisberger in "Del McCoury et al Are Winners, Again," *Country Standard Time*, December 1997.

By the Way:

- Del and his older brother were both named after U.S. presidents: Del after Franklin Delano Roosevelt and G.C. after Grover Cleveland.
- All three McCoury brothers – Del, G.C., and Jerry – play music; Jerry was an integral part of the Dixie Pals in the 1970s and 1980s.
- During the early days of his musical career, Del's primary income came from working as a logger in the Pennsylvania woods.
- Del's wife, Jean, traveled many miles as merchandiser and manager for the Dixie Pals and the Del McCoury Band.
- A limited edition series of 115 Martin D28-DM (Del McCoury) signature guitars was sold out before it began production.

was his tenure with Jack Cooke – a former Blue Grass Boy – that led to Del's joining Bill Monroe in February of 1963. He was originally slated to play banjo but switched to guitar and lead vocals; Monroe had hired Bill Keith a few days before. Del has remained a guitarist ever since. He stayed with Monroe for a year, making numerous appearances on the *Grand Ole Opry* and helping to record six tracks for Decca Records.

When Del's tenure with Monroe ended in February of 1964, he headed for California with fiddler Billy Baker for a short stay with the Golden State Boys (a band that included Chris Hillman). McCoury soon moved on to another California group, the Shady Valley Boys, but by the end of June was back East doing logging work for his father. He worked at this for several years and played nightclubs on the side.

In December of 1967, while living in Glen Rock, Pennsylvania, he made his first recordings under his own name. *Del McCoury Sings Bluegrass*, on the Arhoolie label, with Billy Baker on fiddle, Bill Emerson on banjo, Wayne Yates on mandolin, and Tommy Neal and Dewey Renfro on bass.

1969 saw the formation of the Dixie Pals, Del's group for the next twenty years. Initial members included Del's brother Jerry on bass, Larry Smith on banjo, and Dick Laird on mandolin. With the Dixie Pals Del began to achieve considerable notice within the bluegrass community. Critics praised a string of releases on a variety of independent labels for Del's intense, high lonesome singing and expert backing from the musicians he employed. A highlight of this era was Del's 1972 album for Rounder, *High on a Mountain*. The album's title track, written by Ola Belle Reed, remains a favorite to this day.

Other albums from this period include two for Rebel: 1975's *Del McCoury* and 1978's *Our Kind of Grass*. Standouts from these albums include "Cabin on a Mountain," "Rain and Snow," and "Rain Please Go Away." Notable Dixie Pals from this era included mandolin players Dick Staber and Donnie Eldreth, fiddler Bill Poffinberger, banjo player Bill Runkle, and bass player Dewey Renfro.

The end of the 1970s ushered in new Dixie Pals: Dick Smith on banjo, Herschel Sizemore on mandolin, Sonny Miller on fiddle, and Jerry McCoury on bass. A highlight of their time together was a 1979 tour of Japan. Del signed with Roanoke-based Leather Records. His lone release for the label – *Take Me to the Mountains* – was short-lived, due to the company's demise. It was picked up and reissued by Rebel Records in 1984, followed by a 1985 release on Rebel called *Sawmill*.

The 1980s were transformative years for Del. In 1981 his son Ronnie joined the band playing mandolin. In 1987 another son, Robbie, joined on bass but switched to banjo a year later. Also in 1987, Del began a nearly ten-year relationship with Rounder Records with a duet album called *The McCoury Brothers* (Del and Jerry). By the end of the decade, the group would be rechristened The Del McCoury Band.

In 1992 the family relocated to Nashville. This and three high-profile releases on Rounder (*Don't Stop the Music, Blue Side of Town,* and *A Deeper Shade of Blue*) brought much attention to Del and his music. During the 1990s, the Del McCoury Band dominated the IBMA awards. Del was a four-time winner of the Male Vocalist award, five-time winner of Entertainer of the Year, two-time winner of Instrumental Group, and a winner of the Album of the Year and Recorded Event of the Year awards. Ronnie McCoury won the Mandolin Player award seven times, while band members Jason Carter and Mike Bub each won twice for Fiddle Player and Bass Player. The end of the decade brought a pairing of Del with folk-rock-country singer Steve Earle. Their CD, *The Mountain*, was nominated for several IBMA awards and introduced Del to audiences beyond the bluegrass field.

> *"What's made me keep at this is a love of the music. When I started out, you know, it never entered my mind that you could make any money playing music… In the early days, I'd drive forty miles to make seven dollars. And I still feel that way."*
>
> - Quoted by Dana Andrew Jennings, in "Bluegrass, Straight and Pure, Even if the Money's No Good," in *The New York Times*, April 23, 1995.

In 1999 and 2001 Del made two albums for Ricky Skaggs's Ceili label, *The Family* and *Del and the Boys*. In 2003 Del released the first CD under his own imprint, McCoury Music. Since then, all of his recordings have appeared on that label, including *It's Just the Night, The Company We Keep, The Promised Land* (his first all-gospel recording), *By Request, Celebrating 50 Years of Del McCoury* – a five-CD boxed set with new recordings of Del's most popular songs, *Family Circle, American Legacies* – recorded with the Preservation Jazz Hall Band, and *Old Memories: The Songs of Bill Monroe*.

The awards kept coming in the 2000s. There were four more IBMA Entertainer of the Year awards, as well as Song and Album of the Year wins. In 2006 Del received a Grammy award for *It's Just the Night*. In 2010, he received a National Heritage Fellowship and in 2011 he was inducted into the Bluegrass Hall of Fame. One of his best "awards" was induction into the cast of the *Grand Ole Opry* in 2003.

In addition to his active recording career, Del maintains a busy touring schedule. Fans flock to see McCoury not only at bluegrass festivals and concerts, but also at rock clubs, college campuses, large youth-oriented events like Bonnaroo, and highly successful tours such as the *Down From the Mountain* tour.

— GARY REID

- Del likened his 2002 appearance at Tennessee's Bonnaroo festival – with an estimated crowd of 70,000 youths – to his 1960s appearances on the *Grand Ole Opry* as a member of Bill Monroe's Blue Grass Boys; both crowds were wild with excitement for bluegrass music.

George Saunders Shuffler \ 2011

George Shuffler was known for his flamboyant walking-style bass playing and distinctive cross-picking guitar, both popularized during his sixteen-year association with the Stanley Brothers. He was born in the Western North Carolina community of Valdese, situated not far from Hickory, Charlotte, and Asheville. George was the second of nine children. Music abounded in his family; his mother sang, his father was an old-time banjo player, and most of George's brothers and sisters played. George attended singing schools that were held at a church, where he enjoyed harmonizing in quartets.

At ten he got his first guitar and learned the basic chords. Along with music at home and in church, the radio offered inspiration to the young Shuffler. Merle Travis, the Delmore Brothers and Grandpa Jones were particular favorites.

George's first opportunity to play in a band came in about 1941. At sixteen, he played electric guitar in a group called The Carolina Boys. He soon moved on to The Melody Mountain Boys, an outfit which included his brother John as well as future Stanley Brothers' fiddler Lester Woodie. In 1946, at age twenty-one, he joined the brother duo of Charles and Danny Bailey, then featured on the *Grand Ole Opry*. When the Bailey Brothers left the *Opry* later that year, George came back to North Carolina and

"I think that Ralph would be the first to admit it just wasn't the same without Carter. We were always the prank pullers, the jokesters. Ralph and I tried, but it wasn't the same. We three were like brothers. I never worked for the Stanleys, I worked with them."

– Quote by Ron Gould in "The Shuffler Family: Foothills Gospel," *Bluegrass Unlimited*, November 1977.

Born: April 11, 1925, Valdese, NC

Died: April 7, 2014, Valdese, NC

Primary instruments:
Bass and Guitar

"I liked the tone of a Martin [guitar] for bluegrass. It's louder and deeper."

– Quoted by Larry Mitchell in "George Shuffler," *Pickin'*, April 1978.

Composed:
BMI's database credits George Shuffler with 46 published compositions, co-compositions, and arrangements, including:

"Give the World a Sunny Smile"

"Just a Phone Call Will Do"

"When I Receive My Robe and Crown"

Early influences:
Merle Travis
Sons of the Pioneers
Blue Sky Boys

Photo: Frank and Marty Godbey

Left to right: Don Reno, George Shuffler, Bill Harrell, Columbus, OH, 1968.

Came to fame with:
The Stanley Brothers, 1952-1966

Performed with:
Carolina Boys, c.1941

Melody Mountain Boys, c.1942, 1947-1949

Bailey Brothers, c.1946

Mustard and Gravy, c.1949-1950

Jim and Jesse and the Virginia Boys, c.1951

The Stanley Brothers and the Clinch Mountain Boys, 1952-1966

Ralph Stanley and the Clinch Mountain Boys, 1967, 1969-1970

Don Reno and Bill Harrell and the Tennessee Cut-Ups, 1967-1969

Shuffler Family, 1974-c.1988

"Right now we're [the Shuffler Family] having to turn down more dates than we can book. We try to keep it to weekends, but it's about got out of hand. Looks like we're going to have to make a decision."

- Quoted by John Wright in *Traveling the High Way Home*, University of Illinois Press, 1993.

Led the way:
- Stellar bass player, famous for his walking style which influenced others, notably Tom Gray.
- Developed a cross-picking guitar style which continues to be echoed by bluegrass lead players.
- Toured and recorded with a number of bluegrass legends including the Stanley Brothers, Bill Clifton, and Reno and Harrell.

reassembled the Melody Mountain Boys. The group performed on several regional stations, including WKBC (North Wilkesboro), WMNC (Morganton), WIRC (Hickory), and WJRI (Lenoir).

George Shuffler had occasion to work with several other professional bands between 1949 and 1951. One, Mustard and Gravy, was described in Bruce Eder's online biography of the duo as "country-novelty with a hillbilly edge." The team's forte was blackface comedy and they worked from Florida to New York. Several of their shows were done in conjunction with Eddy Arnold, one of the top country stars of the day.

Shuffler also worked with Jim and Jesse and the Virginia Boys, along with banjoist Hoke Jenkins. In the summer and fall of 1951, the group

Bluegrass Hall of Fame Inductee Biographies

- IBMA Distinguished Achievement Award, 1996.
- North Carolina Heritage Award, 2007.
- Bluegrass Hall of Fame, 2011.

By the Way:
- In George's first band, The Carolina Boys, he played electric guitar.
- George's first recording session occurred on his twenty-seventh birthday, in 1952, when he helped out on a session with the Stanley Brothers.
- George's brother, John, also played bass with the Stanley Brothers.
- While working a show date with the Stanley Brothers, George filled in for the one of the Carter Sisters, who were also on the program, thus acquiring the nickname of "Aunt" George Shuffler.
- One of the first bluegrass sidemen to be portrayed and prominently named on an album cover.
- Bandmates knew he would soon leave and return to animal trading when George started watching horses and cows from the window of their touring vehicle.

appeared on WWNC in Asheville. It was while working with Jim and Jesse that George began developing his unique cross-picking guitar style. (Jesse McReynolds cross-picked the mandolin in a slightly different pattern; both echoed the roll of the newly popular Scruggs-style banjo.)

In the spring of 1951, George married Sue Benfield. Shortly after Christmas that year, he received a phone call at Sue's parents' house in Hickory. It was from Carter Stanley, who invited George to accompany the Stanley Brothers to Versailles, Kentucky, to appear on WVLK Radio. It was to be the first of many stints with the Stanleys. This first tour of duty lasted for most of 1952. From January to April, they worked out of the Versailles-Lexington area.

At the end of their stay in Kentucky, the band journeyed to Nashville to record the Stanleys' final session for Columbia Records. Included on the session was a song that George – although uncredited – helped to put together, "A Life of Sorrow." Other radio shows included WLSI in Pikeville, Kentucky, and WOAY in Oak Hill, West Virginia. As often happened, George missed horse trading and returned home to North Carolina, only to be lured back to music and the road within a number of months.

"We were doing these old, slow, drawn-out mournful songs… I tried Merle Travis-style guitar and Mother Maybelle Carter-style guitar; but single-string leads were just not getting it. So I tried that two notes down, one up, crossing over strings. At first Carter did not like it. 'Is that all you do?' he asked. 'It's all I want to do,' I said. And after it started selling, I could not do it enough to satisfy him."

– Quoted by David Menconi in "The Picker Who Set the Beat," *Charlotte News-Observer*, October 21, 2007.

George participated in the Stanley Brothers' first session for Mercury records in August of 1953. Heralded as one of the Stanleys' best trips to the studio, it prominently showcased George's driving 4/4 walking bass on songs like "(Say) Won't You Be Mine" and "I'm Lonesome Without You."

The summer of 1955 found George again touring with the Stanleys. In the fifties and sixties, Shuffler regularly appeared on recording sessions at Carter Stanley's request, even when he wasn't currently a member of the group. Chuck Seitz, a recording engineer at King Records, overheard George doodling around with his guitar cross-picking and encouraged the Stanleys to feature it on record (Bill Napier, primarily a mandolin player at the time, was the first to record guitar cross-picking with the Stanleys, in September of 1959, at a session where Shuffler played bass). Carter and Ralph were initially opposed to the idea but warmed to it after it caught on with their fans.

In 1958, the Stanley Brothers relocated to Live Oak, Florida. George joined them there in the early part of 1961. In addition to touring and recording he did radio and television work with the group, appearing on their *Jim Walter Jamboree* programs. It was in 1961 that George switched from bass to lead guitar as his primary instrument with the Stanleys. The Shuffler style of guitar playing has remained a part of the Stanley sound ever since.

Throughout the early and middle 1960s George appeared on most of the Stanley Brothers' recorded output. He became so identified with the Stanleys that he received prominent billing on a 1964 album release, *Hymns of the Cross*.

The Stanley Brothers' act came to an end with the passing of Carter Stanley on December 1, 1966. George continued with Ralph for several months, helping him to get established as a bandleader. When Larry Sparks – a capable lead guitarist – joined the band as featured vocalist, George felt it was time to move on.

After a brief rest George signed with the newly formed team of Don Reno and Bill Harrell. Over a roughly two-year period (1967-1969) he recorded three albums with them for King Records and at least as many for other labels such as Jalyn and Rural Rhythm. A *Bluegrass Unlimited* magazine readers' poll in 1967 named George the Best Bass Player of the Year.

In the middle of 1969 Ralph's bass player of the last three years, Melvin Goins, departed the Clinch Mountain Boys, leaving an opening once again for George. He stayed for about a year and appeared on one recording session during this period.

George's last professional group began in 1974 when he put together the Shuffler Family, a traditional country gospel act featuring his daughters (Jennie and Debbie), son (Steve), brother (Dude) and nephew (Dude's son, Joe Shuffler). The group stayed together for nearly fifteen years and recorded four albums for Rebel.

Throughout the 1990s, 2000s, and into the 2010s George kept busy musically, often appearing as a solo, in a duet with Asheville-based Laura Boosinger, and at workshops. He was a fixture in the traditional tent at MerleFest and usually held down the vendor's spot next to Ralph's long-time guitarist James Alan Shelton at Stanley's Memorial Day festival. He also released a number of guitar-oriented albums, including a solo outing for Rex Nelon and three for Copper Creek, including a duet album with James Shelton and one with Laura Boosinger.

George was presented with an IBMA Distinguished Achievement Award in 1996, a North Carolina Heritage Award in 2007, and in 2011 he was inducted into the Bluegrass Hall of Fame. In 2014 he died peacefully at home, of natural causes, four days short of his eighty-ninth birthday.

— GARY REID

Doyle Wayne Lawson \ 2012

Born: April 20, 1944, Ford Town, TN

Primary instrument: Mandolin

Composed:
BMI's database credits Doyle Lawson with 135 published compositions, co-compositions, and arrangements, including:

"Georgia Cracker"

"Picking Wild Cherries"

"Tennessee Dream"

"Welcome to New York"

Early influences:
Leonard and Minnie Lawson (parents)

Bill Monroe

Jimmy Martin

Grand Ole Opry

Came to fame with:
The Country Gentlemen, 1971-1979

Performed with:
Jimmy Martin and the Sunny Mountain Boys, 1963-1966, 1969

J.D. Crowe and the Kentucky Mountain Boys, 1966-1969, 1969-1971

Doyle Wayne Lawson was born on April 20, 1944, in Ford Town, near Kingsport, Tennessee, to Leonard and Minnie Lawson. For as long as he can remember, Doyle has been avidly interested in music. Early exposure came in the form of his parents' singing in local gospel trios and quartets and radio broadcasts such as the *Grand Ole Opry*. Bill Monroe's performances on the *Opry* captivated the young man and fueled his desire to one day become a professional musician.

Doyle acquired a mandolin when he was eleven or twelve years old. In 1954 the family relocated to Sneedville, Tennessee, about an hour's drive west of Kingsport. It was here, in 1958, that Doyle met Sneedville native Jimmy Martin. He recalls that Martin spent several hours helping with his picking techniques. This cemented Lawson's passion to make music a career. He set about learning guitar and banjo, in an attempt to make himself a more versatile and desirable player. These efforts paid off several years later in 1963 when he went to work playing banjo for Jimmy Martin.

Doyle's next musical job came in 1966, when he joined J.D. Crowe and the Kentucky Mountain Boys. His first recording was the 1968 album *The Kentucky Mountain Boys: Bluegrass Holiday*, which included Crowe on banjo, Lawson on mandolin, vocalist/guitarist Red Allen, and bass player Bobby Slone. Lawson stayed with Crowe through 1969, at which time he returned to Jimmy Martin's group for about six months. Doyle came back to J.D. Crowe and stayed until 1971, this time on guitar, while Larry Rice played mandolin. He recorded two more albums with J.D.: *Model Church* — heralded to this day as a bluegrass gospel classic — and *Ramblin' Boy*.

"I remember how much fun it was recording the first album... the [first albums we did] were cut pretty much live, and came off being a little bit rough. But I think the soul in them will stand the test of time."
– Quoted by Tim Stafford in liner notes to *Doyle Lawson and Quicksilver: The Original Band*, Sugar Hill Records, 1990.

Country Gentlemen, 1971-1979

Doyle Lawson and Quicksilver, 1979-present

"When Bill [Emerson] left [the Country Gentlemen], it fell into my lap to get the music together, and I was inquisitive about what it took to get it done in the studio. I did some mixing, and was on the ground floor of the whole process. The expanse of knowledge I gained from that... to this day, no one mixes my vocals but me."

- Quoted by Michael Brantley in "Light on His Feet, Ready to Fly... Farther," *Bluegrass Unlimited*, June 2011.

Led the way:

- Introduced contemporary styles that set the tone for much of bluegrass music in the 1980s and beyond.
- Mentored dozens of musicians who have gone on to lead successful careers in bluegrass and country music.
- Started a bluegrass festival in Denton, North Carolina, 1980.
- Member of the Bluegrass Album Band, an all-star ensemble which made six best-selling albums and limited public appearances.
- Recipient of fourteen IBMA awards, thirty-seven SPBGMA awards, four Grammy nominations, and four Dove nominations.
- National Heritage Fellowship, National Endowment for the Arts, 2006.

On September 1, 1971, Doyle began an eight-year stint with one of the most popular bands in bluegrass, the Country Gentlemen. When he joined, the configuration included Charlie Waller, Bill Emerson, and Bill Yates. Doyle enjoyed a special bond with Emerson, who had a knack for finding and arranging great material such as "Fox on the Run." When Emerson left the group to join the U.S. Navy Band, Lawson considered doing the same, but decided to stay with bluegrass as a civilian.

Doyle recorded six albums with the Country Gentlemen: *Award-Winning* (with 1972 Song of the Year "Legend of the Rebel Soldier,") *Live in Japan*, the self-titled *Country Gentlemen*, *Remembrances and Forecasts*, *Joe's Last Train*, and *Calling My Children Home* – a celebrated gospel release that bore Doyle's distinctive imprint in terms of material and style.

In 1979 Doyle made the decision to strike out on his own. In April of that year he launched Doyle Lawson and Foxfire, only to find that another band was using that name. At his mother's suggestion he adopted the name Quicksilver. Original band members included Jimmy Haley on guitar and lead vocals, Lou Reid on bass and harmony vocals, and Terry Baucom on banjo and baritone and bass vocals. The group secured a recording contract with newly formed Sugar Hill Records. Early releases – including *Doyle Lawson and Quicksilver* and *Rock My Soul* – met with immediate critical acclaim.

"[My band members must] have character, dependability, must be willing to do things my way. I expect them to represent me and the music I play in a professional manner at all times. The fans watch you offstage just like they do when you're performing."

- From "The Doyle Lawson Interview" posted on the *Mandolin Café* website, accessed December 11, 2012.

Doyle embarked on several other new ventures. 1980 saw the inauguration of his own bluegrass festival in Denton, North Carolina. The event quickly established itself as one of the top festivals in the Southeast and featured many of the trendsetting bands of the day. The same year brought Doyle's participation in Rounder Records' *The Bluegrass Album Band*. It allowed top-flight musicians Tony Rice, J.D. Crowe, Doyle, Bobby Hicks, and Todd Phillips to recreate classic songs and tunes from the early days of bluegrass. The release became one of the best selling albums of the early 1980s and led to five follow-up recordings, the last in 1996.

Doyle followed up the success of *Rock My Soul* with 1983's *Heavenly Treasures*. The album was a mix of bluegrass gospel and – in an overture to the southern gospel audience – tracks with pedal steel. Gospel music became an increasingly important component to his sound, so much so that he began to cater to that segment specifically. Where most bluegrass artists would release one album per year, and might alternate every other or every third album with gospel, Doyle took the unprecedented step of simultaneously releasing two albums at a time, one bluegrass and one gospel. In 1985, his love of gospel music took on a new meaning when he rededicated his life to Jesus Christ and viewed his work as a musical ministry to lead others to Him.

During this time period, Doyle averaged between 125 and 175 booking dates per year. A 1979 Ford van racked up so many miles that the engine had to be replaced four times.

In more than three decades as a bandleader Doyle earned a reputation for producing a top-notch sound. His recordings are meticulously produced and he has a knack for choosing and developing stellar talent. Just as Bill Monroe's Blue Grass Boys were a proving ground for many performers who went on to become headliners in bluegrass in the 1950s and 1960s, the same can be said of Doyle Lawson's Quicksilver from the 1980s onward. Among many bluegrass notables who apprenticed with Doyle were Lou Reid, Terry Baucom, Randy Graham, Russell Moore, Scott Vestal, Jamie Dailey, John Bowman, Jim Mills, Ray Deaton, Barry Abernathy, Steve Gulley, and Jimmy Van Cleve.

Doyle's twenty-two year association with Sugar Hill Records came to an end in 2002 when he contracted for two albums with the all-gospel Brentwood label. From there he jumped to another gospel imprint, Horizon, while at the same time releasing straight-ahead bluegrass albums on Rounder. Most recently, his bluegrass and gospel recordings have appeared on the Crossroads label.

A recent career highlight was Doyle's participation in the Children's Hospital and Arena Tour, which combined National Anthem performances at major sporting arenas with performances for boys and girls at children's hospitals in the same regions. The 2011 tour consisted of six performances, which put Doyle before 108,000 people.

In addition to a spate of awards and nominations from the International Bluegrass Music Association, the Society for the Preservation of Bluegrass Music in America, and Grammy and Dove award nominations, Doyle is the recipient of a National Heritage Fellowship from the National Endowment for the Arts (2006) and an Honorary Ph.D. in Fine Arts from King College in Bristol, Tennessee (2007). Doyle and Quicksilver were recognized by the Tennessee State Senate with a Joint Resolution that honored them for "their many contributions to this state and nation through their fantastic gospel bluegrass music." The bluegrass community acknowledged Doyle's lifetime commitment to the music with induction into the Bluegrass Hall of Fame in 2012.

— GARY REID

- Honorary Ph.D. in Fine Arts, King College, 2007.
- Bluegrass Hall of Fame, 2012.

By the Way:

- As a shy young mechanic in Tennessee, repaired a touring vehicle for his heroes the Osborne Brothers without mentioning his own involvement in bluegrass.
- Began his professional bluegrass career playing banjo with Jimmy Martin.
- Appeared in the movie *Bluegrass Country Soul* (1971) in his first weekend with the Country Gentlemen.
- Collects memorabilia of western stars such as Roy Rogers and Gene Autry.
- Enjoys old cars; once restored a 1946 Ford Coupe from the ground up.
- An avid golfer who plays every chance he can get.

Ralph Charles Rinzler | 2012

Ralph Rinzler sought out, recorded, advocated for, booked and wrote about the old-time and bluegrass performers whose music he cherished as a musician and a scholar. He brought Doc Watson to the world; he got Bill Monroe to speak.

Rinzler introduced bluegrass to many people. In 1957 he helped produce the first bluegrass LP album, *American Banjo Scruggs Style*. From 1959 to 1963 he performed in the first nationally touring and recording bluegrass band from outside the South, the Greenbriar Boys. In 1961 he launched Doc Watson's career. Between 1963 and 1965, as a manager and writer, he revitalized Bill Monroe's career. In 1964-65 he helped Carlton Haney start the festival movement that transformed bluegrass. As he moved on to other cultural activities, Rinzler never lost his interest in bluegrass. Among his last productions before dying in 1994 were Smithsonian/Folkways albums of live recordings by Bill Monroe and the Blue Grass Boys and Bill Monroe and Doc Watson.

Today Ralph Rinzler is best remembered for his work at The Smithsonian Institution in Washington, where he played a major role in establishing folklife research and presentation in American public life. He led the development of the Smithsonian's Festival of American Folklife, created its Office of Folklife Programs (now The Center for Folklife Programs and Cultural Studies), and managed its acquisition of Folkways Records in 1988. In 1993 he was awarded the Smithsonian Secretary's Gold Medal for Exceptional Service.

Ralph Charles Rinzler was born on July 20, 1934, in Passaic, New Jersey. Son of a doctor, he grew up in a family with deep interests in the arts. Samuel Joseph, an uncle who had studied folklore at Harvard,

Born: July 20, 1934, Passaic, NJ

Died: July 2, 1994, Washington, DC

Primary instrument: Mandolin

Composed:
BMI's database credits Ralph Rinzler with two published compositions, co-compositions, and arrangements:
"Coot From Tennessee"
"Stewball"

Early influences:
Roger Abrahams
Pete, Mike, Peggy, and Charles Seeger
Ewan MacColl
Alan Lomax

Came to fame with:
The Greenbriar Boys, 1959-1963

Performed with:
The Greenbriar Boys, 1959-1963

Photo: Carl Fleischhauer

Left to right: Ralph Rinzler, Ludwig van Beethoven (on wall), Bill Monroe, 1979.

encouraged his interest in folk music with yearly gifts of newly published Library of Congress field recording albums.

As a teen Rinzler attended folk music concerts in nearby New York City. At Swarthmore College, near Philadelphia, he heard Pete Seeger in concert, took up the five-string banjo, and began performing at folksong revival events. He moved to mandolin after seeing Woody Guthrie play that then-novel folk instrument.

At Swarthmore's Folk Festival, Rinzler met Mike Seeger, who was deeply involved in old-time and bluegrass music in the Washington-Baltimore area. Seeger took him to nearby country music parks where he heard Bill Monroe, the Stanley Brothers, and other bluegrass performers. Their music and its audiences gave him a deeper understanding of the field recordings he'd heard as a child, and moved him to begin making his own recordings of traditional musicians. Between 1956 and 1959 he learned field research techniques by working with Mike Seeger, Alan Lomax, and the great British scholar-performers A. L. Lloyd and Ewan MacColl.

At the same time his musical performing activities grew. He worked as a mandolin accompanist at concerts and recording sessions in Europe and the U.S.

Led the way:

- The first person to identify bluegrass as a style of music in print, 1957.
- Rediscovering Clarence Ashley, "discovered" Doc Watson; managed Watson from 1959 to 1966.
- Performed in one of the first urban bluegrass bands: The Greenbriar Boys.
- Managed Bill Monroe and revitalized his career in the early 1960s.
- Director of field research for the Newport Folk Festival, 1963-1966.
- Consultant to the first three Smithsonian folk festivals, 1967-1969.
- Engineered the Smithsonian Institution's acquisition of the Folkways label.

Bluegrass Hall of Fame Inductee Biographies \ 203

- IBMA Distinguished Achievement Award, 1987.
- Awarded a Grammy as producer for *Folkways: A Vision Shared*, 1988.
- Bluegrass Hall of Fame, 2012.
- *Old Time Music at Clarence Ashley's*, a Folkways album produced by Rinzler, was added to the Library of Congress's National Recording Registry, 2013.

"Newport was a wonderful experience, because I kind of learned a part of the cultural map of the country, and I traveled fairly extensively. But there was something about bringing the best of tradition into the midst of an entertainment-oriented scene with a lot of kids drinking beer or smoking pot that was just really offensive to me. And I stuck with it for four years."

– Quoted by Richard Gagne' in "Ralph Rinzler, Folklorist: Professional Biography," *Folklore Forum* 27:l, Indiana University, 1996.

By the way:
- Sidelined by music while intending to obtain a graduate degree in French.
- Learned to play mandolin by watching Woody Guthrie perform in New York City's Washington Square.
- Bob Dylan was a warm-up act for the Greenbriar Boys in the early 1960s.
- Chose not to be employed by the Smithsonian – a government agency – during the Vietnam war.

In 1959 he was invited to join the Greenbriar Boys, the first non-southern bluegrass band to achieve national popularity. In 1960 they took their sound to the Union Grove Fiddlers' Convention in Iredell County, North Carolina, and walked away with first place in the band contest. When they played Gerde's Folk City in Greenwich Village in the fall of 1961, Bob Dylan opened for them.

Signed to record for Vanguard Records, the Greenbriar Boys released their first album in early 1962. Around the same time they recorded on several tracks of Joan Baez's second Vanguard album. In spring 1962 they toured nationally with Baez as her opening act. When she came to Nashville for a concert at Vanderbilt, the Greenbriars guested on the *Grand Ole Opry*. By 1963, when Ralph left the band to work for the Newport Folk Festival, they had taken bluegrass to folk music audiences all over North America.

"There's nothing wrong with pop music, radios, juke boxes, television and mass culture but it shouldn't kill the small worlds of music and craft that exist in tiny communities across the states."

– Quoted by Barbara Marsh in "Folk Crafts Share Festival Scene," *Newport Daily News*, July 21, 1966.

Through his years with the Greenbriar Boys, Rinzler continued to follow his interest in researching traditional music. In a back-room jam at Union Grove in 1960 he rediscovered Tom "Clarence" Ashley. Ashley's recordings from the late 1920s had made him an authentic folk music icon, but no one had been able to track him down. Ralph arranged to record him, and thus met Doc Watson, who was playing in Ashley's band.

In 1961 Folkways published Ralph's recordings of Ashley's band. Working with the newly formed Friends of Old Time Music, he brought the band to perform in New York. Watson was an immediate hit. Over the next three years Ralph helped guide Doc to a solo career on Vanguard records.

Rinzler's liner notes to the Greenbriars' first album devoted much space to Bill Monroe; he felt that not enough was known about this influential artist. In 1962 he interviewed Monroe for an article in the folk music magazine *Sing Out!* It was Monroe's first published interview and the beginning of an enduring relationship between Rinzler and Monroe.

In 1963 Ralph began introducing Monroe to folk music audiences at festivals and concerts. Moving to Nashville, he became Monroe's manager and helped him assemble a band that included Del McCoury as singer and guitarist and Bill "Brad" Keith as banjoist. McCoury went on to become one of bluegrass music's leading singers. Keith, the first "Yankee" Blue Grass Boy, introduced a style that revolutionized five-string banjo. Rinzler booked Monroe at festivals, coffeehouses, and concerts, showcasing this band and encouraging Bill to talk about his music on stage.

Rinzler stayed in Nashville as Monroe's manager for only six months, but continued to represent Monroe as an agent, and began booking Doc Watson, whom he also represented, to open at Bill's shows, where Doc and Bill began recreating the old Monroe Brothers' duet sound.

While in Nashville, Rinzler began working to edit reissues of Bill Monroe's old recordings. The first fruit of this work came in *Blue Grass Instrumentals* (1965), the first historically oriented collection of bluegrass recordings. The second, *High Lonesome Sound* (1966), compiled Bill's most influential early Decca singles, and introduced the phrase by which Monroe and his music became widely characterized.

In the summer of 1963, Rinzler began working for the Newport Folk Festival as Director of Field Research, a post he held until 1967. Folk had become one of the nation's most popular musical genres, and Newport was its premier showcase. The large crowds who came to see folk stars like Dylan and Baez generated ample income. This gave Newport the means to introduce festival audiences to lesser-known traditional artists from whose music the young stars drew. Ralph's field research was targeted at finding such artists, and to using the festival's resources to help communities preserve and develop their traditional arts.

It was in this spirit that Rinzler invited Carlton Haney to attend the 1964 Newport Folk Festival and then worked behind the scenes with Haney as he created the first multi-day bluegrass festival at Fincastle, Virginia, on Labor Day weekend 1965. That year and the following Ralph helped backstage with Haney's "Story of Bluegrass," a dramatic recreation of Monroe's musical history that brought onstage former Blue Grass Boys like Jimmy Martin, Carter Stanley, Don Reno, and Mac Wiseman to recreate their performances with Monroe.

In 1967 Rinzler moved to the Smithsonian Institution where he forged an innovative career in the public preservation and promotion of traditional culture. He died of HIV/AIDS in Washington, D.C., on July 2, 1994, a few weeks before his sixtieth birthday.

— NEIL V. ROSENBERG

- Named a *Washingtonian of the Year* following the success of the Smithsonian's 1976/Bicentennial festival.

"The meaning of these experiences was clear and powerful. Here was the context of the folk music I had heard in recorded and concert performances for twenty of my twenty-six years. The distinctions between traditional and urban revival performances have long been obvious to me, but never had I been in a community whose music – repertoire, vocal and instrumental styles – was part of its everyday life. Never had it been possible to hear a brilliant, innovative, traditional stylist – like Doc, for example – alongside his own as well as another generation of musicians from whom he had absorbed both style and repertoire."

– Discussing Doc Watson in liner notes to *The Original Folkways Recordings of Doc Watson and Clarence Ashley, 1960-1962*, Smithsonian Folkways Records, 1994.

David Anthony "Tony" Rice ⟩ 2013

Born: June 8, 1951, Danville, VA

Primary instrument:- Guitar

Composed:
BMI's database credits Tony Rice with 48 published compositions, co-compositions and arrangements, including:

"Backwaters"

"Bullet Man"

"California Autumn"

"Manzanita"

"Mar West"

Early influences:
Herbert Rice (father)
Flatt and Scruggs
Clarence White/Kentucky Colonels
Ry Cooder
Chris Hillman
Herb Pedersen

Tony Rice was born in Danville, Virginia, on June 8, 1951. In his infancy, the family headed west to Los Angeles where Tony's earliest musical memory is the guitar playing of his uncle, Hal Poindexter, who played in the Golden State Boys. The band, headed by Tony's guitar and mandolin-playing father Herbert Rice, also included uncles Walter Poindexter on banjo and Leon Poindexter on bass.

Tony started out learning to play mandolin but soon switched to guitar. He made his performing debut at age nine when he sang "Under Your Spell Again" on the *Town Hall* radio show. It was here that he met the Kentucky Colonels and their lead guitarist, Clarence White, who would have a profound impact on his playing. Shortly after, Tony played in a group with his brothers Larry, on mandolin, and Ronnie, on bass, plus banjo player Andy Evans. The youngsters played a number of California venues including the Ash Grove and Troubadour nightclubs and Disneyland.

The pursuit of work created somewhat of a transient lifestyle for the Rice family, and Tony's teenage years found them living in Florida, Georgia, Texas, and North Carolina. In 1970 Tony attended Carlton

> *"When I first started working with [J.D. Crowe], if the timing was not what he was used to, if it didn't have exceptionally good drive, he didn't feel comfortable playing until you did have it. I guess it was through him, indirectly... he was the main one-on-one influence that made me realize the importance of that."*
>
> – Quoted by Bryan Kimsey in "Tony Rice: Flatpicking Master," *Flatpicking Guitar Magazine*, November/December 1998.

Photo: Pamela Hodges Rice, 2002

"The first music that I ever heard – pure bluegrass that turned me on – was the old Flatt and Scruggs stuff. We had a 78 of 'Foggy Mountain Special' and the other side was 'You're Not a Drop in the Bucket.' That was music that really got to me."

– Quoted by Jack Tottle in "Tony Rice: East Meets West," *Bluegrass Unlimited*, October 1977.

Came to fame with:

J.D. Crowe and the Kentucky Mountain Boys (later New South), 1971-1975

Performed with:

Bluegrass Alliance, 1970-1971

J.D. Crowe and the Kentucky Mountain Boys (later New South), 1971-1975

David Grisman Quintet, 1975-1979

Bluegrass Album Band, 1980-1996

Tony Rice Unit, 1978-present

Led the way:

- Major influence on modern bluegrass artists, especially lead guitarists.
- An integral performer on the legendary album, *J.D. Crowe and the New South*.
- Co-founded and produced the Bluegrass Album Band, an all-star recording group.
- Pioneered the fusion of jazz and other acoustic styles to arrive at a new medium he called "spacegrass."
- Established himself as a bandleader, performing in both bluegrass and jazz idioms.

Bluegrass Hall of Fame Inductee Biographies

- Topped the list of the *Frets* Readers Poll Awards for Country Flatpicking Guitar, Jazz/Pop/Progressive Guitar, and Best Acoustic Album, and added to the magazine's Gallery of the Greats, 1984.
- Received numerous IBMA awards, including Guitar Player of the Year in 1990, 1991, 1994, 1996, 1997, and 2007.
- The subject of an authorized biography, *Still Inside: The Tony Rice Story*, by Tim Stafford and Caroline Wright, 2010.
- Bluegrass Hall of Fame, 2013.

"I've always enjoyed playing guitar so much more than my voice anyway. I think back to the Grisman years when I rarely sang. I didn't miss it then, and I can honestly say that I don't miss it all that much now."

- Quoted by Caroline Wright in "A Day in the Life of the World's Best Guitarist," *Listener*, July/August 2002.

By the way:
- Born one day (plus seven years) after one of his guitar heroes, Clarence White, whose legendary Martin D-28 he purchased in 1975.
- Appears with both the Bluegrass Alliance and J.D. Crowe's Kentucky Mountain Boys in the movie *Bluegrass: Country Soul*, filmed the very weekend Rice changed bands, 1971.
- Repairs and reconstructs Accutron watches.
- A big fan of vinyl, long-play albums.

Haney's festival in Reidsville, North Carolina, where he met and joined the Bluegrass Alliance, taking the place of exiting guitar wizard Dan Crary. Tony had previously performed as a rhythm player, while developing his lead guitar work in private. Through the Alliance, Tony came in contact with Sam Bush, another musician who shared his now widening eclectic tastes in music.

After a year with the Bluegrass Alliance, Tony left to begin a four-year stint with J.D. Crowe, whose group already included Tony's older brother, Larry. Tony credits Crowe for teaching him to play perfectly in time and with soul, to hit his notes clearly and cleanly, and how to use the guitar efficiently. Crowe's group maintained a busy schedule, playing six nights a week with amplified instruments in hotel lounges in the Lexington area. During the summer they hit the bluegrass festival circuit.

By 1975, with Ricky Skaggs a new member, the band was all-acoustic when the landmark album *J.D. Crowe and the New South* was released. Rounder 0044, as it has come to be known, set the tone for contemporary bluegrass for much of the next decade and beyond. Tony contributed some of the album's most successful material, including "Old Home Place," "You Are What I Am," "Ten Degrees and Getting Colder," and "Summer Wages." He earned high marks for his vocals, which by

Ralph Emery: "What is flatpicking?" Tony Rice: "Well this is a flat pick right here, so… the rest is self-explanatory."

- Dialogue between Ralph Emery and Tony Rice on a circa 1984 appearance of The Nashville Network's *Ralph Emery Show*.

now were as compelling as his instrumental work.

In 1975, Tony headed back to California to become a member of the David Grisman Quintet. The outfit was described as a combination of Miles Davis, Bill Monroe, Django Reinhart, and more. As a member of this group Tony was able to explore more deeply his interest in jazz. Tony's playing by this time was a combination of flatpicking, cross-picking, and harmonic intervals. He released three solo recordings in the 1970s. *Guitar* and *California Autumn* included members of the Crowe band. The self-titled *Tony Rice* featured members of the Grisman Quintet, fiddler Richard Greene, and others. At the end of the decade the albums *Manzanita* and *Acoustics* heralded the formation of the Tony Rice Unit.

As he continued to explore new avenues of playing, which eventually morphed into a style he called "spacegrass," Tony also embarked on a project that paid homage to the roots of bluegrass. In 1981, along with J.D. Crowe, Doyle Lawson, Bobby Hicks, and Todd Phillips, he formed a recording supergroup, which came to be known as the Bluegrass Album Band. *The Bluegrass Album* featured stellar renderings of classics originally recorded some twenty-five to thirty years earlier by Bill Monroe,

Flatt and Scruggs, and Jimmy Martin. Over a fifteen-year period, six volumes were issued. All met with critical acclaim and were among the bluegrass genre's best sellers.

The decade of the 1980s was a good one for Tony. It began with a widely acclaimed duet album that recreated classic bluegrass and old-time duets with fellow Crowe alumnus Ricky Skaggs. Following were four Bluegrass Album Band releases, four Tony Rice Unit recordings (*Mar West, Still Inside, Backwaters*, and a compilation disc called *Devlin*), a pairing with guitar legend Norman Blake, and a release titled *The Rice Brothers* that brought Tony back together with brothers Larry, Wyatt, and Ron. *Church Street Blues* featured just Tony and his guitar and vocals. With additional releases: *Cold on the Shoulder, Me and My Guitar, Native American*, and *Tony Rice Plays and Sings Bluegrass*, Tony became one of the most widely recorded artists in bluegrass.

In the 1990s, the International Bluegrass Music Awards were initiated to recognize artists' current popularity. The first program, in 1990, recognized Tony and the Bluegrass Album Band as Instrumental Group of the Year and Tony as Guitar Player of the Year. He went on to win the Guitar Player award four more times in the 1990s. The Tony Rice Unit received the Instrumental Group of the Year Award in 1991 and 1995. Instrumental Recording of the Year awards went to *Blake and Rice 2* in 1991 and to *Bluegrass Album Band, Volume 6* in 1996.

Although the 1990s were marked by numerous awards and a multitude of CD releases, the era was noted for a forced change in the direction of Tony's music. Early in the decade he was diagnosed with a muscle tension dysphonia, a condition that affected his vocal chords. Tony's last performance as a singer took place in 1994. He continues to be highly regarded as an instrumentalist.

With the start of the new millennium, Tony began to relax the frenetic pace of his recorded output. A recording that was produced in 1993 with David Grisman and Jerry Garcia finally saw the light of day in 2000 as *The Pizza Tapes*. Tony and Larry Rice, Chris Hillman and Herb Pedersen teamed for a second time, and a pair of releases showcased the talents of Tony with Peter Rowan. Despite his reduced public appearances, Tony picked up the 2007 IBMA award for Guitar Player of the Year.

In addition to the vast number of albums and CDs he has recorded over the years, Tony has appeared on several performance and instructional videos and DVDs. The authorized biography *Still Inside: The Tony Rice Story* by Tim Stafford and Caroline Wright was released in 2010. It offered an in-depth account of Tony's award-winning life in bluegrass and beyond.

— GARY REID

- When his home in Florida was destroyed by a 1993 hurricane and his guitar was underwater for three hours, Tony dried it slowly and "it sounds better than ever."
- Still performs instrumentally, although his singing was curtailed in 1994 by muscle tension dysphonia.

Dorris Paul Warren | 2013

Paul Warren was born forty miles from Nashville in Hickman County, Tennessee, in the community of Lyles, on May 17, 1918. He was reared in a musical family that included a father who played guitar and banjo, a mother who played clawhammer banjo, a brother who played banjo, and a sister who played guitar. As the family had no electricity, it was a neighbor who lived several miles away that afforded Paul his first opportunity to hear the *Grand Ole Opry* on the radio. He was captivated by the sounds of *Opry* musician Fiddlin' Arthur Smith. At age thirteen Paul developed an interest in becoming a fiddler himself, and was soon playing for local dances and public events.

Upon graduation from Hickman County High School in 1938, Paul got his first job in music playing with Johnnie Wright and the Happy Roving Cowboys. Over the next several years, the band went through several name changes and eventually morphed into one of the most popular country acts of the 1950s, Johnnie and Jack and the Tennessee Mountain Boys. Paul stayed

"None was his equal when it came to playing the old time, double-stop breakdowns... He was superb at playing with blinding speed if the tune called for it. His greatest characteristics were his ability to retain the piquant and stimulating 'old time flavor' of a breakdown or country jig, while at the same time applying flawless professionalism and dogmatically insisting on learning what he felt was the most authentic version of the melody line of each tune."

- Lance LeRoy in liner notes to *Paul Warren - America's Greatest Breakdown Fiddle Player*, CMH Records, 1979.

Born: May 17, 1918, Lyles, TN

Died: January 12, 1978, Nashville, TN

Primary instrument: Fiddle

"Plain old country fiddle is what I like, and it takes a lot of practice and staying with it. You got to live the fiddle, that's the way I look at it; keep your ears open, learn all you can. It doesn't come to you; you have to go get it."

- Quoted by Doc Hamilton and Dick Spottswood in "Fiddlin' Paul Warren," *Bluegrass Unlimited*, February 1978.

Composed:
BMI's database credits Paul Warren with one published co-composition:

"Fiddle And Banjo" (a version of the tune variously known as "Buck Creek Gal," "Wild Horse," "Stoney Point" or "Pigtown Fling")

Photo: Doc Hamilton, 1967

with the group until 1942, when World War II dictated that he enter military service. He was sent to North Africa, where he was captured and served twenty-nine months as a prisoner of war. He traded a pack of cigarettes to an enemy soldier for a fiddle; his playing of "Under the Double Eagle" – composed by Austrian bandmaster Josef Franz Wagner – earned him preferential treatment.

Following the end of the war, Paul rejoined the group that was now called Johnnie and Jack and the Tennessee Hillbillies. The band had hired another fiddler in Paul's absence and, for a period of time, the group operated with twin fiddles. Paul temporarily found employment with Homer Briarhopper on WPTF in Raleigh, North Carolina, but was soon back in the employ of Johnnie and Jack. The group joined

Early influences
Fiddlin' Arthur Smith
John W. Warren (father)
Lula Crow Warren (mother)
Hubert Warren (brother)
Mrs. W.K. Pinkerton (sister)

Came to fame with
Lester Flatt, Earl Scruggs and the Foggy Mountain Boys, 1954-1969

Performed with:

Johnnie Wright and the Happy Roving Cowboys (later Tennessee Hillbillies), 1938-1942

Johnnie and Jack and the Tennessee Mountain Boys, 1946-1954

Lester Flatt, Earl Scruggs and the Foggy Mountain Boys, 1954-1969

Lester Flatt and the Nashville Grass, 1969-1977

"Paul Warren has remained one of my chief musical inspirations since the early-mid 1970s. Not many people emulated him then, or today for that matter... His authenticity – both noting and bowing – while playing an old-time tune was second to none... I visit his grave several times a year to reflect and to just say thanks for all his music has meant to me."

- Eddie Stubbs, quoted by Walt Saunders in "Notes and Queries," *Bluegrass Unlimited*, September 2009.

Led the way:

- Worked with three seminal country and bluegrass bands: Johnnie and Jack, Flatt and Scruggs, and Lester Flatt and the Nashville Grass.
- Through constant touring and media exposure, became one of the most popular and well-known fiddlers in history.
- With Earl Scruggs, pioneered the popularity of fiddle and banjo duets.

the *Grand Ole Opry* in 1952; Paul maintained his affiliation with that program for the next twenty-five years.

While working with Johnnie and Jack, Paul participated in nineteen recording sessions, which resulted in the creation of seventy-six masters. Among them were "What About You," "Poison Love," "Lonesome," "Ashes of Love," "Heart Trouble," "S.O.S.," and "South in New Orleans." The group emphasized Johnnie and Jack's unique vocals and the dynamic dobro work of Shot Jackson; Paul's abilities as a fiddler weren't fully utilized.

During the Johnnie and Jack years, Paul also played fiddle on sessions for Kitty Wells, who was Johnnie Wright's wife and a member of their touring ensemble. These releases included "How Far is Heaven," "Searching For a Soldier's Grave," "It Wasn't God Who Made Honky Tonk Angels," "Crying Steel Guitar Waltz," "You're Not Easy to Forget," "One By One" (with Red Foley), "Release Me," and "After Dark."

"Lester had the idea for us to play some fiddle and banjo tunes, because that was mainly what they used back in the old days. I remember sitting around in our dressing rooms trying it out and, oh boy, it sounded kind of authentic, and Lester said we ought to do something like it onstage."

- Quoted by Eddie Stubbs in liner notes to *Johnnie and Jack and the Tennessee Mountain Boys*, Bear Family Records, 1992.

At the start of 1954, Paul Warren and fiddler Benny Martin switched jobs. Martin went to work for Johnnie and Jack and Paul went to work with Lester Flatt, Earl Scruggs and the Foggy Mountain Boys. Paul worked with Flatt and Scruggs until the group's breakup in 1969. He is reported to have never missed a show during this entire period. Working with such a high-profile group made him one of the most visible fiddlers of the 1950s and 1960s.

The group performed radio shows for Martha White Flour that were aired up to seven days a week over radio station WSM in Nashville. With the rise in popularity of television, the band traveled a grueling 2,500 miles a week to do a circuit of live broadcasts for Martha White. Appearing in a different city each night of the week, the group returned to Nashville each Saturday for appearances on the *Grand Ole Opry*. Later on the programs were videotaped, cutting down on the extensive travel schedule.

Starting in May of 1954, Paul appeared on all of the 250 recordings Flatt and Scruggs made for Columbia Records. In contrast to the Johnnie and Jack releases, Paul's work with Lester and Earl was prominent, especially on the instrumentals. He appeared on influential albums such as *Foggy Mountain Banjo, Carnegie Hall, Live at Vanderbilt*, and *Strictly*

Instrumental (with guest Doc Watson). Paul was one of the musicians who recorded the theme song for the *Beverly Hillbillies* television program in 1962. "The Ballad of Jed Clampett" went to #1 on the *Billboard* country singles chart, the highest charting bluegrass record in history.

A stylistic innovation Paul helped bring to the Flatt and Scruggs show was the featuring of banjo and fiddle duets with Earl Scruggs. The practice resonated with older fans, who remembered the fiddle and banjo as sole musical accompaniment at country dances. Younger listeners also enjoyed the vibrant interplay between Paul and Earl on the old-time instrumentals. Among Paul's signature breakdown tunes were "Black Eyed Susie," "Durham's Reel," "Liberty," "Dusty Miller," "Grey Eagle," and "Hoedown in Hickman County."

Following the 1969 breakup of the Flatt and Scruggs group, Paul stayed on with Lester Flatt and his new group, the Nashville Grass. The band maintained a busy schedule, which included *Opry* appearances, festivals, concerts, and college dates. Paul's fiddle work appeared on all of Lester's recordings from 1969 to 1977, including releases on Columbia, Nugget, RCA, Canaan, Flying Fish, and CMH. Notable highlights during this era were three albums on RCA that paired Lester with Mac Wiseman and a live two-LP set recorded at Bill Monroe's 1973 Bean Blossom Bluegrass Festival. With the exception of a few days off for surgery in 1972, Paul never missed a show.

Ill health necessitated Paul's retirement from active touring. His last performance with Lester Flatt was on February 23, 1977, in Lynchburg, Virginia. He died almost a year later, on January 12, 1978. With his wife, the former Eloise Hill of Spencer, Tennessee, Paul raised three children. One of them, Johnny, followed in his father's footsteps as a master fiddler.

Due to Lester Flatt's policy of restricting the outside recording activities of his band members, Paul never got the opportunity to record an album of his work. After his passing, Lester's manager Lance LeRoy assembled a collection of Paul's work recorded on personal appearances and radio performances. The album, released on CMH Records, was called *America's Greatest Breakdown Fiddle Player*.

— GARY REID

- Recorded 76 tracks with Johnnie and Jack, 37 with Kitty Wells, 250 with Flatt and Scruggs, and more than 100 with the Nashville Grass.
- Bluegrass Hall of Fame, 2013.

By the way:
- Rode his bicycle 40 miles each way from his home to perform on WSIX, Nashville, 1938.
- One of the few early country musicians to graduate high school.
- Served 29 months as a prisoner of war in World War II.
- One of the few true bass singers in bluegrass, heard on many rousing quartets.
- With the exception of a few days off for surgery in 1972, never missed a showdate with the Foggy Mountain Boys or Nashville Grass.
- Heard on the theme of the *Beverly Hillbillies* TV show, 1962-1971.
- Never recorded a fiddle album due to his employers' policies; a posthumous collection of broadcast and live performances was released in 1979.

For more information on the history of Flatt and Scruggs, see profiles of Lester Flatt, Earl Scruggs, Josh Graves, Curly Seckler, and Louise Scruggs.

THE ORIGINAL SELDOM SCENE

Michael Dennis "Mike" Auldridge ⟩ 2014

The child of a banker, Mike Auldridge was born in 1938 in Washington, D.C. When he was seven or eight, his large family (there were nine children) moved to the suburb of Kensington, Maryland. It was here, on a jukebox in the local drugstore, that he was first exposed to what was then termed "hillbilly music." Although he didn't care for it at first, the music grew on him.

Among his earliest musical influences was an uncle on his mother's side of the family, Ellsworth Cozzens, who played Dobro on some of Jimmie Rodgers' earliest recordings. In addition to country music on the radio and on jukeboxes and the music of his uncle at family gatherings, Mike also heard and appreciated the music of Benny Goodman.

In 1950, Mike Auldridge heard bluegrass music for the first time. He was already familiar with country groups such as Roy Acuff and the Smoky Mountain Boys, Johnnie and Jack, and Wilma Lee and Stoney Cooper, and felt that the Dobro guitar he heard in these bands would sound good in bluegrass as well.

In his teen years, Mike took up the guitar and banjo and, at age fifteen, was performing once a week on radio station WDON in Wheaton, Maryland. The group, the South Mountain Boys, included Mike and

"In 1950 when I first heard bluegrass, it was still brand new music. And I used to think that it would be real neat to put in Dobro music... So, when I heard Josh Graves with Flatt and Scruggs in '55, I thought, 'Yeah, there it is. My idea of a neat band: Dobro and bluegrass.'"

- Quoted by Michael J. Weiss in "Mike Auldridge: Cruising On a Dobro," *Pickin'*, April 1978.

Born: December 30, 1938, Washington, D. C.

Died: December 29, 2012, Silver Spring, Maryland

Primary Instrument:
Dobro (resonator guitar)

"Mike changed everything... He was the first guy to use the Dobro in a more modern way, to phrase it more like a saxophone or some other instrument... He was able to play more modern material and that freed me. It unchained me from traditional bluegrass music."

- Jerry Douglas, quoted by Bill Friskics-Warren in "Dobro's Standard Setter," *The Washington Post*, January 30, 2011.

Composed:
BMI's database credits Mike Auldridge with 36 published compositions, co-compositions and arrangements, including:

"Eight String Swing"
"Lloyd's of Nashville"
"Spanish Grass"
"Swing Scene"

214 ⟩ Bluegrass Hall of Fame Inductee Biographies

Photo: Jim McGuire, 1982

Early Influences:
Ellsworth Cozzens
Benny Goodman
Josh (Buck) Graves
Flatt and Scruggs

Came to fame with:
Seldom Scene, 1971-1996

Performed with:
South Mountain Boys, mid-1950s
Emerson and Waldron, 1969-1970
Cliff Waldron and the New Shades of Grass, 1970-1971
Seldom Scene, 1971-1996
Chesapeake, 1994-1999
Auldridge-Bennett-Gaudreau, 2000
John Starling and Carolina Rose, 2007
Good Deale Bluegrass Band, c. 2008
Darren Beachley and Legends of the Potomac, 2008-2010

Led the Way:
• A founding member of the Seldom Scene, one of the most popular and influential bands in bluegrass history.
• The second major bluegrass Dobro player, known for his unique and smooth style.
• Based for his entire career in the Washington, D.C. region, contributing to its reputation as a major bluegrass music capital.
• Recorded with Linda Ronstadt, Lyle Lovett, Emmylou Harris, Hank Williams, Jr., James Taylor and Ry Cooder, among others.
• Appeared in a series of instructional videos.

his brother Dave, both on guitars. The group would practice all week in preparation for their weekly broadcast.

In 1955, Mike heard what would be his biggest musical influence, the Dobro playing of Buck "Uncle Josh" Graves when he was a new member of the Flatt and Scruggs show. Mike bought his first Dobro from Graves for $150, in 1961.

From 1963 to 1967, Mike attended the University of Maryland, where he majored in music and art. During this time he became acquainted with banjoist Ben Eldridge and attended picking parties in the area, honing his talents on the Dobro. After graduation he was relatively inactive musically, concentrating his energies on a job at a commercial art firm.

"We liked James Taylor as much as we liked Ralph Stanley, and we attracted an audience of like-minded people. We were college-educated. We were contemporary and urban. We weren't singing about mother and log cabins, because that's not where we came from."

– Quoted by Bill Friskics-Warren in "Dobro's Standard Setter," *The Washington Post*, January 30, 2011.

1969 was a busy year for Mike. He joined the staff of the *Washington Star* newspaper as a graphic artist. He also joined the band of Bill Emerson, Cliff Waldron and the New Shades of Grass and participated in the recording of two of the group's albums for Rebel. Mike was touted by reviewers for his talent, imagination, and his "smooth country style singing."

When Bill Emerson left to rejoin the Country Gentlemen in 1970, Ben Eldridge came on board to take his place in the retitled Cliff Waldron and the New Shades of Grass. Also joining the group was Mike's brother Dave on mandolin.

In the fall of 1971, Mike was a founding member of the Seldom Scene. Initially a once-a-week gig to satisfy the musical urges of a group of Washington area pickers, the Scene quickly achieved status as one of the top bands.

While working with the Seldom Scene, Mike released his first solo album, *Dobro* (1971). It featured guest appearances by Josh Graves, Vassar Clements, and David Bromberg. A follow-up, *Blues & Bluegrass* (1974), also on the Takoma label, included cameos by country-rock stars Linda Ronstadt and Lowell George. Among the highlights were Mike's laid-back vocals on "Take Me" and "Bottom Dollar," leading no doubt to his 1975 Grammy nomination for Best Male Vocalist in Country Music.

Mike Auldridge's playing matured during his tenure with the Seldom Scene. His first recordings reflected admiration for his idol Josh Graves. His work with the Scene was noted for its smoother qualities and chime-like tones. His refined stylings evidently found favor with the readers of *Muleskinner News* magazine, who voted Mike the Best Dobro Player every year from 1974 to 1978.

In 1975, one of Mike's brothers left a steel guitar at his house, which set him on a whole new musical trajectory. While he still loved the Dobro, he awoke each morning anxious to explore the new instrument. Soon, he was adding steel to recordings of the Seldom Scene.

The following year, the newspaper where Mike had worked for the last seven years closed up shop. In some ways it was a scary proposition but it also allowed him to concentrate on the Seldom Scene and session work. Having already guested on Linda Ronstadt's *Heart Like a Wheel* (1972), his newfound freedom found him recording with a host of artists, including Emmylou Harris, Jonathan Edwards, Lyle Lovett, the Country Gentlemen, Dolly Parton, Mary Chapin Carpenter, Hank Williams, Jr., Suzy Boggus, and Merle Travis.

In the 1980s, Mike was a featured columnist in *Frets* magazine, where he offered advice on playing the Dobro and provided tablature for a variety of songs. Not surprisingly, he was also a recipient of top honors in a *Frets* readers' poll which named him Best Dobro Player.

By the early and middle 1990s, Seldom Scene co-founder John Duffey wanted to cut back on the number of performances the group was playing. To pick up the slack, Mike formed a folk-pop-country fusion group with T. Michael Coleman and Moondi Klein. The band, Chesapeake, released three CDs on the Sugar Hill label. In 1996, Mike retired from the Seldom Scene after twenty-five years of service.

Entering the 2000s, Mike returned to a more mainstream bluegrass style with a group called Auldridge-Bennett-Gaudreau. Later in the decade, he was part of John Starling and Carolina Rose, as well as the Good Deale Bluegrass Band. His last performances were with the Washington-based group Darren Beachley and Legends of the Potomac.

In addition to recordings with the Seldom Scene and Chesapeake, Mike made five solo albums, two duet projects, and two others that featured him in collaboration with other Dobro players. Mike also shared his knowledge of the instrument by producing a series of instructional VHS tapes and DVDs.

A lengthy battle with prostate cancer took Mike Auldridge's energy and his speaking voice, but he was able to attend the National Endowment for the Arts event where he was presented with the National Heritage Award in October of 2012. Two months later, Mike died at home under hospice care.

— GARY REID

- *Muleskinner News* Best Dobro Player, 1974-1978.
- *Frets* magazine Dobro Player of the Year, c. 1980s.
- IBMA Instrumental Recorded Performance and Recorded Event of the Year, 1995.
- Grammy award for Best Bluegrass Album, 1995.
- IBMA Distinguished Achievement Award, 2007.
- National Heritage Fellowship, 2012.

"On the radio, Stoney Cooper called it an 'old-time steel.' I pictured it as some ornate-looking thing with legs that probably had feet on it, like an old-time bathtub. In fact, I used to draw pictures in school of what I imagined it looked like. I was fascinated with the sound of something that I wasn't even sure existed."

– Mike Auldridge, in Josh Graves, *Bluegrass Bluesman*, 2012.

By the Way:
- A graphic artist by trade, designed several Seldom Scene album covers.
- John Duffey nicknamed him "Larry the Legend" for his neat appearance and pressed jeans.
- Studied steel guitar with ex-Texas Troubadour Buddy Charleton.
- Applied steel and bluegrass techniques to the eight-string Dobro, 1981.
- Toured with Lyle Lovett, 1998.
- Worked with Beard Guitars to produce the Mike Auldridge Models of square-neck resophonic guitars

THE ORIGINAL SELDOM SCENE

Benjamin "Ben" Eldridge | 2014

Born: August 15, 1938, Richmond, Virginia

Primary instrument: Banjo

"I love to play banjo, and I'm perfectly happy doing that, but if I know I have to sing I get scared to death!"

- Quoted by Robert Kyle in "Music is One Side of Ben Eldridge: 5-String Banjo Picker," *Frets*, May 1979.

Composed:

BMI's database credits Ben Eldridge with 10 published compositions, co-compositions and arrangements, including:

"Cross Country"

"Joshua"

"Rider"

"Smokin' Hickory"

Early Influences:

Earl Scruggs

Don Reno

Ralph Stanley

Bill Keith

Sonny Osborne

Allen Shelton

Mac Wiseman

Ben Eldridge's first memory of music is of hearing his cousin Mike playing "Red River Valley" on the harmonica. Growing up in Richmond, Virginia, Ben had ready exposure to the *Old Dominion Barn Dance*, a weekly live broadcast on radio station WRVA. Starting at age nine or ten, he would attend once a month and see performers such as Looney Luke and Roly Poly Reed, Crazy Joe Maphis, Grandpa Jones, Benny Kissinger and Curly Collins, Sunshine Sue, and Mother Maybelle and the Carter Sisters (who lived on the Eldridges' street). Later, in the early 1950s, bluegrass groups such as Mac Wiseman, Flatt and Scruggs, and the Stanley Brothers were regulars on the program.

"Some of the most enjoyable moments in a Seldom Scene set are likely to occur when, in the middle of a song, Ben gets that tickled-pink gleam in his eye, that possum grin on his face, hunches part way over his banjo, and sets eagerly forth to see if his brand new idea for the song at hand will actually work."

- Bill Vernon, "Part-Time Professionals: The Seldom Scene," *Muleskinner News*, March 1973.

At about the same time that Ben starting to go to the *Old Dominion Barn Dance*, he got a guitar and began learning how to play it. Mac Wiseman's performance of "I'll Still Write Your Name in the Sand" hooked Ben on bluegrass. At age sixteen, in 1954, Ben got a banjo and formed a band with some high school buddies. At the same time, Flatt and Scruggs had a live evening program on WRVA and Ben was able to watch the group perform live in the studio. The first tune Ben learned on the banjo was the Flatt and Scruggs number, "Dear Old Dixie."

Additional exposure to the music came during Ben's senior year of

Bluegrass Hall of Fame Inductee Biographies

Came to fame with:
Seldom Scene, 1971 to present

Performed with:
Cliff Waldron and the New Shades of Grass, 1970-1971

Seldom Scene, 1971 to present

Led the Way:
- A founding member of the pathbreaking Seldom Scene, performed with the group for 40+ years.
- Made bluegrass music and the banjo popular among economic and political elites in the nation's capital and beyond.
- Performed at the White House on numerous occasions.
- Received Grammy nominations for the CDs *Like We Used to Be*, 1995 and *Scenechronized*, 2007.
- Famous (perhaps infamous) for his hip-shaking rock and roll impressions on songs like "Lay Down Sally."

By the Way:
- Grew up on the same Richmond, Virginia, street as Mother Maybelle and the Carter Sisters.
- Shares with Tex Logan the dual professions of mathematician and bluegrass musician.
- Son Chris "Critter" Eldridge plays guitar with the Punch Brothers, appeared with the Seldom Scene, was a founding member of the Infamous Stringdusters, and holds a degree in music performance from Oberlin Conservatory.

high school when WXGI, another Richmond station, aired a half-hour program of acoustic country music. Despite having seen a number of the top bands in person at the *Barn Dance*, it was while listening to one of the DJs on WXGI that he first heard the term "bluegrass."

"I think the reason we've been successful is that we haven't really been trying to prove anything to anybody. When we started off, nobody needed to play music to make money. It was something we were all doing for fun, and I think we've pretty much maintained that attitude."

- Quoted by Robert Kyle in "DC's Best Banjo Picker," *Blueprint Washington's Bluegrass Newspaper*, July 1979.

Following graduation from high school, Ben attended the University of Virginia in Charlottesville, where he studied Mathematics. The campus was home to a number of picking parties over the next four years. Among the regulars was another banjo picker by the name of Paul Craft, who later played with Jimmy Martin and gained fame as a Nashville songwriter.

In 1961 Ben moved to the Washington, D.C., area where he took a job with Johns Hopkins University in their Applied Physics Laboratory. Several years later, he met two other D.C. area pickers, Mike and Dave Auldridge. By 1967 Ben was hosting weekly jam sessions in the basement of his Maryland home. Regular participants included John Starling, the Auldridge brothers, and local DJ Gary Henderson on bass.

Ben's first work as a professional musician came in 1970, when he became the banjo player for Cliff Waldron and the New Shades of Grass, replacing Cliff's partner Bill Emerson, who left to join the Country Gentlemen. Ben recorded three albums while working with the New Shades of Grass. The notes to one had high praise for Ben: "Constantly striving for improvement, he has established innovations

"I love the old Flatt and Scruggs stuff and Jimmy Martin and the Stanleys and Osborne Brothers and Don Reno and Red Smiley -- that's what I cut my teeth on. I can still listen to some of those old records that Flatt and Scruggs made back in the early fifties/late forties and get that same feeling that I had when I was a teenager."

- Quoted by Penny Parsons in "Ben Eldridge - Getting that Magic Feeling," *Bluegrass Unlimited*, February 1985.

which are a key to the drive in the group. His ideas are unique and full of vitality and, in every aspect, his playing is performed with thought, originality, and a strong sense of professionalism."

In September of 1971 Ben, along with bandmate Mike Auldridge, left Cliff Waldron, citing a conflict between too much music and the

"I don't know how much longer I can do this. It hurts when I play. It's frustrating because I can't do a lot of things I used to do."
- Quoted by David Morris in "Catching Up With Ben Eldridge," *BluegrassToday.com*, posted August 22, 2012.

responsibilities of their day jobs. The parting was amicable and, less than a month later, Ben found himself sitting in with a pick-up band that held down a spot for Cliff when he had to be away for another engagement. That ensemble soon morphed into the Seldom Scene, with original members John Duffey, John Starling, Mike Auldridge, Ben Eldridge, Tom Gray, and Dave Auldridge.

For a number of years, the Scene held down a weekly spot at a Bethesda, Maryland, club called The Red Fox Inn. Later, they alternated between the Red Fox and The Birchmere, a club across the Potomac River in Alexandria, Virginia. When original member John Starling left the group after seven years, the band dropped the Red Fox gig and worked exclusively at The Birchmere. Their weekly appearances helped to establish that venue as one of the premier music nightspots in the Washington area.

With over forty years of playing with the Seldom Scene, Ben remains the only original member of the group. To borrow from the frequent play on words that appear in many of their album and CD titles, he has "Scene it all." From the glory days of the group's original configuration, when they were one of the cutting edge progressive bands in bluegrass, through a revolving host of lead singers and bass players, the death of the legendary John Duffey, to the group's long-standing current configuration of guitarist Dudley Connell, mandolin player Lou Reid, bass player Ronnie Simpkins, Dobro player Fred Travers, and, of course, Ben Eldridge on banjo.

— GARY REID

For more information on the Original Seldom Scene, see profiles of John Duffey (page 62) and Tom Gray (page 66).

THE ORIGINAL SELDOM SCENE

John Lewis Starling 2014

Durham, North Carolina, native John Starling began his immersion in music by listening to a number of radio stations that featured Saturday evening live country music programs. These included the *Old Dominion Barn Dance* from WRVA in Richmond, Virginia; the World's *Original Jamboree* from WWVA in Wheeling, West Virginia; and, to a lesser extent, the *Grand Ole Opry* from WSM in Nashville. He was also a fan of rhythm and blues programming from Nashville's WLAC.

Although artists like Bill Monroe and Flatt and Scruggs held his attention, John's first instrument was an electric guitar. After graduation from high school, he took undergraduate and medical degrees at the University of Virginia in Charlottesville. Picking parties there brought him into contact with other bluegrass musicians, notably Paul Craft and Ben Eldridge. When John moved to the Washington, D.C., area in 1968 for his internship, he became a regular at jam sessions in Ben Eldridge's basement.

After a tour of duty in Vietnam and a year of general surgery in North Carolina, John was back in the D.C. area. In his spare time, he made music with several former members of the Country Gentlemen. In

> *"I think, ultimately, if you make a record and nobody knows what bin to put it in, you've succeeded. John Duffey used to say, 'Be different at all costs.' Ben Eldridge and I were listening to Creedence Clearwater Revival and I was listening to Grateful Dead. When we got ready to make a record, we'd try to find original tunes to do."*
>
> – Quoted by Juli Thanki in "An Interview with John Starling, Founding Member of the Seldom Scene," *Engine 145: A Roots Music Publication*, November 7, 2011.

Born: March 26, 1940, Durham, North Carolina

Primary instrument: Guitar

Composed: BMI's database credits John Starling with 16 published compositions, co-compositions, and arrangements, including:
"C & O Canal"
"Gardens And Memories"
"He Rode All the Way to Texas"
"Mean Mother Blues"
"Rider"

Early Influences:
WRVA *Old Dominion Barn Dance*
WWVA *Jamboree*
Bill Monroe
Flatt and Scruggs

Came to fame with:
Seldom Scene, 1971-1977

Performed with:
Seldom Scene, 1971-1977, 1993-1994
Ready Section, 1982-1983

Photo: courtesy of Tom Gray, 1972

John Starling and Carolina Star, 2007

Led the Way:

- Lead vocalist for the Seldom Scene, one of the most influential bluegrass bands of the 1970s.

- Helped to acquaint up and coming country and pop stars Emmylou Harris and Linda Ronstadt with bluegrass.

- While working as a doctor in Alabama, coached Claire Lynch as a singer and songwriter, early 1980s.

- Co-producer of Emmylou Harris, Linda Ronstadt, and Dolly Parton's highly acclaimed *Trio* album, 1987.

- Grammy award for *Spring Training* with Carl Jackson, 1991.

By the Way:

- Served as a U.S. Army Lieutenant Colonel at Walter Reed Hospital in Washington, D.C.

- Maintained dual careers as an Ear, Nose and Throat specialist and musician.

- Operated on Tony Rice to correct a deviated septum, 1988.

- Hosted the party where Ricky Skaggs was introduced to Emmylou Harris, who later employed Skaggs on recording sessions and as a band member.

For more information on the Original Seldom Scene, see profiles of John Duffey (page 62) and Tom Gray (page 66).

October of 1971, this informal group was asked to sit in as a substitute for Cliff Waldron and the New Shades of Grass, a popular D.C.-based group that had a regular gig at the Red Fox Inn in Bethesda, Maryland. The group enjoyed performing in public and soon secured a weekly booking at The Rabbit's Foot on Wisconsin Avenue in Washington, just across the border from Maryland. A dispute over the playing of the club's television during the band's performance soon led to their leaving that establishment.

In January of 1972, the Seldom Scene – given the name by long-time Country Gentlemen stalwart Charlie Waller – relocated to The Red Fox Inn for a legendary six-year stint. The group included John Starling on guitar and lead vocals, John Duffey on mandolin and tenor vocals, Mike Auldridge on Dobro and baritone vocals, Ben Eldridge on banjo and occasional vocals, and Tom Gray on bass and occasional vocals. Also in the group for several months was Mike's brother, Dave Auldridge.

"We decided we'd play one night in a club, we would try to put out as good of records as we could and then limit our playing within a driving distance of Washington, with a few exceptions… And it was enough to the point that we were making a fair amount of money, and it was also enough where it had not reached the point where we were tired of it."

– Quoted by Robert Kyle in "John Starling: Medicine Replaces Music," *Blueprint: Washington's Bluegrass Newspaper,* September 1979.

John Starling's first stay with the Seldom Scene lasted from late 1971 through 1977. During this time, he became one of the most high-profile vocalists in bluegrass. He was routinely a finalist in *Muleskinner News* magazine's annual Bluegrass Music Awards in the Best Lead Singer category. A series of album releases on Rebel Records did much to establish the Seldom Scene's reputation during this period. Highlights include *Act I, Act II, Act III,* and *Old Train.* One of the most consistently best-selling bluegrass albums of all time was recorded over two days in December of 1974 and released as *Live at the Cellar Door.*

The success of the Seldom Scene was an artful blending of talents by a collective group of individuals, each of whom shone brilliantly on his own. John Starling brought a number of important contributions. Foremost were his rich lead vocals. Described as one of the most distinctive stylists in bluegrass, he excelled at delivering expressive renditions of country and contemporary songs. Equally important was his role in selecting repertoire for the group. John was an articulate songwriter and had a knack for mining other genres of music for material. Unlike some writers who work strictly on inspiration, John usually wrote out of necessity, to provide material for recording projects. Despite his musical and medical accomplishments, he possessed a self-effacing, low key personality.

John was on hand for the last two albums that the Scene recorded for Rebel. *The New Seldom Scene Album*, a bluegrass/country project, charted new territory for the group with the inclusion of Mike Auldridge's pedal steel guitar and the radio favorite "California Earthquake." In 1977, as the group was finishing its first and only all-gospel album, *Baptizing*, John relocated to Montgomery, Alabama, and exited the Seldom Scene to devote more time to his ear, nose, and throat medical practice.

After leaving the Scene, John was by no means musically inactive. In Alabama, he became friends with members of the Front Porch String Band. In addition to giving pointers on the band's performance techniques, he was instrumental in bringing Claire Lynch's songwriting talents to the attention of Nashville-based publishers. For a brief period in the early 1980s, John and Claire had a country-oriented group called Ready Section. He served as musical consultant for the 1987 *Trio* release by Linda Ronstadt, Emmylou Harris, and Dolly Parton, and recorded two solo albums: *Long Time Gone* (1977) and *Waitin' On a Southern Train* (1979). A third disc, *Spring Training*, with banjoist/songwriter Carl Jackson, won a 1991 Grammy for Best Bluegrass Album.

John guested on two anniversary collections that the Seldom Scene issued in the late 1980s and early 1990s. *Fifteenth Anniversary Celebration*, recorded live at the Kennedy Center, featured a bevy of top-notch guest artists. A November 1991 concert at the Birchmere reunited current and past members, including John Starling, and resulted in the double-disc set *Scene 20*. That reunion concert likely led to John's rejoining the band in 1993 and 1994.

Retirement from a successful medical practice and another reunion event led to John Starling's most recent recorded project. A benefit concert for banjoist Eddie Adcock reconnected John with fellow Seldom Scene alumni Mike Auldridge and Tom Gray. The trio decided to join forces and venture into the studio for *Slidin' Home* (2007), with Emmylou Harris as guest vocalist. Although he wasn't seeking top billing, Mike and Tom felt that putting John's name front and center would give John Starling and Carolina Star name recognition and credibility for future personal appearances.

— GARY REID

> *"I've started writing stuff again; I've got two or three things I've written... You never know about your own stuff until you hear it done.... I'm not real happy with my own tunes. I guess it's like people's cooking. People don't like their own cooking."*
>
> - Quoted by Robert Kyle in "'Long Time Gone' John Starling Returns," *Blueprint: Washington's Bluegrass Newspaper*, July 1980.

> *"I always liked bluegrass music, even back when the Kingston Trio were popular. I couldn't stand them – I'd much rather listen to Ralph Stanley, and if the truth be known, it probably had a lot more lasting qualities than the Kingston Trio."*
>
> - Quoted by Sheila Berquist in "John Starling: Music and Medicine," *Bluegrass Unlimited*, February 1986.

Neil Vandraegen Rosenberg | 2014

Born: March 21, 1939, Seattle, Washington

Primary involvement with bluegrass:
Author and historian (also a banjoist)

Composed:
Neil Rosenberg is the writer of four songs and tunes published through SOCAN:

"Queenstown"

"Penniless (But Not Baroque)"

"Farewell Cindy"

"Laughin' And Scratchin'"

Early influences:
Pete Seeger
L. Mayne Smith
Billy Faier
New Lost City Ramblers
Earl Scruggs
Ralph Stanley
Eddie Adcock

Performed with:
Lorain County String Band, 1959
Plum Creek Boys, 1960-1961

Neil Rosenberg was born in Seattle, Washington, but spent his early childhood in nearby Olympia, located some sixty miles southwest. Neil began taking classical violin lessons at age seven. When he was ten, his family relocated to Los Alamos, New Mexico, for two years and then, in 1951, settled in Berkeley, California, where his father, an attorney, worked as legal counsel for a research institute.

Not long after the move to Berkeley, Neil dropped the violin, opting for instruction in folk guitar and voice. This was due to his growing fascination with folk music, which coincided with the stirrings of the folk music boom of the 1950s as well as his friendship with classmate and budding folk enthusiast Mayne Smith.

> *"Perhaps it's only a question of historical detail, but my personal feeling is that the person or persons who started calling their favorite hillbilly music 'bluegrass' really gave the musical style a life of its own because they gave it a name."*
>
> - Neil Rosenberg, "Into Bluegrass: The History of a Word," *Muleskinner News*, August 1974.

From 1957 to 1961 Neil attended Oberlin College in Ohio, where he received a Bachelor of Arts degree in History. Two factors contributed to his choice of Oberlin: his friend Mayne Smith was also attending, and *Sing Out!* magazine had reported on the vibrant folk music scene there. Neil's first year at Oberlin was significant in that he first heard the term "bluegrass" and became aware of the first bluegrass album release, Mike Seeger's anthology *American Banjo Scruggs Style*.

It would be two more years before the banjo became Neil's primary mode of musical expression. When he returned to Berkeley for the

Photo: Carl Fleischhauer, 1972

summer of 1959, he helped organize the Redwood Canyon Ramblers with Mayne Smith, Scott Hambly, and Pete Berg. The group was active again in the summer of 1960.

It was also in 1960 that Neil had a chance to see his first professional bluegrass band, the Osborne Brothers, when his band, the Plum Creek Boys, opened for them at Antioch – the first college bluegrass concert in history. That year Neil was elected president of Oberlin's Folk Song Club. The club booked groups such as the New Lost City Ramblers and the Country Gentlemen (their first college concert) at Oberlin.

Redwood Canyon Ramblers, 1959-1960, 1963

Shorty & Juanita Shehan, 1961

Pigeon Hill Boys/Ramblers, 1961-1967

Stoney Lonesome Boys, 1963-1968

Peter Aceves (Narváez), 1967-1976

Bluegrass Hall of Fame Inductee Biographies | **227**

Country Dream, 1971

Sneed Hearn and the Smiling Liberators, 1971-1972

Crooked Stovepipe, 1973-present

Black Auks, 1994-present

"We were teenage bohemians, hanging out in the Cal campus fringe scene, going to North Beach, having big music parties at a cabin in Redwood Canyon in the hills behind Oakland on weekends, playing on the Midnight Special *at KPFA, [and] playing folk music in school concerts. Sometime during my teenage years, making music became an essential part of my being, something I had to do."*

– Quoted by Bob Carlin in "Interview with Neil Rosenberg," Banjo Newsletter, April 2014.

Led the way:

• Performed (opened for the Osborne Brothers) at the first college bluegrass concert in history, 1960.

• Wrote one of the first scholarly papers on bluegrass music, 1966.

• Authored four books, notes to approximately 50 albums and CDs, and 60 articles and review essays in a variety of publications, 1967-present.

• Helped introduce bluegrass to Atlantic Canada, 1968-present.

• Inaugurated "30 Years Ago" column in Bluegrass Unlimited, 1981.

• Authored the definitive book-length history of bluegrass, 1985.

Following graduation from Oberlin, Neil moved to Bloomington to attend Indiana University, where he earned Masters and Doctorate Degrees in Folklore. His stay in Indiana lasted from 1961 to 1968. While there, he spent a considerable amount of time at Bill Monroe's Brown County Jamboree music park in nearby Bean Blossom. It was here, in June of 1961, that he first saw Monroe perform in person. At an informal jam session following this show Bill opined, "That boy's gonna make a fine banjo player." He was invited to join the house band for that season.

A guest appearance on one of Monroe's shows at the Brown County Jamboree in September of 1961 inspired Neil to research Monroe's recording career. Filling in with the Blue Grass Boys, he realized that he was unfamiliar with a sizeable portion of their repertoire. To remedy the situation, he embarked on what would later become a published discography of Bill Monroe's recording career. At the same time he began tape recording shows by Monroe and others at the Jamboree, creating a large collection that is now on deposit at the Library of Congress's Archive of Folk Culture.

"I'd realized when playing with Bill [Monroe] that I didn't know the repertoire, so I got into discography as a way of figuring out who did what when."

– Quoted by Boris Weintraub in "Neil V. Rosenberg: The Scholar Who Played With Bill Monroe," Bluegrass Unlimited, April 2008.

Other early events in Rosenberg's bluegrass life also occurred at the *Brown County Jamboree.* He won banjo contests held there in 1962, 1963, and 1964. In 1963, he was tapped by Ralph Rinzler, Bill Monroe's new manager, to oversee the park during the 1963 season. He played with the Stoney Lonesome Boys in the house band during that and the 1965 season and was called on by Monroe to assist at his first Bean Blossom festivals, in 1967 and 1968.

During the middle 1960s Neil began writing about bluegrass. His article "From Sound to Style, the Emergence of Bluegrass Music" was one of the first scholarly papers on bluegrass. It traced the evolution of bluegrass from being one man's (Bill Monroe's) music to a full-blown musical genre. The paper was first read at the American Folklore Society meeting in Boston in 1966. Neil also published, in the pages of *Bluegrass Unlimited* magazine, a concise discography of the recordings of the Osborne Brothers.

In 1966, after completing his coursework, Neil joined the staff of Indiana University where he worked until 1968 when he accepted a position teaching Folklore at Memorial University of Newfoundland in St. John's, Atlantic Canada's largest university. He held this position until his retirement in 2004.

Although he was geographically far removed from the heartlands of bluegrass, he was certainly not detached from the genre. He worked to bring bluegrass to Canadian audiences. From 1972 to 1979 he helped organize and run the Nova Scotia Bluegrass and Oldtime Music Festival, Canada's first such event. In 1973, he co-founded Crooked Stovepipe, a Newfoundland-based bluegrass band that continues to this day. From 1984 to 1991 he hosted a weekly bluegrass radio show on St. John's commercial country station CKIX-FM. And in 2003 he was a founding member of the Bluegrass and Oldtime Country Music Society of Newfoundland and Labrador.

Meanwhile his activities as a writer expanded. He began writing liner notes for various album releases. His 1969 compilation for RCA's Vintage Series, *Early Blue Grass*, was the genre's first historical reissue anthology. In 1974, the Country Music Foundation published his *Bill Monroe and His Blue Grass Boys: An Illustrated Discography*.

In 1981 Neil launched a monthly column that appeared in *Bluegrass Unlimited* for the next thirteen years. "30 Years Ago This Month" acquainted current readers with the activities (recording sessions, record releases, personal appearance dates, etc.) of luminaries from the golden days of bluegrass.

In the midst of his other writing and teaching responsibilities, Neil found time to complete his crowning achievement in music, the 450-page book *Bluegrass: A History*. Thirty years after its initial printing, the book remains the definitive study on the birth and development of the style. On its twenty-fifth anniversary, the book was revised to include more recent phenomena, including the rise of bluegrass superstar Alison Krauss.

Other books followed, including *Transforming Tradition: Folk Music Revivals Examined* (1993); *Bluegrass Odyssey: A Documentary in Pictures and Words, 1966-86*, which featured the photography of Carl Fleischhauer (2001); and *The Music of Bill Monroe*, a revised and greatly expanded version of his 1974 Bill Monroe discography, co-written with Charles Wolfe (2007).

Neil's writings also include some sixty published articles and review essays, and the notes to approximately fifty albums and CDs. Rosenberg prepared notes and discographies for boxed-set compilations of vintage bluegrass on the German Bear Family label, including sets by Bill Monroe, Flatt and Scruggs, the Osborne Brothers, and Carl Story.

Despite his accomplishments in the academic world, playing his own music is still a top priority. Rosenberg notes, "I never stopped performing, despite the demands on my time and energy… For me, making music is an essential exercise of the inner self."

— GARY REID

- IBMA Distinguished Achievement Award, 1986.
- Grammy Award for Best Album Notes for *Anthology of American Folk Music*, 1997.
- At-large member of IBMA's board of directors, 2006-2012.
- First international inductee to the Bluegrass Hall of Fame, 2014.

"Since 1969 I've written album notes for about forty LPs or CDs, and this kind of writing that links sound to print is my favorite medium. I'm particularly proud of having won a Grammy for my contribution to Smithsonian/Folkways' reissue of Harry Smith's Anthology of American Folk Music."

- Quoted in "George Lyon talks to Neil Rosenberg," *The Canadian Folk Music Bulletin*, May 2001.

By the way:
- Played in the first Bay Area bluegrass band, Berkeley, California, 1959.
- President of Oberlin College Folk Song Club, 1960-1961.
- Filled in occasionally as a banjo player for Bill Monroe's Blue Grass Boys.
- Managed Bill Monroe's Brown County Jamboree Park in Bean Blossom, IN, 1963.
- Holds dual citizenship in the United States and Canada.

The International Bluegrass Music Museum

Bluegrass music arose in the late 1930s and early 1940s. It took much the form it has today between 1945 and 1947, when the classic edition of the Blue Grass Boys included Bill Monroe, Lester Flatt, Earl Scruggs, Chubby Wise, and Howard Watts. Use of the term "bluegrass" to describe the sound first occurred in the mid 1950s, and it wasn't until the 1970s that bluegrass came to be viewed as an independent genre rather than a part of country or folk music.

The notions of a "home" or museum for bluegrass didn't get much traction until the middle 1980s, almost a half century after Bill Monroe started putting the style together. Owensboro, Kentucky, is the nearest city to Rosine, where Monroe was born and reared. Owensboro itself played a minor role in the history of bluegrass until Terry Woodward and other civic leaders began looking for ways to develop the community and encourage people to visit its somewhat isolated location.

Before long, the brand new International Bluegrass Music Association would make its headquarters in Owensboro (1985). An annual trade exposition (1987) and awards show (1990) for the music industry were also established there. Space was set aside in RiverPark Center for an International Bluegrass Music Museum (incorporated as a nonprofit organization in 1991).

"Bluegrass has a rich and colorful history. Our people are a collection of humor, tragedy, romance, sorrow, and every other story you could imagine. The fabric of some fascinating stories is portrayed at the International Bluegrass Music Museum and it's a place as vital to securing our music's future as it is in preserving our history."
– Dan Hays, previous executive director of the International Bluegrass Music Association

Ralph Stanley and Ricky Skaggs were honorary co-chairs of the Museum's initial fund raising campaign, and Peter Kuykendall of *Bluegrass Unlimited* magazine rallied support from the rest of the industry. The State of Kentucky came on board with significant financial support, and soon a high-quality, two-story museum complex began to take shape, with the International Bluegrass Music Hall of Fame and the Bill Vernon Collection of recordings its crown jewels.

Major historians, patrons, long-term fans, and performing artists pitched in to contribute attractive displays, collections, and interpretive materials that were both authoritative and engaging. A steady stream of visitors from the entire world began to make pilgrimages to Owensboro, the International Bluegrass Music Museum, its gift shop, and attractions

International Bluegrass Music Museum Board of Trustees

Dr. Peter Salovey, *Chairman*
Mike Simpson, *Vice-Chairman*
Terry Gold, *Secretary*
Terry Woodward, *Treasurer*
Gill Holland, *Executive Committee At Large*
Dr. Denise Jarvinen, *Executive Committee At Large*
Chris Love, *Executive Committee At Large*
Rodney Berry
Dr. Richard Brown
Dale Cockrell
Rosemary Conder
Matthew Dudman
Larry Harrington
Peter V. Kuykendall
Ross Leazenby
Jesse McReynolds
John Medley
Dagfinn M. Pedersen
Stephanie Taylor
Ralph Wible
Joe Wilson, *Advisor*

in nearby Rosine which chronicle the Monroe family, Bill Monroe's childhood, musical influences, and his grave. Early staff leaders at the Museum included Tom Adler, Bill Evans, Beck Glenn, and Chuck Hayes.

In 2002 the International Bluegrass Music Museum developed its first strategic plan. The board established a Vision: "to be the world center for the presentation of the history, culture, and future of bluegrass music" and a Mission: "to develop and maintain an environment in which people of all ages can discover the richness of bluegrass music through an exciting and educational experience."

It became clear that it would take more than a building in Owensboro for the Museum to achieve its lofty goals. Ambitious programs were launched. One was the Video Oral History Project (chronicling several hundred pioneers of bluegrass while they are still alive to tell the creation story). Another was the River of Music Party (ROMP), an extravaganza event that combines amazing live performances, film, food, a gathering of legends, and participants from all over the world in indoor and outdoor locations for four days every June. A third was the Bluegrass in the Schools Project (BITS) which ensures that thousands of young people in Western Kentucky learn about the living legacy of bluegrass and have their first intimate contact with its instruments. A fifth was an annual Monroe-Style Mandolin Camp, at which the leading proponents of the bluegrass mandolin impart its secrets to select apprentices from emerging generations.

The International Bluegrass Music Museum today, under the executive leadership of Gabrielle Gray, is a magnet, a leader, and the essential force in the world for preserving and interpreting a vital and growing cultural form. Still in its adolescence, the Museum already has an impact far greater than its physical space, small staff, and limited budget would imply. What does the future hold? Dream with us, become a member, visit, and pitch in your hand toward building that future.

– FRED BARTENSTEIN

Contributors

Martha Hearon Adcock has sung and played guitar with Eddie Adcock since 1973. A native of South Carolina, she is working on a book-length biography of her husband Eddie.

Fred Bartenstein has performed many roles in bluegrass music, including magazine editor, broadcaster, musician, festival MC, talent director, scholar, and consultant. Bartenstein lives in Yellow Springs, Ohio.

Gabrielle Gray, professionally trained as a concert violinist, has been executive director of the International Bluegrass Music Museum since 2003. She lives in Owensboro, Kentucky.

Gary Reid is a bluegrass music historian, journalist, and producer, based in Roanoke, Virginia.

Neil Rosenberg, professor emeritus of Folklore at Memorial University (St. John's, Newfoundland and Labrador, Canada), is a leading scholar of bluegrass music, author of *Bluegrass: A History* (1985, 2005), co-author of *The Music of Bill Monroe* (2007) and *Bluegrass Odyssey* (2001), and numerous articles and liner notes.

Steve Spence is a former managing editor of *Bluegrass Unlimited*. He lives in the Shenandoah Valley of Virginia.

Index

35 Years of the Best in Bluegrass, 1960-1995 (sound recording), 135
Abrahams, Roger; influence, 202
Acme Records, 99
Acuff, Roy, 142, 169, 214; influence, 40, 51; and the Smoky Mountain Boys, 76, 141
Adcock, Edward Windsor "Eddie," 4, 55, 58-61, 62, 68, 72, 164; Blue Grass Boy, 60; influence, 226; style, 58
Adcock, Martha, 59, 61, *77*, 89, 233
Adelman, Ben, 64
Adkins, Paul, 127
Adkins, Sammy, 21
Admiral Grill (Bailey's Crossroads, Virginia), 56, 62, 72
Akeman, David "Stringbean," *See* Stringbean
Alcoholism, 17, 142-143
Allen Grass, 139
Allen, Harley "Red", 44, 48, 56, 122, 126, 136-139, 198; and the Kentuckians, 138
Allen, Harley Lee, 127
Allied Artists, 92
American Banjo, Scruggs Style (sound recording), 202, 226
American Federation of Musicians, 33, 85, 152
American Record Corporation, 99
American Tobacco Company, 82
Andy Griffith Show (television program), 177, 180-181
Anthology of American Folk Music (sound recording), 105
Anthony, Donald Lee "Chubby," 118
Archive of Folk Culture, 228
Arhoolie Records, 192
Arnold, Jimmy, 88
Ash Grove (Los Angeles, California), 177, 206
Ashley, Clarence "Tom," 96, 204
Atkins, Chester "Chet" Burton, 107, 108, 140, 182; influence, 94, 96
Auldridge, Michael Dennis "Mike," 69, 135, 165, 214-217, 220-221, 224-225
Auldridge-Bennett-Gaudreau, 217
Automobile accidents, 34, 55, 60, 62, 115
Baez, Joan, 105, 115, 204, 205
Bailes Brothers; influence, 35
Bailey Brothers, 129, 194
Bailey, Charlie, 48
Bailey, DeFord; influence, 166
Baker, Billy, 192
Baker, Kenneth Clayton "Kenny," 4, 61, 77, 86-89, 123, 165
Baltimore, Maryland, vii, 70, 118, 126, 162, 190, 203
Banjo; clawhammer style, 18; melodic style, ix; Scruggs style, 4, 8, 117, 158, 182, 188
Barrier Brothers, 143
Bartenstein, Fred, xiii, 53, 83, 134, 139, 233; influence, 132
Baseball, 5, 23, 81, 82, 156, 161
Baucom, Terry, 200
Beachley, Darren and Legends of the Potomac, 217
Bean Blossom, Indiana, 5, 12, 17, 48, 53, 57, 83, 89, 134, 213, 228, 229
Bear Family Records, 161, 229
Belle, Gloria (Flickinger), 53
Berline, Byron, 4, 177
Berryville, Virginia, 80, 83, 84, 85, 134
Betts, Keeter; influence, 68
Beverly Hillbillies (television program), 8, 10, 188, 189, 213
Big Barn Frolic (Detroit, Michigan: radio program), 171

234 \ Bluegrass Hall of Fame Inductee Biographies

Big Jeff and the Radio Playboys, 140
Billboard Magazine, 17, 44, 52, 134, 184, 188, 213
Birchmere Tavern (Alexandria, Virginia), 69, 221, 225
Blake, Norman, 184, 209
Blankenship, Junior, 21
Blue Grass Boys, 4, 32, 90, 140, 155, 156, 158, 174, 181, 188, 193, 201, 202, 228, 229, 231; alumni, 4, 8; influence, 15, 35
Blue Mountain Boys, 28, 136
Blue Ridge Institute (Ferrum, Virginia), 135
Blue Sky Boys; influence, 23, 28, 35, 40, 112, 194
Blue Star Boys, 59, 60
Bluebird Records, 99
Bluegrass: Country Soul (motion picture), 81, 85, 112, 113, 118, 135
Bluegrass Album Band, 127, 200, 207-209
Bluegrass Alliance, 207, 208
Bluegrass and Oldtime Country Music Society of Newfoundland and Labrador, 229
Bluegrass Cardinals, 90, 92-93
Bluegrass Hall of Fame; elections, xii
Bluegrass music; compared with jazz, x; defined, vii, 2, 4; early development, 4-5
Bluegrass Unlimited (magazine), xiii, 56, 57, 69, 131, 167, 197, 228-229, 231
Bluegrass with Bill Vernon (Roanoke, Virginia: radio program), 135
Blues; influence on bluegrass, 76
Boatwright, Ginger, 180
Boehm, Carl, 162
Bonnaroo (music festival), 193
Bonnie and Clyde (motion picture), 8, 10, 177
Boone Creek, 127
Boone, Claude, 158
Boosinger, Laura, 197
Border radio stations, 99, 104, 107
Boston, Massachusetts, ix, 114-115, 118, 228
Boyd, Jim and the Melody Boys; influence, 154
Bradley, Dale Ann, 45, 49
Branham, Eddie, *See* Kentucky Slim
Brentwood Records, 201
Brewster Brothers, 161
Brewster, Bud, 161
Briarhopper, Homer, 211
Briarhoppers; influence, 128
Britt, Elton, 80, 92
Brock, Jim, 41
Bromberg, David, 216
Brooks, Rex; influence, 8
Brown County Jamboree Park (Bean Blossom, Indiana), 5, 17, 83, 183, 228, 229
Brown, Dewey, 21
Brown, Don and the Ozark Mountain Trio, 182
Brown, Frank "Hylo," 81, 131, 174
Brown, James "Godfather of Soul," 150
Brunswick Records, 102, 104, 106
Bryan, James, 88
Bryant, Donnie; influence, 55
Bryant, Felice and Boudleaux, 44
Bryant, Jimmy and Speedy West; influence, 58
Bryant, Johnny and the White Oak Mountain Boys, 153
Bryant, Steve, 127
Bub, Mike, 193

Buchanan, Jimmy, 41, 139
Busby, Buzz, and the Bayou Boys, 55, 59, 60, 62, 68, 70, 72, 117, 118
Bush, Sam, 184, 208
Buskirk, Paul; influence, 112
Butler, Dennis, 6; influence, 8
Byrds, 177
Cabin Creek Records, 143
Cain, Benny and Vallie, 54, 55, 56, 68
Callahan Brothers; influence, 112
Camp Springs, North Carolina, 84, 85, 134
Campbell, Glen Goodtime Hour (television program), 184
Campbell, Ola Belle, *See* Reed, Ola Belle
Canaan Records, 148
Capitol Records, 35, 38, 40, 41
Capitol Transcriptions (Washington, D.C.), 56
Carlisle, Cliff; influence, 74, 76
Carnegie Hall (New York, New York), 60, 68, 138, 181, 188, 212
Carolina Boys, 194, 195, 196
Carter, Alvin Pleasant "A.P.," 98-105, 162
Carter, Janette, 98, 99, 102, 103, 104, 105, 122
Carter, Jason, 143, 193
Carter, Maybelle Addington "Mother Maybelle," 8, 98-99, 101, 102, 104-108, 136, 177, 188, 218, 220; guitar style, 99, 106, 108, 196
(Carter), Mother Maybelle and the Carter Sisters, 107
Carter, Sara Dougherty, 98-105
Carter Family, 99-108, 122; influence, 16, 32, 35, 40, 42, 94, 112, 140, 162
Carter Family Fold (Hiltons, Virginia), 102, 165
Cash, Johnny, 70, 105, 108, 161, 181
Ceili Records, 193
Chatman, Lucky and the Ozark Mountain Boys, 64
Chesapeake (band), 216, 217
Chuck Wagon Gang; influence, 40, 145
Church, Porter, 138
Cincinnati, Ohio, vii, 16, 26, 28, 40, 43, 44, 48, 136, 150-152
Civil War (television program), 185
CKIX (St. John's, Newfoundland), 229
CKLW (Windsor, Ontario), 44, 52
Clark, Gene, 177
Clark, Johnny, 162, 164; banjo style, 165
Clayton, Paul, 162
Clear Creek Crossin,' 115
Clements, Vassar, 4, 9, 41, 97, 127, 184-185, 216
Clifton, Bill, 57, 63, 64, 68, 69, 88, 105, 119, 162-165, 195; influence, 63
Cline, Charlie, 171, 174, 175
Cline, Ezra, 170-174
Cline, Ireland "Lazy Ned," 170
Cline, Ray "Curly Ray," 20, 170-175
CMH Records, 33, 38, 49, 61, 92, 142, 142, 148, 161, 213
Codack, Clinton, *See* Adcock, Eddie
Coleman, T. Michael, 69, 87, 177, 216
Columbia Records, 5, 8, 9, 10, 12, 16, 18, 21, 32, 35, 41, 68, 74, 76, 79, 97, 99, 105, 108, 113, 114, 130, 141, 156, 157, 160, 161, 188, 189, 196, 212
Comedy, 23, 29, 64, 74, 77, 107, 115, 140, 145, 154, 155, 157, 174, 176, 184, 195
Confederate Mountaineers, 114
Connell, Dudley, 221

Bluegrass Hall of Fame Inductee Biographies \ **235**

Consolidated Coal Company, 86
Constable, Billy, 180
Cooder, Ry; influence, 206
Cooke, Jack and the Virginia Mountain Boys, 190
Cooper, Wilma Lee and Stoney, 32, 76, 77, 135, 214
Copas, Lloyd Estel "Cowboy," 150, 153, 156, 157
Copper Creek Records, xiii, 197
Country Boys, 33
Country Cousins, x
Country Gentlemen, xiv, 55, 56-57, 59-61, 63-66, 68, 69, 72-73, 96, 127, 135, 137, 164, 198, 200, 201, 216, 217, 220, 222, 224, 227
Country Gentlemen Reunion Band, 61
Country Music Association, 33
Country Music Foundation, 229
Country Music Hall of Fame, xiii, 105, 135, 189
Country News and Views (Magazine), 122, 134
County Records, 88, 115, 119, 120-123, 131, 138, 165
County Sales, 122-123
Cozy Records, 43, 170
Cozzens, Ellsworth; influence, 216
Craft, Paul, 53, 220, 222
Crary, Dan, 94, 208
Crase, Noah, 136
Cravens, Red and the Bray Brothers, 183
Cream (band), 57
Crook, Herman; influence, 166
Crooked Road, Virginia's Music Heritage Trail, 21, 123
Crooked Stovepipe, 229
Crossroads Records, 201
Crowe, James Dee "J.D.," 9, 52, 58, 114, 124-127, 139, 177, 198, 200, 207, 208; banjo style, 124; and the New South, 127, 177, 207, 208
Daniels, Keith and the Blue Ridge Ramblers; influence, 190
Davis, Ray; influence, 132
Davis, Steve; influence, 160
Davis Sisters, 171
Dayton, Ohio, vii, 40, 42, 44, 46, 48, 136, 139
Daywind Records, 148
Decca Records, 5, 44, 48, 52, 99, 118, 126, 142, 157, 174, 192, 205
Delmore, Alton, 167
Delmore Brothers, 150; influence, 23, 28, 35, 40, 42, 94, 170, 171
Derrick, Vernon, 53
Design Records, 61
Detroit, Michigan, vii, 44, 52, 99, 124, 126, 171
Devil's Box (magazine), 167, 168
Dickens, Hazel and Alice Gerrard, 166
Dickson, Jim, 177
Dillard and Clark, 177
Dillard, Doug Band, 180
Dillard, Douglas Flint "Doug," 176-181
Dillard, Rodney Adean, 176-182, 185, 189
Dillards, ix, xiv, 176-181, 185
Disc Collector (magazine), 54
Discography, 99, 228-229
Disneyland (Anaheim, California), 206
Dixie Mountain Boys, 162
Dixie Ramblers, 177, 182
Dixie Records, 72
Dobro, *See* Resophonic guitar

Dot Records, 33, 152, 185
Douglas, Jerry, 126, 127
Duffey, John Humbird, 56, 60-61, 62-65, 68-69, 72-73, 164, 165, 217, 220-221, 224
Eanes, Homer Robert "Jim," 4, 8, 84, 134-135; influence, 132
Earle, Steve, 193
Easter, Jeff and Sherri, 148
Edwards, Billy, 174
Eldreth, Donnie, 192
Eldridge, Benjamin "Ben," 192, 200, 216, 218-221, 222
Electric instrumentation, 41, 44-45, 48, 61, 180
Elektra Records, 177
Elf Records, 119, 165
Emerson, William "Bill," 53, 56, 60, 62, 68, 69, 72, 73, 138, 192, 198
Emerson, Bill, Cliff Waldron and the New Shades of Grass, 216
Epic Records, 35, 41
Ethridge, Floyd, 79
Evans, Andy, 206
Event Records, 115
Faier, Billy; influence, 226
Farm and Fun Time (Bristol, Virginia: radio program), 15, 18, 130, 160
Farm Hands, 83
Faurot, Charles, 122
Federal Jazz Commission, 69
Federal Records, 28
Ferris, Ed, 26, 69
Festival of American Folklife, 202
Festival! (motion picture), 105, 113
Festivals; as performance venues, 20, 84, 134, 205
Fincastle, Virginia, 17, 20, 26, 85, 97, 143, 205
First Generation (band), 117, 119, 163, 165
Flatt and Scruggs, 5, 7, 8-13, 18, 32, 74-76, 77, 80, 92, 97, 113, 114, 118, 129-130, 141-142, 145, 152, 156, 157, 168, 171, 177, 186, 188, 189, 209, 212, 213, 218, 229; influence, 35, 42, 63, 68, 72, 124, 128, 132, 136, 145, 148, 182, 183, 190, 206, 214, 216, 220, 222
Flatt, Lester Raymond, 4, 5, 6, 9-12, 23, 33, 52, 76, 79, 81, 90, 91, 92, 97, 131, 134, 135, 138, 139, 140-143, 156, 213, 231; Blue Grass Boy, 4-5, 9-12, 79; guitar style, 10; influence, 15, 183; songwriting, 12
Floyd, Virginia, 123
Flying Fish Records, 143, 180, 185, 213
"Foggy Mountain Breakdown," 8, 157, 177
"Foggy Mountain Top," 8
Foley, Red, 81, 140, 212
Folk music revival, viii, 5, 8, 20, 33, 36, 41, 64, 96, 115, 118, 203
Folkways Records, 56, 61, 64, 68, 72, 96, 97, 105, 115, 138, 139, 202, 203, 204
Ford, Tennessee Ernie Show (television program), 177
Ford tractors, 41
Forrester, Howard Wilson "Howdy," 4, 78-79, 142
Forrester, Sally Ann, 155
Fowler, Wally, 140
Fox, Arnim LeRoy "Curly," 78, 140
Frank, Max; influence, 150
Freeland, Richard "Dick," 57, 64, 123, 134
Freeman, Chet, 123

Freeman, David, 120-123
Frets Magazine, 208, 217
Friendly Inn (Dayton, Ohio), 137
Front Porch String Band, 225
Gallagher Guitars, 97
Garcia, Jerome John "Jerry," 139, 209
Gateway Records, 44, 48
Gaudreau, James "Jimmy," 61, 119, 127, 165
Gay, Connie B., 80
George, Lowell, 216
Gerde's Folk City (New York, New York), 177, 204
Gibson, Don, 88, 168, 169
Ginter, Ott, 46
Glaser Brothers, 183
Goforth, Gene; influence, 183
Goins, Melvin, 20, 171-175
Goins, Ray, 171-175
Golden State Boys, 192, 206
Good Deale Bluegrass Band, 217
Goodman, Benny; influence, 216
Gospel Music Association Dove awards, 148, 200, 201
Governor Morehead School for the Blind (Raleigh, North Carolina), 94
Grammy Awards, 5, 9, 21, 60, 96, 97, 127, 139, 169, 180, 184, 185, 191, 193, 200, 201, 204, 216, 217, 220, 224, 225, 229
Grand Ole Opry (Nashville, Tennessee: radio program), vii-viii, 4, 8, 10, 12, 13, 20, 21, 23, 28, 32, 41, 42, 44, 49, 52, 53, 66, 80, 82, 84, 90, 97, 102, 108, 116, 118, 140, 142, 156, 166, 168, 192, 193, 194, 204, 212; influence, 66, 136, 198, 210, 222
Grappelli, Stephane; influence, 86, 87
Grascals, 45
Grassound (magazine), 85
Grassroots to Bluegrass (video series), 33, 85
Grateful Dead, 122; bluegrass influences, x, 118
Graves, Burkett Howard "Uncle Josh," 8, 61, 74-77, 89, 131, 216; influence, 216; style, 76
Graves, Virgil William "Smokey," 58
Gray, Gabrielle, 232, 233
Gray, Sally Govers, 69
Gray, Thomas L. "Tom," 61, 66-69, 72, 73, 165, 221, 224, 225
Grayson, G. B. and Whitter, Henry; influence, 16, 160
Green Valley Quartet, 153
Green, Doug, 4
Greenbriar Boys, 202-204
Greene, Joe, 88
Greene, Richard, 4, 138, 208
Greenhill, Manuel "Manny," 115
Grier, David, 180
Grisman, David, 138, 208, 209; Quartet, 127; Quintet, 208
Groove Grass Boyz, 33, 45, 48
Gusto Records, 53
Haley, Jimmy, 200
Hall, Tom T., 9
Hammett, Smith; influence, 8
Haney, Lawrence Carlton, 26, 29, 80, 82-85; influence, 132
Hankins, Esco, 76, 77; influence, 124
Harrell, William "Bill," 26, 29, 60, 153, 195, 197; and the Virginians, 118
Harris, Emmylou, 216, 217, 224, 225
Hartford, John, 6, 143, 180, 182-185

Hay, George D., 8
Hayloft Jamboree (Boston, Massachusetts: radio program), 114, 118
Hearon, Martha, *See* Adcock, Martha
Henderson, Gary, 57, 220
Hendley, Fisher; influence, 8
Hensley, Walter, 190
Herzog, Earl; influence, 150
Hicks, Bobby, 4, 84, 127, 200, 208
High Lonesome: The Story of Bluegrass Music (motion picture), 33
Hill Billies; use of solos, x
Hill, Tommy, 138
Hillbilly Ranch (Boston, Massachusetts), 114, 118-119
Hillman, Chris, 192, 209; influence, 206
Hobbs, Smiley, 68
Hollywood Records, 145
Hopkins, Sam John "Lightnin;" influence, 76
Hoppers, Lonnie and the Ozark Mountain Boys, 176
Howard, Paul and his Arkansas Cotton Pickers; influence, 154
Howell, Melvin and the Franklin County Boys, 190
Hurt, John Smith "Mississippi John," 56
II Generation, 61
In and Around Bluegrass (Roanoke, Virginia: radio program), 135
Indian Springs, Maryland, 57
Indiana University, 228
International Bluegrass Music Association, xii, 5, 33, 53, 57, 93, 135, 168, 193, 201, 209, 231
International Bluegrass Music Museum (Owensboro, Kentucky), xii-xii, 57, 231-232
Irvin, Smitty; influence, 55
Jackson, Carl, 225
Jackson, Leon, 153
Jackson, Tommy, 164
Jalyn Records, 197
Jam Up and Honey, 140
Japan; building an audience, 113, 114, 119
Jarrell, Tommy, 88
Jay, Penny, 53
Jayne, Mitchell Franklin "Mitch," 176, 179, 180, 181
Jenkins, Hoke, 129, 158, 195; influence, 18, 20, 35; and His Smoky Mountaineers, 40
Jenkins, Snuffy; influence, 8, 18, 20, 23
Jennings, Ordon L. "Gordon," 170
Jim and Jesse and the Virginia Boys, 35, 38, 40, 41, 130, 152, 195; style, x, 35
Johnnie and Jack, 141, 142, 157, 210-212, 214
Johnson Family; influence, 145
Johnson Mountain Boys, 93, 168
Johnson, Ellis, 50
Johnson, Gene, 127
Johnson, Lois, 53
Jones, Grandpa, 150, 168; influence, 194, 218
Jordan, Victor "Vic," 53
Jubilee Hillbillies, 78
Karl and Harty; influence, 32
Keith, Leslie, 14
Keith, William Bradford "Bill," ix, 118, 138, 165, 192, 204; Blue Grass Boy, 4, 204; influence, 218
Kentucky Mountain Barn Dance (Lexington, Kentucky:

radio program), 124, 136
Kentucky Mountain Boys, 126, 139, 198, 207
Kentucky Pardners, 128-129, 138
Kentucky Records, 40, 136
Kentucky Ridgerunners, 113
Kentucky Slim, 174
Kerosene circuit, viii
Kilpatrick, Dee, 16, 160
Kincaid, Bradley, 163; influence, 32
King Bluegrass Records, 139
King of Bluegrass: The Life and Times of Jimmy Martin (motion picture), 53
King Records, 16-17, 20, 21, 26, 28, 43, 52, 80, 84, 145, 150-153, 196, 197
King, Tony, 127
Kirby, Beecher Ray "Pete"/"Bashful Brother Oswald," *See* Oswald, Bashful Brother
Kitty Records, 46
Klein, Moondi, 217
Krise, Speedy; influence, 76
Kuykendall, Peter Van, 54-57, 68, 138, 231
KWKH (Shreveport, Louisiana), 32, 52, 126
KWTO (Springfield, Missouri), 108
KXEN (Saint Louis, Missouri), 183
Laird, Dick, 192
Lambert, Curley, 135, 164
Lambert, Darrell "Pee Wee," 14, 16, 18
Lancer Agency, 92, 93
Lawrence, Jack, 97
Lawson, Doyle Wayne, 53, 73, 126-127, 139, 198-201, 208; and Quicksilver, 200-201
Lawson, Glenn, 127
Leahy, Larry, 70
Leary Family; influence, 32
Leather Records, 192
Lee, Ricky, 21
Lemco Records, 126, 139
LeRoy, Lansing B. "Lance", 90-93
Lewis Family, 144-149, 161
Library of Congress, 20, 56, 64, 203
Lilly Brothers and Don Stover, ix, 109-113
Lilly, Bea, *See* Lilly, Michael Burt "Bea"
Lilly, Charley Edwin "Everett," 8, 109, 113-115; and the Lilly Mountaineers, 115
Lilly, Everett, *See* Lilly, Charley Edwin "Everett"
Lilly, Michael Burt "Bea", 109, 118
Little Roy and Lizzie Show, 149
Lloyd, Albert Lancaster "A.L.," 203; influence, 202
Logan, Benjamin Franklin "Tex," 113-114, 118-119, 134, 220
Lomax, Alan, viii, 202, 203
Lonesome Pine Fiddlers, 42-43, 46, 48, 51, 52, 126, 170-175
Lonesome Standard Time, 93
Louisiana Hayride (Shreveport, Louisiana: radio program), 32, 52, 70, 118, 124, 126
Louvin, Charlie, 35
Louvin Brothers, 35, 40, 138, 160, 168; influence, 35, 40
Lucas, Nick, 94
Lunn, Robert, 140
Lyle, Rudy; influence, 116
Lynch, Claire, 13, 123, 224, 225
MacColl, Ewan, 203; influence, 202

Macon, David Harrison "Uncle Dave;" influence, 160
Maddox Brothers and Rose, 152
Magaha, Mack, 26, 28, 29
Magness, Tommy, 28; influence, 23; and the Tennessee Buddies, 23, 28, 29
Mainer, J.E.; influence, 16, 20
Mainer, Wade, 152; influence, 16, 20, 116
Mainer's Mountaineers; influence, 23, 32, 40, 171
Malaria, 23
Mandolin; crosspicking, 34
Marburg, William August; *See* Clifton, Bill
Martha White Mills; sponsorships, 8, 10, 12, 13, 35, 41, 130, 212
Martin guitars, 42, 96, 105
Martin, Benjamin Edward "Benny," 4, 8, 26, 140-143, 164, 185, 212; influence, 182, 183, 184; style, 142
Martin, Emory; influence, 116
Martin, James Henry "Jimmy," 4, 16, 43-44, 48, 50-53, 81, 82, 84, 85, 90, 93, 97, 124, 126, 127, 150, 152, 157, 174, 198, 201, 205, 209, 220; Blue Grass Boy, 48, 50; influence, 198, 220; and the Osborne Brothers, 157
Massachusetts Institute of Technology, 114
Masters, The (band), 61, 77, 89
Masters Family; influence, 145
Mauldin, Bessie Lee, 69, 82
MCA Records, 44, 53
McClure, Virginia, 14, 134, 146-147
McCoury Music, 193
McCoury, Del Band, 193
McCoury, Delano Floyd "Del," 4, 93, 123, 134, 190-193; Blue Grass Boy, 192, 204
McCoury, Jerry, 138, 192
McCoury, Robbie, 192
McCoury, Ronnie, 192-193
McGee, Sam and Kirk; influence, 166
McHan, Don, 41
McKnight, Luke, 38
McMichen, Clayton, 167; influence, 78, 140, 171
McPeak, Udell, 174
McReynolds Brothers and the Cumberland Mountain Boys, 40
McReynolds, Amanda, 38
McReynolds, Garrett, 38
McReynolds, James Monroe "Jim," 39-41, 129
McReynolds, Jesse Lester, x, 33, 34-41, 61, 77, 129, 231; mandolin style, 34, 196
McReynolds, Keith, 38
Meade, Todd, 21
Melodeon Records, 57, 138
Melody Mountain Boys, 194
Memorial University of Newfoundland, 228
Menius, Arthur "Art," 93
Mercury Records, 8, 10, 16, 18, 43, 61, 68, 72, 130, 142, 157, 160-161, 164, 196
MGM Records, 44, 48, 137, 138, 141, 142, 157
Microphone; role in bluegrass, viii
Mid-Day Merry-Go-Round (Knoxville, Tennessee: radio program), 108, 136, 142, 158
Middle Tennessee State University, 166
Military service, 14, 18, 23, 28, 35, 40, 43, 48, 86, 164, 170, 211, 222
Miller, Lost John and the Allied Kentuckians, 6

Miller, Sonny, 192
Miller, Wendy, 127
Mississippi Valley Boys, 182
Missouri Ridgerunners, 182
Monroe, Birch, 2, 4, 83
Monroe, Charlie, 112, 128-130, 132, 135, 138, 140; influence, 50, 112, 136
Monroe, James, 4
Monroe, Melissa, 82-83
Monroe, William Smith "Bill," viii, ix, xii, 2-5, 8, 10, 16, 17, 23, 27, 28, 32, 43, 44, 45, 50, 52, 58, 60, 65, 74, 78, 80, 81, 82, 84-85, 88-89, 90, 97, 114, 116, 118, 119, 140, 156, 157, 164, 165, 167, 174, 176, 181, 201, 202-205, 228, 229; childhood, 2; inducted to *Grand Ole Opry*, 4; influence, 2, 4, 5, 15, 16, 20, 35, 42, 46, 48, 51, 63, 68, 72, 79, 136, 145, 168, 170, 176, 198, 203, 208, 213, 222, 231-232; touring, viii-ix
Monroe Brothers, 4, 105, 169; influence, 12, 16, 35, 40, 112, 116, 128, 136, 171, 205
Moody, Clyde, 4, 10, 12, 78, 80, 82, 85, 155, 158
Moore, Lee; influence, 32
Moore, Scotty; influence, 124
Morgan, Ray, 170
Morgan, Tom, 66, 138
Morris Brothers, 8, 23; influence, 128
Morris, Wade, 129
Morris, Wiley; influence, 28
Morris, Zeke, 28, 162
Muleskinner News (magazine), 60, 65, 84, 85, 133, 134, 217, 224
Munde, Alan, 53
Mustard and Gravy, 195
Napier, Bill, 150, 151, 153, 196
Nashville Grass, 10, 90, 92, 130-131, 212, 213; origin of band name, 13
Nathan, Sydney "Syd," 16, 20, 28, 150-153
National Council for the Traditional Arts, xiii, 89
National Geographic Society, 66, 69
Neal, Tommy, 192
Nelson, Ken, 40
New Coon Creek Girls, 93
New Dominion Barn Dance (Richmond, Virginia: radio program), 84, 190
New Grass Revival, 153
New Lost City Ramblers; influence, 226
New River Ranch (Rising Sun, Maryland), viii
Newgrass music, 72, 184
Newgrass Music Festival (Camp Springs, North Carolina), 85
Newport Folk Festival, 17, 20, 38, 84, 97, 105, 108, 115, 119, 164, 177, 203-205
Noel, Joe; influence, 177
Nova Scotia Bluegrass and Oldtime Music Festival, 229
O Brother, Where Art Thou? (motion picture), 21, 55, 97, 184, 185
Oak Leaf Park (Luray, Virginia), 84, 164
Oberlin College, 226-227
O'Day, Molly and the Cumberland Mountain Folks, 32, 112
Okeh Records, 99, 158
Old Dominion Barn Dance (Richmond, Virginia: radio program), 29, 33, 84, 108, 130, 222; influence, 218
Old Dominion Records, 38, 41

Old Homestead Records, 119
Old Time Music (magazine), 167
OMS Records, 89
Osborne, Robert "Bobby" Van, 42-45, 52, 92, 170, 174, 175
Osborne, Roland "Sonny," 42, 44-49, 81, 92, 136-137; Blue Grass Boy, 4, 48; influence, 218
Osborne Brothers, 33, 44-49, 52, 85, 88, 124, 137-138, 143, 157, 174, 201, 227, 228, 229; influence, 45, 63, 65; style, 48
Oswald, Bashful Brother, 166; influence, 76
Owens, Don; influence, 55, 162
Owensboro, Kentucky, xii, 231
Ozark Jubilee (Springfield, Missouri: radio program), 108
Page Records, 113
Palmer, John, 26, 29
Park, Ray, ix
Parker, "Colonel" Tom, 80, 142
Parker, Charles "Rex", 171
Parsons, Penny, 131
Parton, Dolly, 143, 148, 217, 224, 225
Patuxent Records, 61
Paul, Les; influence, 58
Pedersen, Herb, 139, 180, 209; influence, 206
Peer, Ralph, 99, 104, 106-107, 167
Phelps, Jackie, ix, 23, 141
Phillips, Todd, 127, 200
Pick Inn (Gallatin, Tennessee), 38
Pierce, Don, 153, 164
Pinecastle Records, 38, 49, 61, 73, 81
Pioneer Records, 140
Plum Creek Boys, 227
Poffinberger, Bill, 192
Poole, Charlie; influence, 32, 158, 160
Poss, Barry, 122, 123
Potter, Dale, 4, 142
Poverty; role in bluegrass, viii
Prairie Ramblers; influence, 4
Preservation Jazz Hall Band, 193
Presley, Elvis, 40, 70, 108, 142, 143, 149, 168, 184
Prestige Records, 115
Prevette, Ronnie, 53
Price, James, 21
Profitt, Tony "Renfro," 21
Publishing, 188
Puckett, Riley; influence, 32, 160
Punturi, Albert, 171
Purcell, Bryan; influence, 78
Rabbit's Foot (Washington, D.C.), 224
Radio; role in spreading bluegrass, viii, 8, 27, 30, 33, 44, 52, 54, 62, 112, 134, 145, 160, 171, 210, 212, 222
Raines, Missy, 61, 77, 89
Rainwater, Cedric, *See* Watts, Howard Staton "Cedric Rainwater"
Rainwater, Jodie, 8
Rambling Mountaineers, 158, 161
Rasnake, Roger, 180
RCA Victor Records, 10, 33, 44, 48, 52, 76, 80, 92, 99, 108, 142, 157, 171, 174, 183-184, 213, 229
Rebel Records, 21, 56, 57, 61, 64, 65, 73, 120, 126, 123, 133-134, 138, 139, 192, 197, 216, 224, 225
Record collecting, 120, 123, 132, 135
Record Depot (Roanoke, Virginia), 120, 123

Rector, Red, 28, 119, 160, 165
Red Fox Inn (Bethesda, Maryland), 65, 69, 220, 221, 224
Red Slipper Lounge (Lexington, Kentucky), 126
Redwood Canyon Rangers, 227
Reed, Ola Belle, viii
Reid, Gary, xiii, 122, 134, 233
Reid, Lou, 200, 201, 221
Reinhardt, Django; influence, 94, 208
Renfro Valley, Kentucky, 33
Renfro, Dewey, 192
Reno, Dale, 26
Reno, Don, Bill Harrell and the Tennessee Cut-Ups, 26, 195, 197
Reno, Don, Red Smiley and the Tennessee Cut-Ups, 24-25, 28, 29, 84, 150, 152, 153
Reno, Don Wayne, 26
Reno, Don Wesley, 22-26, 28, 61, 138, 143; Blue Grass Boy, ix, 4, 23; influence, 58, 72, 116, 218; songwriting, 22; banjo style, 23
Reno, Ronnie, 26
Resophonic guitar, 74
Rice, David Anthony "Tony," 94, 126, 127, 200, 206-209; Unit, 208-209
Rice, Larry, 126-127, 198, 206, 209
Rice, Ronnie, 206
Richardson, Larry, 42, 170, 174
Rich-R-Tone Records, 15
Riddle, Lesley, 99
Ridge Runner Records, 89
Rigsby, John, 21
Rimrock Records, 29
Rinzler, Ralph Charles, 85, 96-97, 134, 202-205, 228
Riversong Records, 148
Roberts, James, 171
Rock 'n' roll music, 5, 33, 35, 152, 220
Rocky Mountain Boys, 60
Rocky Top X-Press, 45
Rodgers, Jimmie, 74, 76, 100, 103; influence, 4, 42, 94, 140
Rome Records, 61
Ronstadt, Linda, 216-217, 225
Rosenberg, Neil Vandraegen, xiii, 226-229, 233
Rotator cuff injury, 49
Rounder Records, 38, 45, 119, 127, 166, 185, 192-193, 200, 201, 208
Rowan, Peter, 4, 209
Royal Albert Hall (London, England), 165
Runkle, Bill, 192
Rural Rhythm Records, 29, 197
Ryan, Buck, 26
Ryman Auditorium (Nashville, Tennessee), vii, 175, 188
Sally Mountain Show, 92, 93
Sauceman Brothers, 28, 130, 174
Sauceman, Carl, viii, 131
Schatz, Mark, 127
Schultz, Arnold; influence, 4
Scott, Tommy, 128
Scruggs, Ann Louise Certain; See Scruggs, Louise
Scruggs, Earl Eugene, vii, 5-9, 10, 12, 23, 26, 76, 92, 94, 97, 118, 131, 156, 157, 180, 182, 186-189, 212, 213; Blue Grass Boy, ix, 4-7, 10-12, 79; influence, vii, 8, 9, 18, 20, 46, 54, 57, 76, 116, 124, 126, 182, 186, 190, 218, 226; leaves Flatt and Scruggs, 9; Revue, 8, 9, 189

Scruggs, Gary, 9
Scruggs, Horace, 6
Scruggs, Junie, 6
Scruggs, Louise, 8, 92, 186-189
Scruggs, Randy, 9
Scruggs, Steve, 9
Seckler, John Ray "Curly," 8, 13, 40, 128-131, 134, 136, 143, 184
Seeger, Mike, 56, 64, 68, 105, 164, 165; influence, 203
Seeger, Pete; influence, 226
Segovia, Andres; influence, 58
Seldom Scene, 56, 64-65, 69, 134, 216-217, 220, 221, 224-225
Shady Valley Boys, 192
Shamrock Club (Georgetown, Washington, D.C.), 64, 72
Shelton, Allen, 41, 83; influence, 218
Shelton, Curley, 158
Shelton, Jack, 158
Shelton, James Alan, 21, 197
Shelton Brothers; influence, 23
Shenandoah Cut-Ups, 29, 131
Shoney's Restaurant, 5
Shuffler Family, 197
Shuffler, George Saunders, 17, 68, 94, 194-197; influence, 68
Shuffler, John, 68; influence, 68
Shumate, Jim, 79
Silver Dollar City (Branson, Missouri), 180
Simmons, Buster and Lawrence and the Georgia Mountain Boys, 91
Simpkins, Ronnie, 221
Sims, Benny, 8
Sing Out! (magazine), 68, 204, 226
Sizemore, Charlie, 21
Sizemore, Herschel, 192
Skaggs, Ricky Lee, 9, 20, 123, 126, 127, 135, 189, 208, 209, 224, 231
Skillet Lickers; influence, 32
Skinner, Jimmie Music Center, 40
Slone, Bobby, 126-127, 139, 198
Smiley, Arthur Lee "Red," 22, 23, 24-25, 26-29, 28, 84; guitar style, 27; and the Bluegrass Cut-Ups, 84
Smith, Arthur "Fiddlin' Arthur," influence, 20, 26, 167, 171, 210, 211
Smith, Arthur "Guitar Boogie" (and His Crackerjacks), 23, 26, 28, 78, 161, 167, 171, 211
Smith, Dick, 192
Smith, Fred, 28
Smith, Hal, 142
Smith, Larry, 192
Smith, L. Mayne, 226-227
Smithsonian Institution, 202-203, 204
Smoky Mountaineers, 128
Smothers Brothers, 184
Snow, Hank, 80, 81, 114, 168; influence, 72; and the Rainbow Ranch Boys, 80, 157
Society for the Preservation of Bluegrass Music in America (SPBGMA), 60, 80, 118, 148-149, 164, 180, 191, 200, 201
Sons of the Pioneers, 80; influence, 35, 40, 194
South Mountain Boys, 214
Southern Music, 99, 107

Sparkman, Steve, 21
Sparks, Larry, 20, 81, 123, 135, 153, 197
Spears, Willis, 131
Spence, Steve, 233
Spicher, Buddy, 4
Spottswood, Dick, 57, 138
Spurlock, Clifford, 104
Staber, Dick, 192
Stacey, Gladys, 10, 13
Stamper, Art, 137, 165
Stanley, Carter Glen, 14-17, 19, 153, 157, 164, 196, 205; Blue Grass Boy, 4, 14, 16; influence, 162
Stanley, Lee, 14
Stanley, Lucy Smith, 14, 18
Stanley, Nathan, 21
Stanley, Ralph Edmond, 14-21, 153, 164, 175, 197, 231; influence, 58, 218, 226; political activity, 21; style, 18; Museum, 21
Stanley, Ralph II, 21
Stanley Brothers, xiii, xiv, 14, 16-18, 20-21, 35, 43, 46, 57, 68, 85, 102, 105, 130, 136, 141, 142, 150, 151, 152-153, 164, 174, 175, 194-197; influence, 35, 63, 145, 177, 203; style, x, 15-16
Starday Records, 20, 35, 41, 61, 63, 64, 68, 72, 81, 138, 142, 145, 148, 153, 161, 164, 174
Starling, John, 69, 135, 217, 220-225; and Carolina Rose, 217, 225
Stella guitars, 70, 96, 106
Stevens Brothers, 190
Stoneman, Scott, 70, 138
Stonemans, 60
Stoneway Records, 81
Stoney Lonesome Boys, 228
Story, Carl, 4, 78-79, 145, 158-161
Stover, Don, ix, 4, 70, 114-119, 165; Blue Grass Boy, 118
Stringbean (David Akeman), 4, 12, 78, 155
Stripling, Chick, 41
Stroud, Toby, 28
Stuart, Jerry, 68
Stuart, Marty, 13, 92, 97
Sugar Hill Records, 49, 60, 65, 73, 120, 123, 200, 201, 217
Sullivan Records, 144
Sullivan, Hoyt, 145
Summer Olympics, Mexico City, 118
Sumner, Marion; influence, 87, 88
Sunny Mountain Boys, 52, 127, 152
Sunset Park (Oxford, Pennsylvania), viii
Sutherland, David, 41
Suwanee River Jamboree (Live Oak, Florida: radio program), 16, 20
Sykes, Roy and the Blue Ridge Mountain Boys, 14, 18
Takoma Records, 216
Tate, Clarence "Tater", 53, 160
Taylor, Earl, 53, 124, 143; and the Stoney Mountain Boys, 70
Taylor, Merle "Red," 77
Taylor, Paul, 112; influence, 116
Taylor, Tut, 184
Temple University, 26
Tennessee Barn Dance (Knoxville, Tennessee: radio program), 108
Tennessee Cut-Ups, 23-26, 28, 29, 84, 85
Tennessee Folklore Society Bulletin, 167, 187
Terry, Gordon, 4
Tex and Slim and the Sunset Ramblers, 154
Thatcher, Wendy, 61
Thomasson, Ron, 21
Thompson, Robert "Bobby," 41, 161
Top 'o the Morning (Roanoke, Virginia: television program), 29, 84
Towa Kikaku and Company, 114
Travers, Fred, 221
Travis, Merle, 97, 114, 217; influence, 58, 94, 96, 194, 196
Troubadour Club (Los Angeles, California), 206
True Adventures With the King of Bluegrass (motion picture), 53
Tubb, Ernest, 53, 81, 127; influence, 28, 42, 124
Tullock, E.P. "Cousin Jake," 8, 74, 131
UCLA Folk Festival, 177
Union Grove Fiddlers' Convention (Union Grove, North Carolina), 96, 204
United States Army Air Corps, 14
Val, Joe, ix
Valiente, Joseph "Val," *See* Val, Joe
Vanderbilt University Medical Center (Nashville, Tennessee), 61, 204
Vandiver, Pendleton "Uncle Pen;" influence, 4
Vanguard Records, 73, 97, 118, 204
Vernon, Bill, 122, 132-135
Vienna sausages, 60
Vim Herb Products, 128
Virginia Trio, 40
Wagoner, Porter, 29, 85, 138, 143
Wakefield, Frank, 56, 136, 138
Waldron, Cliff and the New Shades of Grass, 216, 220, 224
Waller, Charles Otis "Charlie," 56, 60-61, 63, 64, 68, 70-73, 200, 224
Waller, Randy, 61
Walter, Jim Homes Corporation, 20, 197
WARL (Arlington, Virginia), 30, 60, 64
Warner Brothers Records, 184
Warren, Dorris Paul, 8, 92, 131, 142, 143, 210-213
Warren, Johnny, 213
Warrior River Boys, 174
WATA (Boone, North Carolina), x
Watermelon Park (Berryville, Virginia), 84
Watson, Arthel Lane "Doc," 94-97, 115, 118, 189, 202-204, 213
Watson, Richard, 97
Watts, Howard Staton "Cedric Rainwater," 5, 8, 79, 90, 154-157, 231
WAYS (Charlotte, North Carolina), 160
WBAI (New York, New York, 134
WBT (Charlotte, North Carolina, 104, 107
WCOD (Richmond, Virginia), 164
WCOP (Boston, Massachusetts), 114, 118
WCYB (Bristol, Virginia), 15, 18, 32, 40, 102, 130, 160, 174
WDBJ (Roanoke, Virginia), 28, 84
WDHA (Dover, New Jersey), 134
WDON (Wheaton, Maryland), 214
Webb, Roy Dean "Dean," 176-181
Weisz, Fred, 138
Wells, Kitty, 142, 212, 213
Wesbrooks, Wilbur, 28, 78
West, Hedy, 165
WHIS (Bluefield, West Virginia), 170

Whisnant, Jimmy, 158
White Oak Mountain Boys, 119, 153
White Oak Records, 119
White, Bob, 61
White, Clarence, 57, 94, 208; influence, 206
White, Roland, 4, 92
Whitley, Keith, 13, 20, 126, 127
Whitmore, Tom, 122
WHOW (Clinton, Illinois), 183
WHUB (Cookeville, Tennessee), 140
Wilburn Brothers; influence, 44, 49
Will the Circle Be Unbroken (sound recording), 9, 52, 53, 97, 108
Williams, Dock; influence, 154; and the Santa Fe Trailriders, 154
Williams, Hank, 80, 142, 145, 157
Williams, J.V.; influence, 116
Williams, Paul, 52, 126, 168, 171, 174-175
Williams, Vern, ix
Wills, James Robert "Bob;" influence, 76, 86, 87
Wingfield, Craig, 138
WIRC (Hickory, North Carolina), 195
Wise Records, 33
Wise, Robert Russell "Chubby," 4-6, 23, 78-81, 90, 138, 154-155, 156, 231; Blue Grass Boy, 5, 78-80; influence, 87; style, 78-79
Wiseman, Malcolm B. "Mac," 4, 8, 13, 30-33, 48, 60, 76, 81, 85, 124, 129, 164, 169; Blue Grass Boy, 4, 23, 32, 50; influence, 72, 218
WJAT (Swainsville, Georgia), 144
WJBF (Augusta, Georgia), 145
WJLS (Beckley, West Virginia), 112
WJR (Detroit, Michigan), 44, 52, 171
WJRI (Lenoir, North Carolina), 195
WKBC (North Wilkesboro, North Carolina), 195
WKCW (Warrenton, Virginia), 56
WKIK (Leonardtown, Maryland), 55
WLAC (Nashville, Tennessee), 140
WLS Barn Dance (Chicago, Illinois: radio program), 4
WLSI (Pikeville, Kentucky), 171, 196
WMMN (Fairmont, West Virginia), 113
WMNC (Morganton, North Carolina), 195
WNER (Live Oak, Florida), 16, 20
WNOX (Knoxville, Tennessee), 88, 108, 129, 140-141, 142, 158, 160,
WNVA (Norton, Virginia), 14
WOAY (Oak Hill, West Virginia), 196
Wolfe, Charles Keith, 166-169
Woodie, Lester, 194
Woolbright, Mack; influence, 8
Wooten, Art; influence, 23
WPAQ (Mount Airy, North Carolina), 160
WPFB (Middletown, Ohio), 42, 44, 45, 46, 124
WPTF (Raleigh, North Carolina), 128, 211
Wright, Johnnie, 142, 212; and the Happy Roving Cowboys, 210
WRNL (Richmond, Virginia), 107
WROL (Knoxville, Tennessee), 28
WRUF (Gainesville, Florida), 78
WRVA (Richmond, Virginia), 33, 108, 162, 218, 222
WSAZ (Huntington, West Virginia), 171
WSIX (Nashville, Tennessee), 183
WSJS (Winston-Salem, North Carolina), 128
WSM (Nashville, Tennessee), viii, 4, 10, 12, 45, 79, 108, 130, 183, 212, 222
WSTP (Salisbury, North Carolina), 128
WSVA (Harrisonburg, Virginia), 32
WSVS (Crewe, Virginia), 130
WVLK (Lexington/Versailles, Kentucky), 124, 130, 196
WVWR (Roanoke, Virginia), 135
WWVA Jamboree (Wheeling, West Virginia : radio program), 29, 33, 52, 109, 112, 118, 126, 128, 138, 164, 222; influence, 218
Wynwood Music, 57
Wynwood Recording Studio, 56
WYTI (Rocky Mount, Virginia), 134
Yates, Bill, 53, 73, 138
Yates, Wayne, 138, 192
Yodeling Rangers, 128
York Brothers, 80

"Day job" Index

Accountant: LeRoy, Lance
Blacksmith: Carter, A.P.
Carpenter: Carter, A.P.
Cartographer: Gray, Tom
Coal miner: Baker, Kenny; Lilly, Bea; Lilly, Everett; McReynolds, Jesse; McReynolds, Jim; Stover, Don
Doctor: Starling, John
Engineer: Kuykendall, Pete
Factory worker: Haney, Carlton; Martin, Jimmy
Farmer: Adcock, Eddie; Seckler, Curly; Waller, Charlie
Gas station: Crowe, J.D.; Waller, Charlie
Graphic artist: Auldridge, Mike
Grocery store: Carter, A.P.
Heavy equipment rentals: Crowe, J.D.
Horse Trading: Shuffler, George
Instrument repairman: Duffey, John
Logging: Carter, A.P.; McCoury, Del
Margin clerk: Vernon, Bill
Mathematician: Eldridge, Ben
Mechanic: Lawson, Doyle
Nursery salesman: Carter, A.P.
Nursing: Carter, Maybelle
Oil industry: Monroe, Bill
Painter: Martin, Jimmy
Peacock husbandry: Carter, Sara
Piano tuner: Watson, Doc
Postal worker: Freeman, David; Seckler, Curly
Printer: Duffey, John
Professor: Rosenberg, Neil V.
Radio/Disc jockey: Jayne, Mitch; Wiseman, Mac
Railroad worker: Carter, A.P.
Restaurateur: Cline, Ezra
Retail sales: Nathan, Syd
School teacher: Jayne, Mitch
Taxi driver: Osborne, Bobby; Osborne, Sonny; Wise, Chubby
Textile worker: Flatt, Lester; Scruggs, Earl
Truck driver: Duffey, John; Seckler, Curly